Constructing Early Childhood Science

Constructing Early Childhood Science

David Jerner Martin, Ph.D.
Kennesaw State University

DELMAR

THOMSON LEARNING

Australia Canada Mexico Singapore Spain United Kingdom United States

DELMAR

THOMSON LEARNING

Constructing Early Childhood Science
by David Jerner Martin

Business Unit Director: Susan L. Simpfenderfer	**Executive Marketing Manager:** Donna J. Lewis	**Production Editor:** J.P. Henkel
Acquisitions Editor: Erin O'Connor Traylor	**Channel Manager:** Nigar Hale	**Cover Design:** Judi Orozco
Editorial Assistant: Alexis Ferraro	**Executive Production Manager:** Wendy A. Troeger	**Composition and Production:** Shepherd Incorporated

For permission to use material from this text or product, contact us by
Tel   (800) 730-2214
Fax   (800) 730-2215
www.thomsonrights.com

Library of Congress Cataloging-in-Publication Data
Martin, David Jerner.
    Constructing early childhood science /
    David Jerner Martin.
        p. cm.
    Includes bibliographical references (p.) and index.
    ISBN 978-0-7668-1319-9
    (0-7668-1319-3)
    1. Science--Study and teaching (Early childhood)--United States. 2. Constructivism (Education)--United States. I. Title.

LB1139.5.S35 M27   2001
372.3'5044--dc21   00-043197

NOTICE TO THE READER

Table of Contents

Preface xiii

Acknowledgments xv

To the Student xvii

CHAPTER 1 *Constructing Goals for Early Childhood Science Education* **1**

What Science Do You Remember from the Earlier Grades?   2
How Much Science Does the Early Childhood Education Science Teacher Need
to Know?   3
   Increasing Amount of Scientific Knowledge   5
   Changing Scientific Knowledge   5
   How Much Science Does the Early Childhood Education Science Teacher Need
   to Know?   6
The Processes of Science   8
Goals of Early Childhood Science Education   12
   National Science Teachers Association   12
   American Association for the Advancement of Science   12
   National Science Education Standards   13
   Goals 2000: Educate America Act   14
   National Association for the Education of Young Children   15
Right and Wrong   19
   Perception   20
   Listening   22
Ownership of Knowledge and Thought   22
   Mystery Box   22
   Ownership   24
   Valuing Children's Thinking   24
The Metaphor   27
What Do You Think?   27
Summary   28
Notes   29
References   29

CHAPTER 2   *The Basic Scientific Processes: Observing*   **32**
Notes   45
References   45

CHAPTER 3   *The Basic Scientific Processes: Classifying*   **47**
References   59

CHAPTER 4   *The Basic Scientific Processes: Communicating*   **61**
References   74

CHAPTER 5   *The Basic Scientific Processes: Measuring*   **76**
Measuring Length   77
Measuring Volume   86
Measuring Weight   88
Measuring Temperature   92
Measuring Time   95
Metric vs Conventional Units   98
References   99

CHAPTER 6   *The Basic Scientific Processes: Predicting*   **100**
References   111

CHAPTER 7   *The Basic Scientific Processes: Inferring*   **112**
References   122

CHAPTER 8   *The Process-Oriented Objective*   **124**
Providing a Process-Based Focus   125
References   127

CHAPTER 9   *The Integrated Scientific Processes: Identifying and Controlling Variables*   **128**

The Pendulum   129
Identifying and Controlling Variables   131
References   135

CHAPTER 10   *The Integrated Scientific Processes: Formulating and Testing Hypotheses*   **137**

References   145

CHAPTER 11   *The Integrated Scientific Processes: Defining Operationally*   **146**

References   152

CHAPTER 12   *The Integrated Scientific Processes: Interpreting Data*   **153**

References   163

CHAPTER 13   *The Integrated Scientific Processes: Experimenting*   **164**

References   172

CHAPTER 14   *The Integrated Scientific Processes: Constructing Models*   **173**

Note   182
References   182

CHAPTER 15   *Constructivism*   **183**

Nature of Constructivism   186
Disequilibration   189
Prior Beliefs   191
Conceptual Change   192
Validity of Self-Constructed Conceptualizations   192
Right and Wrong Revisited   193
Summary   195
Note   195
References   195

CHAPTER 16   *Process-Oriented Inquiry*   **196**

The Expository-Discovery Continuum   198
Expository Methodology   199
Free Discovery Methodology   200
Guided Inquiry Methodology   201
Process-Oriented Guided Inquiry Lesson Planning   203
Microteaching   208
Summary   209
Notes   210
References   210

CHAPTER 17   *Learner Differences*   **211**

Learning Modalities   212
   Learning Experiences for Visual Learners   214
   Learning Experiences for Auditory Learners   215
   Learning Experiences for Kinesthetic Learners   216
   Learning Experiences for Visual, Auditory, and Kinesthetic Learners   217
Locus of Control   218
Field Dependence/Field Independence   219
Gender Bias   222
Cultural Differences   224
Multiple Intelligences   228
Science Education for Children with Disabilities   231
Summary   231
Notes   232
References   233

CHAPTER 18   *Assessment*   **235**

What Is Assessed in Early Childhood Science Education?   236
Assessing Process Skills   237
Assessing Inquiry   242
Assessing Attitude   244
Assessing Content   245
The Early Childhood Education Science Portfolio   247
Reporting to Parents   248
Assessing the Early Childhood Education Science Teacher and Program   250
Summary   251
Notes   251
References   252

CHAPTER 19   *The Early Childhood Science Classroom*   **253**

Organizing the Classroom   254
Organizing Bulletin Boards   255
Organizing Materials and Equipment   256
Organizing Time   257
Organizing for Safety   258
Organizing Living Laboratories   259
    Pets   259
    Aquariums   260
    Plants   261
    Terrariums   261
    Ant Farms   263
Organizing Groups   264
Organizing Children's Behavior during Science Activities   264
Organizing Parent Resources   266
    Parent Involvement in Exchanging Information about the Science Program   267
    Parent Nights   269
    Parent Involvement in Classroom Science Activities   269
    Parent Involvement in Establishing Science Assessment Procedures   269
    Getting Parent Involvement Started   270
Organizing Community Resources   270
Summary   271
Notes   271
References   272

CHAPTER 20   *Science beyond the Classroom*   **273**

Outdoor Learning Centers   274
Gardens   280
Field Trips   281
Science at Home   283
Summary   293
Notes   293
References   293

CHAPTER 21   *Technology in Early Childhood Science Education*   **295**

A Technology Inventory   296
Why Use Computer-Based Technology in Early Childhood Science Education?   298
Tutorial and CD Information Programs   301
Word Processing and Desktop Publishing   304
Spreadsheets and Graphing Applications   306

Databases   310
Electronic Mail   312
The Internet and the World Wide Web   313
Video in the Early Childhood Science Education Classroom   317
Evaluating Computer Software   318
Getting Started   320
Summary   321
Notes   321
Sources of Software   321
References   322

CHAPTER 22   *Reading, Writing, and Science*   **324**

Children's Literature   325
   Introducing Cognitive Disequilibration   325
   Introducing Lessons   326
   Validating Conclusions   328
   Presenting Factual Information   329
   Providing Practice in the Processes   329
   Sources of Children's Literature   329
   Evaluating Children's Literature for the Early Childhood Science Program   331
   Multicultural Children's Literature   331
   Children's Magazines   332
Science Textbooks   332
   Traditional Science Textbooks   334
   Activity-Oriented Science Series   335
   Textbooks Review   335
Writing in the Early Childhood Science Program   338
   Recording Children's Responses   338
   Science Journals   338
   Creative Writing   340
   Preparing Written Material on the Computer   341
Conflicting Views on Reading and Writing in Science   341
Summary   342
Note   342
References   343

CHAPTER 23   *Interdisciplinary Integration*   **345**

Toward the Interdisciplinary Curriculum   346
The Daisy Interdisciplinary Model   347
The Rose Interdisciplinary Model   350
Science, Technology, and Society   355
   STS Approaches   355
   Personal Bias in STS Projects   356

Significance of Interdisciplinary Integration in Early Childhood Science Programs 358
Summary 359
Note 360
References 360

CHAPTER 24 *The Early Childhood Science Education Professional* **361**

Decisions about Curriculum and Content 362
Decisions about Methodology 367
Consolidating Curriculum and Methodology Decisions 368
Professional Organizations 369
National Science Teachers Association 370
National Association for Research in Science Teaching 371
Association for the Education of Teachers in Science 371
Academies of Science 371
Other Science-Related Professional Organizations 372
Early Childhood Education Organizations 372
Professional Workshops and Seminars 372
Grants 373
The Early Childhood Science Education Teacher as Researcher 375
Excellence in Science Teaching 380
Summary 380
Afterword 382
Notes 382
Website Addresses for Professional Science Education Societies 383
References 383

APPENDIX A *Activities Cross-Referenced to Content Standards Outlined in the National Science Education Standards* **385**

APPENDIX B *Selected Sources of Free and Inexpensive Materials* **391**

APPENDIX C *Listing of Children's Literature* **396**

Glossary **401**
Index **403**

Dedication

For Katelynn and Joshua

Preface

Children learn science by doing science . . . by asking their own questions about things that interest them, exploring answers to their questions through applying the processes of science in open-ended inquiries, and combining new experiences with information they already possess as they form personally constructed meanings. This is the essence of constructivism: building personal knowledge from one's own experience and thought.

Constructing Early Childhood Education prepares students to teach science from a constructivist perspective in early childhood settings. A wealth of open-ended inquiry activities called "Constructing Your Ideas" are suggested for students to do in class to construct their own personal conceptualizations about teaching early childhood science. Students pursue these activities and discuss their outcomes in small groups and with the whole class—much as teachers conduct their early childhood science classes.

In the end, teachers must be able to apply the methodology they have constructed in their classrooms. More than 150 process-oriented inquiry activities suitable for young children's explorations called "Constructing Science in the Classroom" are suggested. Each is keyed to a range of age levels, and each is open ended so teachers can adapt the suggestions to the children in their classes and can encourage children to develop and perform their own investigations. The activities are placed in the text where the science education concepts they illustrate are discussed so students can immediately see how to apply the concepts in the classroom. Children's literature is referenced extensively throughout the text to encourage the tandem construction of scientific understandings and literacy. Several case histories describe events that actually occurred in science classes.

The text represents the cutting edge of contemporary science teaching. It is aligned with the *National Science Education Standards,* which are referenced throughout, and the principles of Developmentally Appropriate Practice outlined by the National Association for the Education of Young Children.

Each chapter begins with one or more hands-on activities designed to help students begin to construct their conceptualizations. The chapter then is developed in a constructivist manner, asking students to build their own notions from explorations of a variety of specific situations as they progress through the chapter.

Chapter 1 focuses on basic material: the ever-changing body of scientific knowledge and the resulting fact that students can never know all the science that might come up in a classroom; science goals and objectives; the role of the scientific processes; and the importance of children owning their own knowledge. The first chapter sets the stage for the safe and successful study of early childhood science education methods and asks students to begin constructing notions about goals, objectives, methodology, and curriculum. Chapters 2–14 are devoted to investigation of each of the twelve basic and integrated processes of science. In Chapters 15 and 16, students explore the nature of constructivism, inquiry as a primary agent of constructivist learning and the vehicle through which science is learned, and specific science-teaching methodologies. Chapter 17 deals with learner differences; features include contemporary explorations of specific learner differences shown to have an effect on science learning, multiculturalism in early childhood science education, multiple intelligences, and science education for children with disabilities. Chapter 18 is devoted to methods of authentic assessment, showing step-by-step guidance with examples for each assessment technique. In Chapter 19 the student explores ideas and suggestions for organizing the early childhood science classroom, time and materials, classroom plants and animals, safety, behavior during science investigations, and parent and community resources. Chapter 20 deals with teaching science in nontraditional settings such as outdoor learning centers and field trips. In Chapter 21 students explore ways of incorporating technology in early childhood science education. In Chapters 22 and 23, they explore models of interdisciplinarianism, including roles of children's literature and the contemporary science-technology-society thematic thrusts. Chapter 24 is devoted to professionalism, showing the role the professions play in continued professional development, describing ways of writing grant proposals, and urging teachers to undertake action research and publish and present the results. Appendices include the activities cross-referenced to the content standards as outlined in the *National Science Education Standards,* a listing of sources for free and inexpensive science materials, and a listing of children's literature cited.

The text is suitable for undergraduate or graduate studies, and is suitable for both preservice and inservice applications.

In my thirty years in the field of science education at all levels, it has been my experience that the only science children learn is the science they do themselves. Consequently, in this practical text, I have taken the bold and uncompromising position that hands-on, process-oriented, constructivist-focused inquiry must be fostered in early childhood science education. Preservice and inservice teachers who construct their science education conceptualizations and methodologies through the guidance offered in this text will find science teaching to be fun, stimulating, rewarding, and extremely successful.

David Jerner Martin
Kennesaw, Georgia
August 2000

Acknowledgments

This work would not have been possible without the support, help, and input of many people. I am especially grateful to the following people:

Dr. Linda Webb of Kennesaw State University, who read countless drafts and provided much guidance and encouragement.

Mrs. Grace Burkholder of Boulder City, Nevada, and Miss Betty Hesrick of Columbus, Ohio, colleagues who taught early childhood education for many years and embraced the constructivist perspective long before the constructivism label appeared. They both provided meticulous reviews of the draft. My thanks go to them for their extensive and valuable input.

Dr. Emily Johnson of Kennesaw State University for her helpful input concerning contemporary paradigms of early childhood education.

Editor Erin O'Connor Traylor of Delmar/Thomson Learning, who knew just what to say when and provided much encouragement and professional expertise.

The many professional colleagues with whom I have been fortunate to be associated and who have provided much support through the years.

The students in my classes who have helped to show me what works and what doesn't. I have used many of their ideas and vignettes in this text. I am especially indebted to Ms. Julie Stacy, whose work as a graduate student at Kennesaw State University was the source of several of the preschool activities.

Ms. Debbie Ryscamp, first grade teacher, Ms. Sharon Day, Principal, the teaching associates, parents, and children in first grade and kindergarten at American Heritage Academy in Canton, Georgia who opened their doors so I could take pictures of children doing science.

Ms. Beth Puckett, Director, and the teachers and preschool children at Mountain View Preschool in Cobb County, Georgia who opened their doors so I could take pictures of children doing science.

Mr. Paul Hultberg, who understands both children and education, and who supplied much of the photography that so skillfully brings the two together.

Mr. William Reynolds, an elementary art teacher in Rome, Georgia, who supplied many of the line drawings.

Donna Macaluso of MacArt Design who provided many of the drawings.

The teachers, the children, and Ms. Judy Thigpen and Ms. Patti Thomas, principals of Sedalia Park Elementary School in Cobb County, Georgia, who welcomed me as a colleague and provided me with much valuable experience.

Ms. Carey Mills, preschool teacher at Allatoona Elementary School in Cobb County, Georgia, who opened the doors of her classroom to me.

Many of the quotes from children's literature came from the delightful little book, *What the Dormouse Said* by Amy Gash (1999, Chapel Hill, NC: Algonquin Books of Chapel Hill), a book I would recommend for everyone involved in teaching young children.

Finally, my thanks go to my wonderfully patient wife, Mary, whose encouragement and enthusiasm for this work contributed more than she will ever know.

Many professional colleagues provided valuable comments through their reviews; they include

Linda Estes
St. Charles County Community College
Saint Charles, MO

Jennifer Lynch
Moorpark College
Moorpark, CA

Francis H. Squires
Indiana University Southeast
New Albany, IN

Molly Weinburgh
Georgia State University
Atlanta, GA

Elaine Camerin
Daytona Beach Community College
Daytona Beach, FL

To all these people and many more, "thank you."

To the Student

Welcome to this exploration of early childhood education!

Teaching science in early childhood settings need not be difficult. Science is one of the most fascinating pursuits experienced by children. Young children love to tinker, to explore, to try things out, to observe things, to talk about what they observe, to find out what makes things work. They love to play with magnets, discovering that some things are attracted to magnets and some things are not—even through water, plastic, and sand; discovering the idea that some ends of straight magnets attract each other and some ends repel. They are enthralled by the metamorphosis of a caterpillar into a beautiful butterfly. They get excited watching things that swing and things that balance. They are thrilled by the changes that occur during the seasons, by the setting of the sun, by the countless stars in the night sky, by the many shapes of the moon, by the different colors of rocks, by the magic of seeds sprouting. They love to act like scientists, exploring this or that phenomenon and trying something new such as blowing bubbles designed to be bigger or to last longer than anyone else's.

However, in spite of children's natural fascination with exploring on their own, for many years the teaching of science has consisted of the skillful impartation of scientific knowledge to students. Textbooks have contained information for children to learn, and it has been the teacher's job to interpret the textbook and augment it so that every child learns the material presented.

Science education of the 2000s takes a view radically different from this teacher-focused approach. Science education today capitalizes on children's natural curiosity. It encourages children to construct information in ways that are meaningful to them. It consists of experiences children undertake themselves. The focus is on doing rather than acquiring. The competent teacher of early childhood science encourages children to wonder, to ask questions, to explore possible answers to these questions, and to construct their own conclusions.

The way children learn science is through doing science; the way children do science is through using the processes of science in personally constructed inquiries. Therefore, this book is about constructing the process-oriented inquiry method of science teaching. The emphasis is on process skills and hands-on experiences in which children ask their own questions about phenomena that interest them and seek their own answers to their questions by doing activities that they themselves devise. As you will see, inquiry is the agent of constructivism.

The text utilizes a constructivist approach; you will learn to teach science in the same manner as children in your classroom will learn how to do science. You will develop your own personally constructed conceptualizations about teaching early childhood science. Many questions and issues are raised for you to grapple with; there are many more questions than answers, for you have to come to your own conclusions.

Each topic begins with one or more case studies or hands-on activities to help you begin to construct your conceptualizations. Topics are treated inductively, which means you will explore a variety of specific situations pertaining to a phenomenon before the concept is introduced or defined. In this way, you will construct your own generalizations and conclusions as you move through a topic, rather than relying on the author's preconstructed conclusions. Periodically you will be asked to compare your conclusions with the author's. Hopefully there will be a degree of congruence.

The text represents the cutting edge of contemporary science teaching. It is aligned with the *National Science Education Standards,* which are referenced throughout, and the principles of Developmentally Appropriate Practice outlined by the National Association for the Education of Young Children.

Disagreement and debate are encouraged—this is the only way people can crystallize their own ideas. This is the essence of constructivism.

Many class activities called "Constructing Your Ideas" are suggested throughout the text. They are designed to help you in your constructions of your conceptualizations, and it is strongly suggested that you actually do as many as time allows. It also is suggested that you do the "Constructing Your Ideas" activities in small groups of four to six students and share group results with the class as a whole. As you will see, small-group work fosters children's abilities to come to their own valid conclusions, and doing the activities in small groups models the actual elementary class.

AGE

Many suggested children's activities called "Constructing Science in the Classroom" occur throughout the text near the science learning principle they can be used to teach. These "Constructing Science in the Classroom" activities are offered as suggestions only—points of departure; they are not intended to be duplicated. In the constructivist approach, science investigations are designed to meet the unique needs of children in a particular classroom and often are developed jointly between the teacher and the children. Suggested ranges of age levels for each activity are shown with icons. Most of the activities contain suggested children's literature connections to help you utilize an interdisciplinary approach to science.

Many facets of today's science teaching are examined in this text: what to teach, how to teach it, developmental appropriateness, interdisciplinary and multicultural aspects, the use of language arts strands in the science program, the use of technology, parental and community involvement, using schoolyard and field-trip sites to teach science, and the assessment of children, the program, and your teaching.

Chapter 1 presents the fundamentals: the constantly changing body of scientific knowledge and the resulting fact that one can never know all the science that might arise in a classroom; science goals and objectives; the role of the scientific processes; and the importance of children "owning" their own knowledge. The first chapter sets the stage for the safe and successful study of early childhood science education methods and asks you to begin constructing notions about goals, objectives, methodology, and curriculum. Chapters 2–14 are devoted to investigation of each of the twelve basic and integrated processes of science. In Chapters 15 and 16 you will explore the nature of constructivism, inquiry as a primary agent of constructivist learning and the vehicle through which science is learned, and specific science-teaching methodologies. Chapter 17 deals with specific learner differences shown to have an effect on science learning, multiculturalism in early childhood science education, multiple intelligences, and science education for children with disabilities. Chapter 18 is devoted to methods of authentic assessment featuring step-by-step guidance with examples for each assessment technique mentioned.

In Chapter 19 you will explore ideas and suggestions for organizing the early childhood science classroom, time and materials, classroom plants and animals, safety, behavior during science investigations, and parent and community resources. Chapter 20 deals with teaching science in nontraditional settings such as outdoor learning centers, museums, and field trips. In Chapter 21 you will explore ways in which you can incorporate technology in early childhood science education. In Chapters 22 and 23 you will explore models of interdisciplinarianism including roles of children's literature and contemporary science-technology-society thematic thrusts. Chapter 24 is devoted to professionalism, showing the role the professions play in continued professional development, describing ways of writing grant proposals, and urging you to undertake action research and to publish and present the results. Appendices include the activities cross-referenced to the content standards as outlined in the *National Science Education Standards,* a listing of sources that offer free and inexpensive science materials, and a listing of children's literature cited.

The goals of this book are for you to construct your own personal philosophy of teaching science, lose any fears or lack of confidence that may have accompanied you into this course, and construct a methodology and curriculum base that will enable you to enter the classroom a competent teacher of science for elementary children.

Enjoy your explorations!

CHAPTER 1

Constructing Goals for Early Childhood Science Education

Children begin recognizing and sorting out their world from the moment of birth—perhaps even before they are born. They play with their hands and feet and with their fingers and toes, with blankets and toys, and with just about anything placed near them. They look; they manipulate; they move things this way and that; they throw; they chase. Their eyes go wide with excitement when they encounter something new.

Children exhibit natural curiosity about what things are, how things work, and how things are related to each other. They wonder where the rain, the snow, and the hail come from. They wonder why mold grows on old bread and why old apples shrivel up. They wonder why fish can breathe in water and why birds can fly. They wonder why it is hot in the summer and cold in the winter. They wonder why feathers fall more slowly than rocks.

Except for children (who don't know enough not to ask the important questions), few of us spend much time wondering about why nature is the way it is; where the cosmos came from, or whether it was always here; if time will one day flow backward and effects precede causes; or whether there are ultimate limits to what humans can know . . . . In our society it is still customary for parents and teachers to answer most of these questions with a shrug.

Carl Sagan, in Stephen W. Hawking, *A Brief History of Time* (New York: Bantam Books, 1988) p. *ix*

You have brains in your head. You have feet in your shoes. You can steer yourself any direction you choose.

Dr. Seuss, *Oh, the Places You'll Go!* (New York: Random House, 1990)

One of the most important contributions adults can make to the education of very young children is to provide multitudes of rich and varied experiences (Diamond & Hopson, 1998). The experiences to which a child is exposed form the basis of ever-widening curiosity and inquisitiveness. Many of these experiences come from the natural world: trees, grass, flowers, vegetables, fruits, bugs, frogs, insects, birds, butterflies, dogs, cats, cows, rocks, dirt, rain, snow, icicles, stars, the moon, wind, and thousands of other things that are ever present in the child's natural environment. Many more of these experiences come from the child's man-made environment: Ferris wheels, roller coasters, cotton candy, clothes, shoes, houses, fire trucks, streets, stop lights, sidewalks, paints, books, television sets, computers, and thousands of other things the child encounters on the way to growing up.

You may have noticed that the vast majority of the things just listed, which children experience, are included in what is often considered the substance of science.

Thus, children come to school with the experiences of their environment, a natural curiosity, and an innate desire to find out why things happen and how things work. The teacher of early childhood science has a wonderfully rich palate to work with. Given encouragement, sensitive and developmentally appropriate teaching, the power to ask and investigate their own questions, and ownership of their cognitive constructions, this curiosity and desire to explore continues through the early childhood grades and even into adulthood.

Because children are natural-born scientists, we ask, "How are we going to construct the early childhood science education program?"

WHAT SCIENCE DO YOU REMEMBER FROM THE EARLIER GRADES?

Let us start by trying to recall the science experiences you may have had in school.

Constructing Your Ideas 1.1
Remembering Science

What do you remember from your grade-school science? Take about five minutes and recall your preschool, or kindergarten, first-, or second-grade classes. Think of the science you were exposed to. What do you remember? Write these items down, and share them with the class. Make a class list.

What did the class list contain? Chances are that several people remembered looking at pictures in books. Maybe some remembered doing worksheets. Perhaps someone recalled learning a song such as a dinosaur song. But what *science* is on the list? Did anyone report remembering learning the parts of a plant? Or what plants need in order to grow? Or three kinds of rocks? Or the difference between rocks and minerals? Or the effect of forces? Or the causes and effects of friction? Or the things that magnets attract?

Did anyone say they didn't remember *anything* about science in the lower grades? Did anyone say they didn't have science in the lower grades?

Now ask whether you did science-based *activities* in these early grades. For example, did you participate in science activities that dealt with phenomena such as bubbles, balls, animals, plants, rocks, weather, and the like? Did you take science-based field trips? Did your teacher send science materials and activity suggestions home for you and your family to do together? Did any of the "show and tell" experiences you or other children in your classes brought in deal with science topics? How about bugs? Caterpillars? Mechanical toys? Talking dolls? Plants? Were you encouraged to explore these? Did you have class pets?

In all probability, the memories (if they exist) of what you actually *did* are much more vivid than the memories of what you had to learn about science. People remember what they *did* in their early science experiences more than what they had to learn about. Yet, many people are under the impression that the goal of science education is to transmit scientific information to students so the children will learn scientific facts, generalizations, concepts, theories, and laws—the scientific "truths" considered important for children to learn.

How well does this conceptualization of teaching early childhood science correlate with what you remember from science in the early grades? What do *you* perceive your job as a teacher of science in early childhood grades to be? Should you teach content? Or should you focus more on involving children in doing science? These questions will guide our explorations into early childhood science education throughout this text.

HOW MUCH SCIENCE DOES THE EARLY CHILDHOOD EDUCATION SCIENCE TEACHER NEED TO KNOW?

Let us look at the question of how much science the early childhood science teacher needs to know to be able to teach it well.

Constructing Your Ideas 1.2
Unexpected Questions

 Consider this scenario: In your first-grade class, you have decided to teach a lesson on animal camouflage. To prepare for the lesson, you have researched many ways animals camouflage themselves to blend in with their environments, thereby protecting themselves against predators. Your goal is for the children to understand how certain animals camouflage themselves and to understand why camouflage is beneficial. You are about halfway through the lesson when suddenly one of the children asks about the relationship between the **sea anemone** and the **clownfish** (Figure 1.1). It seems he and his family have visited an aquarium where they observed a clownfish darting with complete safety among the tentacles of the sea anemone—tentacles that would paralyze other fish. "Is this," he asks, "a kind of camouflage?" You are in a quandary, for you don't know the answer to his question. What do you do?

a) Tell him it's not part of today's lesson and that he can bring the topic up on a different day.
b) Tell him to please stick to the subject.
c) Tell him to find out for himself.
d) Admit you are not sure of the answer, that you'll look it up and give him the answer tomorrow.
e) Stop the lesson you have prepared and begin a discussion of relationships among sea animals.
f) Something else.

Discuss this situation in groups or as a class. Be aware that there is *no* correct answer to this situation. This is the first of many questions we will pose that have no answers.

FIGURE 1.1 Sea anemone tentacles and clownfish

Increasing Amount of Scientific Knowledge

Regardless of how you decide you would handle this situation, it suggests that no matter how much science you know, it will never be enough.

As we have seen, one reason you can never know enough science is the sheer amount of science known today. In the 1980s there were over 50,000 distinct research fields in science (Hurd, 1990) with over 120,000 science-based journals in print (Hurd, 1985). It has been estimated that in 1995, knowledge was doubling every five years, and that by the year 2020, the amount of knowledge in the world will double every 73 days (Costa & Liebman, 1995, p. 23). Scientific advancement is responsible for a large portion of this knowledge "explosion." The amount of science known today is tremendous, and the amount of scientific knowledge is increasing at an unprecedented rate. It is impossible for anyone to keep up with all of it.

Stephen Hawking, in his White House Millennium Evening address of 1998, said (somewhat whimsically) that if knowledge were to keep growing at the current rate, by the year 2600, "if you stacked the new books being published next to each other, you would have to move at 90 miles an hour just to keep up with the end of the line. Of course," he continued, "by 2600 new artistic and scientific work will come in electronic forms rather than in physical books. Nevertheless, if the exponential growth continued, there would be ten papers a second in my kind of theoretical physics, and no time to read them" (Hawking, 1998).

Changing Scientific Knowledge

Not only is new information being added to our store of scientific knowledge, but scientific information continually is changing. Some becomes obsolete and is refined or replaced with new and more valid information. For example, images of deep-space objects taken by the Hubble telescope are prompting astronomers to challenge current estimates of the age of the universe and to refine current theories about the origin and fate of the universe (Villard, Macchetto, Dressler, & Dickinson, 1994). The theory of **plate tectonics,** developed in the late 1960s, suggests that the continents and oceans lie on **plates** of crustal material that continually move. This theory replaces the formerly well established **continental drift theory** and offers more satisfactory explanations for **volcanoes, earthquakes,** and mountain formation. The discovery in 1953 of **DNA** by Francis Crick, a British investigator, and James Watson, an American, working together at Cambridge University, has completely revolutionized the way people think about the nature of life.

Even factual information is subject to change. For example, in 1956 it was discovered that the number of **chromosomes** in a normal human cell is 46 instead of the previously believed 48 (Thermion, 1986, p. 8). Better technology enabled more precise separation of the chromosomes and thus a more accurate count (Figure 1.2).

sea aner
shallow·
stationa
bright c
ters of tentacles that resemble flowers

clownfish—A small saltwater fish

plate tectonics—A theory of crustal movement of the earth's continents and ocean basins

plates—The crustal material on which the earth's continents and ocean basins sit

continental drift theory—An outmoded theory that suggested that continents wandered about on the earth's crust

volcano—A structure or vent on the earth's crust from which molten rock and gases emerge or formerly emerged

earthquake—A trembling of the earth that is normally caused by volcano eruptions or plate movement

DNA— Deoxyribonucleic acid: the building blocks of genes and chromosomes

chromosome—A cluster of genes that contains the blueprints for the function and reproduction of cells

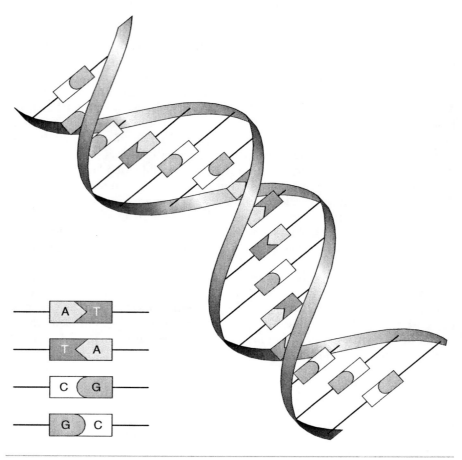

FIGURE 1.2 DNA

How Much Science Does the Early Childhood Education Science Teacher Need to Know?

Scientists, science educators, and other professionals have struggled for decades with the question of how much and what science children and their teachers should know. In the early 1990s the National Commission on Science Education Standards was formed at the request of the National Science Teachers Association and other science and science education professional societies to take the lead in developing national standards for science education. The resulting *National Science Education Standards* (National Research Council, 1996) addressed the question of teacher preparation for science teaching. The *Standards* suggests that "teachers of science must have a strong, broad base of scientific knowledge extensive enough for them to

■ Understand the nature of scientific inquiry, its central role in science, and how to use the skills and processes of scientific inquiry.

▌ Understand the fundamental facts and concepts in major science disciplines.

▌ Be able to make conceptual connections within and across science disciplines as well as mathematics, technology, and other school subjects.

▌ Use scientific inquiry and ability when dealing with personal and societal issues" (National Research Council, 1996, p. 59, Professional Development Standard A).

Thus it seems a good idea that teachers should know some of the basic concepts and principles of **life science, physical science,** and **earth and space science.** Life science includes the study of cells, plants, animals, life cycles, and ecology. Physical science includes topics related to matter, energy, and chemistry. Earth and space science includes topics related to geology, rocks and minerals, the earth, the seas, weather, forces that shape the earth, and space.

Let us return to our question, "How much science does the early childhood education science teacher need to know?" By now you realize that you can never know enough science to be able to answer everyone's questions. This is another of the many questions posed in this book that you will have to answer for yourself; there simply is *no* universal or correct answer to this question. For now, it seems prudent to offer the following proposition: *Early childhood science teachers do not have to have extensive knowledge about science in order to be able to teach it well.*

However, as you will see, scientists, science educators, and other professionals universally agree that it is essential for children to know how to inquire, how to find things out, and how to investigate scientific questions. These experts all attest that it is far more important to know how to inquire than it is to accumulate vast stores of scientific knowledge. As you have seen, the *Standards* indicate that teachers should learn how to inquire in science in order to be able to teach children how to inquire.

A vignette may illustrate our point. Three first-grade teachers report they were reluctant to teach science because they felt they did not know enough science to do a good job. Then they changed their approach to one of learning, experimenting, and inquiring along with the students. They report they became much more successful and felt much more enthusiastic about teaching science when they employed the co-inquirer approach instead of the information-imparting approach to teaching science. They write, "In this way, we [are] increasing our own knowledge as well as inspiring students in science" (Dickinson et. al., 1997, p. 229).

A worldwide study of science achievement may also illustrate our point. The Third International Mathematics and Science Study (TIMSS), a test in mathematics and science achievement, was administered to a half million students in 41 nations at three different grade levels during the 1995 school year. The science sections focused on earth science, life science, and physical science topics. Overall, American seniors scored near the bottom of the test in science, outperforming only Cyprus and South Africa. American eighth-graders

life science—The study of living things and their interrelationships with each other and the environment

physical science—The study of matter and energy; includes the study of mechanical energy (energy of motion), heat, sound, light, electricity and magnetism, nuclear energy, and matter and chemical energy

earth and space science—The study of the earth, the solar system, and the universe

scored near the middle on the science test. But American fourth-grade students performed near the top in science, second only to fourth graders in Korea.[1] There is much discussion as to why American students achieved the scores they did, and whether it is fair or even possible to compare science achievement of students in different countries. Nonetheless, it is worth observing that the children (fourth-graders) taught by teachers who presumably know the least science scored the highest on this measure of achievement in science.

You will read over and over in this book that is far better to teach children how to do science than it is to teach them about science. By learning how to do science children also learn about science. They must learn how to observe, how to create, how to come up with new ideas, how to inquire, how to investigate, and how to analyze and evaluate. It is not necessary for teachers to try to fill children's minds with myriad scientific facts, principles, and concepts to be learned under the mistaken impression that these are essential for survival in today's (or tomorrow's) society. Children must learn how to *do* science. And teachers must learn how to do science so they can facilitate children doing science.

THE PROCESSES OF SCIENCE

What does it mean to *do* science? How do scientists do science? What do people do when they do science? Let us turn our attention to the processes of science.

In 1959, two years after the October 4, 1957 launching of Sputnik, Jerome Bruner, a renowned professor of psychology at Harvard, chaired the now-famous ten-day "Woods Hole" conference in Woods Hole, Massachusetts. The intent of the conference was to "examine the fundamental processes involved in imparting to young students a sense of the substance and method of science" (Bruner, 1965, p. vii). The conclusion reached was that students should learn science the way science is done. Chemistry should be learned the way chemists practice their profession; physics should be learned the way physicists do physics; biology should be learned the way biologists explore their world.

Naturally the question was asked, "How do scientists *do* science?" Over time, the answer emerged that scientists do science by applying the processes of scientific inquiry to the end of understanding a phenomenon, answering a question, developing a theory, discovering more information about something, or challenging conclusions reached by others.

Twelve processes make up the scientific endeavor:

Observing	Identifying and controlling variables
Classifying	Formulating and testing hypotheses
Communicating	Interpreting data
Measuring	Defining operationally
Predicting	Experimenting
Inferring	Constructing models[2]

In the process approach to science education, children are encouraged to do science by applying the processes to inquiries. This approach manifested itself in the 1960s in a number of bold, new elementary science programs such as Elementary Science Study (ESS), Science Curriculum Improvement Study (SCIS), and many others. The Elementary Science Study program was a hands-on discovery approach to elementary science education. Many units such as "Growing Seeds," "Match and Measure," and "Primary Balancing" suitable for early elementary grades were developed to foster children's development of the scientific processes and to guide their own investigations. The emphasis was on discovery, with the teacher facilitating each child's explorations of phenomena according to the child's needs, interests, and prior background.

The Science Curriculum Improvement Study was developed by Dr. Robert Karplus, a theoretical physicist at Berkley. He was dissatisfied with the textbook-based, content-oriented science instruction his daughter and other children in primary school were receiving. He developed SCIS as an inquiry approach to science education that encouraged children to make their own observations and formulate their own conclusions in the manner in which scientists do science.[3]

In developing SCIS, Karplus also created the now-famous "Learning Cycle" to guide teachers in facilitating children's inquiries. The Learning Cycle is a three-phase approach to teaching: (1) exploration, (2) concept explanation and concept invention, and (3) discovering (Figure 1.3). In this model, students first explore a concept presented by the teacher to see what they can figure out. Their hands-on explorations are facilitated (but not directed) by the teacher. After children have had a chance to explore, their discoveries are consolidated with current scientific knowledge under the teacher's direction in the concept-explanation and concept-invention phase. In this phase, the teacher assumes a more traditional role as children compare what they have figured out with accepted scientific conceptualizations. Finally, children are encouraged to explore the concept further through investigating new but related problems and situations. Again, the teacher serves as facilitator more than director. These investigations logically lead to the exploration phase of a new concept, and the cycle begins again. There are many contemporary variations of the learning cycle, and some include an evaluation phase.

In the process approach, scientific information is a springboard for children to use as they explore the processes and learn to master them. Processes are mastered by using science content as a vehicle, and, once mastered, are used to investigate new scientific phenomena. For example, the process of *observing* can be taught using plants, animals, rocks, and moving objects. Children can learn to *classify* using leaves, shells, minerals, and pictures depicting seasons. Children *communicate* the results of their scientific inquiries; they *measure* items they use in their experiments using traditional and **nontraditional** systems; they *predict* what would happen if a plant is deprived of light; and they *infer* the reason soil is composed of many different things.

nontraditional—Units of measurement based on items chosen by children.

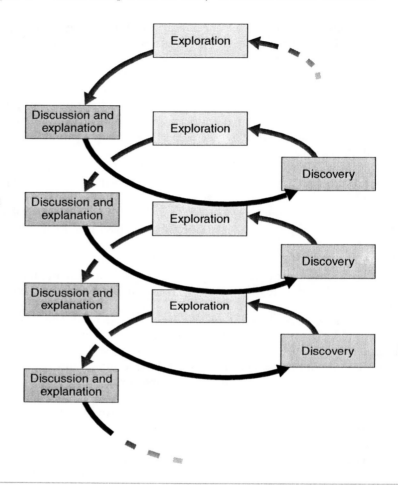

FIGURE 1.3   The Learning Cycle

Constructing Your Ideas 1.3
Investigating Parachutes

To see how the processes are used in investigating scientific phenomena, let us investigate factors that influence how fast parachutes fall.

Divide your class into groups of three or four students. Each group should assemble the following materials:

Several pieces of cloth
A plastic garbage bag
String
A weight such as a toy car, a bolt, or several metal washers

First make one or more parachutes. Cut out several squares of the cloth and garbage bag in different sizes. Measure the side of the square that forms each parachute, and calculate the area using the formula, *area = s^2* (where *s* equals the length of one side). For each parachute cut four pieces of string that are about twice as long as the side of the square. Tie a piece of string to each corner. Gather the strings together, and tie the weight onto the other ends of the string.

Now have a representative of each group select one of the parachutes and then climb onto a table. All students hold the parachutes the same distance above the floor. At a given signal, let them drop. Which parachutes reach the floor first? Try this several times, and employ several variations such as using parachutes of different sizes, timing the length of fall using stopwatches, starting the parachutes from higher places (such as the top of a ladder), using different materials for the parachute, using different weights, and so on. From the results, suggest one or more generalizations (Figure 1.4).

FIGURE 1.4 Exploring Parachutes

In this investigation, you used the processes of science to reach your conclusions. You *observed* the parachutes fall. You may have mentally *classified* the parachutes into small, medium, and large sizes. You *communicated* with each other in discussing the investigation and sharing the results. You *measured* the areas of the parachutes and the lengths of the strings. You probably *predicted* what would happen. You *inferred* why some reached the floor faster than others. You *identified and controlled variables* when you varied size, material, weight, and other factors of the parachute system. You mentally *formulated hypotheses* when you predicted the relationship between size or other variable and how long the parachute would take to fall; you *tested* these hypotheses by dropping the parachutes. You *interpreted data* when you looked at how long it took the parachutes to fall to the floor. Your entire activity was designed in the form of a controlled *experiment*. And the parachutes you made were *models* of real parachutes.

GOALS OF EARLY CHILDHOOD SCIENCE EDUCATION

scientific literacy—The ability to understand science in its day-to-day context

Carl Sagan (1989) wrote, "We live in a society exquisitely dependent on science and technology, in which hardly anyone knows anything about science and technology." The ability to understand science and technology in its day-to-day context is called **scientific literacy**, and the development of scientific literacy is the basic goal of all science education. Scientifically literate people know how and when to ask questions, how to think critically, and how to make decisions based on reason rather than on emotion or superstition.

A number of national organizations have taken positions on goals of science education. Three of these groups have written detailed position statements: the National Science Teachers Association (NSTA), the American Association for the Advancement of Science (AAAS), and the National Commission on Science Education Standards and Assessment (NCSESA). All three position statements are similar and stress teaching less content, teaching more investigation skills, teaching in the inquiry mode, teaching from an interdisciplinary perspective, teaching *all* children, stimulating children's interest in science, and, especially, developing scientifically literate citizens. The material in this book is grounded, in part, in the philosophies and positions of these national organizations. (See Chapter 24 for details concerning these and other professional organizations.)

National Science Teachers Association

The National Science Teachers Association is extremely active in the reform of science education at all levels. The NSTA says that elementary science should emphasize learning science concepts and processes through the use of activities that involve children manipulating materials and thinking about the activity. Curricula should be organized around conceptual themes and should provide opportunities for children to study real-life, personal, and social problems related to science and technology. Children should construct understandings of science concepts and processes, see applications of science and technology to everyday life, form positive attitudes toward science, and learn how knowledge of science helps solve personal and societal problems. Programs should integrate science, technology, mathematics, humanities, and the social sciences and must be responsive to the needs of underrepresented students.

American Association for the Advancement of Science

The American Association for the Advancement of Science, the world's largest federation of scientific and technological societies, engages in a wide variety of activities to advance science and human progress. Responding to grave concerns about the state of science education in the United States, the AAAS embarked on a project named "Project 2061" for the year when Halley's Comet will make its next pass near the earth.[4] The project resulted in the publication of *Science for All Americans* (Rutherford & Algren, 1990), which suggests that science topics should be treated from an interdisciplinary perspective, focusing on systems and interrelationships among the scientific disciplines rather than on isolated facts and concepts from isolated fields of study. Teachers are urged to proceed from the concrete to the abstract, start with questions rather than answers, look for prior information, and engage students in collecting evidence and interpreting data in order to answer the questions.

To augment *Science for All Americans,* the AAAS published *Benchmarks for Science Literacy* (American Association for the Advancement of Science, 1993), which contains statements of what all students should know and be able to do in science, mathematics, and technology in four grade-level spans: K–2, 3–5, 6–8, and 9–12. It presents background information for teachers and offers specific learning objectives for students. A companion volume, *Resources for Science Literacy* (American Association for the Advancement of Science, 1997) augments earlier works and focuses on resources, activities, and course plans. *Benchmarks* has had a huge impact on contemporary science education, and many school districts have developed science programs based on the principles and suggestions outlined in the book.

National Science Education Standards

The *National Science Education Standards* (National Research Council, 1996), is predicated on scientific literacy for *all* students as the primary goal of science education. "All students regardless of age, sex, cultural or ethnic background, disabilities, aspirations, or interest and motivation in science should have the opportunity to obtain high levels of scientific literacy" (National Research Council, 1996, p. 20).

The *National Science Education Standards* are not federal mandates, nor do they represent a national curriculum. Rather, they offer a vision of what it means to be scientifically literate and criteria for judging the quality of six major components of science education: science teaching, professional development for preservice and inservice teachers, assessment, content, science programs, and systems that support science education.

The teaching standards call for inquiry-based science education programs in which teachers facilitate learning rather than impart information, utilize multiple authentic methods of assessment, provide learning environments conducive to inquiry learning, maintain standards of intellectual rigor, and actively participate in the development and planning of their science programs. The professional development standards include criteria for preparing preservice teachers in pedagogy and content and for becoming lifelong learners who keep up with new developments in pedagogical research and scientific knowledge. The assessment standards urge the implementation of assessment practices that are consistent with what is taught, that assess achievement as well as opportunity to learn, and that are accurate and fair.

The science content standards describe desirable student outcomes for Levels K–4, Levels 5–8, and Levels 9–12. The content is identified in eight categories: (1) unifying concepts and processes in science; (2) science as inquiry; (3) physical science; (4) life science; (5) earth and space science; (6) science and technology; (7) science in personal and social perspectives; and (8) history and nature of science.

The science education program standards include specific criteria for appraising the quality of K–12 science programs in terms of program design and conditions necessary to ensure equal opportunities for all students to learn science. The science education system standards address the roles and interactions needed from policy makers at all levels from local schools to district and state levels to effect a lasting and meaningful change in science education. (See inside front and back covers for the individual standards.)

The National Science Teachers Association actively supports the *Standards* and has developed several innovative programs to help science educators move toward the criteria described in the standards. These programs include (1) the "Building a Presence" initiative, through which copies of the *Standards* are provided to school buildings and teachers are made aware of local resources; (2) *NSTA Pathways to the Science Standards*,[5] books that provide classroom ideas to aid teachers in implementing standards-based programs; and (3) workshops and seminars at NSTA conferences designed to help participants implement standards-based programs (National Science Teachers Association, 1998). The *Pathways to the Science Standards* books suggest ways of using the *Standards* to tailor science programs to unique school and community environments, building on the strengths of the teachers in each school. Because each school and each community will follow a different pathway in reaching for the vision of the *Standards,* teachers can "start by building on what works well in your classroom and school" (Lowery, 1997, p. 2).[6]

Goals 2000: Educate America Act

In 1990 President Bush and the nation's governors met for the first time in U.S. history to discuss a national educational policy. Their discussion was summarized in the now-famous six national goals for public education. Two additional goals dealing with teacher education and professional development and parental participation were added to the original six goals, resulting in an expanded Goals 2000: Educate America Act, which was passed into law in 1994. The goals as listed in the *act* are as follows:

1. Ready to Learn
   By the year 2000, all children in America will start school ready to learn.
2. School Completion
   By the year 2000, the high school graduation rate will increase to at least 90 percent.
3. Student Achievement and Citizenship
   By the year 2000, all students will leave grades 4, 8, and 12 having demonstrated competency over challenging subject matter, including

English, mathematics, science, foreign languages, civics and government, economics, arts, history, and geography, and every school in America will ensure that all students learn to use their minds well, so they may be prepared for responsible citizenship, further learning, and productive employment in our nation's modern economy.

4. Teacher Education and Professional Development
   By the year 2000, the nation's teaching force will have access to programs for the continued improvement of their professional skills and the opportunity to acquire the knowledge and skills needed to instruct and prepare all American students for the next century.

5. Mathematics and Science
   By the year 2000, U.S. students will be first in the world in mathematics and science achievement.

6. Adult Literacy and Lifelong Learning
   By the year 2000, every adult American will be literate and will possess the knowledge and skills necessary to compete in a global economy and exercise the rights and responsibilities of citizenship.

7. Safe, Disciplined, and Alcohol- and Drug-Free Schools
   By the year 2000, every school in the United States will be free of drugs, violence, and the unauthorized presence of firearms and alcohol and will offer a disciplined environment conducive to learning.

8. Parental Participation
   By the year 2000, every school will promote partnerships that will increase parental involvement and participation in promoting social, emotional, and academic growth of children. (*Goals 2000* online)

Goal Five states that U.S. students will be first in the world in mathematics and science achievement. The establishment of this goal has had a major impact on science education in U.S. schools. There has been an increase in emphasis and time spent on science; federal funding for science and mathematics initiatives has increased; attention to preservice and inservice teacher training has increased; money for equipment and materials has become more available; and teachers have been encouraged to give attention to all students. This is the goal that was addressed in the Third International Mathematics and Science Study (TIMSS) described earlier in this chapter.

National Association for the Education of Young Children

The National Association for the Education of Young Children (NAEYC), the nation's largest organization dedicated to the education of young children, published a statement on Developmentally Appropriate Practice in 1986 and 1987. The statement was revised in 1997 and provides guidelines for developmentally appropriate practice. The document is intended *not* as a template but as a set of guidelines to foster and encourage flexibility and individualization in teaching young children. There is no single way to implement developmentally appropriate practice. Rather, teachers use the guidelines to help them make sound decisions based on individual children, their developmental and cognitive needs, their families, and the community, social, and cultural context of the children's environment. The guidelines recognize that, though all children progress through the same basic stages of development, each child does so at his or her own rate.

The guidelines are summarized in Figure 1.5. Study the information in this figure. Does it sound familiar? It should, for Developmentally Appropriate Practice and the National Science Education Standards are very similar. The primary differences are that the Developmentally Appropriate Practice guidelines include practices related to all aspects of child development (including cognitive development), and they extend to children younger than those addressed in the National Science Education Standards. As you will see, this text fosters your construction of developmentally appropriate practice in the teaching of science. Thus, you could say that this book could be viewed as a special case of Developmentally Appropriate Practice.

An element of controversy exists over the Developmentally Appropriate Practice statements that parallel the controversy that surrounds *all* national standards. Some of the controversy reflects a tendency of educators to polarize into two groups: those who interpret the document literally and those who accept it as guidance. In an effort to soften this disagreement, the NAEYC has urged people to use "both/and" thinking instead of "either/or" thinking (Bredekamp & Copple, 1997, p. 23). The Developmentally Appropriate Practice position statement continues to receive close examination and will therefore continue to be the subject of much discussion. This is an issue worth discussion in your class. As usual, we take no sides; you will have to develop and defend your own ideas based on solid information and knowledgeable discussion.

1. *Creating a caring community of learners*
   a. The early childhood setting functions as a community of learners in which all participants consider and contribute to each other's well-being and learning.
   b. Consistent, positive relationships with a limited number of adults and other children are a fundamental determinant of healthy human development and provide the context for children to learn about themselves and their world and also how to develop positive, constructive relationships with other people. The early childhood classroom is a community in which each child is valued. Children learn to respect and acknowledge differences in abilities and talents and to value each person for his or her strengths.
   c. Social relationships are an important context for learning. Each child has strengths or interests that contribute to the overall functioning of the group. When children have opportunities to play together, work on projects in small groups, and talk with other children and adults, their own development and learning are enhanced. Interacting with other children in small groups provides a context for children to operate on the edge of their developing capabilities. The learning environment enables children to construct understanding through interactions with adults and other children.
   d. The learning environment is designed to protect children's health and safety and is supportive of children's physiological needs for activity, sensory stimulation, fresh air, rest, and nourishment. The program

FIGURE 1.5   NAEYC guidelines for developmentally appropriate practice for young children (from Bredekamp & Copple, 1997, p. 16–22).

provides a balance of rest and active movement for children throughout the program day. Outdoor experiences are provided for children of all ages. The program protects children's psychological safety; that is, children feel secure, relaxed, and comfortable rather than disengaged, frightened, worried, or stressed.

e. Children experience an organized movement and an orderly routing that provides an overall structure in which learning takes place; the environment is dynamic and changing but predictable and comprehensible from a child's point of view. The learning environment provides a variety of materials and opportunities for children to have firsthand, meaningful experiences.

2. *Teaching to enhance development and learning*

a. Teachers respect, value, and accept children and treat them with dignity at all times.

b. Teachers make it a priority to know each child well.

c. Teachers create an intellectually engaging, responsive environment to promote each child's learning and development.

d. Teachers make plans to enable children to attain key curriculum goals across various disciplines.

e. Teachers foster children's collaboration with peers on interesting, important enterprises.

f. Teachers develop, refine, and use a wide repertoire of teaching strategies to enhance children's learning and development.

g. Teachers facilitate the development of responsibility and self-regulation in children.

3. *Constructing appropriate curriculum*

a. Developmentally appropriate curriculum provides for all areas of a child's development: physical, emotional, social, linguistic, aesthetic, and cognitive.

b. Curriculum includes a broad range of content across disciplines that is socially relevant, intellectually engaging, and personally meaningful to children.

c. Curriculum builds upon what children already know and are able to do (activating prior knowledge) to consolidate their learning and to foster their acquisition of new concepts and skills.

d. Effective curriculum plans frequently integrate across traditional subject-matter divisions to help children make meaningful connections and provide opportunities for rich conceptual development; focusing on one subject is also a valid strategy at times.

e. Curriculum promotes the development of knowledge and understanding, processes and skills, as well as the dispositions to use and apply skills and to go on in learning.

f. Curriculum content has intellectual integrity, reflecting the key concepts and tools of inquiry of recognized disciplines in ways that are accessible and achievable for young children, ages 3 through 8. Children directly participate in study of the disciplines, for instance, by conducting scientific experiments, writing, performing, solving mathematical problems, collecting and analyzing data, collecting oral history, and performing other roles of experts in the disciplines.

g. Curriculum provides opportunities to support children's home culture and language while also developing all children's abilities to participate in the shared culture of the program and the community.

h. Curriculum goals are realistic and attainable for most children in the designated age range for which they are designed.

i. When used, technology is physically and philosophically integrated in the classroom curriculum and teaching.

4. *Assessing children's learning and development*

a. Assessment of young children's progress and achievements is ongoing, strategic, and purposeful. The results of assessment are used to benefit children—in adapting curriculum and teaching to meet the

(continued)

developmental and learning needs of children, communicating with the child's family, and evaluating the program's effectiveness for the purpose of improving the program.

b. The content of assessments reflects progress toward important learning and developmental goals. The program has a systematic plan for collecting and using assessment information that is integrated with curriculum planning.

c. The methods of assessment are appropriate to the age and experiences of young children. Therefore, assessment of young children relies heavily on the results of observations of children's development, descriptive data, collections of representative work by children, and demonstrated performance during authentic, not contrived, activities. Input from families as well as children's own evaluations of their own work are part of the overall assessment strategy.

d. Assessments are tailored to a specific purpose and used only for the purpose for which they have been demonstrated to produce reliable, valid information.

e. Decisions that have a major impact on children, such as enrollment or placement, are never made on the basis of a single developmental assessment or screening device but are based on multiple sources of relevant information, particularly observations by teachers and parents.

f. To identify children who have special learning or developmental needs and to plan appropriate curriculum and teaching for them, developmental assessments and observations are used.

g. Assessment recognizes individual variation in learners and allows for differences in styles and rates of learning. Assessment takes into consideration such factors as the child's facility in English, stage of language acquisition, and whether the child has had the time and opportunity to develop proficiency in his or her home language as well as in English.

h. Assessment legitimately addresses not only what children can do independently but also what they can do with assistance from other children or adults. Teachers study children as individuals as well as in relationship to groups by documenting group projects and other collaborative work.

5. *Establishing reciprocal relationships with families*

a. Reciprocal relationships between teachers and families require mutual respect, cooperation, shared responsibility, and negotiation of conflicts toward achievement of shared goals.

b. Early childhood teachers work in collaborative partnerships with families, establishing and maintaining regular, frequent two-way communication with children's parents.

c. Parents are welcome in the program and participate in decisions about their children's care and education. Parents observe and participate and serve in decisionmaking roles in the program.

d. Teachers acknowledge parents' choices and goals for children and respond with sensitivity and respect to parents' preferences and concerns without abdicating professional responsibility to children.

e. Teachers and parents share their knowledge of the child and understanding of children's development and learning as part of day-to-day communication and planned conferences. Teachers support families in ways that maximally promote family decisionmaking capabilities and competence.

f. To ensure more accurate and competent information, the program involves families in assessing and planning for individual children.

g. The program links families with a range of services, based on identified resources, priorities, and concerns.

h. Teachers, parents, programs, social service and health agencies, and consultants who may have educational responsibility for the child at different times should, with family participation, share developmental information about children as they pass from one level or program to another.

FIGURE 1.5 *continued*

RIGHT AND WRONG

In traditional science programs, teachers present information about science topics that they expect children to learn, and children demonstrate their learning of this information by responding to questions and situations. Some responses are considered "right," and some are considered "wrong."

Let us consider two questions that are fundamental to all of science education: *Are there right answers? Are there wrong answers?*

The Gummy Bears Lesson

A student teacher had developed a fine interdisciplinary math and science lesson for a first-grade class using gummy bears. The object of the lesson was for children to sort various-colored gummy bears given to them in individual plastic bags by color, lay them head-to-toe on vertical columns previously drawn on chart paper, and draw an elementary histogram of the numbers of each of the gummy bear colors in their bags. After they were finished, they would get to eat their "lesson." The student teacher passed out bags of different-colored gummy bears, one to each student. Seizing on a "teachable moment," she asked each child to estimate how many gummy bears there were in his bag as she handed it to him. (Prior to this lesson, the class had explored estimation using common classroom objects.) It was obvious that there were 15 to 20 gummy bears in each bag. She went from child to child. "How many gummy bears do you suppose there are in your bag?" she asked. "Twenty," said one child. "Twenty-five," said another. "Seventeen." "Twenty." "Thirty." "Twenty-five." "Five." "Eighteen." Wait a minute! Didn't Melissa just say "five"? Wisely, the student teacher moved to the rest of the children, not commenting on what Melissa or anyone else had estimated. The class did the lesson while the student teacher facilitated. No one commented on the estimating activity. When they were finished, Melissa raised her hand. "I said there were five gummy bears in the bag," she said. "I thought you meant 'How many colors'!" (Figure 1.6) (From Martin, 2000)

FIGURE 1.6 Sorting gummy bears

This anecdote illustrates a principle that is to be found over and over again in education, not only in science education: *There are no right answers!*

Perception

The way people make sense of a happening or an observation is a direct result of the way they perceive it.

Constructing Your Ideas 1.4
Meanings of Words

Pick and then say a word that is a little unusual but that everyone knows, and ask the rest of the class to write the first word that comes to mind. For example, you might ask the students to write the first thing that comes to mind when you say one of these words:

range	land
foot	play
fun	work
home	pet
jaguar	kitten
the letter *a*	

Suppose you used the word *jaguar.* Responses might include "tiger," "animal," "car," "silver," "money," "rich," or "cat." Each response represents the initial association made with the word. Notice the different ways people in your class perceive the same stimulus.

Constructing Your Ideas 1.5
Constructing Pairs of Words

Create a pair of words from the following, and tell why you paired them.

ants	cats
monkeys	buildings
plastic	rocks
bananas	cast
mice	apples

Someone might have paired "cats" with "plastic" because cats like to play with plastic. Someone might have paired "cats" with "mice" for the obvious "cat-and-mouse" reason. Someone might have paired "cats" with "cast" because they have the same letters. Someone might have paired "ants" with "rocks" because, in their experience, ants are often found under rocks. Someone might have paired "ants" with "bananas" or "apples" because ants are attracted to fruit. Someone might have paired "ants" with "buildings" because they have seen ants crawl up the sides of buildings.

Notice the different ways different people perceive things. Is any one of these responses right? Is any wrong?

Optical illusions also show that different people perceive the same stimulus in different ways (see Figure 1.7).

Perception is "the detection and interpretation of sensory stimuli" (Solso, 1988, p. 6). It is the mental image formed when information is received through the senses and is attended to. No two people, when exposed to the same stimulus, perceive it in the same way.[7] This is because we all have different prior experiences of different strengths that influence how we perceive things.

If this is true with simple things such as words, then it is also true with more complex concepts such as "dog." Suppose in your preschool class you are going to bring in your newly acquired pet puppy, Rusty. You tell the children that Rusty is friendly and cuddly and that he loves children and gives them loving kisses. Your expectation is that all the children will eagerly

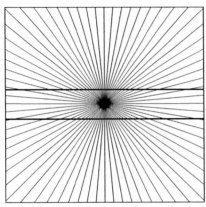

a. Are these lines straight?

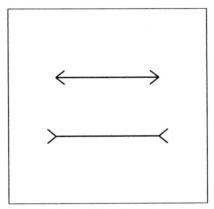

b. Are these lines of different lengths?

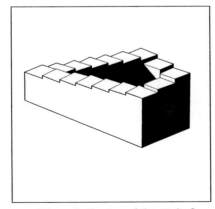

c. Where is the top of the stairs?

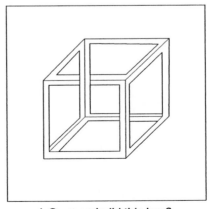

d. Can you build this box?

FIGURE 1.7   Optical illusions

anticipate getting to know Rusty. In fact, every child in the class *is* eager. That is, all except one who, out of the blue, starts to howl an anguished wail. You wonder what the matter can be, and, after questioning, you discover that he has been deathly afraid of dogs ever since he saw his brother get bitten by one last year. Is either of these responses right? Is either wrong? It would be very difficult indeed to say that any of these responses was either *right* or *wrong*. The best we can say is that *to the individual* the response is right. Children are likely to respond in very different ways from what teachers expect. That does not make a child's response wrong; it simply makes it *theirs*.

Listening

A fundamental premise of this text is that teachers of early childhood science must listen to children—listen to their responses—so they can understand what *their* prior experiential bases are, what *their* perceptions are, how *they* are combining new information with their prior experiences and their perceptions, and how *they* are constructing information.

In this way, we see that there are no "right" answers and there are no "wrong" answers; the answers children offer are representative of the way they are thinking. It is far more important for teachers to listen to children and elicit from them their reasons for their responses than to declare their responses either right or wrong.

OWNERSHIP OF KNOWLEDGE AND THOUGHT

One of the goals of education is self-empowerment. In order to be self-empowered, children must develop confidence in their thinking abilities. They must take ownership of their knowledge and their thinking. As we indicated in the beginning of this chapter, children know a great deal of science before they enter school, such as properties of toys, characteristics of seasons, the difference between heat and cold, what cooking does to food, and so on. They need to be told that they know a lot of science so they can begin to develop confidence and take ownership of their abilities to learn.

Mystery Box

A typical box might contain a 1-inch washer taped to the bottom of the box, a loose metal screw, and a small irregularly shaped stone (see Figure 1.8). You may wish to include coins or marbles. Do not put too many items in the box!

What do you have to do to figure out what is in the box? You will probably shake it. You will tilt it, sometimes rapidly, sometimes very slowly, and sometimes at different angles. You will listen to what is happening inside as you tilt it. You will try to balance it. You will use the magnet to see whether anything magnetic is in it. As you proceed with your investigation, you will get more and more refined in focus. You will discuss your ideas with others in your group, arguing, defending, changing your mind in response to their input, and so on.

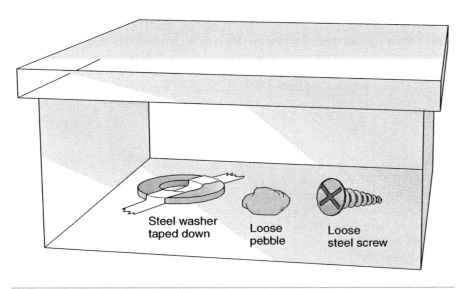

FIGURE 1.8   A mystery box

Constructing Your Ideas 1.6
A Mystery Box

Obtain a small box that has a cover, and place two or three small objects in it. The objects may be any size and any shape and may be made of any material. *Do not tell anyone what is in the box!* Put the cover on the box, tape it shut, and give this Mystery Box to four or five other students in a group. Ask them to draw or write or describe what is in the box. If you put magnetic items in the box, you may wish to provide them with a magnet to help them in their observations.

Please notice that in this activity you used several processes: observing, classifying (identifying objects as magnetic or nonmagnetic), communicating (with members in your group), maybe some measuring (locations of permanent objects; relative strength of magnetic pull), predicting, inferring, formulating and testing hypotheses (if you compared the magnetic strength of known objects with the magnetic strength of objects in the box), interpreting data, and, possibly, constructing models.

Keep pursuing your investigations until you have formulated your very best idea. Are you *right?* How sure are you? What is your confidence percentage? How could you increase your confidence percentage? You could make a model—create an identical box with the same things in yours that you think are in the Mystery Box, and compare the two boxes carefully to see whether they exhibit the same characteristics.

There probably are several notions about what is in the box. Who is right? Who is wrong? Remember, the box is closed. "Rightness" and "wrongness" take on different perspectives—they no longer refer to the correctness of an answer but rather to your thinking and the ways you interrelate your observations and your thinking to form your conclusions. Each student's conclusion is accepted as representative of his or her best thinking.

Ownership

Should you open the boxes? Suppose they were sealed shut, never to be opened! How would you feel? Frustrated? Cheated? You would never know if you were right or wrong. If you are not permitted to open the boxes, you will be required to rely on your own powers of observation, your own reasoning and inferring, and the conclusions that you yourself reach from your own and others' thinking. You will be forced to validate your conclusions from your own thinking. You will be forced to *assume ownership* of your observations, thoughts, and conclusions.

However, suppose you know you will be allowed to open the box at some point. Suddenly *your* thinking is devalued. Instead of observing, inferring, and reasoning, you are trying to "guess." The motivation becomes to compare your answer with the "right" answer, not with your own conclusion. There is a "right" answer, and you compare your answer with *it*. If you guessed correctly, great! If not, oh well!

Should you open the box? Do you have faith in the ability of the scientific processes you used in this activity to provide a "best" answer? Each class will have to decide for itself. As you are deciding, please cite your arguments.

Valuing Children's Thinking

Is it more important that children value the teacher's knowledge or their own? Many students answer "their own." This response comes from a belief that one of the teacher's primary jobs is to help children think for themselves. But what about the teacher? Isn't the teacher's thinking more valid than the children's? Hasn't the teacher had many years of education learning how to think? Shouldn't the teacher teach the children how to think? Shouldn't the teacher encourage the children to emulate correct thinking? These are questions for you to ponder.

If you truly believe it is important for children to take ownership of their own knowledge, then you will be asking how teachers can foster children's belief that their thinking is valuable.

Consider a typical series of questions a kindergarten teacher might ask in introducing a lesson on animals:

Name something you eat that's green.
Name something you eat that's red.
Name something you eat that's yellow.
Name something you eat that's orange.

Name something you eat that you don't have to cook.
Name something you eat that comes from leaves.
Name something you eat that comes from stems.
Name something you eat that comes from roots.
Name something you eat that's cold.
Name something you eat that's frozen.
Name something you eat that's hot.

Let us take a look at these questions. Each question implies there are one or more right answers and that any other answers are wrong.

"Name something you eat that's red."
"Tomato?"
"Right!"
"Strawberries?"
"Right!"
"Carrots?"
"Wrong!"
"Name something you eat that you don't have to cook."
"Carrots?"
"Right!"
"Chicken?"
"Wrong!"
"Name something you eat that's frozen."
"Ice cream?"
"Right!"
"Potato chips"
"Wrong!"

You get the idea: For each question, there are *right* answers and there are *wrong* answers. Who knows the right answers? The teacher, of course. Note in the preceding questioning scenario, the children answered in a questioning tone of voice, and the teacher told them whether they were right or wrong. Teachers indicate "right" or "wrong" answers in a variety of subtle ways, like "Oh, really?" "That's a good answer," "Thank you for answering," and so on until finally a right answer comes along, and the teacher says "Right" or "That's what I was looking for" or "The other answers were good ones, but that is the one I wanted to hear."

Thus, it is the teacher who owns the knowledge. The teacher encourages the children to compare their answers (maybe right and maybe wrong) with the teacher's (always right), thereby giving the children the unmistakable notion that their job is to supply the answers the teacher wants to hear. The teacher owns the knowledge. The teacher is in charge. It is the teacher's thinking that is valued. The same thing happens in hands-on settings that involve children doing activities whose results are already known, in which it is the children's job to come up with the result the teacher expects. "I don't think that's quite right; try it again and see what you get." (Translation: "You haven't yet gotten the result I wanted you to get.")

How can that be reversed? Using Bloom's higher levels in questioning promotes discussion, whereas using Bloom's lower levels leads to right and wrong answers (Bloom et. al., 1956). Using higher-level questioning requires the teacher to provide time for children to prepare answers. Suppose, for instance, you were asked what plants need in order to grow into large and healthy plants. You probably would quickly respond that plants need food, light, and water. But suppose you were asked a higher-order question, such as what might happen to plants if they were left in red light for a week. You would need *time* to assemble your thoughts into a well-constructed and logical answer before you respond. Rowe (1996) reported that "Teachers who have learned to use silence report that children who do not ordinarily say much start talking and usually have exciting ideas" (p. 36). The use of open-ended questions with longer wait time and longer think time goes a long way toward fostering children's beliefs that their own thinking is important. When asking open-ended and higher-level questions, if you, the teacher, resist the temptation to offer "words of great wisdom" (or, better yet, if you don't know the answer to the question), the children will have to work the situation out for themselves. They will own the thought processes as well as the conclusion. They will be well on their way to learning that their knowledge is valuable and is valued by the teacher.

Another way to encourage children's ownership of their own thought processes and knowledge is to reduce the number of affirmations offered, such as "right," "good try," and "wonderful" because these responses subtly but surely suggest to children that their responses are given for the teacher's judgement. To foster children's ownership of their thinking, use simple statements thanking children for their responses or nonverbal responses such as smiles or head nods.

The responses to children's answers that foster the highest degree of ownership are those that probe the children's thinking. "Why did you say that?" "How do you know?" "Give an example of what you just said." "Can you add to Jane's response?" "Do you agree?" "Do you disagree?" "What would happen if. . ." "Tell us how you came up with that idea." "Can you explain your thinking?"

Blasi (1996), a kindergarten teacher, asserts that the way to show children we value their thinking is to encourage them to talk. She writes, "By valuing talk in the classroom, we enrich our curriculum with children's thoughts, raise learning activities to more sophisticated levels, and build strong, supportive relationships that, in turn, help our students grow into independent thinkers, lifelong learners and socioeconomic individuals" (p. 131). Quintero and Rummel (1996) report that, in addition to asking children open questions, they encourage children to share by asking them simply to "say something" about the topics under investigation.

In this course you will construct a way of teaching early childhood science that places ownership of thought and scientific facts, concepts, generalizations, and theories firmly in the laps (or heads) of your children: the process-oriented inquiry methodology. Under the teacher's guidance, children ask their own questions, devise their own ways to explore their questions, and develop their own answers to their questions.

It is not within the scope of this book to discuss at length how children develop or how they learn. But if children are to learn and retain anything, they must own and value what *they* do, not what *we* do. Our job is to lead them to their own sound thinking. We must set the tone in the class that sends the signal to all children that their answers are at least as important as anyone else's—including the teacher's.

THE METAPHOR

Research has examined the influence of the metaphor on teaching (Munby, 1986; Pajares, 1992; Tobin, 1990). A metaphor is a word or a phrase a teacher chooses to characterize his or her role as a teacher. For example, teachers who characterize themselves as "captain of their ship" may be very strong leaders but reluctant to transfer responsibility for learning to children.

Constructing Your Ideas 1.7
Metaphors

Think for minute or so about a metaphor you would use to characterize your role as a teacher of early childhood science. Do you consider yourself the captain of your ship? A bus driver? An explorer? A scout leader? A parent? Record the various metaphors the members of your class come up with, and from that list (which includes your own metaphor) select the metaphor you believe most closely represents your current thinking about what an early childhood science teacher is and does. Write it down.

Refer to this metaphor frequently during this course; see whether you want to change it. This may be one of the better indicators of how you are constructing the content of the course.

WHAT DO YOU THINK?

It is time now for you to consolidate your thoughts about early childhood science education.

Constructing Your Ideas 1.8
Preliminary Philosophy of Early Childhood Science Education

Write your own philosophy of early childhood science education. Think through the issues carefully and thoroughly. Consider these kinds of questions:

■ What is the teacher's role?
■ What is the student's role?
■ What are the goals and outcomes of your science program?
■ What is the role of scientific processes?
■ What content should be taught?

(continued)

- ■ How will you merge process and content?
- ■ What is the role of hands-on activities?
- ■ How will you use textual materials and worksheets?
- ■ What kinds of materials and equipment will you use?
- ■ How involved will the children get in their own learning?
- ■ How will children achieve this involvement?
- ■ How will children learn to value science?
- ■ How will you ensure success for *all* children, especially underrepresented groups such as females, African-Americans, Hispanics, and Native Americans?

The statement should be a well-thought-out synthesis of your thinking about your own teaching of science—*not* a compilation of answers to the questions. The questions are offered merely to stimulate your thinking.

This activity is deliberately suggested at the beginning of the course to give you a chance to reflect on your own thinking and to review your thoughts as you move along. This book is designed to enable you to gain experience in doing science so you can construct your own conceptualization of how science should be taught to young children and how you will teach it. You will use your statement to guide you in the construction and reconstruction of your own thinking about appropriate methodology in quality early childhood science education.

SUMMARY

The goal of this first chapter has been for you to get started on your personal inquiry into the "best" ways of teaching science to children in early childhood classroom settings. You have examined a number of issues dealing with the amount of science known, the constant changes and refinements that scientific information undergoes, and the amount of scientific information early childhood teachers need to know to be able to teach science well. You have examined the goals of early childhood science education as set forth by several important groups and professional organizations. You have looked at the process approach to science education and the notion that it is more meaningful for children to learn how to *do* science than it is for them to learn about science. You have inquired into the meanings of "right" and "wrong," the phenomenon of perception, and ways of fostering children's thinking. You have drawn tentative conclusions for all these notions, and you have started to ask important questions about content, process, goals, outcomes, and methodology of early childhood science teaching.

As you progress through this course, make it your goal to formulate answers to these questions, to resolve concerns, and to develop a system of early childhood science education that meets the needs of today's children as we prepare them to live in the twenty-first century. No one can do this for you; to try to do so would be to do the same thing we are suggesting you *not* do with children: pump them full of previously digested information. You have to make up your own mind; you have to construct this business of early childhood science education in a way that makes sense to you.

The rest of this text will help you in your quest.

Notes

1. The entire TIMSS report, including sample test questions and analyses, can be accessed on the World Wide Web at http://nces.ed.gov/timss.
2. For detailed treatment and additional information concerning the processes of science, refer to Padilla (not dated), McCormack and Yager (1989), and Rezba, Sprague, Fiel, and Funk (1995).
3. Teacher guides for Elementary Science Study and SCIS 3, an updated version of Science Curriculum Improvement Study, are available from Delta Education, Box 3000, Nashua, NH 03061-3000, Telephone 1-800-442-5444. You can access Delta Education on the World Wide Web at www.delta-ed.com. See also Chapter 22.
4. Comets are named for the people who discover them. Halley's Comet is named in honor of Edmund Halley, who discovered it in the late 1600s. He calculated its orbit and successfully predicted its return in 1758. It was last in the earth's vicinity in 1985, and it returns every 76 years.
5. The elementary school edition of *NSTA Pathways to the Science Standards* (Lowery, 1997) focuses on grades K–4, providing much useful material for early childhood science educators.
6. The entire January 2000 issue of *Science and Children* (vol. 37, no. 4) is devoted to using the *Standards* in early childhood and elementary science programs.
7. The concept of uniqueness of perception and its application to education was explored in detail over forty years ago by Kelley and Rasey (1952).

References

American Association for the Advancement of Science (1993). *Benchmarks for science literacy: Project 2061*. New York: Oxford University Press.

———. (1997). *Resources for science literacy*. New York: Oxford University Press.

Blasi, M. J. (1996). Pedagogy: Passivity or possibility. *Childhood Education, 72* (3), 130–132.

Bloom, B. S., Englehart, M. D., Furst, E. J., Hill, W. H. & Krathwohl, D. R. (Eds.). (1956). *Taxonomy of educational objectives: The classification of educational goals. Handbook I: Cognitive domain*. New York: McKay.

Bredekamp, S. & Copple, C. (Eds.). (1997). *Developmentally appropriate practice in early childhood programs* (rev. ed.). Washington, DC: National Association for the Education of Young Children.

Bruner, J. S. (1965). *The process of education*. Cambridge, MA: Harvard University Press.

Costa, A., & Liebman, R. (1995). Process is as important as content. *Educational Leadership, 52*(6), 23–24.

Diamond, M., & Hopson, J. (1998). *Magic trees of the mind: How to nurture your child's intelligence, creativity, and healthy emotions from birth through adolescence.* New York: Penguin Group.

Dickinson, V. L., Burns, J., Hagen, E. R., & Locker, K. M. (1997). Becoming better primary science teachers: A description of our journey. *Journal of Science Teacher Education, 8*(4), 295–311.

Goals 2000. Online at http://inet.ed.gov/legislation/GOALS2000/TheAct/sec102.html.

Hawking, S. (1998). Millennium evenings: Science in the next millennium. On-line at http://www.whitehouse.gov/Initiatives/Millennium/shawking-plain.html.

Hurd, P. D. (1985). *A changing society: New perspectives for science education.* Paper adapted from an address delivered at the PACE Seminar on Educational Policy for a Changing California Economy, Sacramento, CA, June 14, 1984. Eric Document Number: ED 271311.

Hurd, P. D. (1990). Guest editorial: Change and challenge in science education. *Journal of Research in Science Teaching, 27*(5), 413–414.

Kelley, E. C., & Rasey, M. I. (1952). *Education and the nature of man.* New York: Harper & Row.

Lowery, L. F. (Ed.). (1997). *NSTA pathways to the science standards* (Elementary school ed.). National Science Teachers Association, 1840 Wilson Boulevard, Arlington, VA 22201.

Martin, D. J. (2000). *Elementary science methods: A constructivist approach* (2nd ed.). Belmont, CA: Wadsworth/Thompson Learning.

McCormack, A. J., & Yager, R. E. (1989). Towards a taxonomy for science education. *The Georgia Journal of Science, 19*(3), 11–12.

Munby, H. (1986). Metaphor in the thinking of teachers: An exploratory study. *Journal of Curriculum Studies, 18,* 197–209.

National Research Council. (1996). *National Science Education Standards.* Washington, DC: National Academy Press.

National Science Teachers Association. (1998). The National Science Education Standards: A vision for the improvement of science teaching and learning. *Science Scope 21*(8), 32–34.

Padilla, M. (n.d.) The science process skills. "Research Matters . . . to the Science Teacher." National Association for Research in Science Teaching.

Pajares, M. (1992). Teachers' beliefs and educational research: Cleaning up on a messy construct. *Review of Educational Research, 61,* 307–332.

Quintero, E., & Rummel, M. K. (1996). Something to say: Voice in the classroom. *Childhood Education, 72* (3), 146–151.

Rezba, R. J., Sprague, C., Fiel, D. L., & Funk, H. J. (1995). *Learning and assessing science process skills.* Dubuque, IA: Kendall/Hunt.

Rowe, M. B., (1996). Science, silence, and sanctions. *Science and Children, 34*(1), 35–37.

Rutherford, F. J., & Ahlgren, A. (1990). *Science for all Americans*. New York, Oxford University Press.

Sagan, C. (1989, September 10). Why we need to understand science. *Parade*.

Seuss, Dr. [pseud. for Geisel, T. S.]. (1990). *Oh, the places you'll go!* New York: Random House.

Solso, R. L. (1988). *Cognitive psychology* (2nd ed.). Newton, MA: Allyn and Bacon.

Therman, E. (1986). *Human chromosomes*. New York: Springer-Verlag.

Tobin, K. (1990). Research on science laboratory activities: In pursuit of better questions and answers to improve learning. *School Science and Mathematics, 90,* 403–418.

Villard, R., Macchetto, D., Dressler, A., & Dickinson, M. (1994). Hubble identifies primeval galaxies, uncovers new clues to the universe's evolution. On-line at http://oposite.stsci.edu/pubinfo/press-releases/94-52.txt.

CHAPTER 2

The Basic Scientific Processes: Observing

In Chapter 1 you considered the notion that the goal of early childhood science education is for children to learn how to do science the way scientists do science. It was suggested that scientists do science by employing the processes of science. [1]

Our first task will be to investigate the six basic processes of science. They are as follows:

▮ Observing

▮ Classifying

▮ Communicating

▮ Measuring

▮ Predicting

▮ Inferring

The shrewd guess, the fertile hypothesis, the courageous leap to a tentative conclusion—these are the most valuable coin of the thinker at work.

Jerome Bruner, *The Process of Education* (Cambridge, MA: Harvard University Press, 1960), p. 14

Knowledge will not always take the place of simple observation.

Arnold Lobel, "The Elephant and His Son," *Fables* (New York: HarperCollins Children's Books, 1980).

These six processes, referred to as the "basic" processes (McCormack & Yager, 1989; Padilla, n.d.), are fundamental to all scientific investigation. Think of the parachute activity or the mystery box activity suggested in Chapter 1. If we are going to investigate a phenomenon, we must observe what we can about it. We often find it desirable to classify various occurrences relating to the phenomenon. We certainly will want to communicate with other people what we observed and what our ideas are about what we are investigating. Frequently we find it necessary to make careful measurements in order to compare or gather information. Often we find ourselves predicting what would happen if we tried something, and then trying it to see if we were right. But, equally often, something happens in our investigation for which we don't know the reason, and we find ourselves making one or more inferences.

Explorations of each of the processes are contained in the following chapters. Individual chapters begin with one or more Constructing Your Ideas activities that you, the student, should do to gain an idea of what it is like to investigate the process. This is followed by a discussion of the process and ways young children can master and apply it to their scientific inquiries. The chapter then contains suggestions of activities called "Constructing Science in the Classroom" that you can implement to provide opportunities for children to explore and master the process. Suggestions for preparing charts and graphs are included in some of the activities to help organize the inquiries and to help children begin to portray the results of their investigations visually—as scientists do. The charts and graphs are not necessarily meant to be assessed or sent home with the children but are intended primarily for in-class use. The "Constructing Science in the Classroom" activities also contain suggested literature connections that will help you select interesting reading materials that complement the topic under investigation. Finally, for each process you are asked to develop an activity of your own dealing with the process that you can use in the early childhood science classroom.

The ancient Chinese proverb says:

I hear and I forget;

I see and I remember;

I do and I understand.

The goal of this text is for you to construct your own understandings of the nature of science, your understandings of the ways scientists do science, your understandings of the goals of early childhood science education, and your understandings of the most effective ways to teach science to young children. The only way you can do this is to *do*.

So, let's get ready to *do!*

We start by exploring the process of observing. First we will do an activity that involves observing.

heft—Hold an object in one's hand and move the hand up and down to feel the weight of the object

inclusions—Pieces of nonnative materials imbedded within pieces of rock

---

Constructing Your Ideas 2.1
The Rock Hunt

In preparation for this activity, you will need a magnifying glass and a few small rocks. You can either collect the rocks on your own and bring them to your class or go outdoors as a class to find your specimens. Each person should gather approximately 15 different kinds of rocks. While you are looking for your rocks, be sure to pick them up carefully and turn them over to see whether there is anything clinging to the underside. Look for insects and little worms. You might want to make a note of which rocks had insects and/or worms on them or hiding underneath them. You can identify the rock you are examining in several ways. One way is to trace an outline of it. Another way is to write a number on the surface of each rock using permanent markers. Or you can write your initials followed by a number on each rock so you will be able to tell which rocks you yourself collected when your collection is mixed with those of other students later on. Select relatively small rocks, and put them in a bag.

In class, look at your rocks carefully. Use magnifying glasses to help. Describe their characteristics. Many people have a difficult time making observations of things the first time they see them, so you may wish to use a table similar to the one shown in Figure 2.1 to help guide you on what to look for. Do not feel compelled to fill in all the boxes; the sheet is provided only as a guide. "Color" is your general impression of the rock's color. "Texture" refers to how smooth, slippery, rough, chalky, etc. it is. "Relative weight" refers to how heavy it feels when you **heft** it compared with what you would expect and compared with the other rocks in your collection. "**Inclusions**" refer to tiny pieces of material of other colors, brilliances, or textures imbedded within the rock; these can be described in as much detail as you choose. "Smell" is self-explanatory. Finally, list anything else you observe in the rocks.

The purpose of this activity is for you to *observe*. It is *not* for you to try to identify the rocks or to tell whether they are **igneous, metamorphic, or sedimentary** or to tell how they were formed or where they came from or whether they are rocks or minerals. The *sole purpose* of this activity is to observe.

A word of caution is in order: *Do not taste the rocks* because they may harbor germs or other materials harmful to the body. Much as it might be tempting to see what the rocks taste like, you should not taste them. Please also note that teachers should caution children *not* to taste things unless the teacher specifically tells them to.

What did you observe? What characteristics were immediately apparent? Which characteristics revealed themselves only after you had observed them all quite intently? Which rocks were more interesting than others? Which were unique? In what ways were they unique?

Keep your collections for future activities.

Outline or Number	Color	Texture	Relative Weight	Inclusions	Smell	Anything Else
1						
2						
3						
4						

FIGURE 2.1 Partial data sheet for rock observation activity

What senses did you use? Certainly you used the sense of sight as you looked at the rocks. As a matter of fact, you extended your sense of sight by using the magnifying glasses. The sense of sight enabled you to observe such characteristics as shape, color, subtleties of color and differences within and between rocks, as well as the characteristics of any inclusions. You may have used the sense of smell to see which rocks smelled earthy and which did not, or which had other peculiar odors. Did you use the sense of hearing? Some people may have dropped the rocks to see what sound they made when they hit the floor. You did not use the sense of taste.

You used the sense of touch when you explored how smooth and how heavy the rocks are and what their textures are. In addition, maybe some rocks felt warmer or cooler than others when you touched them. Notice that the sense of touch actually includes many senses. We feel something's texture through nerve endings on the skin. We feel how heavy something is through an internal muscular sense. We detect how warm or cold something is through heat-sensitive nerve endings. In addition, we have the sense of pressure, the sense of balance, the sense of muscle contraction, the sense of muscle memory, the sense of direction, and many other internal senses. In all we

igneous—Rocks formed from magma; includes granite, pumice, basalt, obsidian, and others

sedimentary—Rocks formed from materials that have settled and become cemented together; includes sandstone, limestone, conglomerate, shale, gypsum, and others

metamorphic—Rocks formed from changes in other rocks caused by high temperatures or high pressures or both; includes gneiss, schist, quartzite, slate, marble, and others

receptor systems—Systems in living organisms that enable them to detect stimuli

have some 30 different kinds of **receptor systems** in our bodies. Thus, one can say that the human body has over 30 different kinds of senses.

In developing the skill of observation, children learn to use all their senses, and it is critically important that teachers of children in preschool and the early grades provide stimuli that encourage children to observe. Research on brain function has shown that rich and varied experiences are required for optimum brain development, especially during the early childhood years. The more experiences a child can be provided, the more the brain grows and develops, and the better prepared the child will be for more complex cognitive operations as he or she grows and matures (Wolfe & Brandt, 1998). These experiences are acquired through stimulation of the senses by means of the process of observing.[2]

Let us return to our rocks. What words did you use to describe your rocks? Make a class list; you will use this list in the next section.

As an interesting sideline to this activity, were there any people in your class who were not at all interested in rocks? Were *you*? Compare the observations made by the people who were interested in rocks with those made by people who were not interested in rocks. Is there a difference? It seems we are much better observers when we are interested in something than when we are not.

Activities patterned after this rock-observing activity provide excellent ways for children to begin observing. Use pictures, leaves, bells, coins, stamps, buttons, dolls, hardware, or just about anything else. You may want to place individual specimens on paper plates and put them around the room. Children move around the room and make observations to report back to the class. Do you have a collection of something? Use it. Remember the old dictum, "If you're going to be a teacher, never throw anything away," and use things you have saved. When teachers share their collections with children, their enthusiasm is demonstrated, and this encourages participation by the children (Figure 2.2).

FIGURE 2.2   Examining a collection

Constructing Your Ideas 2.2
What Did You See on Your Way to School Today?

Ask this question every class period. You will notice that, as time goes by, there will be more and more responses from the students in your class. When people are challenged to observe, they direct their attention to observing, and they actually *see* things.

Constructing Your Ideas 2.3
What Did You See on the Way to School Today That Has Always Been There but Which You Never Noticed Before?

After your class has been in session for two or three weeks, start asking this question. You will find there are numerous things that have always been present along the route you take to school but which you never noticed before. It is surprising to find these things, and we ask ourselves how we could *not* have noticed them before. The key is deliberate observation. When we look for something, we are more inclined to see things than when we are not focusing our attention on observing.

Constructing Your Ideas 2.4
What Did You See on Your Way to School Today That Made You Wonder about Something?

Begin asking this question after your class has been in session five or six weeks. Then "brainstorm" as a class ways in which you could find the answers to your questions. For example, in one class, students noticed that, in the morning, dew was present on one side of cars that were parked outdoors overnight but not on the other side. They wondered why this happened. In another class, students said they had observed that in the autumn, leaves fall from most of the deciduous trees but not the oak trees, and they wondered why. In southwestern United States, the **ginkgo tree** drops *all* its leaves overnight the night the first frost arrives; why does this happen?

The essence of all science is observation. Ultimately, it is observation that suggests questions and phenomena to be investigated; it is observation that suggests the procedures to be followed during the investigations; it is observation of the outcomes of investigations that enable inferences and conclusions to be formulated. The skill of observation must be developed in children and must be developed so they observe accurately and completely, and especially so they look for the unexpected. Early childhood education teachers must provide children the greatest possible opportunity to observe. Observation must be built into every aspect of the daily program. It is our responsibility to help children develop, sharpen, deepen, and master their skills of observation.

ginkgo tree—A deciduous tree with fan-shaped leaves and yellow fruit; native to eastern China

Several observation activities are suggested in Constructing Science in the Classroom 2.1–2.11. Some are appropriate for preschool children, and some are more appropriate for children in the early elementary grades. The activities suggest ways of providing experiences and practice in using each of the senses for observation.

Constructing Science in the Classroom 2.1
Listening for Different Sounds

AGE

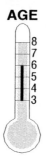

AN OBSERVATION ACTIVITY USING THE SENSE OF HEARING

Objective
The student will observe the sounds made by a variety of objects when dropped onto a tabletop.

Assemble a collection of several objects that make different sounds when dropped on to a table. Suggestions include coins, paper clips, erasers, rubber bands, sticks, M&M®s, keys, pencils, hollow gourds, books, marshmallows, a rock, an empty can, a bell, a plastic cup, and so on. Have children hold each object about two feet above a tabletop and drop it. Ask them to provide one or more words that describe the sounds ("tinkle," "thud," "crash," "bang," "bump," and the like).

Also ask children to tell whether the sound was loud or soft. Ask them to try dropping the objects from different heights to see whether height affects the loudness of the sound.

Literature Connection:
Just Listen by Winifred Morris (1990) is a moving story of a young girl's visit to her grandmother's house. There, grandmother and granddaughter spend time together outside and listen to the "special song" of nature.

Constructing Science in the Classroom 2.2
How Smooth Is That Cloth?

AGE

AN OBSERVATION ACTIVITY INVOLVING TEXTURE

Objective
The student will observe the textures of different fabrics.

Cut two squares each out of fabrics with different textures such as silk, flannel, felt, lace, corduroy, terrycloth, burlap, imitation fur, and so on. Give children one set of the squares to feel; ask them to describe the texture of each (soft, furry, fuzzy, smooth, rough, etc). Put the other set in a paper bag. After children have acquired familiarity with the samples they have been feeling, select one at a time and ask them to find its matching sample in the bag using the sense of touch.

Literature Connections:
Feely Bugs: To Touch and Feel by David A. Carter (1995) is a touch-and-feel book presenting a broad array of textures for children to experience.
I Touch by Rachel Isadora (1991) is formatted as a board-book for readers' interaction. Children react to things they touch.

Constructing Science in the Classroom 2.3
What Sound Is Louder?

AGE

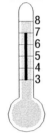

AN OBSERVATION ACTIVITY USING THE SENSE OF HEARING

Objective
The student will observe loud sounds and soft sounds.

Ask children to tap their fingers lightly on a desktop. They must be very quiet to do this activity. Ask them to describe how loud or how soft the sound is. Then ask them to put one ear directly on the desktop and tap their fingers the same way. Is this sound louder or softer than before? Have children try several variations of this activity, including tapping their fingers harder and softer and using other materials such as pencils, paper clips, keys, coins, and so on.

Literature Connections:
It's Too Noisy! By Joanna Cole (1989). A farmer learns to accept the noise made by the many people living in his house when he compares it with the noise made when animals also live in the house.
Crickets and Bullfrogs and Whispers of Thunder by Harry Behn (1984) is a collection of poems about nature, fantasy, and beauty.

Constructing Science in the Classroom 2.4
Observing Animals

AGE

AN OBSERVATION ACTIVITY USING THE SENSE OF SIGHT

Objective
The student will observe different kinds of animals.

The best place for children to observe animals is in their natural habitats. Pets can be observed at home; farm animals can be observed at farms; less common animals can be observed at zoos. (See Chapters 19 and 20 for suggestions on doing science in nontraditional settings and for taking field trips.)
     Ask children to describe what they see when they look at the various animals. Focus initially on physical characteristics such as color, shape, covering (hair, feathers, something else), markings, shape and size of tail, shape and size of ears, and so on. Also ask them to describe how the animals walk, how they run, how they sit, how they lie down, and what sounds they make.
     Older children in late kindergarten through second grade could use photographs in addition to real animals. Provide photographs of animals in their natural habitats cut out from magazines such as *Your Big Backyard* (published by the National Wildlife Federation), *National Geographic, National Geographic World, National Wildlife, Ranger Rick, Smithsonian,* and *Zoobooks.*

Literature Connection:
Brian Wildsmith's Wild Animals by Brian Wildsmith (1967) is a picture book showing lions, leopards, foxes, badgers, and other wild animals.

Constructing Science in the Classroom 2.5
What's That Smell?

AGE

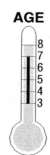

AN OBSERVATION ACTIVITY USING THE SENSE OF SMELL

Objective
The student will use the sense of smell to identify materials.

Press a cotton ball or a single sheet of tissue into the bottom of each of several empty film canisters. (Photo finishing shops normally have an abundance of film canisters that they are happy to give away.) Use a thin nail to poke three or four holes in the tops of the canisters. Sprinkle materials with different smells into each canister, and close them with the perforated tops. Suggestions include apple juice, orange juice, lemon juice, pineapple juice, dishwashing liquid, cinnamon, soy sauce, cooking essences such as almond, vanilla, peppermint, and so on. Number each canister, and ask children to smell each one and identify what is in it.

Safety Note: Be sure children are not allergic to any of the materials you use in this activity. School records should have allergies listed for each child. If someone is allergic to one or more of the materials used, have that child skip over the canister that contains that material.

Literature Connections:
My Five Senses by Aliki (1989) is a very simple text with clear illustrations of how we use our five senses. "When I bounce a ball, I see, hear, and touch."
You Can't Smell a Flower with Your Ear!: All about Your 5 Senses by Joanna Cole (1994) is a fun and simple science book with games and experiments involving the senses.
Snuffles by Joan Anson-Weber (1995). Snuffles, the pig, travels to France to look for truffles using his sense of smell.

Constructing Science in the Classroom 2.6
What Is the Weather Today?

AGE

AN OBSERVATION ACTIVITY USING SEVERAL SENSES

Objective
The student will observe the weather each day.

Ask children what the weather was like on their way to school. Then take them outside to observe. Ask such questions as "What do you feel?" "What do you see?" "What do you hear?" "What do you smell?" Ask them to point out weather indicators such as clouds, rain, dew, or snow, puddles, ice spots, what people are wearing, how the flag or tree branches and leaves are moving, and so on. To enable children to observe how windy it is outdoors, put a pinwheel in the ground in an open area where the children can see it from a classroom window, and have children tell how fast the pinwheel is moving. You may wish to record their observations on a class chart using pictograms or words or both. Occasionally, you may wish to ask children to make an illustration in their science journals (see Chapter 18) of something they observed. Do this each day, and ask children to point out any significant changes in weather that occur from day to day. A four-year-old may draw or color a picture depicting the weather and dictate descriptions for the teacher to write down. Older children can write weather descriptions themselves (see Figure 2.3).

Literature Connections:

Will It Rain? by Holly Keller (1985). Animals become aware of darkening skies and an impending rainstorm. They seek shelter during the storm and reappear when the sun shines again.

Umbrella by Taro Yahsima (1985). Momo, a Japanese girl, eagerly awaits a rainy day so she can use the red boots and umbrella she received for her third birthday.

WEATHER CHART						
Sunday	Monday	Tuesday	Wednesday	Thursday	Friday	Saturday
Cloudy	Rainy	Thunderstorm	Sunny	Sunny	Sunny	Cloudy
Cloudy						

FIGURE 2.3 Daily weather chart

Constructing Science in the Classroom 2.7
What Did You See Today?

AGE

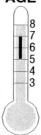

8
7
6
5
4
3

AN ONGOING OBSERVATION ACTIVITY

Objective

The student will observe their natural surroundings.

"What did you see on your way to school today?" Ask this question each day. As time goes on, children will report more and more as they sharpen their senses of observation.

"Did you see the same things on the way home?" Encourage children to share with their parents what they saw on their way home from school.

Literature Connection:

I'm in Charge of Celebrations by Byrd Taylor (1986) is a story of a Native American girl who celebrates beautiful everyday happenings such as seeing rainbows and coyotes.

Constructing Science in the Classroom 2.8
What's That Sound?

AGE

8
7
6
5
4
3

AN OBSERVATION ACTIVITY USING THE SENSE OF HEARING

Objective

The student will use the sense of hearing to identify unknown objects.

Put various items in a dozen plastic eggs. (Note: Empty film canisters can be used instead of the plastic eggs.) Suggested items include tiny marshmallows, rice, beans, pins, cotton, dice, paper clips, a key, matches, a bottle cap, pennies, toothpicks, macaroni, thread, crayon pieces, machine nuts, machine screws, M&M®s, a marble, and so on. Seal the eggs and label them with numbers (see Figure 2.4). Also have available a few empty eggs and samples of each item you put in the eggs. Be sure young children can distinguish between sounds of different qualities before attempting this activity.

In groups, ask the children to shake the eggs and try to identify what is in each egg from the sound it makes when shaken. Ask questions such as "Which eggs have loud sounds?" "Which eggs have soft sounds?" "Which eggs seem empty?" "Which eggs have familiar sounds, like metal, glass, or plastic?" "Are some sounds easy to recognize?" "Are some sounds difficult to recognize?"

If children are uncertain about what is in a particular egg, suggest they put a sample of what they think might be in the egg into an empty egg and compare the sounds made when both are shaken. In this way, they are constructing *models* of the unknown eggs.

Literature Connections:

Click, Rumble, Roar: Poems about Machines by Lee Bennett Hopkins (1987) is a book of poetry about the different sounds machines make.
The Noisy Book by Margaret Wise Brown (1993), is about a blindfolded dog that identifies things from the sounds they make.

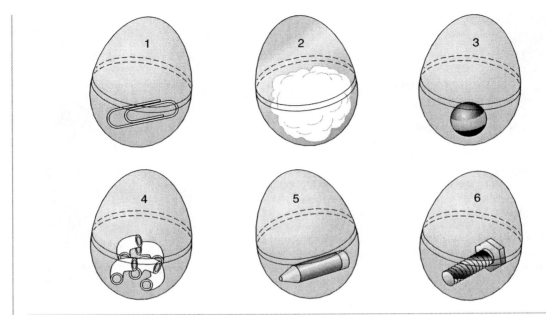

FIGURE 2.4   Materials in plastic eggs

Constructing Science in the Classroom 2.9
What's in the Dirt?

AGE

AN OBSERVATION ACTIVITY USING THE SENSE OF SIGHT

Objective
The student will observe the composition of dirt.

Bring a bag of soil from your home or the schoolyard. Put a spoonful of the soil on a paper plate for each child or group of children. Provide magnifying glasses. Ask the children to examine the soil carefully and to tell the different kinds of things they can find in the soil.

Children can bring soil from where they live, and the class can examine the soils from different places to see what is similar and what is different. You might also want to include some potting soil to show the similarities and differences.

Literature Connection:
We Love the Dirt by Tony Johnston (1997). In this story, the farmer, pig, frog, cricket, earthworm, tree, flower, and scarecrow involve themselves with dirt in special ways.

Constructing Science in the Classroom 2.10
Observing Seeds

AGE

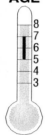

AN OBSERVATION ACTIVITY USING THE SENSE OF SIGHT

Objective
The student will observe seeds.

Obtain a collection of several different kinds of vegetable seeds such as beans, peas, and lima beans. Soak them in water for a few hours or overnight to loosen the skin.
    Ask children to describe (or draw) the outsides of the seeds. Then ask the children to cut the seeds with plastic knives; they should open readily if they have been soaked (Figure 2.5). Ask children to describe (or draw) what they observe on the insides of the seeds. Provide magnifying glasses to help them in their observations.

Literature Connections:
All about Seeds by Melvin Berger (1992) suggests several activities for collecting, planting, and cooking seeds.
Eat the Fruit, Plant the Seed by Millicent Selsam (1980) is an easy how-to book that shows various stages of development from seed to plant in different fruits.

FIGURE 2.5 Examining the insides of seeds

Constructing Science in the Classroom 2.11
Which Rock Is Mine?

AGE

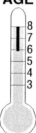

AN ACTIVITY FOR OBSERVING

Objective
The student will observe a rock and select it from a group of similar but unfamiliar rocks.

Take children for a walk around the schoolyard and playground, and ask them to find a rock they really like. Ask them to get to know their rock very well by observing it carefully, using all their senses except taste. Have all the children put their rock in a basket and sit in a circle. Pass the basket around and have the children pick out their rock and explain to the class how they knew it was theirs. If a child selects someone else's rock by mistake, the real owner should remain quiet and challenge the error when his or her turn comes.
    As a variation, use whole peanuts in the shell, raw carrots, raw potatoes, and the like (Figure 2.6).

Literature Connection:
Everybody Needs a Rock by Byrd Taylor (1974) is a story that prescribes rules for finding your own special rock. One of the rules is to sniff a rock. "Some kids can tell by smelling whether a rock came from the middle of the earth or from an ocean or from a mountain where the wind and sun touched it every day for a million years."

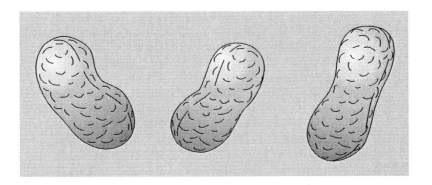

FIGURE 2.6 Which peanut is mine?

Constructing Your Ideas 2.5
An Activity for Observing

Now it's your turn. Write a short activity that can be used to help children sharpen their senses of observation. Specify age/grade level, and be sure the activity is appropriate to the children in the age/grade group you specify. Cite a process-oriented objective for your lesson; this objective will read something like this: "The student will observe _____." Then get together in small groups and do the activities each member of your group has prepared.

Notes

1. A position statement issued by the National Science Teachers Association characterizes science as "the systematic gathering of information through various forms of direct and indirect observation and the testing of this information by methods including, but not limited to, experimentation" (National Science Teachers Association, 2000, p. 15).
2. The entire November 1998 issue of *Educational Leadership* is devoted to the subject of brain research and its application to the learning process.

References

Aliki. (1989). *My five senses.* New York: Crowell.

Anson-Weber, J. (1995). *Snuffles.* Marietta, GA: Cherokee Publishing.

Behn, H. (1984). *Crickets and bullfrogs and whispers of thunder.* Orlando: Harcourt Brace & Co.

Berger, M. (1992). *All about seeds.* New York: Scholastic.

Brown, M. W. (1993). *The noisy book.* New York: HarperCollins Children's Books.

Carter, David A. (1995). *Feely bugs: To touch and feel.* New York: Simon & Schuster Children's.

Cole, J. (1989). *It's too noisy!* New York: HarperCollins Children's Books.

Cole, J. (1994). *You can't smell a flower with your ear!: All about your 5 senses.* Madison, WI: Demco Media.

Hopkins, L.B. (1987). *Click, rumble, roar: Poems about machines.* New York: Crowell.

Isadora, R. (1991). *I touch.* Fairfield, NJ: Greenwillow Books.

Johnston, T. (1997). *We love the dirt.* New York: Scholastic.

Keller, H. (1984). *Will it rain?* (1985). New York: Greenwillow.

Lobel, A. (1980). *Fables.* New York: HarperCollins Children's Books.

McCormack, A. J., & Yager, R. E. (1989). Towards a taxonomy for science education. *Georgia Journal of Science, 19*(3), 11–12.

Morris, W. (1990). *Just listen.* New York: Athenium.

National Science Teachers Association (2000). NSTA position statement: The nature of science. *NSTA Reports!, 11* (6).

Padilla, M. J. (n.d.) The science process skills. "Research Matters. . . . To the Science Teacher." National Association for Research in Science Teaching.

Selsam, M. (1980). *Eat the fruit, plant the seed.* New York: Morrow.

Taylor, B. (1974). *Everybody needs a rock.* New York: Macmillan.

Taylor, B. (1986). *I'm in charge of celebrations.* New York: Charles Scribner's Sons.

Wildsmith, B. (1967). *Brian Wildsmith's wild animals.* New York: Oxford University Press.

Wolfe, P., & Brandt, R. (1998). What do we know from brain research? *Educational Leadership, 56* (3), 8–13.

Yashima, T. (1985). *Umbrella.* Madison, WI: Demco Media.

CHAPTER 3

The Basic Scientific Processes: Classifying

A teacher who can arouse a feeling for one single good . . . poem, accomplishes more than he who fills our memory with rows on rows of natural objects, classified with name and form.
Johann Wolfgang von Goethe, *Elective Affinities,* **Book I, Chapter 7** (1808)

I never Saw a Purple cow;
I never Hope to See one;
But I can Tell you, Anyhow,
I'd rather See than Be one.
Gelett Burgess, "The Purple Cow," *Nonsense and Commonsense: A Child's Book of Victorian Verse* **by John Grossman & Priscilla Dunhill (New York: Workman Publishing, 1992). (Original work published 1901).**

Let us start by doing a few activities involving the process skill of classifying.

Classifying is the process we use when we sort objects or events into groups. Classification is used in many different situations, such as setting up grocery and hardware stores, developing the class schedule, assigning children to buses, identifying the variables that influence the result of an action, and developing controlled scientific experiments. Classification is a skill that can be practiced with increasing proficiency as children grow older and more intellectually mature. To foster children's awareness of their enviornment and their intellectual growth children should be provided many opportunities to classify.

Constructing Your Ideas 3.1
Classifying Rocks

Use the rocks you collected for Constructing Your Ideas 2.1 (The Rock Hunt). Mix up all the individual collections, and divide the rocks randomly into groups of 30 to 40 specimens. Form groups of three or four students.

First, sort the rocks in any way you wish. Compare your arrangement with the arrangements of other groups in your class.

How many different ways did your class have of sorting the rocks?

Keep the arrangements intact for the next activity.

Sorting into groups is a simple form of classifying. To accomplish this task, children need to be able to see similarities and differences among similar objects. These distinguishing properties may be color, shape, weight, size, use, location, and other properties that children can readily recognize. For example, if you had provided children with a collection of foreign coins to sort, they might have formed groups of square coins, round coins, coins with holes in them, coins with pictures of people, coins with pictures of animals, silver-colored coins, copper-colored coins, and so on.

Very young children need much practice in describing the characteristics of objects, telling what is alike and what is different among objects, and sorting and grouping objects.

A preschool teacher cut out 6 red leaves, 6 yellow leaves, and 6 green leaves, all the same size. After ensuring that the children could recognize and name each color, she put the 18 leaves in a bag, shook them, and dumped them out in front of a small group of children. She asked the children to sort them. After some discussion, the children ended up with a pile of red leaves, a pile of yellow leaves, and a pile of green leaves.

Next, the teacher cut out 6 leaves, 6 pumpkins, and 6 hats, all the same color. After ensuring that the children could recognize and give meaningful names to each of the shapes, she put the 18 items in a bag, shook them, and dumped them out in front of a small group of children. She asked the children to sort them. After some discussion and some trial and error, the children ended up with a pile of leaves, a pile of pumpkins, and a pile of hats.

The teacher did the same thing with different colors and with different shapes, always keeping either the color or the shape the same while varying the other.

After the children gained some proficiency in sorting by a single property, the teacher put equal numbers of red leaves, yellow leaves, green leaves, red pumpkins, yellow pumpkins, green pumpkins, red hats, yellow hats, and green hats in a bag, shook them up, and dumped them out in front of a group of children (Figure 3.1). She asked the children to sort them. After much discussion, one group ended up with a pile of red shapes, a pile of yellow shapes, and a pile of green shapes. But when she did the same thing with another group of children, they ended up with a pile of leaves, a pile of pumpkins, and a pile of hats. Each group thought their way was right and the other way was wrong.

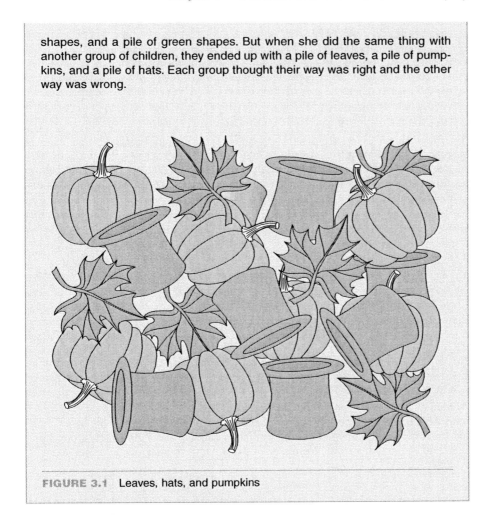

FIGURE 3.1   Leaves, hats, and pumpkins

In order for children to be able to sort the cutouts just described in more than one way, they must recognize that each of the cutouts has two characteristics—shape and color. The preoperational (young) preschool child typically is able to recognize only one of the characteristics. Thus, some will sort on the basis of color, and others will sort on the basis of shape. One of Piaget's experiments illustrates this point. Preoperational children are shown a collection of 20 wooden beads that consists of 17 brown ones and 3 white ones. The children are asked, "Can you make a longer necklace with the brown beads or the wooden beads?" Preoperational children typically reply "brown beads" because they are not yet able to recognize that each bead has two **attributes:** its color and the material it is made of (Bybee & Sund, 1982, p. 87). Preoperational children typically can deal with only one attribute at a time (Salkind, 1985, p. 203).

attribute—A characteristic of an object

Children do a great deal of classifying in their everyday activities in school. Asking children who are wearing different-colored shirts to form separate lines is an activity in classifying. So is asking children with different hair colors to form different lines. Having children keep pictorial logs of the weather requires them to classify weather according to categories previously selected, such as sunny, cloudy, rainy, or snowy, and hot, warm, cool, or cold. Having them put jigsaw puzzles together requires children to recognize attributes of shape and design similar to both the piece and the place where it belongs. Daily playtime cleanup when children put blocks in their proper places, put cars in the car container, plastic bears in the bears box, and plastic animals, train pieces, and other objects in their proper containers all foster development of the process skill of classifying.

It is important that you provide many different kinds of things for children to sort. You can even have a "sorting" center in which you change the materials being sorted every week. Some suggestions include foreign coins, shells, buttons, feathers, bolts, screws and washers, bowls of dried corn, peas, and beans, macaroni of different sizes and shapes, and so on. You can also use boxes of mixed nuts, bags of mixed snacks such as TrailMix, and the like, but be sure to tell children *not* to taste or eat the food materials; instead, provide something similar for them to eat when the activity is finished.

Constructing Your Ideas 3.2
Classifying Rocks into Two Distinct Groups

 Next, use the collection of rocks you have sorted, and form *two distinct* groups. Give a descriptive name to each group. Again compare your arrangement with those of other groups in the class.

What different ways did people have of sorting the rocks into two sets? Ask each group to explain why they sorted the way they did. Were any of these ways "righter" or "wronger" than those of other groups?

Take a look at the two sets the groups made and the names that were given to them. Are the two sets of rocks *parallel* in construction? In other words, is one set the opposite of the other? For example, to be parallel in construction, one of the two groupings might be a set of "light-colored rocks" and another a set of "dark-colored rocks." Or, in the example of the foreign coin collection, the sets may be "coins that are round" and "coins that are not round." In these cases, the groupings are "opposites" of each other. Suppose, however, the rocks are sorted into "light-colored rocks" and "rough rocks." Or, in the example of the foreign coin collection, the two groups may be "coins that are round" and "coins with pictures of people." These groupings are not parallel in construction, and, in both cases, each group has attributes that also belong to the other group. There may be "light-colored rocks" that also are rough, and there may be "rough rocks" that are light in color. The groups are not **mutually exclusive**. There is no clear line of demarcation between them. Children who create groups that are not mutually exclusive might have difficulty deciding in which group to place a new rock.

mutually exclusive— Characteristics of different objects or concepts that do not overlap

For children to devise parallel classification systems, they must be able to recognize the general characteristics common to objects in a collection. For example, each rock has several attributes such as color, texture, relative weight, and presence of inclusions. Each coin has several attributes including color, shape, size, and design of surfaces. Children must be able to isolate those characteristics possessed by each item in the collection that make some different from the others, such as light and dark colors in the case of the rocks, or silver and copper colors in the case of the coins. They must also learn to recognize that objects have more than one attribute. For example, the same rock can be light or dark in color and also be rough or smooth; the same coin can have both a certain shape and a certain design. This ability occurs during the concrete operational stage, which emerges for most children at around age 7. You can tell that young, preoperational children should be encouraged to devise classification systems without regard to parallelism; as they grow in cognitive ability, they will be able to classify in parallel groups.

Constructing Your Ideas 3.3
Classifying Rocks into Subgroups

 Now, divide the two groups of rocks you formed and named in the previous activity into two subgroups. This level of classifying is referred to as *class inclusion*. Name each of the subgroups with meaningful and descriptive words. As before, compare the arrangements various people had of grouping similar objects.

You will end up with an arrangement something like this:

Main Group A	Main Group B
Subgroup 1	Subgroup 1
Subgroup 2	Subgroup 2

Are Subgroup 1 and Subgroup 2 mutually exclusive within each main group? For example, if Subgroup 1 is a set of "dark-colored rocks," is Subgroup 2 a collection of "light-colored rocks?" Also look at Subgroup 1 within each main group; are they the same? Look at each Subgroup 2; are they the same? If so, you have classified in parallel.

Notice that the absence of parallelism does *not* make a classification system wrong. Nor does it even make it necessarily weak. The important result of a classification system is that it describes the collection such that each group is distinct from every other group. The best way to tell whether this is so is to try to place a new item in the system. If there is only one group into which it can be placed, your classification system is solid. Consider, for example, a collection of leaves. There are many different kinds of leaves—leaves with **serrated** (sawlike) edges, leaves shaped like palms of hands, leaves with smooth edges, thick leaves, thin leaves, leaves that are pine needles, and so on.

serrated—Sawlike edges

A classification system for a collection of leaves may well not exhibit parallelism. Such a classification system might look like this:

Broad Leaves	Pine Needles
Straight Edges	Fat
Crooked Edges	Thin

There is no question as to which of the four groups any new leaf would be placed in. Thus, the system is an adequate representation of the collection.

Classification is a skill that is used throughout the scientific enterprise. It is a skill that children need in order to form conclusions from observation of multiple cases of an event, and it is a skill that is essential in identifying variables as children form hypotheses and design experimental procedures. For example, you used the process skill of classifying when you investigated parachutes in Chapter 1. In order to explore factors that affect how fast different parachutes fall, you mentally classified the different parachutes according to their attributes, forming some groups based on size, other groups based on weight, and still other groups based on how fast they fall. To do this, you needed to recognize that each parachute has several attributes including size, weight, and speed of fall. Once having classified the attributes, you were able to investigate them one at a time. As you explore the processes of science, you will become increasingly aware of the role skillful classification plays in process skill mastery.

Several classification activities appropriate for children of different age groups are suggested in Constructing Science in the Classroom 3.1–3.9. Some are appropriate for preschool children, and some are more appropriate for children in the early elementary grades. The activities suggest ways of providing experiences and practice in classifying.

Constructing Science in the Classroom 3.1
Classifying Plastic Food

AGE

8
7
6
5
4
3

A CLASSIFYING ACTIVITY INVOLVING ITEMS OF PLASTIC FOOD

Objective
The student will classify items of plastic food according to self-determined criteria.

Use the big container of plastic food. Ask children to place each item into one of two boxes marked "Group 1" and "Group 2." Ask the children to explain why they chose to group the food in the way they did.

Literature Connection:
Play With Your Food by Joost Elffers (1997). Readers observe foods in new and whimsical ways as they learn how to make creatures out of the food they eat.

Constructing Science in the Classroom 3.2
Classifying Seeds

AGE

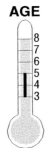

A CLASSIFYING ACTIVITY INVOLVING SEEDS

Objective

The student will devise a classification system for a collection of seeds.

Provide children with a collection of several different kinds of seeds, such as peas, lima beans, sunflower seeds, corn, radish seeds, marigold seeds, and seeds for other flowers and vegetables. Ask children to group the seeds by placing similar ones together in separate piles. Ask them to give a descriptive name for each kind of seed (Figure 3.2).

To incorporate mathematics in this activity, you may wish to ask children to count the number of seeds in each of their groupings. They then record the number of each kind and draw a bar graph (histogram) of the data.

Literature Connections:

Seeds and More Seeds by Millicent Selsam (1969). An inquisitive young boy discovers through experimentation how to find and plant seeds that grow into bears, fruits, trees, and flowers. The story uses the processes of observing, classifying, communicating, and measuring.

Is it Red? Is It Yellow? Is It Blue?: An Adventure in Color

Is It Rough? Is It Smooth? Is It Shiny? Both books are written by Tana Hoban (1978, 1984). The vibrant photographs in these books offer many opportunities for introductory classification activities.

FIGURE 3.2 Sorting seeds

Constructing Science in the Classroom 3.3
Classifying Stuffed Animals

AGE

8
7
6
5
4
3

A CLASSIFICATION ACTIVITY INVOLVING STUFFED ANIMALS

Objective
The student will classify stuffed animals according to self-determined criteria.

Using a collection of Beanie Babies® and other stuffed animals, ask children to form groups according to whatever attributes they observe (Figure 3.3). Attributes to look for might include size, color, presence or absence of a tail, number of legs, and the like. Children may form several groups of animals; the only requirement is that each group should have at least two animals in it. Ask children to explain why they formed the groups they did.

Literature Connections:
My Feet by Aliki (1990). In this delightful story, Aliki explains how we use feet and describes the many variations in size and appearance. This would be a great introduction to classification for younger children.
How Teddy Bears Find Their Homes by David Kenneth Wald (1994). Carol's grandma tells how Teddy bears search for a home with human 5-year-old children.
Beanie Mania II: A Comprehensive Collector's Guide by Becky Phillips (1998) contains pictures and facts about all Beanie Babies® made to date.

FIGURE 3.3 Sorting stuffed animals

Constructing Science in the Classroom 3.4
Classifying Animals

AGE

8
7
6
5
4
3

A CLASSIFYING ACTIVITY INVOLVING ANIMAL PHOTOGRAPHS

Objective
The student will classify animals shown in photographs.

Obtain (or prepare) a collection of laminated photographs of different kinds of animals. Sources of photographs include *Your Big Backyard* (published by the National Wildlife Federation), *National Geographic, National Geographic World, National Wildlife, Ranger Rick, Smithsonian,* and *Zoobooks* (see Constructing Science in the Classroom 2.4.). Discuss each animal with children relative to attributes such as color, presence or lack of fur, number of feet, kind of tail, habitat, food preferences, and the like. Let the children provide the focus for the discussion. Then mix up the laminated photographs and place them on a tray. Ask children to sort them into groups, give a name to each group, and tell why they formed the groups they did.

Literature Connection:
Benny's Animals and How We Put Them in Order by Millicent Selsam (1966). In this story, a young boy with a passion for neatness and order learns how to classify animals.

Constructing Science in the Classroom 3.5
What's Magnetic? What's Not Magnetic?

AGE

8
7
6
5
4
3

A CLASSIFYING ACTIVITY INVOLVING MAGNETIC OBJECTS

Objective
The student will classify common objects as magnetic or nonmagnetic.

Provide each child with a magnet and allow time to explore objects in the classroom to see which are attracted to the magnet and which are not. Then place an assortment of objects, some of which are magnetic and some of which are nonmagnetic, on a tray. Suggestions include nail, screw, metal washer, paper clip, scissors, rubber band, pencil, eraser, piece of paper, wooden block, plastic block, crayon, leaf, key, penny, nickel, dime, and quarter. Children in a small group select each item, one at a time, try the magnet on it, and tell whether the magnet picks it up. To help children organize their results, have a laminated, reusable chart available with two columns labeled "Magnetic" and "Not Magnetic" in words or pictures or both (see Figure 3.4). After testing each item, ask the child to place it on the appropriate half of the chart.

This lesson also can foster the process of predicting. Children select each item, one at a time, and predict whether it will be attracted to the magnet before they try the magnet on it. Then they try out their predictions and place the item on the appropriate half of the chart as before.

This activity also is a good place to discuss the use of magnets in everyday life, such as the magnets that hold refrigerators shut and those that hold cupboard doors closed. Ask children to share what they know about the use of magnets and how magnets help people.

(continued)

Literature Connection:

Mickey's Magnet by Franklin Blankly and Eleanor Vaughn (1956). Mickey discovers some of the properties of magnets when he accidentally spills a box of straight pins that he has to pick up.

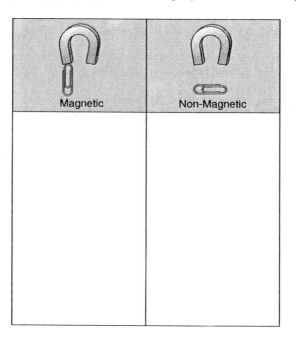

FIGURE 3.4   "Magnetic/Non-magnetic" chart

Constructing Science in the Classroom 3.6
Classifying Leaves

AGE

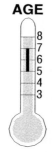

A CLASSIFYING ACTIVITY INVOLVING LEAVES

Objective

The student will classify a collection of leaves according to self-identified criteria.

Take children on a walk around the school to collect leaves. CAUTION: You should inspect this area before you take children to it to be sure there are no dangerous plants such as poison ivy or poison oak. Also caution them not to taste or chew on the leaves, for many leaves are poisonous. Upon returning to the classroom, ask children to group their leaves according to one or more characteristics they themselves identify. Children then explain why they grouped the leaves as they did (Figure 3.5).

If desired, children can make rubbings of their leaves: Place a leaf, underside up, under a piece of paper, and rub the paper gently with the side of a crayon. Adults can press the leaves, or you can explain to parents how they can press the leaves for preservation: Place leaves between squares of waxed paper with the waxed sides toward the leaves. Put a cloth over the squares and iron with a hot iron. (Be sure only adults use the hot iron.) Let the assembly cool, and then gently remove the waxed paper to obtain well-preserved leaves.

Literature Connections:

Crinkleroot's Guide to Knowing the Trees by Jim Arnosky (1992). Take a tour through a forest as Crinkleroot introduces broad-leafed and evergreen trees.
Why Do Leaves Change Color? By Betty Maestro (1994) is a story of how leaves change color when they are exposed to less water and sunlight.

Maple   Oak   Birch

Sycamore   Sweet gum

FIGURE 3.5 Some kinds of leaves

Constructing Science in the Classroom 3.7
The Grocery Store

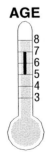

AGE

8
7
6
5
4
3

A CLASSIFYING ACTIVITY INVOLVING GROCERIES

Objective
The student will classify common grocery items.

Ask each child to bring empty food containers such as empty cereal boxes, empty canned goods cans from which the top has been removed (check the edges to be sure they are not sharp), empty salt and pepper containers, boxes from TV dinners and other frozen foods, and so on. You may want to save your own empties to add to the collection. Put all the empty containers in one place. Form groups of two or three children, and ask each group to pretend they are going to set up a grocery store. They are to group the items in a way that they would use

(continued)

to put them out on shelves. They must put them out such that customers could find what they are looking for when they come in the store. Children group the items and label each group with a descriptive name. They set up the store and invite other classes to come in to browse.

Literature Connection:

Tommy at the Grocery Store by Bill Grossman (1989). In this humorous tale, little Tommy is accidentally left at the grocery store, where he is mistaken for a salami, a potato, a banana, and an ear of corn.

Constructing Science in the Classroom 3.8
Classifying Materials in Soil

AGE

8
7
6
5
4
3

A CLASSIFYING ACTIVITY INVOLVING SOIL

Objective

The student will devise a classification system for materials found in soil.

Extend the observing activity, "What's in the Dirt?" (Constructing Science in the Classroom 2.9) by asking children to group the materials they found in the dirt (see Figure 3.6). Alternatively, you or the children may provide fresh bags of soil for this activity. Children first spread a small amount of the soil on a paper plate or piece of paper. Using pencils and magnifying glasses, they examine the soil carefully. When they find something recognizable such as grains of sand, pieces of leaves, pieces of bark, rocks, worms, roots, or seeds, they name it and put it aside. If children find something they are not sure of, they form another group labeled with a question mark. The result is a grouping of the materials in the soil. Ask children to share their groupings with the whole class, explaining why they grouped the materials in the soil the way they did.

Literature Connection:

There's a Hair in My Dirt! A Worm's Story by Gary Larson (1998). A worm who is extremely angered over finding a hair in the dirt he has to eat is told an ecological fable by his father.

FIGURE 3.6   Making groups of similar things found in soil

Constructing Science in the Classroom 3.9
The Hardware Store

AGE

8
7
6
5
4
3

A CLASSIFYING ACTIVITY INVOLVING HARDWARE

Objective
The student will classify common hardware items.

Ask each child to bring as many surplus hardware items from home as can be spared. You may want to bring in some inexpensive hardware items as well, such as an assortment of screws, nuts, bolts, washers, and so on. You can also use hardware items you have on hand at school.

Put everything in one large container. Form groups of two or three children, and ask each group to pretend they are going to set up a hardware store. They are to group the items in a way they would use to put them out on shelves. They must put them out such that customers would readily find what they are looking for when they come into the store. Children group the items and put them in small open boxes or transparent bags, each labeled with a descriptive name. After each group has done this, list the categories on chart paper and ask the class to decide on a single grouping system. Then set up the store and invite other classes to come in to browse.

This activity is a good opportunity for older children to investigate marketing techniques, especially the devices retailers employ to attract customers.

Literature Connection:
Uncle Lester's Lemonade Lure by Susan Ginny (1988) is a story of a small-town hardware store owner whose business spirit enables him to survive advanced competition.

Constructing Your Ideas 3.4
An Activity For Classifying

Now it's your turn. Write a short activity that can be used to help children sharpen their skills of classifying. Specify age/grade level, and be sure the activity is appropriate to the children in the age/grade group you specify. Cite a process-oriented objective for your lesson; this objective will read something like this: "The student will classify _____." Then get together in small groups and do the activities each member of your group has prepared.

References

Aliki. (1990). *My feet*. New York: Crowell.

Arnosky, J. (1992). *Crinkleroot's guide to knowing the trees*. New York: Bradbury.

Blankly, F., & Vaughn, E. (1956). *Mickey's magnet*. New York: Scholastic.

Burgess, G. (1901). In J. Grossman & P. Dunhill (Eds.), (1992). *Nonsense and commonsense: A child's book of Victorian verse*. New York: Workman Publishing.

Bybee, R.W. & Sund, R. B. (1982). *Piaget for educators* (2nd ed.). Columbus, OH: Charles E. Merrill.

Elffers, J. (1997). *Play with your food.* New York: Stewart, Tabori, & Chang.

Ginny, S. (1988). *Uncle Lester's lemonade lure.* Medina, MN: S Y F Enterprises.

Grossman, B. (1989). *Tommy at the grocery store.* New York: Harper & Row.

Hoban, T. (1978). *Is it red? Is it yellow? Is it blue?: An adventure in color.* New York: Greenwillow.

Hoban, T. (1984). *Is it rough? Is it smooth? Is it shiny?* New York: Greenwillow.

Larson, G. (1998). *There's a hair in my dirt! A worm's story.* New York: HarperCollins.

Maestro, B. (1994). *Why do leaves change color?* New York: HarperCollins.

Phillips, B. (1998). *Beanie mania II: A collector's guide.* Naperville, IL: Dinomates, Inc.

Salkind, N. J. (1985). *Theories of human development.* New York: John Wiley & Sons.

Selsam, M. (1966). *Benny's animals and how we put them in order.* New York: HarperRow.

Selsam, M. (1969). *Seeds and more seeds.* New York: HarperRow.

Wald, D. K. (1994). *How Teddy bears find their homes.* San Francisco: Rebecca House, Inc.

CHAPTER 4

The Basic Scientific Processes: Communicating

We begin by investigating how we can communicate in science through language.

Communicating is the process we use to let people know what we are doing and what we are thinking. It can take many forms in addition to language. Multiple forms of communication are encouraged in early childhood science so that children learn that accurate and complete communication is essential in their scientific investigations.

Language is only the instrument of science, and words are but the signs of ideas.
Samuel Johnson, Preface to the *Dictionary of the English Language* (1755).

"I never knew words could be so confusing," Milo said . . .

"Only when you use a lot to say a little," answered Tuck.
Norman Juster, *The Phantom Tollbooth* (New York: Random House, 1961).

Constructing Your Ideas 4.1
Favorite Rocks

Using the rocks you collected for Constructing Your Ideas 2.1, "The Rock Hunt," choose your favorite rock. Why is this one your favorite? Without removing it from your collection, describe your favorite rock to a partner, and ask your partner to pick out the right one. If your partner picks out the wrong one, *do not* tell which is the right one; instead, describe the right one better. When your partner selects the right one, reverse roles.

Was it easy to describe your favorite rock? Was it easy to pick out the rock your partner described? This activity shows what a precise and exquisitely difficult skill it is to communicate accurately.

One of the primary goals of early childhood education is to foster the development of communications skills. This is often translated to mean language development: speaking, reading, and writing. In the sections dealing with the processes of observing and classifying, the importance of children developing descriptive vocabularies was stressed. To develop the skill of verbal communication, children need to have words to describe what they observe. Asking children to describe their observations in their own words, and asking them to explain their classification systems fosters the development of these very important language skills. Do not be dismayed if young children use non-words or words you would not use to describe something. Remember that the development of symbolic representation of concrete phenomena requires huge cognitive leaps. In time, children will discover the more commonly used terminology; meanwhile, they are inventing their own symbolism—and it works if everyone has the same understandings. After all, communication can be defined as any and all ways people let others know their thoughts. Accurate communication is best fostered by providing children opportunities to express themselves, some of which are successful and some of which are not. When a given attempt at communicating fails to provoke the expected understanding, the child must try a different way, thus strengthening the skills.

Four-year-old Andrew is sitting on top of an assemblage he created out of large wooden blocks; it looks like a cross between a boat and an airplane. He is holding a large Y-shaped block with both hands that he rotates occasionally while staring straight ahead. There are several adults in the room, and one asks, "Andrew, what are you doing?" Andrew replies he is driving a boat. Later, another adult asks, "Andrew, are you flying an airplane?" Andrew replies, "Yes."

This anecdote points to the importance of listening to children. If the teacher's goal is to find out what children are thinking, then the only way we can find this out is to listen to them. Communication is *not* fostered by supplying responses for children so they don't have to think for themselves. Communication is fostered by *listening* to children and requiring that they express themselves in understandable ways.

Constructing Your Ideas 4.2
Ways of Communicating

How many different ways do people use to communicate? In groups, list as many ways as you can think of in, say, 2 minutes. Then make a master class list.

What means of communicating did your class think of? Of course, you listed speaking and writing. Did you also include gesturing, drawing, telling stories, pantomiming, singing, puppeteering, play acting, and putting on different facial expressions? How about making posters, preparing bulletin boards, developing symbols, drawing maps, and, for older children, writing mathematical expressions? Did you include graphing? Charting? Creating diagrams? A daily chart of the weather or outdoor temperatures tells legions about weather patterns. (See Constructing Science in the Classroom 2.6 and 4.9.) Charts of daily food groups eaten by children tell legions about their nutrition habits. (See Constructing Science in the Classroom 4.10.)

A wide variety of communicating activities should be included in the early childhood science program so children can be given the maximum opportunity to express their thoughts in a way that others can understand them. If you avoid supplying "correct" responses, you will help children learn to express their own thoughts. If you avoid repeating children's responses, you will help foster children's ownership of their thoughts (see Chapter 1). The more opportunity children are given to describe, explain, and discuss, the better their communications skills will become.

Several activities designed to foster skill in the science process of communicating are given in Constructing Science in the Classroom 4.1–4.12. Some are appropriate for preschool children, and some are more appropriate for children in the early elementary grades.

Constructing Science in the Classroom 4.1
Tell About the Bubbles

AGE

AN ACTIVITY FOR COMMUNICATING

8
7
6
5
4
3

Objective
The student will describe bubbles.

Provide a bottle of bubble preparation and a round wand. Dip the wand into the preparation, and blow a few bubbles (Figure 4.1). Ask children questions such as the following:
What shape are the bubbles?
What colors did you see in the bubbles?
How big are the bubbles?
How do the bubbles move?
When you pop the bubbles, what do you suppose happens to them?

(continued)

Literature Connections:

Bubble Trouble by Joy N. Hulme (1999) is an easy-to-read story about bubbles.

Troubles with Bubbles by Frank B. Edwards (1998). The animals at the zoo get help in taking baths, and soon the zoo is filled with bubbles.

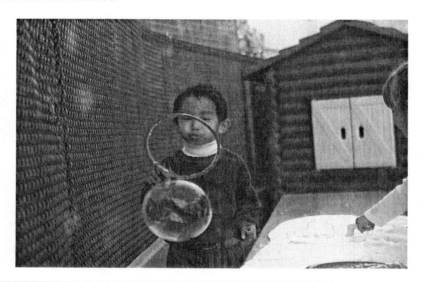

FIGURE 4.1   "Look at the bubbles!"

Constructing Science in the Classroom 4.2
What Falls out of a Flower When You Shake It?

AGE

8
7
6
5
4
3

AN ACTIVITY FOR COMMUNICATING

Objective

The student will describe the material that falls out of the center of a flower when it is shaken.

Obtain an assortment of flowers with obvious amounts of **pollen.** Suggestions include daisies, lilies, tulips, dandelions, clover, poinsettia (in winter), flowers with long **stamens** (the slender stalks with pollen-bearing sacs on them), and old baskets or bouquets of flowers. Ask the children to describe the flowers. Then provide a piece of black paper, and ask children to turn the flower upside down and shake it over the paper or scrape the tips of the stamens over the paper. Ask them to observe the material (pollen) that falls off the flower. Be sure children

pollen—Fine dust in a seed plant whose function is reproduction

stamens—Slender stalks on flowers with pollen-bearing sacks on them

know how to use magnifying glasses, and encourage their use so they can see the pollen better. Ask them to describe what they observe. Questions such as the following may help facilitate the discussions:

What color is the material?
How large are the particles?
How much pollen fell from the flower?

Be sure to check for allergies to pollen before you do this activity. You will need to offer a different communicating activity for children with pollen allergies.

Literature Connection:

Barney Bipple's Magic Dandelions by Carol Chapman (1977). In this story, a little boy makes wishes by blowing on a dandelion. The wishes get the boy into situations he would not like to be in.

Constructing Science in the Classroom 4.3
Making Egg Shells Soft

AGE

8
7
6
5
4
3

AN ACTIVITY FOR COMMUNICATING

Objective

The student will describe changes in an eggshell after it has been submerged in vinegar.

Provide an egg for each child in your class. They can be fresh or hard-boiled. Let children feel their eggs carefully and gently and describe what they feel. Then put the egg in a glass of vinegar. Cover the glass loosely with plastic wrap so the odor of the vinegar does not become objectionable.

What are the bubbles that come from the egg?

Using a plastic spoon, children lift the egg out of the vinegar twice a day, rinse it with water, and gently feel the shell. Ask them to describe what they feel. If children get vinegar on their hands, have them rinse their hands in water.

What does the egg-feel like at the end of two days in the vinegar?

Teacher note: The vinegar dissolves the **calcium carbonate** (the material that makes the shell hard) of the egg, leaving it soft after one to two days. The bubbles that come from the egg are carbon dioxide gas resulting from the reaction of the vinegar, which is acetic acid, with the calcium carbonate in the eggshell.

calcium carbonate—$CaCO_3$, the chemical name for calcite, found in bones and shells and used for making Portland cement and lime

Literature Connections:

Daisy and the Egg by Jane Simmons (1999). Mama Duck and Aunt Buttercup sit on a new egg as Daisy eagerly awaits the arrival of her new brother or sister.

Bently & Egg by William Joyce (1997). While egg-sitting for Kack Kack the duck, Bently Hopperton, the frog, paints his friend's egg. The egg is mistaken for an Easter egg and is kidnapped, taking Bently on an adventure of a lifetime.

Green Eggs and Ham by Dr. Seuss (1960). Sam-I-Am tries to persuade his friend to try eating green eggs and ham.

Constructing Science in the Classroom 4.4
Growing Marigolds

AGE

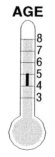

AN ACTIVITY FOR COMMUNICATING

Objective

The student will describe the growth of marigold plants.

Provide each child with a clear plastic bag that can be sealed, three or four marigold seeds, and a piece of paper towel or a tissue. Ask children to put the paper towel or tissue inside the plastic bag, and pour enough water into the bag that the towel becomes soaked. Then ask them to "plant" the marigold seeds by carefully placing them on the top of the wet paper. Seal the bags, and put them in a light place. Some teachers hang them in a window, and others hang them on a bulletin board.

Each day, ask children to describe what they see. (Note: The marigold seeds take several days to sprout. Once sprouted, they will continue to develop inside the sealed bag until good root and leaf systems are developed. It is not necessary to unseal the bags during this period of initial growth.) Ask children to describe the different parts of the plant they see: the roots (if visible), the stem, and the leaves.

Literature Connections:

The Enormous Carrot by Vladimir Vagin (1998) is an adaptation of the traditional Russian folktale, "The Turnip." Animals each try to pull up an overgrown carrot, but, finally, teamwork accomplishes the task.
How a Seed Grows by Helen J. Jordan (1960) introduces children to different kinds of seeds and experiments they can do at home with seeds.

Constructing Science in the Classroom 4.5
Do the Buttons Match?

AGE

AN ACTIVITY FOR COMMUNICATING

Objective

The student will describe one of a pair of buttons to another student.

Form pairs of children and give each child a card with a large number "1" or number "2" on it to identify their respective roles in the activity. Give a button to each child in the pair. The buttons may be different or matching. Ask each child to silently examine the button given to her. Then ask the Number 1 child to describe her button to her partner in enough detail that the partner can decide whether his button matches or is different. When the pair has decided, give them two more buttons and ask the Number 2 child to do the verbal describing until the Number 1 child can decide whether her button matches or is different.

Literature Connections:

The Button Box by Margarette S. Reid (1990). A boy and his grandmother enrich their communication with each other as he explores the many pleasures that can be found in her button box.
Brass Button by Crescent Dragonwagon (1997). Mrs. Moffett's new red coat loses a button that travels to many places throughout the neighborhood before Mrs. Moffett finds it again a year later.

Constructing Science in the Classroom 4.6
What Can I See with the Magnifying Glass?

AGE   AN ACTIVITY FOR COMMUNICATING

8
7
6
5
4
3

Objective
The student will describe what he sees with a magnifying glass.

Magnifying glasses are important tools of observation, for they extend our sense of sight.
    First be sure children know how to look at things through the magnifying glass. Provide a magnifying glass and a page of a newspaper, a leaf, a pine cone, and some soil. Ask children to examine these items with and without the magnifying glass and describe what they see. Also extend this activity to the process of classifying by asking children to describe the differences between what they see without the magnifying glass and what they see when they use the magnifying glass.

Literature Connection:
Exploring With a Magnifying Glass by Kenneth E. Rainis (1991). This nonfiction book describes numerous activities that can be done using a magnifying glass and common materials found around the house.

Constructing Science in the Classroom 4.7
What's in the Bag?

AGE   AN ACTIVITY FOR COMMUNICATING

8
7
6
5
4
3

Objective
The student will communicate the characteristics of unseen objects.

Secretively, place a familiar object in a paper bag. Suggestions include toy dishes such as plates, saucers, cups, and glasses, plastic or paper drinking cups, toy or real tools, stuffed animals, and the like. Ask a child to reach in the bag, feel the object, and describe its attributes out loud (long, short, round, flat, fat, thin, hard, soft, rough, smooth, etc.) (see Figure 4.2) one at a time. Be sure to tell children *not* to reveal what the object is. Other children try to guess what the object is from the description. The demonstrator continues to provide clues until the object has been guessed correctly.
    Alternatively, the children can bring objects from home so that even the teacher doesn't know what they are.

Literature Connection:
Sense Suspense: A Guessing Game for the Five Senses by Bruce McMillan (1994). Using close-up pictures, the reader is required to figure out what the whole picture is of and what senses can be used to solve the mystery. The beautiful pictures are from the Caribbean, and the text is in both English and Spanish.

(continued)

FIGURE 4.2 Describing what's in the bag

Constructing Science in the Classroom 4.8
Twenty Questions

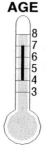

AGE

A COMMUNICATIONS GAME

Objective
The student will communicate characteristics of unknown objects and events.

The game "Twenty Questions" is an excellent way of helping children sharpen their communications skills. Provide objects such as a toy truck, a teddy bear, a candy bar, a magnet, a magnifying glass, a shell, and so on. Select one object unknown to the children, place it in a bag or a box so it cannot be seen, and begin the game. Children continue to ask questions until someone guesses the object.

Literature Connections:

What In the World? By Barbara J. Phillips-Duke (1998). Young children utilize the delightful text and fold-out illustrations as they take part in this simple guessing game.

The Wise Woman and Her Secret by Eve Merriam (1991). Many people seek the advice of a wise woman who says, "The secret of wisdom is to be curious; to take the time to look closely; to use all your senses to see and touch and taste and smell and hear; to keep wandering and wondering."

Constructing Science in the Classroom 4.9
Weather Charts and Graphs

AGE

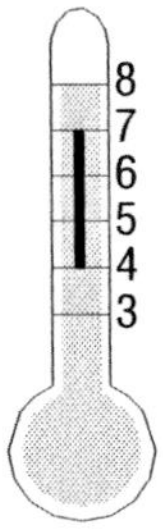

8
7
6
5
4
3

AN ACTIVITY FOR COMMUNICATING WITH CHARTS

In conjunction with the daily calendar, include questions about the weather. Ask children to record factors such as temperature, cloud cover, whether the wind is calm, moderate, strong, or gusty, and whether it is raining or snowing. Ask them to record this information on a large "Weather Chart" each day to try to discover weather patterns. Figure 4.3 shows a sample chart. Temperature can be read from a thermometer after children learn how. Prior to that, they can record such terms as "warm," "hot," "cool," "cold," and other temperature terms that are meaningful to the children in your area. Cloud cover can be recorded as "none," "some," or "lots." Wind can be detected from the way plants, tree branches, flags or a pinwheel stuck in the ground move. Record such terms as "none," "light," "medium," and "heavy."

Day and Date	Temperature	Cloud Cover	Wind	Raining? Snowing?
Monday				
Tuesday				
Wednesday				
Thursday				
Friday				
Monday				
Tuesday				

FIGURE 4.3 A weather chart

As children gain skill in making graphs, ask them to graph temperatures on a class graph (see also Constructing Science in the Classroom 5.18.) The one shown in Figure 4.4 was prepared using a computer graphing application (see Chapter 21).

Also ask children to discuss the role weather plays in their lives. Discuss the importance of accurate weather forecasting and ways in which we rely on weather forecasts.

Literature Connections:

Cloudy With a Chance of Meatballs by Judi Barrett (1978). The town of Chewandswallow has very unique weather conditions that open children's imaginations to "what if?"

What Makes the Weather? by Janet Palazzo (1989). A little bear takes the reader on a trip in which weather concepts and weather forecasting indicators in the sky are the focus of attention.

(continued)

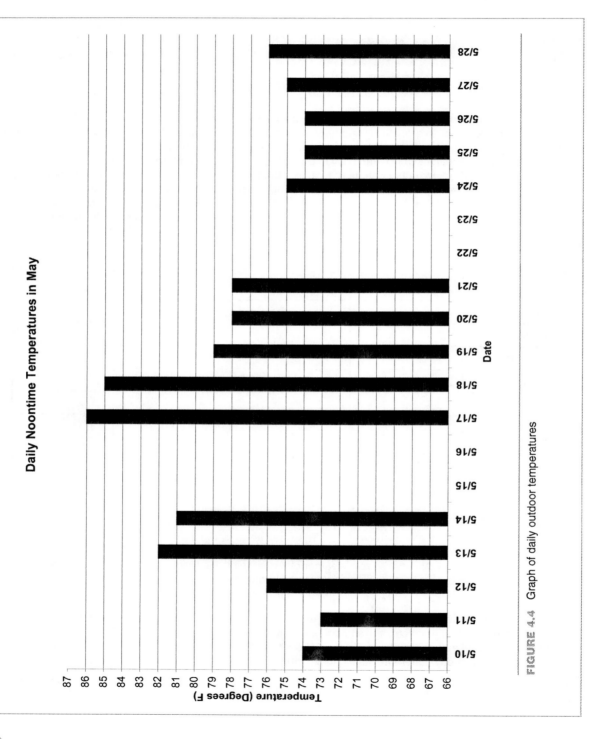

FIGURE 4.4 Graph of daily outdoor temperatures

Constructing Science in the Classroom 4.10
Charting Food Groups

AGE

8
7
6
5
4
3

AN ACTIVITY FOR COMMUNICATING WITH CHARTS

Objective
The student will construct a chart showing the food groups in a lunch meal.

First, discuss the food groups with the children so they become familiar with the food pyramid. The food groups generally recognized are the Bread and Cereal Group; Vegetable Group; Fruit Group; Milk and Milk Products Group; Meat and Meat Alternatives Group; and Fats, Oils, and Sweets. Show children the pyramid and explain that the closer to the bottom a food group is located, the more of that food group they need to eat to maintain healthy eating habits (see Figure 4.5).

Classifying foods into the food groups is a necessary component of this activity. Ask children to classify the foods they eat at various meals—both at home and at school—into the six basic food groups. Because most of the foods we eat contain elements of more than one food group, children can categorize given foods according to the predominant food group; for instance, a hamburger would contain food from both the bread and cereal group (the bun) and also from the meat and meat alternatives group (the meat).

On the appointed day, ask children to analyze the food they eat for lunch that day relative to the basic food groups. Give each child a blank food pyramid, and ask them to mark on it the relative amount of each food group they consumed during lunch. Older children can write the name of the food (hamburger, hamburger bun, lettuce, etc.) on the pyramid. Younger children can place check marks on the pyramid to indicate what they ate.

Literature Connections:
Gregory, the Terrible Eater by Mitchell Sharmat (1980). Gregory, the goat, is a very picky eater who prefers fruits, vegetables, eggs, and orange juice to shoes and tin cans.

The Edible Pyramid: Good Eating Every Day by Loreen Leedy (1996). Animal characters in a restaurant are offered foods grouped in sections of the food pyramid and learn how many servings of each they need every day.

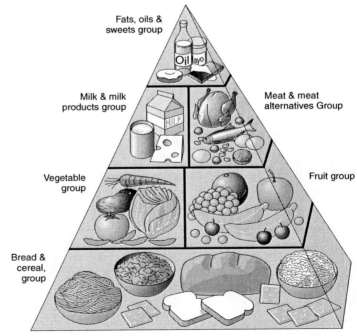

FIGURE 4.5 The food pyramid

Constructing Science in the Classroom 4.11
Funny Figures

AGE

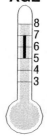

AN ACTIVITY FOR COMMUNICATING

Objective
The student will describe line drawings accurately and will identify line drawings from descriptions.

Prepare a number of laminated cards, each with a "funny figure" drawn on it such as those pictured in Figure 4.6.

Form pairs of children, and give each child a complete set of cards. Designate one child of the pair as Number 1, and the other as Number 2. Ask the Number 1 child to pick a card, hide it from view, and describe the figure on it to the Number 2 child. The idea is that the Number 2 child must find the matching card in her own set. Number 1 must continue to refine the description of the figure until Number 2 selects the correct match. Continue until all children have had a chance to be both Number 1 and Number 2 and they have used all the cards.

As a variation, ask the Number 2 children to put their cards away, and ask Number 1 to select a card and describe it to Number 2 while holding it so the partner cannot see it. Number 2 draws *exactly* what was communicated by Number 1 and then compares the drawing with the card. Continue until all children have had a chance to be both Number 1 and Number 2.

Literature Connection:
The Seasons of Arnold's Apple Tree by Gail Gibbons (1988) is a wordless book showing what happens to the apple tree through the four seasons. It also includes recipes for applesauce and apple pie.

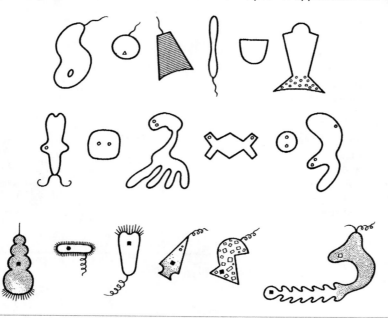

FIGURE 4.6 Funny figures
Courtesy Delta Education, Inc., Box 3000, Nashua, NH 03061, 1–800–442–5444

AGE

8
7
6
5
4
3

AN ACTIVITY FOR COMMUNICATING

Objective

The student will describe his or her fingerprints.

Provide each student with a stamp pad and a sheet of paper. Help them to "roll" their finger-prints onto the paper after they have inked the tips of their fingers with the inkpad. As an alter-native, ask children to rub 5″ × 7″ cards thoroughly with soft lead pencils, rub their fingertips on the pencil smears, and roll their fingertips on the sticky part of a piece of transparent tape. They then tape the lifted fingerprints to the sheet of paper, and label them with the finger des-ignation and the hand (right or left). You may wish to use a chart to help children keep track of the fingers and hands from which the fingerprints come.

Left Hand	Finger	Right Hand
	Thumb	
	Index Finger	
	Middle Finger	
	Ring Finger	
	Pinkie	

Ask children to observe their fingerprints. Provide magnifying glasses if desirable. Ask children to describe what their thumbprints look like. Ask them to describe their other fingerprints. Ask them to look at someone else's fingerprints and describe theirs.

To extend this activity to the process skill of classifying, ask children to compare their thumbprint with the prints of the fingers and with the thumbprints of other children. Describe how they are alike. Describe how they are different.

If desired, you can ask children to draw some of their fingerprints.

(continued)

Teacher note: No two fingerprints are alike. The three primary fingerprint patterns are (1) the arches (lines that start up on one side of the fingerprint and exit on the other side) (2) loops (lines that enter and exit on the same side of the fingerprint) and (3) whorls (lines that do not exit on either side of the fingerprint) (see Figure 4.7). Through very complex classification and retrieval systems, law enforcement officers can identify criminal suspects from the fingerprints they leave at the scenes of crimes. This would be a good place to engage children in discussions of crime fighting, crime prevention, and personal safety. An FBI "Kids & Youth" site dealing with fingerprinting at a very fundamental level can be accessed on the World Wide Web at http://www.fbi.gov/kids/crimedet/finger/fingerpt.htm.

Literature Connection:

Ed Emberly's Great Thumbprint Drawing Book by Ed Emberly (1994). This nonfiction book contains directions for creating a variety of shapes and figures using thumbprints.

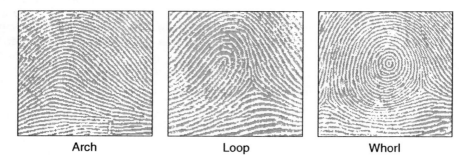

Arch   Loop   Whorl

FIGURE 4.7   Basic fingerprint patterns

Constructing Your Ideas 4.3
An Activity for Communicating

Now it's your turn. Write a short activity that can be used to help children sharpen their communicating skills. Specify age/grade level, and be sure the activity is appropriate to the children in the age/grade group you specify. Cite a process-oriented objective for your lesson; this objective will read something like this: "The student will communicate _____." Then get together in small groups and do the activities each member of your group has prepared.

References

Barrett, J. (1978). *Cloudy with a chance of meatballs.* New York: Macmillan.

Chapman, C. (1977). *Barney Bipple's magic dandelions.* New York: E. P. Dutton.

Dragonwagon, C. (1997). *Brass button.* New York: Simon & Schuster Children's.

Edwards, F. B. (1998). *Troubles with Bubbles.* Buffalo, NY: Firefly Books.

Emberly, E. (1994). *Ed Emberly's great thumbprint drawing book*. New York: Little, Brown & Co.

Gibbons, G. (1988). *The seasons of Arnold's apple tree*. San Diego: Harcourt Brace & Co.

Hulme, J. N. (1999). *Bubble trouble*. Danbury, CT: Children's Press.

Johnson, S., & McDermott, A. (Eds.). (1996). *Dictionary of the English language* (on CD ROM). Cambridge, England: Cambridge University Press. (Originally Published 1755).

Jordan, H. J. (1960). *How a seed grows*. New York: HarperCollins.

Joyce, W. (1997). *Bently & egg*. Madison, WI: Demco Media.

Juster, N. (1961). *The phantom tollbooth*. New York: Random House.

Leedy, L. (1996). *The edible pyramid: Good eating every day*. New York: Holiday House, Inc.

McMillan, B. (1994). *Sense suspense: A guessing game for the five senses*. New York: Scholastic.

Merriam, E. (1991). *The wise woman and her secret*. New York: Simon and Schuster.

Palazzo, J. (1989). *What makes the weather?* New York: Troll.

Phillips-Duke, B. (1998). *What in the world?* New York: Harper Growing Tree.

Rainis, K. G. (1991). *Exploring with a magnifying glass*. Danbury, CT: Franklin Watts, Inc.

Reid, M. S. (1990). *The button box*. New York: Dutton Children's Books.

Seuss, Dr. [pseudo. for Geisel, T. S.]. (1960). *Green eggs and ham*. New York: Random House for Young Readers.

Sharmat, M. (1980). *Gregory, the terrible eater*. Madison, WI: Demco Media.

Simmons, J. (1999). *Daisy and the egg*. New York: Little, Brown & Co.

Vagin, V. (1998). *The enormous carrot*. New York: Scholastic.

The Basic Scientific Processes: Measuring

Measuring is the scientific process that enables us to find out such things as how big something is, how much it weighs, how much space it takes up, how hot or cold it is, and long it takes something to occur. We measure to find quantitative information about objects and events; we measure to find the effects of something we do; and we measure to compare objects or events with other objects or events.

There are five basic entities that children in early childhood programs measure in science: length, volume, weight, temperature, and time.

When you can measure what you are speaking about, and express it in numbers, you know something about it; but when you cannot measure it, when you cannot express it in numbers . . . you have scarcely, in your thoughts, advanced to the stage of science.

William Thompson, Lord Kelvin, *Popular Lectures and Addresses, 1899–1894*

"As for me, I am concerned with matters of consequence. There is no time for idle dreaming in my life."

"Ah! You mean the stars?"

"Yes, that's it. The stars."

"And what do you do with five-hundred millions of stars?"

"Five-hundred-and-one million, six-hundred-twenty-two thousand, seven-hundred-thirty-one. I am concerned with matters of consequence: I am accurate."

Antoine de Saint-Exupéry, *The Little Prince* **(Dan Diego, CA: Harcourt Brace, 1971).**

Constructing Your Ideas 5.1
Measuring Rocks

Select a rock from the collection you have been using and mark it so you can recognize it. Ask the students to contribute their marked rocks to a class collection.

(1) Which rock is the biggest? How do you know? How can you be sure?
(2) Which rock is the shortest? How do you know? How can you be sure?
(3) Which rock is the heaviest? How do you know? How can you be sure?
(4) Which rock is the coldest? How do you know? How can you be sure?

Tackle these questions one at a time. Work out strategies as a class or in groups, and then implement your strategies to obtain solutions you can be confident of.

How did you approach answering these questions? Did you find it necessary to take some measurements? Perhaps you measured length in some creative way. Some may have measured **circumference** (distance around) in one or two directions. You probably discovered that you could not tell which rock is the heaviest just by hefting them—that you had to devise some method of comparing their actual weights. How did you tell which rock is the coldest? Because you can't thrust a thermometer into the inside of a rock, thermometers won't work.

This activity shows the significance of obtaining measurements in scientific investigations.

circumference—The distance around an object

MEASURING LENGTH

Length is defined as the distance between two points. Examples are the length of a table top, the length of a floor tile, the width of a door, the distance between two cities, a person's height, the circumference of a beach ball or a rock, and so on.

Length may be measured in **metric** units or in **conventional** units. The metric system is a system of measurement based on the meter as the standard. In the metric system, units are expressed as decimal multiples of each other such as 10, 100, 1000, ⅒, ⅟₁₀₀, ⅟₁₀₀₀, and so on (see Figure 5.1). The conventional system, formerly known as the British system, is based on the standardized foot. The conventional system uses a wide variety of units, and each uses a different multiple for conversion to other units.

The most commonly used metric units are the meter (m); the kilometer (km), which equals 1000 meters; the centimeter (cm), which is ⅟₁₀₀ of a meter; and the millimeter (mm), which is ⅟₁₀₀₀ of a meter. It takes 100 cm to make 1 m; it takes 1000 mm to make 1 m; and it takes 10 mm to make 1 cm.

metric units of measurement—Units of measurement based on the meter as the standard
conventional units of measurement—Units of measurement based on the standardized foot as the standard; formerly known as the British system

Prefix	Meaning
kilo	1000 times
hecto	100 times
deca	10 times
deci	$\frac{1}{10}$
centi	$\frac{1}{100}$
milli	$\frac{1}{1000}$

FIGURE 5.1   Table of metric conversions

Factoid: The meter was originally defined as one ten-millionth of the distance from the earth's north pole to the equator measured along a **great circle** extending through Lyons, France. Today the meter is defined as the distance light travels in 1/299,792,458 of a second in a vacuum.

great circle—An imaginary circle surrounding the globe that passes through both the north and south poles

The basic unit of length in the conventional system is the foot. Three feet equals one yard, and 5,280 feet equals one mile. One foot contains twelve inches. A meter is a little longer than a yard.

Factoid: The foot as the fundamental unit of length was developed by the Greeks; legend has it that the original foot was based on an actual measurement of Hercules's foot. Today it is defined as 1200/3937 of a meter, or the distance between two fine lines on gold plugs in a bronze bar kept at 62° F in a vault in Westminster, England.

Children should be encouraged to measure many things. But before young children can gain skill in measurement, they must first gain skill in comparisons. Ask questions of comparison in preschool and kindergarten classes frequently: "Which is longer?" "Which is shorter?" "Who is taller?" "Who is shorter?" "Which is closest?" "Which is farthest away?" Provide many opportunities for children to make comparisons of length: sticks, leaves, desks, blocks, crayons, pencils, strips of paper, large and small balls, and so on. Avoid asking young children to make comparisons of the sizes of objects they see in pictures or photographs with the sizes of the actual objects, for they first need to develop the ability to abstract images of real objects from the images they see in the photographs. For instance, if a 3-year-old is shown two photographs, one of a cat and one of a cow, and the images are shown the same size, he may infer that the cat and the cow are in fact the same size. For young children, always have real materials available to compare and later to measure.

Elizabeth had just turned four. Mother was working on a college report at her computer while Elizabeth was playing in the room. Mother printed a draft of her report on connected perforated computer paper. Elizabeth looked at the sheets as they came out of the printer, and she watched Mother tear off two sheets and put them to one side. She took them and held them up next to her.

"Am I this tall?" Elizabeth asked.

"What do you think?" asked Mother.

"I think I'm bigger. Could I have more paper to see?"

"How many sheets do you think?"

"Three."

Elizabeth held three connected sheets next to her.

"It's not enough. I need some more."

"Okay. How many?"

"Five."

Elizabeth held five connected sheets next to her.

Mother said, "What do you think?"

"It's too big. Draw a line right here." Elizabeth pointed to the top of her head.

After the line was drawn, Elizabeth cut the top sheet off at the line. She regarded her height of 3½ sheets and wrote her name on the paper.

To gain a sense of the nature of measuring length, children should be encouraged to devise their own systems of "unconventional" measurement. They can measure length in terms of number of Legos®, plastic bears, blocks, paper clips, precut lengths of string, nose-to-fingertip span, lengths of feet, and so on. In this way children internalize the idea that the lengths of things can be expressed in numbers (quantified) and that the number of units of length can be compared and even graphed. It is far more important for children to gain a fundamental understanding of the nature of length and to be able to express length in quantitative terms than to memorize the number of inches in a foot or the conversions within metric units. Of course, foot rulers, yardsticks, and meter sticks can and should be used, but these instruments are treated simply as another way to measure length.

Body Measurement Olympics

A student teacher assigned to a second grade challenged her class to participate in a *Body Measurement Olympics* competition. She intended the activity to provide practice in the process skill of measurement and also to enable children to experience at first hand the need for standardization of measurement. Four separate competitions involving distance were set up, and each distance was measured using an obsolete, nonstandardized unit of measurement based on the length of a body part. The competitions were as follows:

(continued)

Contest	Unit of Measurement
Cotton Ball Throw	Hand
Paper Plate Disk Throw	Pace
Broad Jump	Foot
Straw Javelin Throw	Cubit

The teacher explained the measurement units to the children:

One *hand* is the width of the four fingers held together flat.
One *pace* is the distance from the toe of one foot to the toe of the other foot in an ordinary walking pace.
One *foot* is the length of a person's foot (with shoes on).
One *cubit* is the length of a person's forearm from the tip of the longest extended finger to the elbow (see Figure 5.2).

She gave a tally sheet to each child and instructed the children to record their distances for each event on the tally sheet. Each child was to measure distances using the units of hand, pace, foot, and cubit. The winner for each event was the child who accomplished the farthest distance.

She left it up to the children to decide how the measurements could be fair for all the children—the shortest as well as the tallest. Ideas included asking the same individual to be the official "measurer" for each event (the tallest or the largest); splitting the class into groups and competing as groups rather than as individuals; and other suggestions to compensate for the lack of standardization of the units of measure.

When the children had established all the rules, the *Olympics* began.

(Thanks to Ms. Donni Quinney, who developed this game as an undergraduate preservice teacher at Kennesaw State University.)

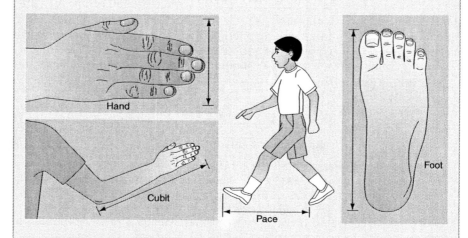

FIGURE 5.2 *Body Measurement Olympics* units of measurements

Several inquiry activities appropriate for helping children explore and master the skill of measuring length are suggested in Constructing Science in the Classroom 5.1–5.7. Some are appropriate for preschool children, and some are more appropriate for children in the early elementary grades.

Constructing Science in the Classroom 5.1
Which Is Longer? Which Is Shorter?

AGE

8
7
6
5
4
3

AN ACTIVITY FOR MEASURING LENGTH

Divide the class into groups of three or four children. Be sure they understand the names of body parts such as arm, hand, thumb, leg, foot, and so on. Then name a body part, and ask children to find something in the room that is either longer or shorter than that body part. Suggestions include, "Find something longer than your foot." "Find something shorter than your hand." "Find something about as long as your thumb." "Find something shorter than your foot." "Find something longer than your thumb." "Find something longer than your arm."

Keep the activity going until all children have had an opportunity to respond to at least six such questions.

Literature Connection:
Inch by Inch by Leo Lionni (1995). A little inchworm takes the reader on a real-world investigation.

Constructing Science in the Classroom 5.2
Measuring Your Partner's Height

AGE

8
7
6
5
4
3

AN ACTIVITY FOR MEASURING LENGTH

Objective
The student will measure her partner's height using unconventional units.

Form pairs of children. Provide a dozen or so die-cut hands. Ask one of the pair to lie down on the floor. The other child lays the die-cut hands, palm to finger, on the floor next to the partner and counts the number of hands that were used. The child whose height was just measured finds her name on the class chart and records the number of hands high (or long) she is. Then the children switch roles. Continue until all children have been measured.

You also may wish to ask children to use the die-cut hands to measure different things in the classroom such as stuffed animals, desks, or door openings (From Tryba, Davis, & Sikes, 1996).

Literature Connection:
Mr. Tall and Mr. Small by Barbara Brenner (1994). Mr. Tall, a giraffe, and Mr. Small, a mouse, constantly argue over who has the better height until a fire threatens them, and they discover that there are benefits to both sizes.

Constructing Science in the Classroom 5.3
How Long Is My Arm? How Long Is My Foot?

AGE

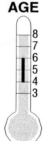

AN ACTIVITY FOR MEASURING LENGTH

Objective

The student will measure the length of another student's arms, feet, and other body parts.

Provide each student a piece of string 6 inches long. Divide the class into pairs. Ask children to use this piece of string to measure the length of their partner's body parts such as foot, arm, leg, hand, finger, forearm, and so on. Ask children to measure the same body part for each of the two children in the pair and decide whether they are the same length or, if not, whose is longer and whose is shorter.

Children may encounter difficulties such as remembering the length of the string or marking or measuring lengths that are longer than the string. Before suggesting solutions to the difficulties, ask children to come up with their own ideas.

Literature Connection:

How Big Is a Foot? By Rolf Myller (1962). This is a comical story of the use of nonstandard measurement. A king orders a carpenter to build a bed based upon the length of the king's foot. However, the carpenter builds the bed based upon the length of his own foot.

Constructing Science in the Classroom 5.4
How Many Pennies?

AGE

AN ACTIVITY FOR MEASURING LENGTH

Objective

The student will measure length using common objects.

Provide each child with about twenty pennies and several objects to be measured, such as a clothespin, a napkin, a paper clip, a sheet of construction paper, or a banana. Explain to the children that the unit of measure is "one penny." Ask them to select an object and lay pennies end-to-end next to the object. They measure how many pennies long each of the objects is by counting the number of pennies. (See Figure 5.3)

If a whole number of pennies falls short of the length of the object they are measuring, round up to the next number. Explain to them that they are counting the *total* number of pennies it takes to equal a given length and that if a portion of a penny is left over, it still takes part of a whole penny to cover it (see Figure 5.4).

Literature Connection:

The Hundred Penny Box by Sharon Bell (1986). An elderly woman explains to her grandson that a penny is placed in a box every year of her life. The passage of time is explained well in this moving story.

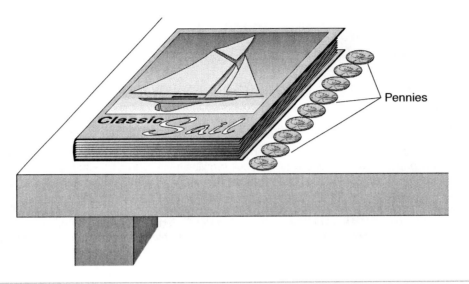

FIGURE 5.3 How many pennies long is the book?

FIGURE 5.4 Measuring objects with unconventional units of length

Constructing Science in the Classroom 5.5
Graphing Plant Growth

AGE

8
7
6
5
4
3

AN ACTIVITY FOR MEASURING AND GRAPHING LENGTH

Objective

The student will measure the length of growing plants over time and will graph the results.

In this activity, children measure plant height in terms of anumber of squares on a piece of graph paper. Provide seedlings of quick-growing plants, such as marigolds, beans, mung beans, or morning glories. Children place thin strips of graph paper behind the plants each day, mark where the top of the plant comes on the strip, and cut the strips off at the mark. They paste the strips onto a large chart, count the number of squares, and enter that number together with the day and date at the bottom of the strip. The resulting graph is a histogram that shows in graphic form the relative heights of the plant over time (see Figure 5.5).

Literature Connection:

The Carrot Seed by Ruth Krauss (1945). A little boy plants a carrot seed and cares for it regularly. The seed grows into a huge plant despite everyone's telling him it won't come up.

FIGURE 5.5 Charting plant growth

Constructing Science in the Classroom 5.6
How Long Is My Shadow?

AGE

8
7
6
5
4
3

AN ACTIVITY FOR MEASURING LENGTH

Objective
The student will measure the lengths of shadows using conventional or nonconventional units.

This activity is best done in the early morning or late afternoon when the shadows are longest. To show the apparent movement of the sun in the sky, children can do it every hour throughout the day and can compare the lengths and directions of shadows.

Separate the class into pairs of children. Provide each pair with a length of string 6 to 8 feet long and a pair of scissors. Have one member of the pair stand tall and step on one free end of the string. The other member of the pair stretches the string out as far as the shadow extends, cuts the string off at that length, and gives the cut piece of string to the first person, who retains it for future use. Then have children trade positions. Back in the classroom, children mount their strings on a class poster and label them with their names, or they measure the length of their string in inches or centimeters and record the lengths on a class chart. You could choose to have children measure their shadows at different times during the day and compare the lengths of the shadows formed. Did the shadows stay the same length? Did the shadows stay in the same place? Ask children to offer reasons for their answers.

Literature Connection:
Footprints and Shadows by Anne Wescott Dodd (1992) contains beautiful watercolors that illustrate footprints and shadows playing their own game of hide-and-seek.

Constructing Science in the Classroom 5.7
How Long Is a Kilometer? How Long Is a Mile?

AGE

8
7
6
5
4
3

A SERVICE ACTIVITY INVOLVING MEASURING LENGTH

Objective
The student will measure a kilometer and a mile.

This activity requires that you have a straight measurable distance of one mile or more along the street the school is located on.

Provide students with a few meter sticks and a few yardsticks. Take the students and the instruments outside to a curb adjacent to the school. CAUTION: Be sure the school administration asks the local police to block off the streets while the children are doing this activity!

Drive a stake into the ground next to the curb at a point near the school. Children lay the meter sticks end-to-end along the curb until 1000 lengths have been counted. Drive a stake into the ground next to the curb to indicate the end of the measured kilometer. Starting with the same beginning stake, a different group of children lays the yard sticks end-to-end along the curb until 1760 yardstick lengths (which equals 5280 feet) have been counted. Again, drive a stake into the ground by the curb to represent the end of the measured mile. As part of the preparation, ask children to devise a method they can use to keep accurate count. Finally, prepare large weatherproof signs that indicate the

(continued)

beginning and end of both the measured kilometer and the measured mile. Publicize the existence of these measurements next to your school, and invite people to check the accuracy of their vehicle odometers by comparing with the measured lengths.

Literature Connections:

The Half-Mile Hat by Bernard Lodge (1995). Yorrick, the shepherd, hires a giant with a huge hat to protect her city during a rainstorm. But she is faced with the difficulty of getting the sleeping giant to leave when the sun comes out.

Mushroom in the Rain by Mirra Ginsburg (1990). Animals hide under a tiny mushroom to stay dry during a storm, but the mushroom expands as the rain falls.

MEASURING VOLUME

The volume of an object is a measure of how much space it takes up. In the metric system, the basic unit for volume is the liter (which is about the same as a quart). One liter (l) contains 1000 milliliters (ml). One milliliter is the same volume as one cubic centimeter (cc). In the conventional system, the basic unit of volume is the quart. One quart contains two pints or four cups, and one cup contains eight ounces of liquid. Four quarts make a gallon.

As with length, it is desirable to have children invent their own units for volume such as paper cups, coffee cans, milk cartons, soda bottles, measuring cups, and measuring spoons.

Young children have difficulty dealing with the concept of volume because of their limited ability to conserve. You will recall the classic Piagetian experiment about children's ability to conserve volume. When the experimenter pours water from a tall glass into a large tank, young children perceive that there is less water in the tank than there was in the glass because the water in the tank is not as deep as it was in the glass, (see Figure 5.6). They do not understand that the amount of material in something does not change when it changes shape. Thus, it is inappropriate to ask young children to compare volumes of different materials, to ask them to do activities that

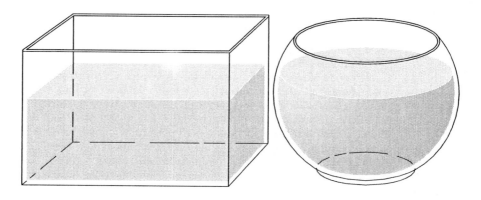

FIGURE 5.6 How do the capacities of the two containers compare?

require recognizing that the volume of a material does not change when its shape changes, or to ask them to do activities involving water displacement. Volume activities for young children center around the question, "How much does this hold?"

Inquiry activities appropriate for helping children explore and master the skill of measuring volume are suggested in Constructing Science in the Classroom 5.8–5.10. Some are appropriate for preschool children, and some are more appropriate for children in the early elementary grades.

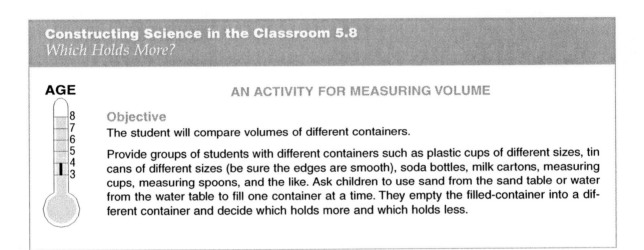

Constructing Science in the Classroom 5.8
Which Holds More?

AGE

AN ACTIVITY FOR MEASURING VOLUME

Objective

The student will compare volumes of different containers.

Provide groups of students with different containers such as plastic cups of different sizes, tin cans of different sizes (be sure the edges are smooth), soda bottles, milk cartons, measuring cups, measuring spoons, and the like. Ask children to use sand from the sand table or water from the water table to fill one container at a time. They empty the filled-container into a different container and decide which holds more and which holds less.

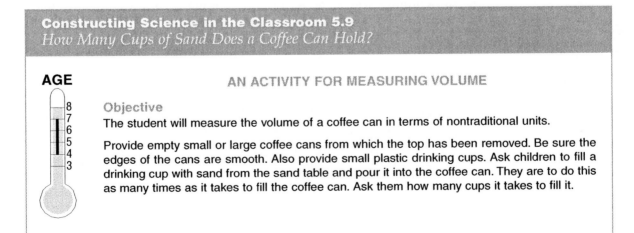

Constructing Science in the Classroom 5.9
How Many Cups of Sand Does a Coffee Can Hold?

AGE

AN ACTIVITY FOR MEASURING VOLUME

Objective

The student will measure the volume of a coffee can in terms of nontraditional units.

Provide empty small or large coffee cans from which the top has been removed. Be sure the edges of the cans are smooth. Also provide small plastic drinking cups. Ask children to fill a drinking cup with sand from the sand table and pour it into the coffee can. They are to do this as many times as it takes to fill the coffee can. Ask them how many cups it takes to fill it.

Constructing Science in the Classroom 5.10
How Much Soda Is in a Liter?

AGE

8
7
6
5
4
3

AN ACTIVITY FOR MEASURING VOLUME

Objective
The student will measure the volume of a liter in terms of number of paper cups.

Provide children with a liter bottle (or a 2-liter bottle) of soda. Also provide a number of paper cups of the size children in your class would normally use to drink out of. Ask them to pour the soda from the bottle into the paper cups. Then ask them to count the number of cups they filled with soda. "Is there enough soda in this bottle for everyone in the class to have a cup of it?"

MEASURING WEIGHT

Weight is the pull of gravity on something. The unit of weight in the conventional system is the pound. One pound contains 16 ounces of weight. Two thousand pounds equals one ton.

The weight of an object depends on two factors: the amount of material in that object and the pull of gravity. The pull of gravity varies on the earth according to elevation; the higher up something is, the less it weighs. This is because the higher an object's elevation, the farther away it is from the earth's center of mass and the less gravitational pull there is on it. These differences in weight are extremely minor on the earth. However, the differences are very great in orbiting spaceships. Spaceships orbit the earth several hundred miles above the earth. (For example, the space shuttle *Endeavour* orbits the earth at altitudes between 190 miles and 330 miles, depending on its mission.) At these altitudes, the earth's gravitational pull is extremely small. When coupled with the force of its orbital motion, the force of gravity on the spaceship is reduced to about one-millionth of that felt on earth and is perceived as zero.

Gravity on the moon is about ⅙ as much as on the earth. Thus, things weigh about ⅙ as much on the moon as they do on earth, and people can jump higher and hop farther on the moon than they can on earth because there is less gravity to hold them down.

However, regardless of gravitational pull, an object has the same amount of material in it whether it is on the seashore, in Denver, on the top of Mt. Everest, in a space ship, or on the moon. The amount of material in an object is called its mass. As you can see, weight varies from place to place, but mass does not. The basic unit of mass in the metric system is the kilogram (kg). One kilogram contains 1000 grams (g). One gram is about the mass of a good-sized mosquito. A kilogram of mass has a weight of 2.2 pounds on earth at sea level.

Although the pound is a unit of weight and the kilogram is a unit of mass, they are often used interchangeably in the United States. For example, we weigh 125 pounds at home, but at the doctor's office, we are told that we weigh 57 kilograms. The label on a pound package of butter says "Net Weight 1 Pound (454 grams)," even though the pound is a unit of weight and the gram is a unit of mass. Because of this popular, yet erroneous, interchangeability between units of weight and mass, it is suggested that early childhood educators not spend much effort in trying to get children to understand the difference between the two. This is a topic better treated in later grades.

As with length and volume, it is possible and desirable for children to invent their own units of weight. They should be encouraged to weigh things in terms of number of plastic bears, Legos, paper clips, plastic cubes, and the like. The most significant weight-related concept for young children is comparison. Preschool teachers should frequently ask, "Which is heavier?" "Which is lighter?" Children can heft rocks of different sizes to see which is heavier and which is lighter. Similarly, they can compare the weights of books, rocks of different sizes, large and small washers, and so on.

There are many excellent devices available for measuring weight. The two-pan balance is the most appropriate instrument for measuring weight in early childhood science activities. Some come with pans and some with hanging buckets. The principle is the same. The object to be weighed is placed on one pan or bucket, and the units of weight (plastic bears, Legos, paper clips, and the like) are placed on the other pan or bucket, one at a time, until the arm connecting the pans or buckets is level or the pointer shows the pans are balanced. Children count the number of weighing units it takes to achieve balance (see Figure 5.7).

Inquiry activities appropriate for helping children explore and master the skill of measuring weight are suggested in Constructing Science in the Classroom 5.11–5.13. Some are appropriate for preschool children, and some are more appropriate for children in the early elementary grades.

FIGURE 5.7 A balance

Constructing Science in the Classroom 5.11
Which Is Heavier? Which Is Lighter?

AGE

AN ACTIVITY FOR COMPARING WEIGHTS

8
7
6
5
4
3

Objective
The student will compare the weights of different objects.

Provide an assortment of objects that have different weights such as a large stone, a small stone, a stuffed toy, a plastic hamburger, a book, a paper clip, a pencil, a crayon, and the like. Ask each child to select one object and heft it by holding it in his hand and moving his hand up and down to get the feel of its weight. Then ask the child to select a different object that he believes will weigh more and one that he believes will weigh less. Ask the child to test his decisions by hefting each in a different hand and comparing their weights.

Alternatively, children can place each object on a different pan or bucket of the balance to see which is heavier. First, be sure children know how to use the balance.

Literature Connection:
Weigh It Up, Bear's Playschool Kits by Andy Cooke (1997). Little Bear picks up different objects and discovers they all have different weights.

Constructing Science in the Classroom 5.12
How Much Does a Penny Weigh?

AGE

AN ACTIVITY FOR MEASURING WEIGHT

8
7
6
5
4
3

Objective
The student will measure the weight of an object using nonconventional units.

First show children how to use the two-pan balance scale. Then ask them to put a penny in one pan of the scale and add paper clips to the other pan until balance is achieved. Children record the number of paper clips. Do all pennies weigh the same?

Encourage children to experiment with how much two, three, and four pennies weigh. Also encourage them to explore the weights of other coins and many different things using different kinds of "weights" on the balance scale. If desirable, children may wish to mix up the units to achieve greater accuracy in weighing. For example, a toy truck may turn out to weigh seven plastic bears, two Legos, and three paperclips.

Literature Connection:
Let's Find Out What's Light and What's Heavy by Martha and Charles Shapp (1975). With attention-getting pictures and humorous text, children will discover that what may be light for one person may be heavy for another person.

Constructing Science in the Classroom 5.13
Who Has the Biggest Cookie?

AGE

8
7
6
5
4
3

AN ACTIVITY FOR MEASURING WEIGHT

Objective

The student will weigh cookies using a pan balance.

Provide each group with a two-pan balance scale, and show the children how to use it. Provide each child with one fairly large cookie such as a chocolate chip cookie. All cookies should be taken out of the same container so they appear to be identical. (Be sure to tell them *not* to eat it; you can have cookies available for eating after the activity is complete.) Ask children to guess whether the cookies all weigh the same. Then ask each child to find the weight of her cookie in terms of the units you have chosen to use (Legos, plastic bears, paper clips, and the like). If desirable, you may wish to mix up the units to achieve greater accuracy in weighing. For example, a cookie may turn out to weigh four Legos and three paper clips. Children record the weight of their cookies on a large class chart and decide whether all the cookies are the same weight or whether some are lighter than others (see Figure 5.8).

Literature Connection:

The Biggest Cookie in the World by Linda Hayward (1995). Cookie Monster sets out to bake the biggest cookie in the world.

FIGURE 5.8 Whose cookie weighs more?

MEASURING TEMPERATURE

Temperature can be measured either in degrees Fahrenheit (in the conventional system) or in degrees Celsius (in the metric system). Of course, a given temperature is the same whether it is measured in degrees Fahrenheit or degrees Celsius. The primary points of reference on both scales are the freezing point and the boiling point of pure water at sea level. On the Fahrenheit scale, the freezing point of water is 32° and the boiling point of water is 212°. On the Celsius scale, the freezing point of water is 0° and the boiling point is 100°. Common temperatures on both the Fahrenheit and Celsius scales are shown in Figure 5.9.

Young children have difficulty with the concept of temperature because it is an abstract concept. They should begin to explore temperature by comparing things that are hot or warm with things that are cold or cool. Ask the questions "Which is warmer?" "Which is cooler?" "Which is hotter?" "Which is colder?" Ask young children to compare how hot or cold some-

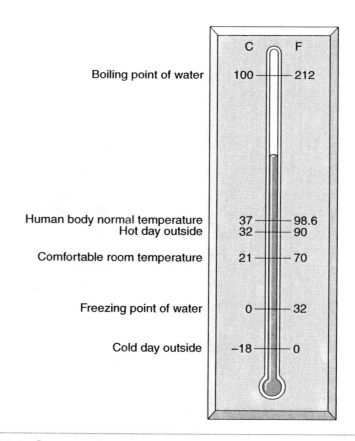

FIGURE 5.9   Common temperatures in Celsius and Fahrenheit degrees

thing is with their own body temperature by asking questions such as "How do things feel?" Also ask questions such as "What foods and drinks do you like hot?" "What do you like cold?" "What season is it when it is hot outside?" "What season is it when it is cold outside?" In this way, children begin to recognize that there are different temperatures and that different things have different temperatures.

As children grow older, they can make the transition from comparing temperatures to making actual temperature measurements. School supply companies offer a variety of inexpensive and safe thermometers suitable for children. Children need practice in using thermometers. This practice can be provided in a variety of ways. Ask children to write down the temperature that was forecast on the radio or TV to be today's high temperature, and then mark this temperature on a large wall-mounted model thermometer at school. Because reading thermometers requires **interpolation** (inferring readings that are not printed on the scales), children need skill in estimation to be able to read thermometers. Once they acquire this skill, they will be able to count the lines between degrees that are marked on the thermometer and obtain the actual reading. Digital thermometers are available that provide accurate temperature readings and may be used until children learn how to use thermometers.

interpolation—Inferring information between two known points, such as inferring temperature between labeled marks on thermometers

Several inquiry activities appropriate for helping children explore and master the skill of measuring temperature are given in Constructing Science in the Classroom 5.14–5.16. Some are appropriate for preschool children, and some are more appropriate for children in the early elementary grades.

Constructing Science in the Classroom 5.14
Is It Warmer in the Sun or in the Shade?

AGE

8
7
6
5
4
3

AN ACTIVITY FOR MEASURING TEMPERATURE

Objective

The student will measure the relative temperatures of water under different conditions.

Provide two Styrofoam cups for each child. Children fill each of their cups about half full of water. Ask them to put their finger in the water in both cups and see whether there is a difference in temperature or whether they are the same temperature. Then place one cup in the sun and the other cup in the shade. Let the cups stand there for about an hour. Then ask children to test the temperatures of the water in each cup with their finger again. Which is warmer? Which is cooler? Why do you suppose the water in the cup in the sun got warmer than the water in the cup left in the shade?

Constructing Science in the Classroom 5.15
How Does Ice Affect the Temperature of Water?

AGE

8
7
6
5
4
3

AN ACTIVITY FOR MEASURING TEMPERATURE

Objective

The student will measure the temperature of water.

Fill a glass partly full of water and measure its temperature. Add an ice cube to the water, and ask children what they think will happen to the temperature of the water. Record the temperature and the time on a class chart every minute. Keep recording temperature and time readings until the last three readings stay the same.

Literature Connection:

Winter Barn by Peter Parnall (1986). The winter barn is a safe haven for all of the creatures that seek shelter from the brutal subzero winds as they wait for the first signs of spring.

Constructing Science in the Classroom 5.16
Does the Color of the Cover Affect How Fast Water Heats up in the Sun?

AGE

8
7
6
5
4
3

AN ACTIVITY FOR MEASURING TEMPERATURE

Objective

The student will measure temperature of water under different conditions.

Provide children with large Styrofoam cups, a bucket of water, thermometers, an assortment of paper of different colors (including white and black), and a piece of aluminum foil. Children fill their cups to about the three-quarter level with water, cover the top with a piece of colored or white paper or a piece of aluminum foil, and insert the thermometer through the top of the cover so it is in the water. Record the initial temperature. Then place the cups in the sun, and ask children to record the temperatures every minute. Provide a data table such as the following one to help them. Children continue recording temperatures every minute until the last three temperatures are the same.

Back in the classroom, children look at their data to answer the question, "Does the color of the cover affect how fast the water in the cup heats up in the sun?" They can also make a group graph of their data to see the results in graphic form.

DOES THE COLOR OF THE COVER AFFECT HOW
FAST WATER HEATS UP IN THE SUN
DATA TABLE

Color of Cover _____

Time	Temperature

MEASURING TIME

The unit of time is the second. This is a universal unit and is the same in both the metric system and the conventional system. The length of a second is about the length of time it takes to say "one-one-thousand." Intervals of time measured in science activities done at school, such as the time it takes a toy parachute to fall to the floor, can be approximated by having children count, "one-one-thousand, two-one-thousand, three-one-thousand . . ." rhythmically. As children gain skill in this rhythmic method of counting seconds, they can compare their counting with the sweep second hand on the wall clock to demonstrate for themselves that their method is in fact very close to "real" time. This method of counting seconds can also be applied in many nonschool situations. For example, in estimating how far away a thunderstorm is, the interval between seeing lightning and hearing the resulting thunder is counted using the rhythmic method. For every five seconds of delay between lightning and thunder, the storm is one mile away.

A second aspect of measuring time involves time of day. One of the skills children start to learn in early schooling is telling time using clocks. When children have mastered this skill, they can engage in activities that involve time of day. For example, in investigating how long it takes water to evaporate, children measure the depth of water left in a pan at regular intervals of time such as 9:00 AM, 11:00 AM, 1:00 PM, and 3:00 PM.

Measuring time is difficult for young children, so teachers should be sure children are ready before asking them to do time-related activities. Several inquiry activities appropriate for helping children explore and master the skill of measuring temperature are suggested in Constructing Science in the Classroom 5.17–5.21.

Constructing Science in the Classroom 5.17
How Long Does It Take Sand to Run through a Funnel?

AGE

8
7
6
5
4
3

AN ACTIVITY FOR MEASURING INTERVALS OF TIME

Objective

The student will measure the time it takes for sand to run through a funnel.

Divide the class into pairs of children. Provide a plastic cup and a funnel with a narrow spout for each pair. One child holds the funnel with one hand and closes the tip of the funnel with the thumb of the other hand. The other child measures one cupful of sand and pours it carefully into the funnel. At a signal, the thumb is released, and the children begin counting seconds using the "one-one-thousand, two-one-thousand . . ." method. How many seconds does it take for all the sand to go through the funnel?

Literature Connection:

In the Next Three Seconds by Rowland Morgan (1999) is a book of predictions of what could happen in three units of time. For example, Americans will eat 3,600 eggs in the next three seconds; seventeen species of rainforest life will disappear in the next 3 hours; and a rat could have 20 million descendents in the next 3 years.

Constructing Science in the Classroom 5.18
Recording Time and Outdoor Temperature

AGE

AN ACTIVITY FOR MEASURING TIME OF DAY

Objective
The student will record the outdoor temperature at the same time each day.

Provide an outdoor thermometer that is large enough that children can easily read the numbers. Tell children they are going to keep track of the outdoor temperature every day for a month (or so). To compare daily temperatures fairly, the readings have to be taken at the same time each day. Ask children to choose the best time; they may want to obtain outdoor temperatures around midday, such as just before or just after lunch. At the agreed-upon time, children bring the thermometer outdoors and hold it *in the shade* for 2–3 minutes to be sure the final thermometer reading has been reached. They record the temperature and transfer it to a large chart in the classroom. Graphing the results will enable children to see how the temperature changes from day to day (Figure 5.10) (see also Constructing Science in the Classroom 4.10.).

Literature Connection:
Temperature and You by Betsy and Guillo Maestro (1990). This is an introductory story (appropriate for lower grades) of what temperature is and how it is measured.

FIGURE 5.10 Checking the outdoor temperature

Constructing Science in the Classroom 5.19
How Long Does It Take to Run across the Playground?

AGE

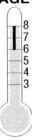

AN ACTIVITY FOR MEASURING INTERVALS OF TIME

Objective

The student will measure the time it takes for another student to run a given distance.

Divide the class into pairs of children. One of each pair runs from one end of the playground to the other end while the partner counts the number of seconds using the "one-one-thousand, two-one-thousand . . ." method. If the child reaches the other end before a given count is completed, this can be counted as half a second. Each child records his or her time on a large class chart.

Literature Connection:

Clocks and More Clocks by Pat Hutchins (1970). Mr. Higgins buys many clocks, but they show different times when he moves from room to room. He consults the clock maker, who teaches him about elapsed time.

Constructing Science in the Classroom 5.20
How Long Does It Take a Toy Car to Roll down a Ramp?

AGE

AN ACTIVITY FOR MEASURING INTERVALS OF TIME

Objective

The student will measure the length of time it takes an object to roll down a ramp.

Provide a wide board and a toy car or truck. Put one end of the board on a stack of books to elevate it. Place the toy car at the top of the board, and let it roll down. Children start counting the number of seconds the moment the car is released. Young children can use the rhythm method of counting "one-one-thousand, two-one-thousand. . . ." Older children can measure the time interval using a stopwatch or by counting seconds using the sweep second hand of a watch or clock. After all children have done the activity, check the results for consistency. Change the height of the elevated end of the ramp to determine whether height makes a difference in the time it takes the car to roll down the ramp.

Literature Connection:

Pushing and Pulling (in *Science for Fun*) by Gary Gibson (1996) contains directions for experiments dealing with gravity, weights, and friction.

Constructing Science in the Classroom 5.21
What Happens to Chocolate Chips Left in the Sun?

AGE

8
7
6
5
4
3

AN ACTIVITY FOR MEASURING INTERVALS OF TIME

Objective

The student will measure an interval of time.

Provide a bag of chocolate chips and a plastic baggie that can be sealed shut. Children place a few chocolate chips in the baggie, seal it, and place it in the sun. They decide how long to leave their bags in the sun—say, 10 minutes. They record the time they placed it in the sun and also what the time will be 10 minutes later. At the end of the determined period of time, they retrieve their baggies and describe what, if anything, happened to the chocolate chips.

Literature Connection:

Curious George Goes to a Chocolate Factory by Margaret Rey (1998). Curious George causes a problem at the chocolate factory, but his quick thinking and speedy action save the day.

METRIC vs CONVENTIONAL UNITS

Many science educators feel children should learn to think in terms of the metric system. Science uses the metric system almost exclusively, and most of the world's countries use the metric system in everyday living. The United States is one of the very few countries that still uses the conventional system. Even our closest neighbors, Canada and Mexico, uses the metric system.

Those who favor using the metric system in science education point out that the world of science uses the metric system. Thus, in keeping with our premise that children should do science the way scientists do science, children should make all measurements in science using the metric system. The metric system is easier to use than the conventional system, and children enjoy working with it. In addition, with increasing diversity, more and more families use the metric system at home, reflecting their countries of origin. Thus, the metric system is relevant to some children. However, learning theory suggests that children learn best that which is meaningful to them. Children in the United States are much more familiar with the units of the conventional system than the units of the metric system. A person is four feet three inches rather than 130 centimeters tall. She weighs 80 pounds rather than 36 kilograms. The temperature of a room is 72 degrees Fahrenheit rather than 22 degrees Celsius. Children measure everyday things in units of the conventional system. To insist the metric system be used in early childhood science classes even though it is not used consistently in the children's daily lives may be to ask children to think in terms of units that are less meaningful to them than conventional system units.

So it is your decision whether the metric system or the conventional system should be used in your science activities. If you use the metric system because it is used by scientists in doing science, you have a strong argument for you decision. If you use the conventional system to foster meaning based on prior experience and familiarity, you have a strong argument for this choice. The decision is yours. You will have support either way.

Constructing Your Ideas 5.2
An Activity for Measuring

 Now it's your turn. Write a short activity that can be used to help children sharpen their measuring skills. Specify age/grade level, and be sure the activity is appropriate to the children in the age/grade group you specify. Cite a process-oriented objective for your lesson; this objective will read something like this: "The student will measure _____." Then get together in small groups and do the activities each member of your group has prepared.

References

Bell, S. (1986). *The hundred penny box.* New York: Puffin.

Brenner, B. (1994). *Mr. Tall and Mr. Small.* New York: Henry Holt.

Cooke, A. (1997). *Weigh it up, Bear's playschool kits.* Hauppage, NY: Barron's Educational Series, Inc.

Dodd, A. W. (1992). *Footprints and shadows.* New York: Simon & Schuster.

Gibson, G. (1996). *Pushing and pulling* (in *Science for fun*). Highland Park, NJ: Copper Beach Books.

Ginsburg, M. (1990). *Mushroom in the rain.* New York: Aladdin.

Hayward, L. (1995). *The biggest cookie in the world.* Madison, WI: Demco Media.

Hutchins, P. (1970). *Clocks and more clocks.* New York: Macmillan.

Krauss, R. (1945). *The carrot seed.* New York: Harper & Row.

Lionni, L. (1995). *Inch by inch.* Madison, WI: Demco Media.

Lodge, B. (1995). *The half-mile hat.* New York: Whispering Coyote Press.

Maestro, B., & Maestro, G. (1990). *Temperature and you.* New York: Lodestar.

Morgan, R. (1999). *In the next three seconds.* New York: Puffin Books.

Myller, R. (1962). *How big is a foot?* New York: Atheneum.

Parnall, P. (1986). *Winter barn.* New York: Atheneum.

Rey, M. (1998). *Curious George goes to a chocolate factory.* Wilmington, MA: Houghton Mifflin.

de Saint-Exupéry, A. (1971). *The little prince.* Orlando: Harcourt Brace.

Shapp, M., & Shapp, C. (1975). *Let's find out what's light and what's heavy.* New York: Franklin Watts.

Tryba, C., Davis, A., & Sikes, L. (1996). Science sacks: Hands-on approach to teaching the processes of science to elementary students. Presentation made at regional conference of Kappa Delta Pi, November 2, 1996, Kennesaw, GA.

CHAPTER 6

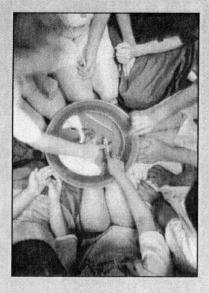

The Basic Scientific Processes: Predicting

Predicting is the process we use when we offer our best guess as to what will happen as a result of some action. We can find out how correct our prediction is by trying it. If the evidence we observe when we try it out supports our prediction, our thinking is probably valid. If we observe something different than what we predicted, we probably need to refine, augment, or change our thinking.

It is a test of true theories not only to account for but to predict phenomena.

William Whewell: *Philosophy of the Inductive Sciences,* 1840, aphorism 39.

"You've got to be able to make those daring leaps or you're nowhere," said Muskrat.

Russell Hoban, *The Mouse and His Child.* (New York: Bantam Doubleday Dell Books for Young Readers, 1967).

Constructing Your Ideas 6.1
Predicting What Would Happen If . . .

In groups, discuss answers to the following questions, and try one or two to see what happens.

- What would happen if you were to add water to a sand pile?
- What would happen if you were to put sugar on a plate with mealworms crawling on it?
- What would happen if you were to line up dominoes on end in a curved pattern, a half inch away from each other, and then push the first one down?
- What would happen if you were to blow bubbles from a square-shaped wand?

Think up a few more "What would happen if . . ." questions. Ask the students to explain why they predicted what they did.

These are questions that involve the scientific process of predicting.

A prediction is your best guess as to what would happen if you were to do something. The questions you just discussed all involve predicting what would happen if you were to do certain actions. Some have only one logical response, but several logical predictions can be made for others. For example, some students might predict that the mealworms will move toward the sugar. Some might predict that they will move away from the sugar. And some might predict that nothing will happen. All these predictions are logical, depending on the reason.

Perhaps the single most important question an early childhood teacher can ask in science is "What would happen if. . . ." These "What would happen if . . ." questions stem from curiosity and observations, that lead to questions someone would like to find out about. When these questions are asked, they seem to require some sort of answer. Answering such questions involves the process of predicting.

We can make certain predictions with some degree of accuracy. For example, we can predict with reasonable assurance that, in the continental United States, the weather will be cold in the winter and hot in the summer. Astronomers used complex calculations involving speed and orbit to predict that Halley's Comet will next be seen from earth in the year 2061.

However, some predictions are less accurate. Results of close political races cannot be predicted with any degree of accuracy. **Meteorologists** provide the public with their best prediction about what the weather will be like in the next day or two. But weather predictions depend on many factors that can change suddenly and cause the actual weather to be different from the prediction.

meteorologist—Scientist who studies weather

The Case of the Mysterious Crayons

Often an activity can have unexpected results, thus opening up whole new avenues of inquiry that people had not thought of before. In a first-grade class, a teacher was engaging his students in a prediction "sink-or-float" activity. Included in the assemblage of items for children to predict and then try were several kinds of crayons. The activity proceeded as expected with the wooden objects, the buttons, the Ivory soap, the paper clips, and so on. But when it came to the crayons, the children observed a most remarkable thing: Some of the crayons sank and some floated. Attempting to understand this newly discovered phenomenon, the teacher asked children to suggest reasons why some crayons would sink and others float. "Maybe it's the paper." So they removed the paper from all the crayons. Some still sank and some floated. "Maybe it's the length." So the children gathered several crayons of the same length with the papers removed. Again some sank and some floated. "Maybe it's how fat they are." So the children tried crayons of the same length with their papers removed but of different thicknesses. Once more some sank and some floated. After some time of trying several things, someone noticed that the yellow and orange colors floated while the blue and purple colors sank. More experimentation showed that this indeed was the case. The darker colors of the same brand of crayon sank, and the lighter colors floated. In fact, some of them (such as the red and green crayons) floated half way between the top and the bottom of the water.

Many inservice and preservice teachers have since asked first-grade children to predict whether crayons sink or float and test their predictions. The results are mixed. In some cases, children find that *all* crayons sink if the paper has been removed. In other cases, children have found that dark-colored crayons float and light-colored crayons sink. In one detailed activity, first-grade children found that, when they removed the paper wrapper, the yellow and orange crayons floated for a while but eventually submerged and came to rest in the water part way to the bottom.

Why does this happen? I don't know.

Prediction is essential in doing science, and children should be encouraged to predict before they test. Prediction charts are often prepared to help children stay focused. For example, children should predict whether an object will sink or float before they try it, and they should predict whether an object will be attracted to a magnet before they try it. In this way, children learn to compare what actually happens with what they thought would happen rather than merely accepting what happened without thinking about it. If there is a discrepancy between what children predict and what actually happens, questions arise in the child's mind that require resolution. This resolution often can occur through further inquiry. Such is the nature of science.

Several predicting activities are suggested in Constructing Science in the Classroom 6.1–6.9. Some are appropriate for preschool children, and some are more appropriate for children in the early elementary grades. The activities suggest ways of providing experiences and practice in fostering the process of predicting.

Constructing Science in the Classroom 6.1
What Can Sprout and Grow?

AGE   AN ACTIVITY FOR PREDICTING

8
7
6
5
4
3

Objective
The student will predict which of given items can sprout and grow.

Provide children with a collection of several items including some seeds. Suggestions include several kinds of bean seeds, corn seeds, pea seeds, roasted peanuts, other nuts, a piece of gum, a shell, a button, a rubber band, a screw, a crayon, and so on. Ask children to pick out the things they think will sprout and grow. Ask why they think these items will sprout and grow. Then ask children to pick out the things they think will not grow and to tell why they think they will not grow. Glue the items to a large piece of poster paper on the appropriate sides labeled "Will Sprout and Grow" and "Will Not Sprout and Grow." Finally, for each item that children predicted will sprout and grow, "plant" a duplicate in a wet tissue or paper towel, place the towel with the "seed" in a plastic baggie that can be sealed, seal it, and place it in a well-lit area. Ask children to check the results of their predictions each day until they see whether something happens in the bags.

Literature Connection:
The Biggest Pumpkin Ever by Steven Kroll (1984). Two mice grow the same pumpkin plant without knowing it. They feed it sugar water to encourage its growth and end up with the biggest pumpkin anyone has ever seen.

Constructing Science in the Classroom 6.2
Mixing Colors

AGE   AN ACTIVITY FOR PREDICTING

8
7
6
5
4
3

Objective
The student will predict the color that results when two colors are mixed.

Provide children with a small portion of red, yellow, and blue tempera paint, several toothpicks, and a sheet of plain white paper. Ask them to scoop up a blob of one color of the paint with the toothpick and spread it on the sheet of paper. Then ask them to scoop up a blob of a different color with a different toothpick and mix it with the color that already is on the paper. Also ask them to do the same with other pairs of colors. After each mixture has been made, ask them to identify the color that results. Then provide clean toothpicks and a clean sheet of paper. Do the same as before, but this time ask children to predict the color that will result from mixing each pair of colors. Encourage children to come up with their own mixtures and colors. Finally ask them to make given colors, such as orange, green, and purple. Can they make brown? Can they make black? Can they make gray? Can they make white?

As an alternative to tempera paint, use colored frosting and plastic spoons. Children mix them on paper plates to obtain new colors.

Literature Connection:
Mouse Paint by Ellen Stoll Walsh (1989). This story is about mice who walk into red, yellow, and blue paint. As they walk from color to color, they mix the paints, forming new colors.

Constructing Science in the Classroom 6.3
Sink? Or Float?

AGE

8
7
6
5
4
3

AN ACTIVITY FOR PREDICTING

Objective
The student will predict whether given objects will sink or float.

Provide a dishpan about two-thirds filled with water and a tray with a number of different kinds of objects, some of which sink and some of which float. Suggestions include metal spoon, plastic spoon, wooden spoon, metal fork, plastic fork, wooden fork, piece of wood, penny, dime, nickel, quarter, empty shampoo bottle, liquid soap, regular soap, wooden clothespin, pencil, paper clip, crayons, eraser, magic marker, and so on.

Children select one object at a time, predict whether it will sink or float in the water, and then drop it into the water to see if their prediction was accurate (see Figure 6.1). It is best to provide a laminated chart with columns marked "sink" and "float" to help children keep track of their predictions. Children place each object either in the "sink" columns or in the "float" columns in accordance with their predictions. They then put each object in the water, one at a time, to check their predictions. Encourage children to try other things in addition to what you provided.

Literature Connection:

Mr. Gumpy's Outing by John Burningham (1970) is a humorous tale of an outdoor adventure on a boat on a river. One by one, children and animals join Mr. Gumpy in the boat. Everything is fine until they upset the balance of weight in the boat.

FIGURE 6.1   Will it sink? Or will it float?

Constructing Science in the Classroom 6.4
Do Plants Move?

AGE

AN ACTIVITY FOR PREDICTING

8
7
6
5
4
3

Objective
The student will predict the effect of sunlight on the movement of plants.

Plants experience a phenomenon known as **phototropism** in which they move toward bright light sources.

Provide each child with a plastic cup, a paper towel, and two to three lima bean seeds or other fast-growing seed. Soaking the seeds overnight will hasten their germination. Ask children to stuff the paper towel into the cup, wet it thoroughly, and "plant" the seeds between the wet paper towel and the inside surface of the cup. Place the cups on a windowsill or a table near a window. After a few days, the seeds will sprout primary roots, stems, and leaves. If the cup is transparent, children can see the roots. (see Figure 6.2).

Leave the seedlings in the sunlight, and notice that they grow toward the light; the stems actually bend toward the light. Ask children to predict what would happen if they turned the cups around so the curved stems were facing *away* from the light. Then ask them to turn their cups around and wait a day or two to see whether their predictions were accurate.

Literature Connection:
The Berenstain Bears Grow-It: Mother Nature Has Such a Green Thumb (1996). A brother and sister plant a variety of seeds, cuttings, and tubers and watch them grow. The book contains suggestions for children's own experimentation with plant growth.

phototropism—The bending of a plant toward a light source

FIGURE 6.2 The plant bends toward the light

Constructing Science in the Classroom 6.5
Do Crayons Sink or Float?

AGE

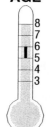

AN ACTIVITY FOR PREDICTING

Objective
The student will predict whether given crayons will sink or float.

Provide children with an assortment of crayons and a pan of water. Ask them to select the crayons one at a time and predict whether each will sink or float. Then ask them to try each to see what happens.

When children put the crayons in the pan of water, it may occur that some may sink and some may float. Ask children to suggest reasons why some sink and others float. Is it because of the color? Is it because of the paper wrapping? Is it because of the lengths? Is it because of how thick they are? Ask children to investigate each reason by eliminating the variable. For instance, they can remove the paper to see whether the wrapper had an effect, and they can break the crayons so they are all the same length to see whether length had an effect. (See "The Case of the Mysterious Crayons" earlier in this chapter.)

Literature Connections:
The Crayon Box That Talked by Shane DeRolf (1997). Crayons in a box of crayons convey the message that results are better when we all work together.
My Crayons Talk by Patricia Hubbard (1996). A young girl's crayons talk about colors, feelings, and images.

Constructing Science in the Classroom 6.6
Mixing Liquids with Water

AGE

AN ACTIVITY FOR PREDICTING

Objective
The student will predict whether given liquids will mix with water.

Provide a clear transparent plastic cup and a plastic spoon for each group of children. Ask them to fill the cup about half full with water. Have available a variety of other liquids such as vinegar, cooking oil, corn syrup, liquid soap, and the like. Ask children to select one liquid at a time and predict whether it will mix with the water or float on top. After predicting, children try the liquid to check their prediction. Suggest that they drizzle the liquid slowly down the side of the cup onto the water to see what happens and then stir it gently to see what happens. You might want to provide a data table for children to record their predictions and results. Encourage children to try this activity at home *under adult supervision,* using other liquids. The next day ask children to share their experiences.

Constructing Science in the Classroom 6.7
What Kinds of Materials Absorb Water?

AGE

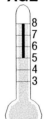

AN ACTIVITY FOR PREDICTING

Objective

The student will predict whether given materials absorb water.

Provide an assortment of materials such as waxed paper, paper towels, paper bags, napkins, typing paper, plastic wrap, cloth, oil cloth, a roofing shingle, and the like. Children place the material on a piece of cardboard held at an angle. Using an eyedropper or a straw, children place one or two drops of water on the material at the top of the incline and observe what happens to the water. You might want to demonstrate this first with one of the materials to show that the water runs down the incline quickly or slowly depending on how rapidly it is absorbed by the material. Ask children to predict which materials will allow the water to run down the incline rapidly and which will cause the water to run down the incline slowly or be absorbed almost immediately. Children then test their predictions. Encourage children to do many variations on this activity, such as laying the material flat on the table, holding the material over the top of an open coffee can, using oil instead of water, and other variations. Encourage children to try their own variations and to suggest different materials that they might use.

Literature Connection:

Desert Giant: The World of the Saguaro Cactus by Barbara Bash (1989). This is a wonderful book on the life cycle of the saguaro cactus and the haven it produces for desert life. The book has an abundance of information such as how the cactus skin expands to store rainwater for the dry spans.

Constructing Science in the Classroom 6.8
How Much Will It Rain? How Much Will It Snow?

AGE

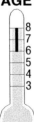

AN ACTIVITY FOR PREDICTING RAINFALL AND SNOWFALL

Objective

On a day when the weather forecast calls for rain or snow for the next day, record (or ask children to record) the amount of rain or snow that is forecast. Then measure the amount that falls at school, and compare your measurements with the forecast amount.

To measure rainfall, set out a commercial or a homemade rain gauge in the open, making sure it is empty. To measure snowfall, set a board approximately 3 feet square out in the open (see Figures 6.3 and 6.4).

At the end of 24 hours, measure the amount of rain in the rain gauge or the depth of the snow on the board. Compare the amount measured at school with the amount predicted by the weather forecast. Are they the same? Are they different? If they are different, ask children to suggest reasons why the accumulation at school might be different from the forecast.

(continued)

Literature Connections:

Cat and Mouse in the Rain by Tomasz Bogacki (1997). Cat and Mouse meet to play. But when the rain falls, a frog teaches them how to have fun in the rain.

Cat and Mouse in the Snow by Tomasz Bogacki (1998). Cat and Mouse go out to play in the meadow but discover something new that's fun to play in.

Come On, Rain! By Karen Hesse (1999). Tess pleads to the sky for rain. Clouds roll in, the rain pours, and Tess, her mother, and her friends celebrate the shower with a rain dance.

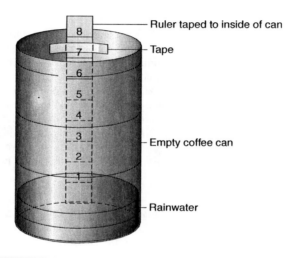

FIGURE 6.3 A homemade rain gauge

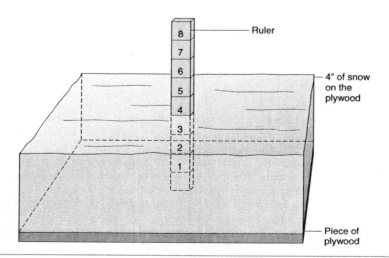

FIGURE 6.4 Snow accumulation on a board

A Homemade Rain Gauge

A rain gauge is simply a container set out in the open that collects the rain. Its diameter makes no difference, for the depth that accumulates is the same whether the diameter is large or small. The reason is that it rains the same amount in the same place, and the depth is the same whether it is collected in a small container or a large one. Obtain an empty coffee can and be sure the edges are smooth. Or use a 1–2-quart plastic container. Set the container in an open area. This is the rain gauge (see Figure 6.3).

To measure rainfall, put a plastic ruler vertically into the can so it rests on the bottom, and read the depth of the water from the ruler. Alternatively, you can tape a flexible ruler to the inside of the can, or you can mark a piece of masking tape as a ruler, with each inch divided into 10 tenths (for easier comparison with the forecast), and tape that to the inside of the can. If the container you use is transparent, you can measure the depth of the rainfall from the outside, or you can tape the measuring device to the outside for easy reading.

Measuring Snow Accumulation

The accumulation of snow is measured in two ways; the context of the forecast will tell you which way is used. One way is to measure the actual depth of the snow. Children in your class can do this by inserting a ruler vertically down through the center of the snow, all the way to the board to see how deep the snow is (see Figure 6.4). The other way to measure snowfall is through equivalent rainfall accumulation. Snow is one-tenth as dense as water. It takes 10 inches of snow to equal 1 inch of water. So, divide the depth of the snow that accumulates on the board by 10 to find its rainfall equivalent.

transparent—A material that permits clear images to pass through
translucent—A material that permits scattered light to pass through but not whole images
opaque—A material that does not permit light to pass through

Constructing Science in the Classroom 6.8
Transparent-Translucent-Opaque

AGE

8
7
6
5
4
3

AN ACTIVITY FOR PREDICTING

Objective
The student will predict whether given materials are transparent, translucent, or opaque.

When we shine a light on an object, one of three things can happen: (1) All the light will go through the material, and images will be clear if the material is **transparent;** (2) some of the light will go through the material, and images will be hazy if it is **translucent;** (3) none of the light will go through the material, and there will be no image if it is **opaque.** (Note: These definitions are not precise, but they are fine for purposes of this activity.)

Provide transparent, translucent, and opaque materials such as a clear plastic cup, a sheet of white paper, a plain overhead transparency, cardboard, poster board, aluminum foil, waxed paper, facial tissue, tissue paper, a glass of water, a mirror, plastic wrap, an eyeglass lens, Scotch tape, a magnifying glass, and the like. Children predict whether each object is transparent, translucent, or

(continued)

opaque and tell why they predicted what they did. Then they shine a flashlight beam at each object in turn to check their prediction. A data table that can help children in their explorations is shown in Figure 6.5.

Literature Connection:

Keep the Lights Burning, Abbie by Peter Roop (1985). Abbie keeps the light on in the lighthouse during a storm.

ITEM	PREDICTED			ACTUAL		
	Transparent 	Translucent 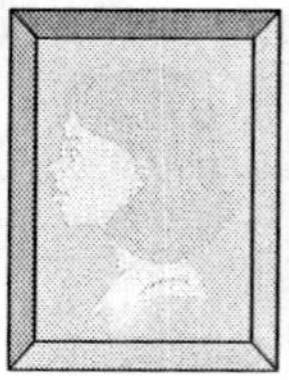	Opaque 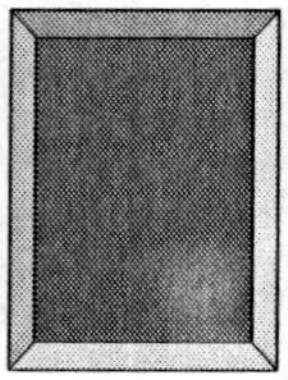	Transparent 	Translucent 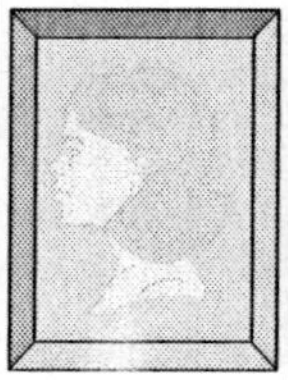	Opaque 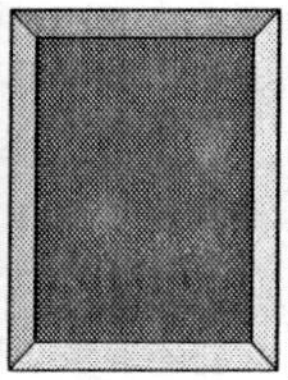

FIGURE 6.5   Data sheet for "Transparent? Tranlucent? Opaque?" activity

Constructing Your Ideas 6.2
An Activity for Predicting

Now it's your turn. Write a short activity that can be used to help children sharpen their skills of predicting. Specify age/grade level, and be sure the activity is appropriate to the children in this grade group. Cite a process-oriented objective for your lesson; this objective will read something like this: "The student will predict _____." Then get together in small groups and do the activities each member of your group has prepared.

References

Bash, B. (1989). *Desert giant: The world of the giant saguaro cactus.* San Francisco: Sierra Club/Little Brown.

Berenstain, S., & Berenstain, J. (1996). *The Berenstain bears grow-it: Mother Nature has such a green thumb.* New York: Random House.

Bogacki, T. (1997). *Cat and mouse in the rain.* New York: Farrar Straus & Giroux.

Bogacki, T. (1998). *Cat and mouse in the snow.* New York: Farrar Straus & Giroux.

Burningham, J. (1970). *Mr. Gumpy's outing.* New York: Henry Holt.

DeRolf, S. (1997). *The crayon box that talked.* New York: Random House.

Hesse, T. (1999). *Come on, rain!* New York: Scholastic.

Hubbard, P. (1996). *My crayons talk.* New York: Henry Holt & Co.

Kroll, S., & Bassett, J. (1984). *The biggest pumpkin ever.* New York: Scholastic.

Roop, P. (1985). *Keep the lights burning, Abbie.* Minneapolis: Carolrhoda.

Walsh, E. S. (1989). *Mouse paint.* San Diego: Harcourt Brace.

CHAPTER 7

The Basic Scientific Processes: Inferring

Inferring is the process we use when we try to figure out what caused something to happen, but where we can't observe the cause directly. In inferring, we take into account *all* the evidence as we develop conclusions and theories for why something happened. Our conclusions and theories are valid as long as they offer logical explanations of what happened and take into account all the evidence.

The method of scientific investigation is nothing but the expression of the necessary mode of working of the human mind.

Thomas Henry Huxley, *Our Knowledge of the Causes of the Phenomena of Organic Nature*, 1863

"I don't mind him just thinking," said Mrs. Brown, with a worried expression on her face. "It's when he actually thinks of something that the trouble starts."

Michael Bond, *A Bear Called Paddington* (New York: Bantam Doubleday Dell Books for Young Readers, 1958).

Constructing Your Ideas 7.1
A Wordless Story

 Look at the illustration in Figure 7.1. Take a piece of paper, and cover the illustration entirely. Then move the paper slowly from left to right, uncovering more and more of the picture as you move it. What is happening? Write or draw or play-act what you think caused what you observe in the picture. Share your inferences with the rest of the class. Remember: There are no right answers.

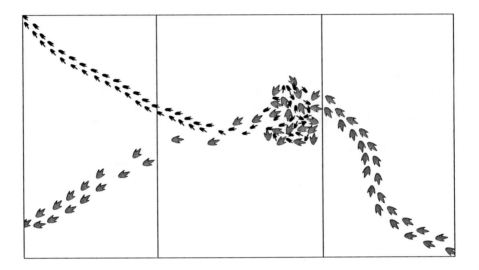

FIGURE 7.1 Footprints

From *Investigating the Earth Teacher's Manual, Fourth Edition* by the American Geological Institute. Copyright © 1984 by Houghton Mifflin Company. All rights reserved. Reprinted by permission of McDougal Littell Inc.

Did everyone's inference take account of *all* of the evidence? Or did some students make more "selective" inferences, adroitly skipping one or two pieces of evidence? Did anyone unconsciously *add* a bit of evidence that is not in the diagram to bolster his or her interpretation?

Inference is a person's best guess as to *why* something happened. This is contrasted with predicting, in which a person guesses what will happen next. In inferring, we have to figure out what caused something to happen. And our guess must be based solely on the evidence we have. If you think of criminal investigations and trials, you will get a good idea of the precision required of accurate inferring. The perpetrator and cause of a crime are often inferred from indirect evidence, but the inferences must take account of "the facts and only the facts," as Joe Friday, the famous detective on the television show, *Dragnet,* put it.

Many times we can observe directly what happens in a scientific activity without having to infer. For example, if we blow up a balloon and then let it go, we can see that it scoots around the room in directions opposite to the direction from which the air escapes. We can infer that the escaping air propels the balloon forward. However, many times we cannot observe what happens directly.

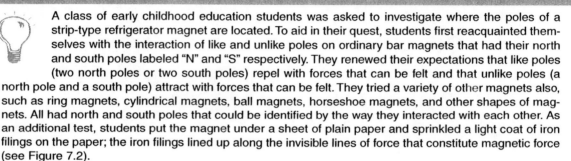

Constructing Your Ideas 7.2
Where Are the Poles on a Strip Magnet?

A class of early childhood education students was asked to investigate where the poles of a strip-type refrigerator magnet are located. To aid in their quest, students first reacquainted themselves with the interaction of like and unlike poles on ordinary bar magnets that had their north and south poles labeled "N" and "S" respectively. They renewed their expectations that like poles (two north poles or two south poles) repel with forces that can be felt and that unlike poles (a north pole and a south pole) attract with forces that can be felt. They tried a variety of other magnets also, such as ring magnets, cylindrical magnets, ball magnets, horseshoe magnets, and other shapes of magnets. All had north and south poles that could be identified by the way they interacted with each other. As an additional test, students put the magnet under a sheet of plain paper and sprinkled a light coat of iron filings on the paper; the iron filings lined up along the invisible lines of force that constitute magnetic force (see Figure 7.2).

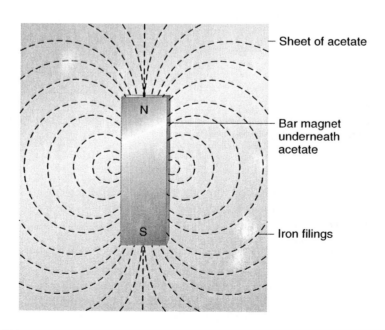

FIGURE 7.2 Magnetic force patterns

Then each student was given a pair of flat, strip-type refrigerator magnets, all of which sported advertising on one side and were plain and dark in color on the other side. The students were asked to determine that these were magnets by fooling around with them. Students found that the strip magnets are attracted to metallic surfaces (such as the door of a refrigerator) and that they attract magnetic items (such as paper clips). From their inquiries, students determined that these were indeed magnets. Then students were asked to fool around with these strip magnets for a few more minutes to see whether they could infer where the north and south poles were. They had already concluded that *all* magnets have north and south poles and that, because these were magnets, they must have north and south poles. They laid them on a table next to each other in different attitudes, placing them so the advertising surface sometimes faced up and sometimes faced down and so that different edges were brought near each other. They put the magnets on top of each other, sometimes with similar surfaces facing each other, and sometimes with nonsimilar surfaces facing each other. They tried to pull them apart and found that it took forces similar to the forces encountered with the other magnets to pry them apart. They tried sliding them in different directions while they were on top of each other, sometimes with similar surfaces touching, and sometimes with the different surfaces touching. They found that in some directions, the magnets slid over each other easily. They found that in other directions, it took quite a bit of force to slide the magnets over each other, and it felt bumpy, like driving a car over a corrugated road, even though the surfaces were smooth.

Over a period of several weeks, the students investigated the strip-type refrigerator magnets at home and at school, discussing their observations and findings with each other and posting summaries of what they found out on the class Internet site to keep other students informed. Eventually, these students came up with several ideas about where the north and south poles of strip-type refrigerator magnets are located. Statements found on the class Internet site (with responses) are as follows:

I assume the gravitational pull towards the center of the magnet proves the north and south poles are in the middle. However, you know what happens when you assume. HaHaHa.

I believe the North and South poles are in the direct middle. I am truly guessing because I have not a clue as to where they might be located.

I think the center of the magnets are the north and south poles. That's just my educated guess.

I originally thought the poles were on the top and bottom of the magnet. As I started playing, that didn't seem right. I felt a definite pull on the parallel sides of the magnet. I would say the poles are on the parallel sides—on the edges and then in the middle of the magnet.

I tried the magnets at home and found the same thing. The two magnets I had pushed away from each other when I put the two long sides together. Both magnets were in the shape of a rectangle—one was quite a bit larger than the other. When I put the two short sides together they stayed put.

I think there is more than one magnet. I wonder if you can have several microscopic magnet pieces on the surface. Who knows?

I have two theories on the location of the north and south poles of refrigerator magnets. My first guess was that the poles are arranged in alternating rows. One of the refrigerator magnets I observed seems to have small lines or rows on it. Secondly, my husband and I discussed that maybe magnets were ground into a powder (with the north and south poles mixed), and then bound together with some type of adhesive to form the magnetic bar of the refrigerator magnet that seems not to have poles.

Try this investigation in your class. See what you can infer about where the north and south poles of strip-type refrigerator magnets are.

Inferential reasoning is basic to all scientific understanding. Many of the activities you do with children in early childhood science classes require inferential reasoning on the part of the children. Be sure to ask them what they observe in each activity and *why* they think it happened. In this manner, you will foster the process of inferring.

Children's literature is also a great source of opportunities for children to develop their skill of inferring. Avoid the temptation to explain what you read in stories; instead, ask children for their explanations. Two examples of children's literature that can help foster the process of inferring are as follows:

The Mitten: A Ukrainian Folktale adapted by Jan Brett (1989). As each animal comes to crawl inside the lost mitten, it walks across the snow, leaving its footprints. Ask children to infer whether the pictured tracks are those of the animal that has just made its way to the mitten.

Animal Tracks and Traces by Kathleen Kudlinski (1991). This book encourages children to become good detectives by discovering where to look for animal clues including tracks, nests, skin, feather or fur coverings, and food remnants.

Several inferring activities are suggested in Constructing Science in the Classroom 7.1–7.10. Some are appropriate for preschool children, and some are more appropriate for children in the early elementary grades. The activities suggest ways of providing experiences and practice in fostering the process of inferring.

Constructing Science in the Classroom 7.1
What Season Is It?

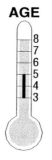

AGE

8
7
6
5
4
3

AN ACTIVITY FOR INFERRING

Objective
The student will infer seasons from photographs.

First, review the names and characteristics of the four seasons. You may wish to include only the seasons you experience in your area. Then provide children with photographs of landscapes showing the different seasons. Ask them to tell what season it is and *why* they think it is the season they inferred. Have them discuss any discrepancies in responses with each other.

Literature Connections:
A Bear for All Seasons by Diane Marcial Fuchs (1995). Bear tries to determine his favorite season, remembering the edible delights of each. He finally decides that the best times are those he has with his friend Fox.

Grandfather Four Winds and Rising Moon by Michael Channin (1994). Rising Moon worries about what will happen to his home because of the drought. Grandfather Four Winds tells him a story about the ability of the old apple tree to continue to thrive throughout the seasons.

Constructing Science in the Classroom 7.2
What's That Animal?

AGE

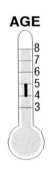

8
7
6
5
4
3

AN ACTIVITY FOR INFERRING

Objective
The student will infer the kind of animal from simulated movement.

First ask children to name some animals with which they are familiar. Remind them different animals move in different ways; for example, turtles crawl very slowly, elephants normally walk slowly with giant steps while swinging their trunks, dogs and cats walk and run, birds walk and fly, rabbits hop, frogs hop and swim, snakes crawl and swim, and so on.

One at a time, give each child a picture of an animal and ask her to demonstrate how the animal moves. Tell her *not* to show the picture to the other children or to tell them the name of the animal. The other children are to guess (infer) which animal is being portrayed and to tell *why* they guessed what they did. After each child has had a turn, ask children to select their own animals to portray. They should whisper its name to the teacher first.

(Note: this activity can be incorporated with the physical education program.)

Literature Connection:
On the Move: A Study of Animal Movement by Joyce Pope, Stella Stilwell, and Helen Ward (1992). This book describes the different methods various animals use to move around.

Constructing Science in the Classroom 7.3
Keeping a Paper Towel Dry in the Water

AGE

8
7
6
5
4
3

AN ACTIVITY FOR INFERRING

Objective
The student will infer the reason a paper towel stays dry in the bottom of a cup when the cup is submerged in water upside down.

Provide a pail of water, several large plastic cups, and some pieces of paper towel. Stuff a piece of paper towel in the bottom of a cup. Then put the cup, upside down without tilting it, into the pail of water. What happens? Does the paper towel stay dry? Why?

Constructing Science in the Classroom 7.4
Shadows

AGE

8
7
6
5
4
3

AN ACTIVITY FOR INFERRING

Objective
The student will infer the height and position of a light source from the shadow it forms.

Provide a funnel, a flashlight, and a large sheet of tagboard with a slit cut into it slightly narrower than the width of the lens end of the flashlight. In groups, children put the funnel upside down on a sheet of paper. Another child holds the flashlight behind the tagboard so others cannot see the flashlight and shines it onto the funnel at different angles and from different heights (see Figure 7.3). From the shadow made by the funnel, children infer the position from which the flashlight was aimed to produce that shadow. It may be necessary for children to "fool around" with flashlights and objects such as the apparatus just described before they try the inferring activity to get the general idea of shadows and how they are formed.

To follow up on this activity, take children outdoors to infer the position of the sun from the length and direction of their shadows. *Caution them not to look at the sun!!* (See Chapter 20 for descriptions of ways of viewing the sun's image without looking directly at the sun.)

Literature Connection:
Shadows and Reflections by Tana Hoban (1990). Objects are compared with their shadows and reflections.

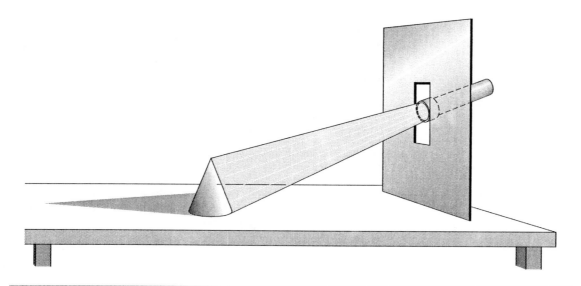

FIGURE 7.3   How is the flashlight pointed to form the shadow?

Constructing Science in the Classroom 7.5
Wind

AGE

8
7
6
5
4
3

AN ACTIVITY FOR INFERRING

Objective
The student will infer the direction the wind is blowing.

First discuss the effects of wind. Bring up such effects as leaves fluttering on trees, flags blowing in the wind, pinwheels twirling, clothes blowing on clotheslines, and so on. All these effects can help us infer how strong the wind is.

Ask how we could tell the *direction* the wind is blowing toward and the direction the wind is blowing from. To investigate this, have children make simple weather vanes. Provide each child with an empty thread spool, a plastic straw, and a wide arrow cut out of tagboard. Tape the arrow to one end of the straw, and put the straw in the hole in the spool (see Figure 7.4). Have children blow on the arrow from different directions, and watch the arrow turn in the direction of the wind.

Put some of the weather vanes outdoors, and check them during the day. Ask children to use their weather vane observations to tell which direction the wind is blowing.

Relate this activity to weather vanes children may have seen around their homes.

(Teacher note: Wind direction is named for the direction *from* which it blows. For example, a north wind is a wind that blows *from* the north.)

Literature Connections:
Gilberto and the Wind by Maria Hall Ets (1963). Gilberto has many adventures with the wind, his constant companion.
Feel the Wind by Arthur Dorros (1989) explains what causes wind and how wind affects our environment. The book includes directions for making a weather vane.

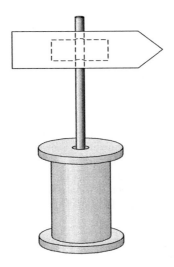

FIGURE 7.4 Homemade weather vane

Constructing Science in the Classroom 7.6
What's That Unknown Object?

AGE

AN INFERRING ACTIVITY USING SEVERAL SENSES

Objective
The student will use the senses to identify unknown objects.

Obtain a collection of several materials from nature, such as leaves, pine cones, sticks, rocks, blades of grass, flowers, dirt, and the like. Place individual samples in each of several small brown bags such as sandwich bags. The object is for children to identify what is in the bag without looking inside. They can use all their senses *except taste* and *sight*. Ask them to shake, feel, and smell the object inside the bag *without looking inside*. Ask them to identify the object or material, and ask them to tell how they know and what senses they used. Typical questions might include, "What do you think is in this bag?" "What does it sound like inside the bag?" "What does it smell like inside the bag?" "What does it feel like inside the bag?" At the end, children are permitted to look inside to confirm their conclusions. (See also Constructing Science in the Classroom 4.7, What's in the Bag?)

You may wish to suggest to parents that they do similar activities with their children at home; see Chapter 20 for suggestions on involving parents.

Literature Connection:
What's What? A Guessing Game by Mary Serfozo (1996). This is a guessing game book involving use of the senses. "What's hard?" A sidewalk is as hard as a rock or a wall.

Constructing Science in the Classroom 7.7
What's the Weather Outside?

AGE

AN INFERRING ACTIVITY USING SEVERAL SENSES

Objective
The student will infer the outdoor weather from clues.

Have the children look out of the classroom window and tell what they think the weather is like from what they observe. (See Constructing Science in the Classroom 2.6 "What Is the Weather Today?" for an activity on weather observation.) Most will probably tell what the weather was when they came to school. Suggest that they look for specific clues, such as clouds, what people are wearing, puddles, ice patches, fallen leaves, how the flag or tree branches and leaves are moving, and so on. You might secretly have one or two people casually walk by the window dressed in unseasonable clothes to add an element of discrepancy.

Then bring the children outdoors to confirm their inferences.

Literature Connections:
Boat Ride with Lillian Two Blossoms by Patricia Polacco (1989). A mysterious Native American woman takes William and Mabel on a strange boat ride and answers their questions about the wind, the rain, and the changing nature of the sky.

Eyewitness Readers: Whatever the Weather by Karen Wallace (1999). This text deals with the nature of the weather; it is one of a series of learning-to-read texts.

Constructing Science in the Classroom 7.8
The Origin of Soil

AGE

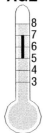

AN ACTIVITY FOR INFERRING

Objective

The student will infer the origin of given samples of soil.

Provide several different kinds of soil samples, paper plates, magnifying glasses, and plastic spoons. Tell the children they are going to be detectives. Children put a spoonful of the soil on the plate and examine it carefully with and without the magnifying glass to try to identify the different kinds of things in the soil. (See Constructing Science in the Classroom 2.9 "What's In the Dirt?" for an activity on observing soil.) Ask children to describe what they see in the soil, to infer where these things came from, and also to cite their reasons for inferring what they did. Finally, ask them to infer where the soil sample itself may have come from, based on what they found in it.

Literature Connection:

Who Is the Beast? By Keith Baker (1990). Several animals identify various parts of a beast. Children infer what the beast is from the progressive clues.

Constructing Science in the Classroom 7.9
How Old Was That Tree?

AGE

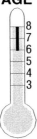

AN ACTIVITY FOR INFERRING

Objective

The student will infer the age of a tree from the tree rings in a cross section of its trunk.

A tree ring is a layer of wood produced by a tree in one year. One ring normally contains a thin layer (produced early in the growing season) and a thicker layer (produced later in the growing season) (see Figure 7.5.)

After a discussion about the nature of tree rings and the seasonal growth of trees that results in tree rings, give students a cross-sectional piece of a tree trunk. Ask them to count the number of complete tree rings. From this count, ask them to infer how old the tree was. Depending on the nature of the rings, children may also be able to infer the length and weather conditions of the seasons during which the tree grew. Wide rings suggest a growing season with plentiful rainfall; narrow rings suggest hard times such as draught.

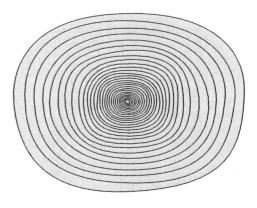

FIGURE 7.5 Tree trunk cross-section showing the growth rings

Literature Connection:

The Giving Tree by Shel Silverstein (1986) is a story of a boy who grows to manhood and a tree that gives him its bounty through the years.

Constructing Science in the Classroom 7.10
Causes of Soil Erosion

AGE

CAUSES OF SOIL EROSION

Objective
The student will infer causes of soil erosion in the environment around the school.

Take the class outdoors and help them find examples of soil erosion around the school. Good places to look are on slopes and at the ends of drainage pipes. Ask them for their observations about the soil, the general area, the slope of the ground, and so on. Ask them to infer what caused the soil to erode in the way they observed and to provide reasons for their inferences.

Literature Connections:
Follow the Water from Brook to Ocean by Arthur Dorros (1991). This story tells of the journey of water and the erosion water causes in the rivers, waterfalls, canyons, dams, and oceans it flows through.

Come a Tide by George Lyon (1990). When the snow melted and the water overflowed by the banks of the creeks and river, a little rural town flooded. Gardens were washed away, and homes were full of water, but the townspeople began the slow process of rebuilding their homes.

Constructing Your Ideas 7.3
An Activity for Inferring

Now it's your turn. Write a short activity that can be used to help children develop their skills of inferring. Specify age/grade level, and be sure the activity is appropriate to the children in the grade group you specify. Cite a process-oriented objective for your lesson; this objective will read something like this: "The student will infer _____." Then get together in small groups and do the activities each member of your group has prepared.

References

Baker, K. (1990). *Who is the beast?* San Diego: Harcourt, Brace, Jovanovich.

Bond, M. (1958). *A bear called Paddington.* New York: Bantam Doubleday Dell Books for Young Readers.

Brett, J. (1989). *The mitten: A Ukrainian folktale.* New York: G. Putnam and Sons.

Chanin, M. (1994). *Grandfather Four Winds and Rising Moon.* Tiburin, CA: H. J. Kramer.

Dorros, A. (1989). *Feel the wind.* New York: HarperCollins Children's Books.

Dorros, A. (1991). *Follow the water from brook to ocean.* New York: HarperCollins Children's Books.

Ets, M. H. (1963). *Gilberto and the wind*. New York: Viking Press, Inc.

Fuchs, D. M. (1995). *A bear for all seasons*. New York: Henry Holt & Company.

Hoban, T. (1990). *Shadows and reflections*. New York: Greenwillow.

Kudlinski, K. (1991). *Animal tracks and traces*. New York: Franklin Watts.

Lyon, G. (1990). *Come a tide*. New York: Orchard.

Polacco, P. (1989). *Boat ride with Lillian Two Blossoms*. New York: Putnam.

Pope, S., Stilwell, S., & Ward, H. (1992). *On the move: A study of animal movement*. Austin, TX: Stech-Vaughn.

Serfozo, M. (1996). *What's what? A guessing game*. New York: Simon & Schuster Children's.

Silverstein, S. (1986). *The giving tree*. New York: HarperCollins

Wallace, K. (1999). *Eyewitness readers: Whatever the weather*. New York: D. K. Publishing, Inc.

CHAPTER 8

The Process-Oriented Objective

The processes of observing, classifying, communicating, measuring, predicting, and inferring are the building blocks on which all of scientific inquiry rests. If our goal in early childhood science education is teaching children how to do science rather than teaching them about science, it is absolutely essential to engage children in activities that foster development and mastery of these basic process skills at increasing levels of sophistication.

In action, be primitive; in foresight, a strategist.
Renè Char, *Leaves of Hypnos, 72,* in *Hypnos Waking: Poems and Prose,* 1956.

Everything's got a moral, if only you can find it.
Lewis Carroll, *Alice's Adventures in Wonderland* (Old Tappan, NJ: Simon & Schuster Children's, 1962). (Original work published in 1865).

PROVIDING A PROCESS-BASED FOCUS

Robert Mager, considered by many to be the "father" of the instructional objective, tells the following story:

Once upon a time a Sea Horse gathered up his seven pieces of eight and cantered out to find his fortune. Before he had traveled very far, he met an Eel, who said,

"Psst. Hey, bud. Where 'ya goin'?"

"I'm going out to find my fortune," replied the Sea Horse, proudly.

"You're in luck," said the Eel. "For four pieces of eight you can have this speedy flipper, and then you'll be able to get there a lot faster."

"Gee, that's swell," said the Sea Horse, and paid the money and put on the flipper and slithered off at twice the speed. Soon he came upon a Sponge, who said,

"Psst. Hey, bud. Where 'ya goin'?"

"I'm going out to find my fortune," replied the Sea Horse.

"You're in luck," said the Sponge. "For a small fee I will let you have this jet-propelled scooter so that you will be able to travel a lot faster."

So the Sea Horse bought the scooter with his remaining money and went zooming thru the sea five times as fast. Soon he came upon a Shark, who said,

"Psst. Hey bud. Where 'ya goin'?"

"I'm going to find my fortune," replied the Sea Horse.

"You're in luck. If you take this short cut," said the Shark, pointing to his open mouth, "you'll save yourself a lot of time."

"Gee, thanks," said the Sea Horse, and zoomed off into the interior of the Shark, and was never heard from again.

The moral of this fable is that if you're not sure where you're going, you're liable to end up someplace else.

Reprinted with permission from *Preparing Instructional Objectives.*© 1984 Published by The Center for Effective Performance, 2300 Peachford Road, Suite 2000, Atlanta, GA 30338 (1-800-558-4237).

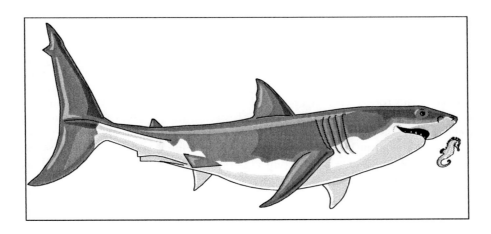

This fable suggests that, in planning any lesson, we must have a well-defined focus. We have to know where we're going. If we want to construct lessons that foster children's facility in the processes of science, we have to provide a process-based focus. We must construct the lessons so that the goal is increased skill in the scientific processes. Lesson planning is critical to the educative process, and well-constructed lessons stipulate desired learning outcomes, goals, or objectives, often stated as one or more behavioral, or learning, objectives. The best way to ensure that science lessons are built to foster development of process skills is to express the outcomes in the form of process-oriented objectives.

Simply put, the process-oriented objective is an ordinary learning objective in which the verb is a process skill. "The student will *observe* rocks." "The student will *classify* leaves according to a self-developed system." "The student will *communicate* how to put on a jacket so others can do the task successfully." "The student will *measure* the weight of a cookie in terms of number of pennies." "The student will *predict* which of several objects will sink and which will float in Karo syrup." "The student will *infer* from its tracks which animal was walking through the snow." You have written process-oriented objectives for each of the processes you have explored thus far. Furthermore, each of the activities described has a process-oriented objective as its goal.

The process-oriented objective enables both the teacher and the children to focus on one or more processes of science during a lesson. It is easy to get sidetracked and focus on acquisition of scientific knowledge. For example, in a lesson on classifying objects as magnetic or nonmagnetic, the temptation might exist to have children focus on identifying which objects are magnetic and which are nonmagnetic so they know these characteristics and can recall them at a later time. But if the objective stresses the process of classifying ("The student will *classify* given objects as magnetic or nonmagnetic."), the focus of the lesson shifts from learning the magnetic characteristics of the objects to grouping objects that have similar magnetic characteristics (magnetic objects in one group and nonmagnetic objects in a different group). Of course, at the same time, the children will also be learning which objects are magnetic and which are nonmagnetic. The science content, then, is viewed as the vehicle by which the children master the process skills. This results in student achievement in both process and content.

Most of the activities you have done in this text utilize more than a single process. For example, in the rock-observing activity, you not only observed the rocks with increasing skill and detail, but you also discussed your observations with others, thereby fostering the process of communicating. In the classifying activity, you had to call upon your skills of observing and communicating as well as classifying. Describing your favorite rock so other people could identify it required detailed observation as well as skill in communicating.

The scientific processes are interdependent and thus are seldom taught totally in isolation from one another. They are taught in an interdependent manner similar to the way you yourselves explored them. However, in early childhood science education, activities focus primarily on one of the processes, even though other processes may also be involved. Thus, when planning science activities for young children, the process-oriented objective represents the lesson's *primary* focus.

If children are to learn to do science the way scientists do science, they must acquire facility in the scientific processes. To ensure that this happens, you are strongly encouraged to write a process-oriented objective for each science lesson you prepare (suggestions for lesson planning are found in Chapter 16). As children acquire facility in the six basic processes, they are able to inquire into scientific phenomena the way scientists do. The next six chapters are devoted to the integrated processes that enable children to master the process of scientific investigation so they can do their own complete scientific inquiries.

References

Carroll, L. (1962). *Alice's adventures in wonderland.* Old Tappan, NJ: Simon & Schuster Children's.

Char, R. (1956). *Hypnos waking: Poems and prose.* New York, Random House.

Mager, R. F. (1984). *Preparing instructional objectives* (rev. ed.). Center for Effective Performance, Inc., 2800 Peachford Road, Suite 2000, Atlanta, GA 30338.

CHAPTER 9

The Integrated Scientific Processes: Identifying and Controlling Variables

In Chapters 2–7 you explored the processes of observing, classifying, communicating, measuring, predicting, and inferring. As we indicated earlier, these are sometimes referred to as the "basic" scientific processes. All scientific inquiry rests upon the investigator's ability to implement these processes carefully, accurately, and appropriately.

But scientific investigations require more than these basic processes. In investigating something to find cause and effect or relationships among various phenomena, we must also utilize the "integrated" processes. The integrated process skills include the following:

- Identifying and controlling variables
- Formulating and testing hypotheses

The whole of science is nothing more than a refinement of everyday thinking.
Albert Einstein, *Out of my Later Years,* 1950. Carol Publishing Group.

Without a doubt, there is such a thing as too much order.
Arnold Lobel, "The Crocodile in the Bedroom," *Fables* (HarperCollins Juvenile Books, 1980).

■ Defining operationally

■ Interpreting data

■ Experimenting

■ Constructing models

THE PENDULUM

As an example of using the integrated processes, suppose we have a home-made pendulum similar to the one depicted in Figure 9.1, and we want to know what factors influence the **period of the pendulum** (how long it takes the pendulum to swing back and forth). After watching the pendulum swing for a minute or so, we get a "feel" for how it works. Now we can "brainstorm" ideas about what we think might affect how fast it swings back and forth. These factors are termed *variables,* and our first step is to identify them. Variables we identify might include the weight of the bob, how far back we pull the pendulum before letting it swing, the length of the string, the thickness of the string, the presence of wind, the force of gravity, and so on. You and your colleagues could list more if you thought about it for a few minutes. Having listed the variables we *think* might influence the swing of the pendulum, we then pick out *one* of these variables to test. Let us say we want to see whether the weight of the bob affects how fast the pendulum moves back and forth. When we experiment, we will put different weights on the bob, and we will be very careful to keep *all* the other variables unchanged. This whole

period (of a pendulum)—Time it takes a pendulum to make one complete back-and-forth swing

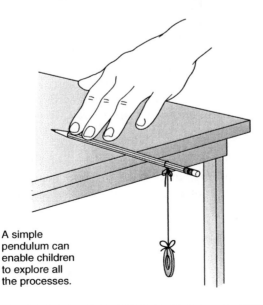

A simple pendulum can enable children to explore all the processes.

FIGURE 9.1 A pendulum

process of identifying the factors we think might influence the swing of the pendulum, picking out one to experiment with, and controlling all the rest, is the scientific process called *identifying and controlling variables.*

Although it is not always necessary, it helps guide our investigation if we formulate a hypothesis concerning the variable with which we are experimenting. In fact, we may want to give the investigation a few quick trial runs to see whether it is worth doing more completely. In the case of our pendulum investigation, we identified the weight of the bob as the variable we want to investigate. So we will form a hypothesis that suggests an answer to the question, "What would a heavier bob do to the swing?" Let's say we decide that the heavier the bob, the slower the swing. We have now formulated a hypothesis. We can test it by adding washers to the string, thereby increasing the weight of the bob, and letting it swing (with all other variables constant) to see what happens. This process is termed *formulating and testing hypotheses.*

Now we have to decide what we mean by the speed of the swing. The speed of a moving object is equal to the distance it travels divided by the time it takes to travel that distance. Obviously it would be both cumbersome and inaccurate for us to calculate distance and time for every swing of the pendulum. So we will want to find something easier to measure that tells us how fast or slowly the pendulum swings under different conditions. There are several ways to do this. One way is to count the number of swings in a given unit of time, say 15 seconds. (Can you explain how this gives us the same information?) In this manner, we have defined the speed of the pendulum in terms of the number of swings in 15 seconds. This is called an *operational definition.*

Having decided what variable to investigate, having formulated a hypothesis, and having defined the swing of the pendulum in operational terms, we are ready to set up an *experiment.* This involves setting up the apparatus, planning how we are going to make systematic changes to the selected variable, planning what data we need to be able to draw conclusions and how we are going to obtain it, and setting up a simple data table in which to record our data. Then we actually do the investigation, keeping in mind the very real possibility that we may have to change the procedure once we get into the investigation if something doesn't work the way we want it to. This process is called *experimenting.*

When we have collected the data, we can look at it to see what we can conclude. Was there a definite relationship between changes in the weight of the bob and changes in the number of swings the pendulum made in 15 seconds? Or were there no changes or only inconsistent and fairly small changes? From the data, we can draw conclusions. This is the scientific process called *interpreting data.*

We proceed in the same manner to investigate each of the other variables we have listed.

Finally, having collected swing information from all the variables, we are able to make a general conclusion concerning what variables affect how fast the pendulum swings and how the variables affect this rate. We can then set up a laboratory pendulum that will serve as a model for understanding the behavior of all pendulums. This is the scientific process called *constructing models.*

In Chapters 9 through 14 you will explore the integrated processes. While exploring these processes, you will be constructing your own understanding of what they are, how they are employed in scientific investigations, and how young children can work with them. Working with the integrated processes requires deeper and more mature levels of thinking than working with the basic processes. Many young children will not yet have the cognitive capabilities they need to work proficiently with these skills. However, most will be able to devise simple but well-thought-out investigations that employ the integrated process skills.

IDENTIFYING AND CONTROLLING VARIABLES

Let us start out with an activity in which you identify and control variables that affect how much sugar dissolves in water.

Constructing Your Ideas 9.1
What Affects the Amount of Sugar That Will Dissolve in Water?

Obtain the following materials for each group of three or four students:

Plastic cups   Some hot water
A small container of sugar   Some cold water
A spoon   Some lukewarm water

Make a list of everything you think might have an effect on the amount of sugar that will dissolve in water. Some factors that you might list are (a) amount of water, (b) temperature of water, (c) how fine the sugar crystals are, (d) type of sugar, and (e) how fast you stir the mixture. Think of as many as you can, and write them down. Share them with the rest of the class.

How would you find out which of these factors actually influence the amount of sugar that will dissolve in water? You would have to try each factor out, one at a time. For example, if you want to see whether the temperature of the water has an effect on the amount of sugar that will dissolve in it, you will keep the amount of the water, the size of the sugar crystals, the rate of stirring, and all other factors the same while you vary the water's temperature.

Assign one variable to each group, and ask the group to determine whether the variable has an effect on how much sugar dissolves in water. While you are doing this, you may think of other variables that might have an effect. If you do, add these to your list.

Listing the factors that might have an influence is called *identifying variables.* Selecting one of them to investigate and figuring out ways of keeping all the others unchanged (or constant) is called *identifying and controlling variables.*

There once was a student who became ill with flulike symptoms shortly before she was to begin student teaching. Panicked at the thought of missing her first day, she asked her friends how to get over her illness. One suggested taking aspirin. Another suggested going to bed for a whole day and keeping herself overly warm to "sweat it out." Her mother suggested eating chicken soup. So the student took two aspirins, ate a big bowl of her mother's homemade chicken soup, and went to bed, piling on two extra blankets. After a day, she felt much better.

What cured this student? Was it the aspirin? The chicken soup? The rest? The heat? She will never know, for she did *all* of them at the same time.

If we want to know what causes something to happen, we have to isolate the factors (variables) involved and test them one at a time. Before we can set up any experimental procedure, we must decide which variable we are going to manipulate and which variable we are going to observe the effect of this manipulation on.

Young children do not intuitively know that they must try things out one at a time to isolate cause and effect. However, they do have the capability to develop a basic understanding of the concept of identifying and isolating variables.

Several activities to help children learn to identify and control variables are suggested in Constructing Science in the Classroom 9.1–9.4. Some are appropriate for preschool children, and some are more appropriate for children in the early elementary grades.

Constructing Science in the Classroom 9.1
How Can We Increase the Speed with Which Sand Flows through a Funnel?

AGE

8
7
6
5
4
3

AN ACTIVITY FOR IDENTIFYING AND CONTROLLING VARIABLES

Objective
The student will identify variables that affect how fast sand flows through funnels.

This activity will be done at the sand table. Provide funnels of different sizes with stems of different diameters.

Ask children to fill a funnel with sand while keeping their fingers over the bottom of the stem. Ask them to uncover the bottom of the stem and watch the sand run through the funnel, noting how fast it runs through. Then ask them what they could do so the sand would run through the funnel faster. Write all responses on chart paper. Responses might include "Have a wider funnel," "Have a longer stem," "Use wet sand," "Use dry sand," "Put a hose on the end of the funnel," "Put a wider hose on the end of the funnel," "Put a smaller hose on the end of the funnel," and so on.

Ask children to try each of the variations they suggested, one at a time. (If children suggest variations for which you do not have the necessary materials, consider extending the activity to the next day to give time to obtain the needed materials.) Record the results next to each variable listed on the chart paper, and discuss the results of all the trials with the class as a whole.

Literature Connections:

The Sand Children by Joyce Dunbar (1999) is a fantasy about a sand giant (created by a boy and his father) who comes to life and makes seven sand children.

Swimming in the Sand by Marcia Leonard (1989) is a story about a hippopotamus who cools off in the sand and mud at the beach. Readers are asked to predict what happens next at various points in the book.

Constructing Science in the Classroom 9.2
Floating Eggs

AGE

AN ACTIVITY FOR IDENTIFYING AND CONTROLLING VARIABLES

Objective

The student will identify variables that influence whether an egg will float in water.

For each pair of children, provide a large plastic cup about half filled with water, about 1/3 cup of salt, a spoon, and an egg (raw or hard boiled). Ask the children to *carefully* put the egg in to the water. Does it float? (It sinks.) Now ask children to add salt to the water one spoonful at a time, stirring it well after each addition. If the water is warm, the salt will dissolve more easily. Children continue adding the salt a spoonful at a time until all the salt has been added. What happens to the egg? (It floats.) (See Figure 9.2.)

Ask children what they did to the water to cause the egg to float. The addition of salt to the water is called a variable.

Try the same thing with sugar to see whether sugar causes the same thing to happen.

Ask children to name some other factors they might think of that might influence whether an egg will sink or float in water. Try each factor they suggest to see whether the factor causes the expected results.

(Teacher note: Adding salt to the water increases the **buoyancy** [the degree to which objects float] of the water. The phenomenon of buoyancy can be observed by people swimming in ocean water; they float higher and more easily than they do when they swim in fresh water.)

buoyancy—The ability of a liquid to cause something to float in it

FIGURE 9.2 A "floating" egg

(continued)

Literature Connection:
Little Ned Stories: A Chapter-Picture Book for Kids by Edward Allan Faine (1999). The chapter "The Ocean Vacation" is a story of a boy who overcomes his fear of the ocean and learns how to swim.

Constructing Science in the Classroom 9.3
How Can We Make Salt Crystals?

AGE

AN ACTIVITY FOR IDENTIFYING AND CONTROLLING VARIABLES

8
7
6
5
4
3

Objective

The student will identify variables that affect the growth of salt crystals and will test each while controlling the others.

First, set up a crystal farm for children to observe (see Figure 9.3). Collect a few small pebbles and fill a glass pie plate three-fourths full with them. Dissolve 8 tablespoons of salt in one cup of warm water, and pour the solution over the rocks. Place the pan in direct sunlight. As the water evaporates, small crystals of salt form on the rocks. Magnifying glasses may help children with their observations.

(Teacher note: The warmer the water is, the faster it will evaporate, and the smaller the salt crystals will be. To form larger crystals, let the water cool after you have dissolved the salt so it will take longer for it to evaporate. Note that, in evaporating, only the water escapes; the salt and other materials dissolved in the water remain behind, forming the crystals.)

After children have had a chance to observe the crystal farm you set up, ask them to list factors they think might influence how fast the crystals form. (Alternatively, ask children to list factors they think might influence how large the salt crystals grow to be.) Responses might include "Use warmer water," "Use cooler water," "Use more salt," "Use less salt," "Use more rocks," "Use fewer rocks," "Use an aluminum pie tin instead of a glass one," "Use more salt solution," and so on. Write all their responses on chart paper, and ask them to test each one independently while keeping the other factors constant. For older children, you might want to divide the class into groups, with each group testing one of the variables listed on the chart. Record the results next to the appropriate variable on the chart paper, and discuss the results of the entire project with the class as a whole.

Literature Connection:
Snowflakes, Sugar, and Salt: Crystals Up Close by Chu Maki (1992). This nonfiction book shows close-up photographs of crystals and develops a working definition of crystalline materials. The book also suggests experiments dealing with crystals.

FIGURE 9.3 A salt crystal garden

Constructing Science in the Classroom 9.4
What Causes Plants to Grow to Be Healthy?

AGE

AN ACTIVITY FOR IDENTIFYING AND CONTROLLING VARIABLES

Objective

The student will identify and control variables that affect the growth of plants.

Provide an assortment of seedling plants. Children can grow the seedlings from seed, you can grow them yourself, or you can purchase them at a local garden store. Ask the children what they think they would need to do in order for these plants to grow. Responses might include "Give them water," "Put them in the sun," "Fertilize them," "Play music to them," "Talk to them nicely," and so on. As children give their responses, write each one on chart paper.

Divide the class into small groups, and assign each group the project of finding out the effect of one of the factors listed on the growth and health of their plant. Give the group two or three seedling plants, and ask them to figure out how they might determine whether their own particular factor has an influence. Then ask them to actually do what they have suggested.

When they list the factors, children are identifying the variables. They are isolating the variables when they choose one to experiment with.

Literature Connection:

Growing Things by Ting Morris (1994) is a nonfiction book about gardening and growing both ordinary and unusual plants.

Constructing Your Ideas 9.2
An Activity for Identifying and Controlling Variables

Now it's your turn. Write a short activity that can be used to help children learn to identify and control variables. Specify age/grade level, and be sure the activity is appropriate to the children in the age/grade you specify up. Cite a process-oriented objective for your lesson; the objective will read something like this: "The student will identify the variables in _____ and will decide which to manipulate and which to control when investigating this." Then get together in small groups and do the activities each member of your group has prepared.

References

Dunbar, J. (1999). *The sand children.* Northampton, MA: Interlink Publishing Group.

Einstein, A. (1950). *Out of my later years.* Secaucus, NJ: Carol Publishing Group.

Faine, E. A. (1999). *Little Ned stories: A chapter-picture book for kids.* Takoma Park, MD: MD Press.

Leonard, M. (1989). *Swimming in the sand.* Parsippany, NJ: Silver Burdett Press.

Lobel, A. (1980). *Fables.* New York: HarperCollins Juvenile Books.

Maki, C. (1992). *Snowflakes, sugar, and salt: Crystals up close.* Minneapolis: The Leaner Publishing Group.

Morris, T. (1994). *Growing things.* Danbury, CT: Franklin Watts.

CHAPTER 10

The Integrated Scientific Processes: Formulating and Testing Hypotheses

In Chapter 9 you explored the scientific process of identifying and controlling variables. In each activity, someone identified the variables involved, selected one to investigate, and devised ways to investigate it while keeping all the other variables constant. Having done this, people then tested each variable independently of the others. The activities were exploratory in nature—primarily to see what happens when a person manipulates one of the variables. In identifying and controlling variables, people are not asked to predict specifically what will happen when the value of a variable is changed; they are asked only to identify the variables and select one to investigate while keeping the others constant.

Hypotheses are only the pieces of scaffolding which are erected around a building during the course of construction, and which are taken away as soon as the edifice is completed.

Goethe, quoted in Anthony M. Ludovici's introduction to Friedrich Nietzsches *The Will to Power*, trans. and ed. Walter Kaufmann and R. J. Hollingdale. NY: Vintage, 1967.

So many things are possible just as long as you don't know they're impossible.

Norton Juster, *The Phantom Tollbooth* (New York: Random House, 1961).

In this chapter we go one step further by exploring the scientific process of formulating and testing hypotheses. In this process, you predict what you suppose will happen to one variable if you manipulate a different variable in a certain way (formulating a hypothesis), and you test the hypothesis to see whether the evidence suggests that the hypothesis is valid.

Let us look at the activity on dissolving sugar in water that you explored in Chapter 9. In identifying the variables that might influence the amount of sugar that will dissolve in water, we can formulate hypotheses that predict whether this amount will increase, decrease, or remain the same for each manipulation for each variable. For example, we might predict that more sugar will dissolve in hot water and less sugar will dissolve in cold water. These are hypotheses and are different from simply stating that we think the temperature of water would somehow affect the amount of sugar that dissolves in it. The hypothesis states our best guess as to *how* the change in temperature will affect the amount of sugar that dissolves in the water.

Constructing Your Ideas 10.1
How Much Sugar Dissolves in Water?

 Select one of the variables you listed in Constructing Your Ideas 9.1, *What Affects the Amount of Sugar That Will Dissolve in Water.* Remember, the idea is to find out what factors influence the amount of sugar that will dissolve in water and how they influence it. Keeping all the other variables constant, dissolve as much sugar as you can for at least three different values of the variable you selected. For example, if you are investigating whether the temperature of the water has an effect on the amount of sugar that will dissolve in it, you will want to measure out equal amounts of hot water, lukewarm water, and cold water into the same kinds of cups, stirring at the same rate of speed for the same period of time with the same kind of spoon for each of your trials. Of course, you will have to decide on how to measure the amount of sugar you are adding to the water. Perhaps a level teaspoon will be your unit of measure. You will add the sugar to the water one measured amount at a time, until the last measured amount will not dissolve. To ensure accuracy, you will need to measure the amount of sugar that dissolves in each temperature of water at least three times (called *trials*) and average the results. You will find it helpful to record your data in a data table such as the one shown in Figure 10.1.

Temperature	Predicted Number of Spoons of Sugar	ACTUAL NUMBER OF SPOONS OF SUGAR			
		Trial 1	Trial 2	Trial 3	Average
Hot					
Lukewarm					
Cold					

FIGURE 10.1   Data table for Constructing Your Ideas 10.1. How Much Sugar Dissolves in Water?

Have each group investigate a different variable so you can get a better picture of the factors that influence the amount of sugar that dissolves in water. Share your results with the class. What can you conclude about these factors?

Several activities to help children learn to formulate and test hypotheses are suggested in Constructing Science in the Classroom 10.1–10.5. Some are appropriate for preschool children, and some are more appropriate for children in the early elementary grades.

Constructing Science in the Classroom 10.1
Making Butter

AGE

8
7
6
5
4
3

AN ACTIVITY FOR FORMULATING AND TESTING HYPOTHESES

Objective

The student will formulate and test hypotheses concerning how fast butter can be made.

In this activity, children will make butter out of cream as people did in the "Old West."

Fill a Tupperware container half full of very cold whipping cream. Place a marble in the cup and put the lid on tightly. Pass the container around the class, and ask each child to shake it six or eight times. After all children have had a turn shaking the container, you may wish to complete the shaking yourself. Butter will form in a few minutes. You can tell because you will feel and hear the "thump" of the butter. You can spread the butter on crackers or warm biscuits for children to eat.

Now ask the children what they could do to speed up the process of turning cream into butter. Responses might include making the cream colder, making the cream warmer, shaking the container faster, shaking it more slowly, adding more marbles, not using any marbles, and so on. Children are formulating hypotheses to show a possible relationship between changing one of the variables involved in making butter and how fast the butter forms.

Provide the materials the children need to test their hypotheses, and ask them to test each one. Be sure children keep track of how long it takes for butter to form in each case so they can compare the effects of the different variables. For younger children, you may choose to keep track of the time yourself.

(continued)

Literature Connection:

Like Butter on Pancakes by Jonathon London (1998). This delightful book describes a day on a farm, from waking up to bedtime.

FIGURE 10.2   Making butter

Constructing Science in the Classroom 10.2
How Can We Increase the Rate of Evaporation of Water?

AGE

AN ACTIVITY FOR FORMULATING AND TESTING HYPOTHESES

Objective

The student will formulate and test a hypothesis that predicts how the rate of evaporation of water can be increased.

First, soak a paper towel in water, wring it out, and hang it up to dry. Have children check it every half hour. When it is dry, record how long it took for it to dry. Young children may want to develop creative ways of telling how long it takes the paper towel to dry.

Ask children how they would speed up this drying. Responses might include "blowing on it," "putting it in a warm place," "putting it outdoors," and so on. Children are identifying the variables they think might influence how fast the paper towel dries.

As children identify the variables, ask them to come up with an educated guess as to *how much* faster the towel would dry under each of the circumstances suggested by the children. Their responses may take the form of "much faster," "some faster," "no faster," "slower," and so on. Or, with older children, the responses could take the form of elapsed time, such as 1 hour, 2 hours, ½ hour, 10 minutes, and so on.

Record all this information on a class chart similar to the one in Figure 10.3.

DATA TABLE FOR INVESTIGATING FACTORS THAT SPEED UP HOW LONG IT TAKES A PAPER TOWEL TO DRY		
Variable	Predicted Effect	Actual Effect
Blow on it		
Put it in a warm place		
Put it outdoors		
Put it in front of a fan		

FIGURE 10.3   Data table for investigating factors that speed up how long it takes a paper towel to dry

Then give children wet paper towels, and ask them to test their hypotheses by drying one of them using each of the variables listed. Be sure they isolate the variable they want to test and keep all the others constant. The only variable they will be recording is the length of time it takes the paper towel to dry. Ask them to check their paper towel every 10–15 minutes or so and to record which one dried first, second, third, and so on.

Finally, ask children to answer the question, "How can we increase the rate of evaporation?"

Literature Connection:

Wet Foot, Dry Foot, Low Foot, High Foot: Learn about Opposites and Differences by Linda Hayward (1996). Based on the works of Dr. Seuss, this book introduces the young reader to opposites, including wet and dry.

Constrcting Science in the Classroom 10.3
How Long Does It Take an Ice Cube to Melt?

AGE

8
7
6
5
4
3

AN ACTIVITY FOR FORMULATING AND TESTING HYPOTHESES

Objective

The student will formulate and test a hypothesis concerning the effect of an identified variable on the length of time it takes an ice cube to melt.

Give each child a small ice cube in a paper cup. Ask the children how long they think it will take for the ice cube to melt completely. Record their responses, and then let the ice cubes melt to see how long it takes. Record each result.

Now ask what they could do to speed up the melting. They will be identifying variables that could influence the melting of the ice cube. Responses might include "heat it," "put it in warm water," "put it in hot water," "put it in cold water," "put it on the windowsill," "put it in a warm closet," and so on. As each variable is identified, ask children to provide their best guess as to how long it would take the ice cube to melt under the circumstances of that variable. Then ask children to test their hypotheses and record the length of time it takes their ice cube to melt. Compare this time with the time it took the first ice cube to melt.

Literature Connections:

Ice Is Whee by Carol Greene (1993). This book describes the nature of ice and the fun children can have with it.

Constructing Science in the Classroom 10.4
Mealworms

AGE

8
7
6
5
4
3

AN ACTIVITY FOR FORMULATING AND TESTING HYPOTHESES

Objective

The student will formulate and test hypotheses concerning the response of mealworms to different stimuli.

Mealworms are larvae of beetles and can be purchased at pet stores.

Provide the following materials for each child or group of children: 6–8 mealworms, paper plates, and some sand, salt, sugar, water, vinegar, a flashlight, and black paper. Children first put the mealworms on the paper plates and observe their behavior. It may take a few minutes for the mealworms to warm up and become active. Ask children to observe and describe the mealworms' behavior (Figure 10.4).

Now ask children to put each of the materials in separate areas of the plate and again observe the mealworms' behavior. The mealworms may move toward the sugar, burrow under the sand, or move toward the water but away from the salt and the vinegar. Also ask them to cover the plate with the black paper and to shine the flashlight on the mealworms and observe their behavior under changed light conditions. Children may find it useful to prod the mealworms *gently* toward the stimuli so they can observe behavior.

Ask children to formulate hypotheses concerning the behavior of the mealworms when they are exposed to each of the stimuli. For example, hypotheses might be "When mealworms come near sand, they burrow under the it," "When mealworms come near vinegar, they crawl away from the it," or "Mealworms move toward bright light." Record these hypotheses on a class chart.

Then ask groups to select *one* of the stimuli and test their hypothesis using clean paper plates, fresh mealworms, and the stimulus they are testing.

Discuss the results as a class. Encourage children to continue their investigations using stimuli not originally provided.

Literature Connection:

Mealworms: Raise Them, Watch Them, See Them Change by Adrienne Mason (1983) is a book of ideas about investigating the behavior of mealworms and raising them to witness the mealworm-beetle life cycle.

 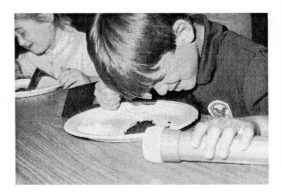

FIGURE 10.4 Watching the behavior of mealworms

Constructing Science in the Classroom 10.5
What Affects Our Heartbeat Rate?

AGE

AN ACTIVITY FOR FORMULATING AND TESTING HYPOTHESES

Objective

The student will formulate and test hypotheses concerning the effect of exercise on heartbeat rate.

First teach children how to find their pulse, which can be found on the inside of the wrist or in the small of the neck just below the ear (Figure 10.5). Also, be sure children can measure heartbeat rate, which is the number of times the heart beats in 1 minute.

Ask children what they think exercise would do to their heartbeat rate. Suggest they consider several kinds of exercise, such as stretching in place (light exercise), doing deep knee bends in place (moderate exercise), and running or jumping in place (heavy exercise). Also suggest they consider the effect of doing the different kinds of exercises for different periods of time on

(continued)

heartbeat rate. Now ask each child or each group of children to formulate both a hypothesis that represents their best guess about the relationship between heartbeat rate and kind of exercise and also a hypothesis that represents their best guess about the relationship between heartbeat rate and length of time for the kind of exercise they are investigating. The hypothesis will take a form such as the following: If I do heavy exercise for 1 minute, my heartbeat rate will be greater than if I do heavy exercise for half a minute. Or it could take a form such as the following: If I do heavy exercise for 1 minute, my heartbeat rate will be greater than if I do light exercise for 1 minute.

Now ask children to test their hypotheses. They will need to devise a way of measuring and recording heartbeat and also a way to be sure the kind of exercise and the length of time are consistent. You may wish to provide a data sheet for them to use.

Ask children to share the results of their hypothesis testing with the class. Can they formulate any generalizations from these specific tests?

Literature Connection:

The Magic School Bus: Inside the Human Body by Joanna Cole (1989). The magic school bus is accidentally eaten by Arnold and travels through his body to get a first-hand look at major body parts.

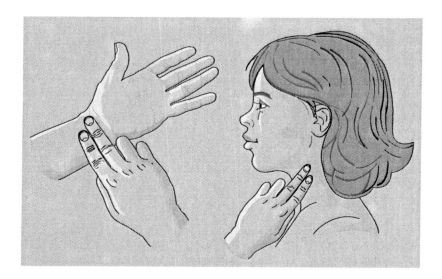

FIGURE 10.5 Feeling for a pulse

Constructing Your Ideas 10.2
An Activity for Formulating and Testing Hypotheses

Now it's your turn. Write a short activity that can be used to help children learn to formulate and test hypotheses. Specify age/grade level, and be sure the activity is appropriate to the children in the age/grade you specify. Cite a process-oriented objective for your lesson; the objective will read something like this: "The student will formulate a hypothesis concerning _____ and will test it." Then get together in small groups and do the activities each member of your group has prepared.

References

Cole, J. (1989). *The magic school bus: Inside the human body.* New York: Scholastic.

Greene, C. (1993). *Ice is whee.* Danbury, CT: Children's Press.

Hayward, L. (1996). *Wet foot, dry foot, low foot, high foot: Learn about opposites and differences.* New York: Random House.

Juster, N. (1961). *The phantom tollbooth.* New York: Random House.

London, J. (1998). *Like butter on pancakes.* Madison, WI: Demco Media.

Mason, A. (1998). *Mealworms: Raise them, watch them, see them change.* Buffalo, NY: Kids Can Press.

Nietzsche, F. (1967). (W. Kauffman & R. J. Hollingdale, Trans. & eds.). *The will to power.* New York: Vintage.

CHAPTER 11

The Integrated Scientific Processes: Defining Operationally

Defining operationally is the scientific process that enables us to express precisely what we mean by something. We define variables we cannot see or measure easily in ways that we can see or measure and that relate directly to the variables. Through this process, we can be consistent throughout an investigation and we can communicate accurately with other people.

I hate definitions.
Benjamin Disraeli, *Vivian Grey, Book II, Chapter 6* (1826)

All doors are hard to unlock until you have the key.
Robert C. O'Brien, *Mrs. Frisby and the Rats of NIMH* (Old Tappan, NJ: Simon & Schuster's Children's, 1971)

Constructing Your Ideas 11.1
What Do You Mean By . . . ?

Try to answer these questions:
1. You are driving down a freeway that has a posted speed limit of 65 mph, and the passenger in your car says you are driving too fast. How fast are you driving?
2. You ask a 4-year-old to wash her hands until they are clean. What do you mean by "clean"?
3. You water and fertilize the plants in your room so they will stay healthy. How can you tell whether they are "healthy"?
4. You tell the children in your kindergarten class to talk quietly. How quiet is "quiet"?
5. You are preparing an activity for your class of 4-year-olds that involves the use of hot, lukewarm, and cold water. How will you tell what these temperatures are?

In much of our daily activity, we come across phenomena that seem to require definitions. "Fast," "clean," "healthy," "quiet," and "lukewarm" can all mean different things to different people. They can also mean different things to the same people at different times. In scientific investigations, it is critically important that everyone have the same understandings of the same things.

Defining a variable that cannot be measured or easily seen in terms that everyone understands in the same way, leaving no room for ambiguity, is called *defining operationally*.

To see the importance of defining variables in operational terms, let us return to our explorations concerning factors related to how much sugar can dissolve in water. Perhaps you already have had to define what you mean by "dissolve." Does "dissolve" mean that the water is clear and there is no sugar in the bottom of the glass? Or does it mean the water is clear and there is a thin layer of sugar on the bottom? Or does it mean the water is cloudy and won't clear up even after several minutes? When you define what you mean by "dissolve," you are providing an operational definition. It is easy to see that the entire investigation into how much sugar can be dissolved in water hinges on how you define "dissolve."

Have you done a "Sink-or-Float" activity with children? In most such activities we ask children to predict whether objects will sink or float in water, after which they try each one to test their predictions. (See, for example, Constructing Science in the Classroom 6.3, "Sink? or Float?" and Constructing Science in the Classroom 6.4, "Do Crayons Sink or Float?") When children actually test their predictions, they very quickly find that they need to devise operational definitions of "sink" and "float." In many cases, the item stays submerged so that it is completely below the surface of the water, yet it does not go all the way to the bottom. Does this item sink? Does it float? We need to define these terms. In addition, most items that float do so with varying amounts of the object below the surface of the water. What is meant by "float"? Can an object be said to "float" if *any part* of it remains above the surface of the water? It is recommended that you enlist the assistance of children when you develop these kinds of operational definitions.

Operational definitions also define things we cannot see directly. For example, we cannot see magnetic forces, and so we define magnetic force in terms of something we can see, such as the number of paper clips a magnet will pick up, or how far the magnet can be from a paperclip and still cause it to move toward the magnet.

Children often compare characteristics of different people and different objects: "He's tall." "This rock is heavy." "This soup is too hot." "She's a fast runner." These and countless other exclamations express young children's comparisons of attributes with that they believe is normal. When children make such statements, ask them what they mean by the attribute they are describing, such as "What do you mean by 'tall'?" "What do you mean by 'heavy'?" "What do you mean by 'hot'?" What do you mean by 'fast'?" This questioning gently leads children to form operational definitions of the attributes and, perhaps more important, helps them understand the necessity of defining attributes so that everyone has the same understanding.

Take a few minutes and look through the activities you have done thus far. Which of them required operational definitions? Chances are you will find you employed operational definitions in many of these activities, beginning as early in your inquiries as observing rocks, when you undoubtedly had to tell what you meant by "smooth" or "rough" or even what you meant by colors, such as "gray" or "brown."

As we indicated earlier, operational definitions define variables or phenomena that cannot be directly measured. If we can measure an occurrence directly, there is no need for an operational definition, for the occurrence can be defined in terms of standard units of measurement. We would not need to define the length of a desktop in operational terms, for example, because we can measure it with a ruler or in terms of a number of pennies or paper clips. Similarly, we would not need to define the a person's weight in operational terms because the person can stand on a scale and we can read the "real" weight. We might not need to define water temperature in operational terms because all we need to do is use a thermometer to read the temperature. However, young children cannot always read temperature from thermometers, so we may choose to define temperature in terms of something they can relate to, such as "warmer than my hand," "cooler than my hand," "as cold as an ice cube," "as hot as a bowl of soup," and so on.

The purpose of operational definitions is to provide consistency and accuracy in scientific investigations.

Several activities to help children learn to define variables in operational terms are suggested in Constructing Science in the Classroom 11.1–11.4. Some are appropriate for preschool children, and some are more appropriate for children in the early elementary grades.

Constructing Science in the Classroom 11.1
What Happens to our Hands When We Leave Them in Water?

AGE

8
7
6
5
4
3

AN ACTIVITY FOR DEFINING OPERATIONALLY

Objective

The student will define "wrinkled hands" in operational terms.

Ask children what they think will happen to a hand that is left in a pan of warm water for several minutes. Provide pans of lukewarm water for each group of children. Ask each child to place one hand in the water for, say, 5 minutes and leave the other outside. After the time is up, ask them to remove their hand from the water and compare it with the dry hand. What is different? The wet hand will probably have a wrinkled appearance.

Now let them hold their hands outside the water until the wrinkles disappear. Once the wrinkles are gone, ask them to put one hand in the water again and remove it as soon as wrinkles start to form. In order to do this, they will have to decide what they mean by "wrinkled."

Encourage children to try several variations such as using cold water and putting on gloves. Have them try their hypotheses and record their results.

Literature Connections:

Hands! by Virginia Kroll (1997). This multicultural text explores different ways people use their hands. *Here Are My Hands* by Bill Martin Jr. and John Archambault (1995) invites readers to respond as they learn the parts of the body.

Constructing Science in the Classroom 11.2
Cleaning Pennies

AGE

8
7
6
5
4
3

AN ACTIVITY FOR DEFINING OPERATIONALLY

Objective

The student will define "clean penny" in operational terms.

Obtain a dozen or so pennies, some of which are bright and shiny and some of which are dull and corroded. Ask the children to think of different ways they might be able to clean the tarnished pennies (Figure 11.1). Responses might include "washing them with soap," "washing them without soap," "brushing them," "soaking them," and so on. Introduce some new ideas such as cleaning them with lemon juice, cleaning them with vinegar, cleaning them with salt, and cleaning them with a mixture of vinegar and salt. Provide the materials children would need to try these options. In small groups or with individuals, have the children try each option. Provide plastic trays to work on, and be sure children wash their hands well after they have done the activity.

Now ask children what they mean by "clean pennies." Ask which method produced the cleanest pennies? Alternatively, you can ask what children mean by "clean pennies" before they investigate for themselves. (Teacher note: The mixture of salt and vinegar produces the cleanest pennies, for this mixture chemically reacts with the tarnish to remove it.)

(continued)

FIGURE 11.1   Cleaning a tarnished penny

Literature Connection:

Water Magic by Carole Mitchener, Virginia Johnson, and Phyllis Adams (1987). Two young children question their dad about how objects appear differently in water and how a tarnished penny can sparkle after it is placed in a glass of water and vinegar.

Constructing Science in the Classroom 11.3
What's Hot? What's Cold?

AGE

8
7
6
5
4
3

AN ACTIVITY FOR DEFINING OPERATIONALLY

Objective
The student will define "hot" and "cold" in operational terms.

Provide three bowls of water. One should contain hot water (quite hot, but not too hot for children to put their hands in). The second should contain lukewarm water. The third should contain ice-cold water.

Ask a child to put her left hand in the hot water and her right hand in the ice-cold water. Ask her to tell which is hot and which is cold. Have her keep her hands in the water for a minute or so. Then ask her to quickly plunge *both* hands into the bowl filled with lukewarm water.

How hot or cold does the lukewarm water feel to your left hand? How hot or cold does the lukewarm water feel to your right hand? From this, how would you define "hot" water? How would you define "cold" water?

Can you think of a reason why the lukewarm water seemed to be at different temperatures to each hand?

(continued)

Literature Connections:

Hot or Not (from the *Toppers* series) by Nicola Baxter (1995) is a book of science activities dealing with hot and cold temperatures.

Hot and Cold (from the *Start-up Science* series) by Jack Challoner (1997) contains activities to introduce the concepts of hot and cold in relation to melting and freezing and other applications.

Constructing Science in the Classroom 11.4
Bouncing Balls

AGE

8
7
6
5
4
3

AN ACTIVITY FOR DEFINING OPERATIONALLY

Objective

The student will define "bouncy ball" in operational terms.

Provide children with an assortment of different kinds of balls such as a baseball, a softball, a ping pong ball, a "superball," a tennis ball, a basketball, a soccer ball, a volleyball, and other balls used in sports. All these balls move rapidly when struck in accordance with the rules of the sport in which they are played: batting, paddling, dribbling, kicked, volleyed, and so on. The question asked in this activity deals with the ability of the ball to bounce on its own.

Children select one ball at a time and drop it from a predetermined height. This height can be determined by the children and can include children standing on chairs or tables to obtain greater heights from which to drop the balls. After each ball is dropped (not thrown), children look to see whether it bounces and, if so, how high it bounces (Figure 11.2). They will observe that there are great differences in the height to which each dropped ball bounces.

From their investigations and observations, ask children to devise a definition for "bouncy ball." Ask them to check out other balls and other situations to see whether their definition maintains itself.

Literature Connection:

Stop That Ball! by Mike McClintock (1989). A boy encounters madcap adventures as he tries to retrieve his runaway bouncing ball. The text is written in rhyming prose.

FIGURE 11.2 How high will the ball bounce?

Constructing Your Ideas 11.2
An Activity for Defining Operationally

Now it's your turn. Write a short activity that can be used to help children learn to define operationally. Specify age/grade level, and be sure the activity is appropriate to the children in the age/grade you specify. Cite a process-oriented objective for your lesson; the objective will read something like this: "The student will define _____ in operational terms." Then get together in small groups and do the activities each member of your group has prepared.

References

Baxter, N. (1995). *Hot or not.* Danbury, CT: Children's Press.

Challoner, J. (1997). *Hot and cold.* Austin, TX: Raintree Steck-Vaughn.

Kroll, V. L. (1997). *Hands!* Honesdale, PA: Boyds Mills Press.

Martin, Jr., B., & Archambault, J. (1995). *Here are my hands.* New York: Henry Holt.

McClintock, M. (1989). *Stop that ball!* New York: Random House.

Mitchener, C., Johnson, V., & Adams, P. (1987). *Water magic.* Parsippany, NJ: Modern Curriculum Press.

O'Brien, R. C. (1971). *Mrs. Frisby and the rats of NIMH.* Old Tappan, NJ: Simon & Schuster's Children's.

CHAPTER 12

The Integrated Scientific Processes: Interpreting Data

Interpreting data is the process by which we decide what data we want to gather in an investigation, and plan how to obtain this data, organize it, and analyze it to make valid conclusions. Data tables, line graphs, and bar graphs help us interpret and analyze the data.

We begin by looking at data we might have obtained in an activity we did earlier.

The facts will eventually test all our theories, and they form, after all, the only impartial jury to which we can appeal.
Jean Louis Rodolphe Agassizi, *Geological Sketches, Chapter 9* (1970)

Think left and think right
And think low and think high.
Oh, the THINKS you can think up
If only you try!
Dr. Seuss, Oh, the THINKS You Can Think! (New York: Random House, 1975)

Constructing Your Ideas 12.1
Making Sense Out of Data

In Chapter 9, you did an activity to test your hypothesis dealing with the effect of the temperature of water on the amount of sugar that can be dissolved in the water. You gathered some information in the form of temperatures and the number of spoons of sugar that dissolved.

Look at this data. What sense can you make of it? Does it appear that as the temperature increases, the amount of sugar that dissolves also increases? Or does it decrease? Or does it stay the same? Perhaps you found that the amount of sugar that dissolves increased to a point (a certain temperature), but when the water was hotter than that point, the additional amount of sugar that could dissolve stayed the same or perhaps even decreased.

Your first look at the data gives you an indication of the general relationship between the temperature of water and the amount of sugar that can be dissolved in it. This is *qualitative* in nature. As one variable changes, the other changes as well. For example, as the temperature increases, the amount of sugar that can be dissolved also increases.

Now look at the data once again. Is there a *quantitative* relationship between temperature and amount of sugar dissolved? Specifically, is there a certain increase in the amount of sugar that dissolves for any given increase in temperature? It would be useful to graph the data to see. Try plotting the amount of sugar on the vertical (*y*) axis and the temperature on the horizontal (*x*) axis as is shown in Figure 12.1. What does this graph show you? How do you interpret the graph?

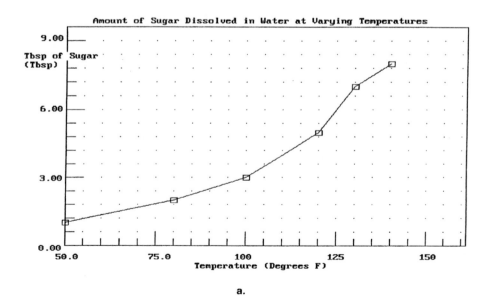

a.

FIGURE 12.1   Amount of sugar that dissolved in water at different temperatures. a. Line graph

(Graphical Analysis application, Vernier Software, 8656 SW Beaverton-Hillsdale Hwy, Portland, OR 97225-2429)

(continued)

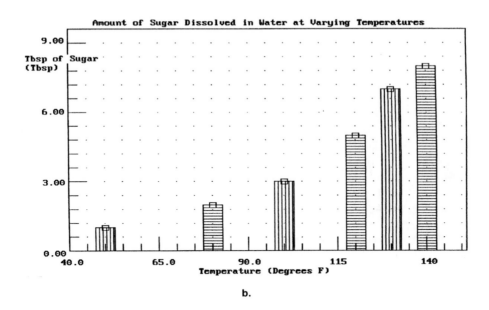

FIGURE 12.1 *(continued)* b. Bar graph c. Data table

Interpreting data involves organizing the data so that you can work with it and then analyzing the data to draw valid conclusions. The first step in organizing data is to decide what data you need. This is a natural outcome of identifying and controlling the variables and formulating a hypothesis. The second step is deciding how you will obtain it. Maybe you can measure the variables directly; otherwise, you will want to develop operational definitions. The third step in organizing data is to set up a data table to help you keep track of the information.

Suppose you are investigating whether playing music to plants affects their rates of growth. The variables of interest are the music being played to plants and the growth of plants. You will need to define the variables "playing music" and "plant growth." Perhaps you will define "playing music" in terms of the number of hours a day you will keep the radio on. You could measure the growth of the plants by measuring their heights each day using a ruler or strip of graph paper. You would then set up a data table to record the heights of the plants grown under different numbers of hours of music played per day, from none to however long you want to keep the radio on. Of course, each plant will have to be isolated from the others. You will record the data on the data table.

You can often interpret data simply by looking at it. If plants that had music played to them 24 hours a day for two weeks showed a 3-inch growth and the same kind of plants that had no music played to them showed a 1-inch growth in the same two weeks, you could safely conclude that some relationship exists between music being played to plants and their rates of growth, providing, of course, that all the other variables such as food, light, and water, remained constant (see Figure 12.2).

To show this visually, you could construct a histogram. Cut out strips of paper equal to the height of the plant each day of the investigation. Paste the strips side-by-side on a horizontal line with each strip representing the next successive day. Do the same for each plant involved in the investigation. At the end of the period of inquiry, compare the histograms.

It is obvious that there is very little point in conducting a scientific investigation unless you plan to conclude something from it. It is equally obvious that the information gained from the investigation has to be interpreted. Children should begin to learn how to interpret data as an integral part of their science activities.

Graphing is one of the primary ways of organizing data for interpretation. Any activity that involves two quantitative variables has the potential for being graphed. Children then interpret the data from the graphs in addition to the real objects and the numbers themselves. Use graphs as often as possible so children begin to construct the relationship between changes in real concepts and the more abstract graphical representation.

Young children begin interpreting data by contrasting "more than" with "less than," by building "living graphs," and by constructing elementary histograms. As an example of a "living graph," you might ask all children who wore blue shirts to school today to stand in a line. Ask all children who wore red shirts to stand in a different line. White shirts should stand in a third line. And so on. When all children have been accounted for, you have a "living graph." Now ask the children to look around. Which are there more of—red shirts or blue shirts? Which shirt color has only one example? Which has only two? Use shoe sizes (if children know theirs), shoe types (sneakers, shoes with buckles, and so on), number of teeth missing, and other common variations children bring to school.

When children know numerals, they can prepare histograms. Using eye-shaped cutouts of different colors to represent eye colors, ask kindergarten and first-grade children to paste histograms showing the number of children who have each eye color. Ask them to develop histograms to portray the num-

FIGURE 12.2 Growing plants under different conditions

ber of boys and girls in the class or the distribution of hair colors of the children in the class (see Figure 12.3).

Several activities to help children learn to interpret data are suggested in Constructing Science in the Classroom 12.1–12.3. Some are appropriate for preschool children, and some are more appropriate for children in the early elementary grades.

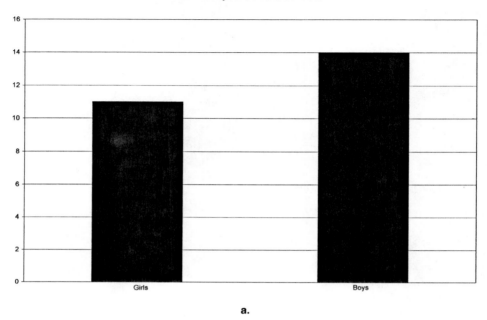

a.

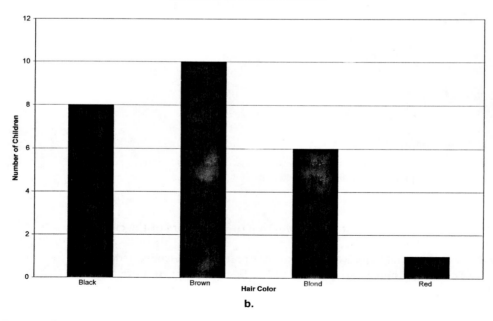

b.

FIGURE 12.3   Bar graphs of number of boys and girls in a class, their hair colors, and their eye colors. a. Number of boys and girls b. Number of children with each hair color (Microsoft Excel application)

(continued)

Eye Color of the Children in Our Class

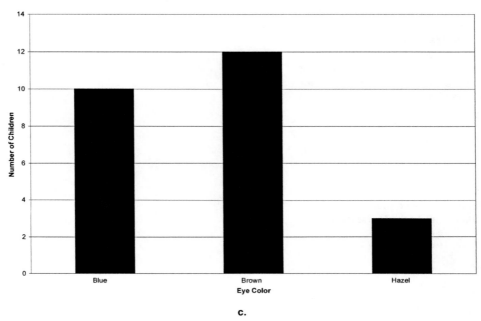

c.

FIGURE 12.3 *(continued)* c. Number of children with each eye color

Constructing Science in the Classroom 12.1
Balloon Rockets

AGE

8
7
6
5
4
3

AN ACTIVITY FOR INTERPRETING DATA

Objective

The student will interpret data concerning the relationship between how full a balloon is blown and how far it goes when the air is let out.

Construct a balloon rocket out of a balloon and a straw as follows: Blow up a balloon, clamp it shut with a small binder clip of the type that can be purchased in office-supply stores, and tape a 2-inch piece of plastic straw to the side of the balloon. You may wish to tape a penny to the opposite side of the balloon to help stabilize it as it flies along the string. Thread a 10–30-foot length of string through the straw. Tie the string to the backs of two chairs, and pull it as tight as possible. Alternatively, ask two children to hold the ends of the string, pulling it tight. Slide the blown-up balloon rocket to one end of the string. Then release the binder clip. If the children cannot make the balloon rocket themselves, you can do it for them. Ask them how far down the string the balloon went. Mark the distance on the string with a magic marker.

Blow up the balloon to several different levels, release the clamp, and let the balloon rocket move down the string. If you are making the balloon rocket yourself, ask the children to tell you when to stop blowing. Each time, put a mark on the string where the balloon rocket stopped.

(continued)

You may wish to transfer the marks on the string to a long strip of adding-machine tape so the children can see the marks better. Make an indication beside each mark, showing how full the balloon was when it sailed down the string that far.

From the data, ask the children whether blowing more air into the balloon changed how far down the string it went. They can answer the question by looking at the marks on the string or at the data recorded on the adding-machine tape (Figure 12.4).

Literature Connection:
Roaring Rockets by Tony Mitton (1997). A variety of personable animals operate digging machinery and soar to the moon in a rocket.

FIGURE 12.4   Balloon rockets

Constructing Science in the Classroom 12.2
Effect of Different Kinds of Cups on the Temperature of Water

AGE

AN ACTIVITY FOR INTERPRETING DATA

8
7
6
5
4
3

Objective
The student will gather and interpret data from an investigation of the effect that different kinds of cups have on the temperature of tap water left standing in the cups.

First be sure the children can read thermometers. Then ask them which kind of container they think is best for keeping drinks warm or cold. Record the responses.

Provide each group with several different kinds of containers; suggestions include Styrofoam cup, drinking glass, coffee mug, plastic cup, empty soft drink can, empty plastic soft drink bottle, empty glass soft drink bottle, a foam sleeve, and so on. Also provide each group a with thermometer.

Run tap water until it is quite hot. Measure the same amount of water into each of the cups. Record the temperature of the water and write it down. Wait five minutes, and record the temperature again. Record the temperature of the water every 5 minutes or so for about 20 minutes. Using the data collected for each cup, ask the children to construct a histogram or a graph to portray the information. The histogram uses the horizontal line as the time line, divided into 5-minute portions. Strips of paper may be cut out to represent the temperatures at each 5-minute increment. If graph paper is used for the histogram, children use the graph paper grid to draw lines to show the temperature at 5-minute intervals.

Using the graphic portrayals, the children interpret the data and come to their conclusions.

(continued)

For a qualitative approach, ask the children to assess the temperature of the water in the various containers by putting their fingers in the water or, if appropriate, by feeling the outsides of the containers. They do this at the beginning and at regular intervals, finding which cools fastest through the sense of feeling. They record information in the form of terms such as "the same," "a little cooler," "some cooler," and "much cooler," or by using some other system the children decide upon. Have the children do a trial run so they can provide operational definitions for the temperature changes they observe.

Literature Connection:

Hot and Cold by Helena Ramsay (1998) is a nonfiction book of projects and experiments children can use to explore the concepts of heat and cold.

Constructing Science in the Classroom 12.3
How Many Peas Are in a Peapod?

AGE

AN ACTIVITY FOR INTERPRETING DATA

8
7
6
5
4
3

Objective

The student will gather and interpret data about the relationship between length of pea pods and the number of peas in them.

Provide each group of students with several pea pods. Ask the children if they think there are more peas in longer pea pods than in shorter ones. Ask them what they would need to do to find out. The children then measure the length of each pea pod. To do this, they will have to develop a measuring system that will permit them to measure lengths of pea pods that are curved. One by one, they record the length of a pea pod and then open it and count the number of peas inside. They do this for all the pea pods in their collection.

Record all the data on a class chart, and look at it to see whether any conclusions can be made. The chances are that the children will find it easier to interpret the data if it is listed in order of pea pod length. This may require rewriting the data so that the shortest pea pods are first on the list. Stress that the data must be transferred to the new chart *accurately*. Now look at the data. It should be much easier to find whether there is a relationship between the length of pea pods and the number of peas.

There are several ways these data can be charted. One is to construct a histogram. On the horizontal axis, children record the lengths of the pea pods in order from shortest to longest. If the histogram is done on graph paper, the number of peas can be plotted by counting squares above the horizontal axis. Alternatively, children can cut strips of paper whose lengths are proportional to the number of peas; for example, they could let each inch of length represent one pea. Children also can graph the data by constructing histograms or a line graphs; these graphs are shown in Figures 12.5 and Figure 12.6.

Literature Connection:

Black and White by David Macaulay (1990). This book is an excellent introduction to the process of interpreting data. The book contains four stories, but in reality it may contain only one story. Attention must be given to interpreting clues given in the story.

(continued)

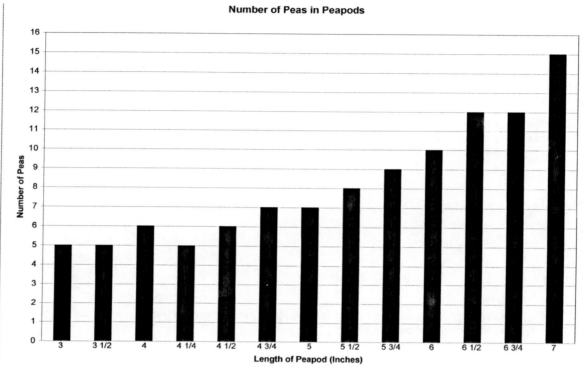

Number of Peas in Peapods

a.

```
DATA TABLE
    Row      Series              Peapod Length          Number of Peas
  Number     Number               (Inches)                (Number)
-----------------------------------------------------------------------------
     1          1                   3.00                     5.00
     2          1                   3.50                     5.00
     3          1                   4.00                     6.00
     4          1                   4.25                     5.00
     5          1                   4.50                     6.00
     6          1                   4.75                     7.00
     7          1                   5.00                     7.00
     8          1                   5.50                     8.00
     9          1                   5.75                     9.00
    10          1                   6.00                    10.0
    11          1                   6.50                    11.0
    12          1                   6.75                    12.0
    13          1                   7.00                    15.0
-----------------------------------------------------------------------------
```

b.

FIGURE 12.5   a. Bar graph of number of peas in peapods b. Data table.

(Graphical Analysis application, Vernier Software, 8656 SW Beaverton-Hillsdale Hwy, Portland, OR 97225-2429)

(continued)

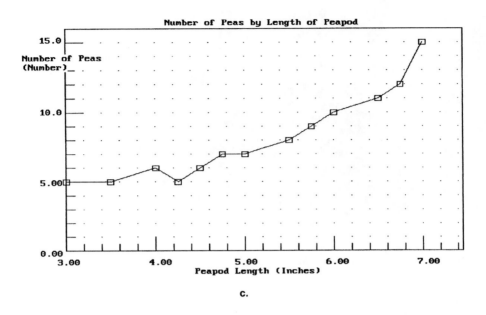

FIGURE 12.5 *(continued)* c. Line graph

Constructing Your Ideas 12.2
An Activity for Interpreting Data

Now it's your turn. Write a short activity that can be used to help children learn to interpret data. Specify age/grade level, and be sure the activity is appropriate to the children in the age/grade you specify. Cite a process-oriented objective for your lesson; the objective will read something like this: "The student will collect, organize, and interpret data dealing with _____." Then get together in small groups and do the activities each member of your group has prepared.

References

Macaulay, D. (1990). *Black and white.* Boston: Houghton Mifflin.

Mitton, T. (1997). *Roaring rockets.* New York: Larousse Kingfisher Chambers, Inc.

Ramsay, H. (1998). *Hot and cold.* Danbury, CT: Children's Press.

Seuss, Dr. [pseud. for Geisel, T. S.] (1975). *Oh, the THINKS you can think!* New York: Random House.

CHAPTER 13

The Integrated Scientific Processes: Experimenting

Experimenting is the scientific process in which we investigate the effect of changing one variable on the change in a different variable. In experimenting we utilize all the processes. We observe; classify what we observe; identify variables and control those we do not plan to manipulate; write hypotheses or tentative guesses worth investigating; gather and analyze data; infer valid conclusions; and utilize all the other processes as required.

Let us start by doing an experiment.

We must never make experiments to confirm our ideas, but simply to control them.
Claude Bernard, from *Bulletin of New York Academy of Medicine, Volume IX* (1928), 997

You must always take risks when experimenting.
Tove Jansson, *Finn Family Moomintroll* (New York: Farrar, Straus & Giroux, 1948)

Constructing Your Ideas 13.1
Blowing Bubbles

A common "recipe" for bubble-blowing solution is as follows:

Mix slowly 1 cup water, 2 tablespoons liquid detergent, 1 tablespoon glycerin (available at most drug stores), and 1 teaspoon sugar. Let the mixture set at room temperature for a half-hour. Dip a bubble-blowing wand into this mixture, and blow on the wand to form bubbles that last quite a while.

Mix up the solution. Form a ring out of the end of a pipe cleaner, and blow bubbles. How long do the bubbles last?

You may be asking why the recipe calls for four different materials. You may be wondering, for example, why you wouldn't get just as good a result if you used only the liquid detergent. Or what would happen if you used only detergent and water. Or detergent and glycerin. Or detergent and sugar. Or any of a number of combinations. You may also be wondering what would happen if you changed the proportions.

To find out, you will have to do an experiment.

Experimenting is the scientific process in which we carefully plan and execute a procedure designed to determine the effect of changing one variable on the *change* in another variable while keeping all the other variables constant.

In our bubble-blowing activity, we may want to know, for example, what effect glycerin has on blowing bubbles. To find this out, we need to devise an experiment. First, we identify the variable we want to investigate—in this case, the amount of glycerin. Then we specify how we are going to vary this variable. In this case we could make several mixtures, each with a different amount of glycerin in it, including one mixture with no glycerin at all in it. First, we "fool around" with blowing bubbles using the different mixtures to see what the effects might be. From our observations, we identify what effect we are going to examine. We may choose, for example, to investigate the effect that adding different amounts of glycerin to the solution has on how long the bubbles last before they burst. So we need to devise a method of measuring the longevity of the bubbles. We may want to use the "one-one-thousand, two-one-thousand . . . " method of time measurement where each "____-one-thousand" is a time period about as long as a second (see Chapter 5). We may also choose to write a hypothesis to help keep us focused. Our hypothesis, for example, might say that the more glycerin we add to the mixture, the longer we expect the bubbles to last.

Having gotten this far, we can construct a table in which to record our data. It might look like the one in Figure 13.1.

As we have already discovered, we must control all the other variables—amounts of other materials in the solution, size and material of wand, method of forming the bubbles, and so on. It would also be a good idea to experiment with your bubble-blowing procedure to develop a consistent technique so you can blow bubbles the same way every time.

How many trials should you do for each variation of the solution? Most scientists feel at least three trials are necessary. If the results from each of the

Amount of Glycerin	HOW LONG BUBBLES LAST			
	Trial 1	Trial 2	Trial 3	Average

FIGURE 13.1   Data table for investigating the effect of amount of glycerin in a bubble solution on how long the bubbles last

three trials are essentially the same, we can be reasonably certain the data is accurate. The results are normally averaged for the final result. On the other hand, if the results are substantially different from one trial to another, it becomes necessary either to do more trials to see which of the results is correct or to revise our procedure to ensure more consistent results.

Constructing Your Ideas 13.2
Experimenting with Bubbles

Go ahead and do an experiment to investigate the relationship of changing one variable in the bubble solution to some variable in the bubbles you blow. Fool around first, ask a few questions, and then write your hypothesis. Set up your plan, and then do the experiment.

What did you find out? How do you know? What evidence do you have? Report to the class, and invite them to critique your work. Are all the variables controlled? Is your technique consistent throughout the investigation? Did you take reliable measurements? If you utilized an operational definition, did it stay consistent throughout the investigation?

Jake, who is nearly four, spends a lot of time exploring the construction of his battery-operated train set. He worked on building an inclined bridge with the track pieces, using plastic blocks for support of the "hill." The hill track was connected to the level part of the track. He set the engine with its eight cars on the level track, turned the engine on, and watched. The engine moved toward the hill and then started up the hill but stopped about half-way up. Jake observed the problem for a few seconds, took one car off, and did it over again. The train went a little farther up the hill but still did not make it to the top. Jake then took three more cars off and started again. This time the train made it all the way to the top of the hill.

Jake was performing an experiment in which he investigated the effect of the number of cars in the train on how far up the incline the engine was able to pull the train.

From Watson (1997).

Young children can develop and execute true experiments that investigate the effect of changing one variable on the change in another variable. Several activities to help children learn the skills involved in experimenting are suggested in Constructing Science in the Classroom 13.1–13.3. Some are appropriate for preschool children, and some are more appropriate for children in the early elementary grades.

Constructing Science in the Classroom 13.1
An Investigation into Magnetism

AGE

AN ACTIVITY FOR EXPERIMENTING

Objective
The student will devise and execute an experiment to investigate the ability of magnetism to penetrate different materials.

Provide magnets for children to fool around with (see also Constructing Science in the Classroom 3.4). As they are discovering which materials are attracted to magnets and which are not, ask the question, "Do magnets attract through different kinds of materials?" (see Figure 13.2). Ask the children to design and execute an experiment to investigate this question.

FIGURE 13.2 Will the magnet attract the paperclips through the cardboard?

(continued)

First they identify the variables that could affect the results, such as distance, type of material, thickness of material, strength of magnet, shape of magnet, and so on. Then they must develop an operational definition for magnetic attraction. Perhaps they will want to use a paper clip as the indicator; they may wish to say, for example, that if the paper clip moves because of the magnet, then the magnet attracts the paper clip. Next ask them to make a list of the various things they would like to try; suggestions include paper, cardboard, plastic, overhead transparency paper, aluminum foil, sand, water in a paper cup, water in a plastic cup, and so on. Assemble the materials and ask the children to plan and execute the experiment. They will find they have to devise ways of keeping the distance between the magnet and the objects being attracted through the different materials the same for all the materials; this is because the ability of a magnet to attract objects increases as its distance from the object decreases. Data collected is *qualitative* rather than quantitative (numerical). In this case, the magnet either does or does not attract the paper clip. From the data, the children make their conclusions. They should be encouraged to develop their own data tables to reflect the experimental procedure they plan.

While children are doing this investigation, they may realize that they must also control for the thickness of the materials. This may lead to another experiment in which they investigate the relationship between the thickness of each material and the ability of a magnet to attract through it.

Literature Connections:

Playing with Magnets by Gary Gibson (1995). This book introduces children to the concept of magnetism with simple experiments to enable the children to explore the north and south poles and their effects on each other. *Mr. Fixit's Magnet Machine* by Richard Scarry (1998). Busytown's repairman sets out on an adventure that is informative and funny.

Constructing Science in the Classroom 13.2
The Inclined Plane

AGE

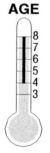

8
7
6
5
4
3

AN ACTIVITY FOR EXPERIMENTING

Objective

The student will investigate the effect of changing the height of the top end of an inclined plane on how long it takes a toy truck to roll down the plane.

Provide a bookshelf or piece of flat wood about 2 feet wide by 5 feet long. Also provide several books and a toy truck or car.

Place the upper end of the inclined plane on a stack of, say, three books. Let the truck roll down the plane. Ask the children to make observations, especially as to whether the truck rolled fast or slowly. At this point, the children will need to define "fast" and "slow" in operational terms. They may decide to measure the time it takes the truck to roll down the plane by counting "one-one-thousand, two-one-thousand" or by clapping their hands rhythmically.

Now ask the questions, "What would happen to the speed of the truck if we raised the top end of the board?" "What would happen to the speed of the truck if we lowered the top end of the board?"

Ask the children to formulate hypotheses and to set up a procedure that controls all the other variables. The height of the top end of the board can be measured either directly with a ruler or in terms of number of books. Set up a data table similar to the one in Figure 13.3. Children should record the time in the terms that were decided upon when they designed the experiment. It could be expressed in terms of seconds, number of "____-one-thousand" counts, number of hand claps, or descriptive words such as "much faster," "faster," "the same," "slower," and "much slower."

Does it take a longer or a shorter time for the truck to roll down when the top end is higher? Lower? (Figure 13.4)

(continued)

| Height | TIME TO ROLL DOWN PLANE | | | |
	Trial 1	Trial 2	Trial 3	Average

FIGURE 13.3   Data table for investigating the effect of height of the top of an inclined plane on the time it takes a toy truck to roll down the plane

FIGURE 13.4   How long will it take the truck to roll all the way down?

Literature Connections:

All Aboard Trucks by Lynn Conrad (1989) is a collection of easy-to-study pictures of familiar and unfamiliar trucks.

Dirt Movers by Bobbie Kalman (1994). A variety of construction vehicles such as snowplows, cement mixers, backhoes, and bulldozers is discussed and illustrated.

Constructing Science in the Classroom 13.3
An Investigation into Friction

AGE

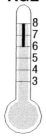

8
7
6
5
4
3

AN ACTIVITY FOR EXPERIMENTING

Objective
The student will plan and execute an experiment to show the relationship between surface roughness and force needed to move an object across the surface.

Provide a few blocks of wood around 3″ wide by 5″ long by 1″ thick. Screw a cup hook into one end of each block. To enable children to gain familiarity with the investigation, ask them to place the blocks one at a time on a smooth desk top, and use a rubber band looped into the cup hook and held *parallel* to the desk top to pull the block. How far did the rubber band stretch? Children measure the length of the stretched rubbed band with a ruler. They do the same for each of the blocks.

Then put a piece of fine sandpaper about 12″ long on the desk top, and ask the children to do the same thing, this time pulling the blocks of wood across the sandpaper. How far did the rubber band stretch?

Ask the children what other materials they might try. Suggestions include a piece of carpet, plastic wrap, a sheet of paper, a piece of cardboard, rough sandpaper, waxed paper, and so on.

RUBBER BAND SCALE

SCIENCE IS A SNAP!
Snappy Spring Scales
Tape a rubber band to the zero end of a ruler. Attach an opened paper clip to the other of end the rubber band to act as a hook. Hang small objects on the hook. Observe how far the rubber band is stretched. The amount of stretch is an indication of the relative weight of the object. Relate weight to earth-pull on the object.

Snappy Investigations
Have students investigate to find out:

▮ How does thickness of a rubber band affect its strength?
▮ What effect does temperature have on rubber band stretch?
▮ Does the thickness of a rubber band affect its pitch when plucked?

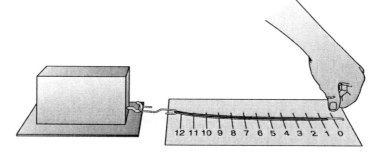

(continued)

Material	Nature of Surface	Trial	Force (Length of Stretched Rubber Band)
Tabletop	Smooth	1	
		2	
		3	
		Average	
Fine Sandpaper	Rough	1	
		2	
		3	
		Average	

FIGURE 13.5   Data table suggested for experiment investigating the relationship between surface roughness and force needed to move an object across the surface

In planning the actual experiment in which the children investigate the relationship between surface and force, they will have to come up with two operational definitions. One deals with how smooth the surface is. They will want to designate the smoothness or roughness of surfaces with qualitative terms, such as "very smooth," "smooth," "rough," "very rough," and so on. The other deals with the force. They might want to measure force in terms of how far the rubber band stretches. To do this, they can hold a ruler next to the rubber band to measure its stretch. Younger children can mark the stretch of the rubber band on strips of graph paper and count the squares; the number of squares represents the force. Of course, all other variables will have to be identified and controlled. Of particular importance is using the same rubber band for each of the trials, for rubber bands differ greatly in how far they can stretch under the same amount of force.

Now ask the children to set up the experiment and do it. Have them develop their own data tables or use one similar to that shown in Figure 13.5.

What conclusions can be reached?

Literature Connection:

The Magic School Bus Plays Ball by Joanna Cole (1998). Mrs. Frizzle's class plays baseball in a world without friction, learning about friction and forces.

Constructing Your Ideas 13.3
An Activity for Experimenting

Now it's your turn. Write a short activity that can be used to help children learn to plan and conduct experiments. Specify age/grade level, and be sure the activity is appropriate to the children in the age/grade you specify. Cite a process-oriented objective for your lesson; the objective will read something like this: "The student will plan and conduct an experiment to investigate the relationship between _____ and _____." Then get together in small groups and do the activities each member of your group has prepared.

References

Bernard, C. (1928). *Bulletin of New York Academy of Medicine, IX*.

Cole, J. (1998). *The magic school bus plays ball*. New York: Scholastic.

Conrad, L. (1989). *All aboard trucks*. New York: Putnam Publishing Group.

Gibson, G. (1995). *Playing with magnets*. Madison, WI: Demco Media.

Jansson, T. (1990). Finn family Moomintroll. New York: Farrar, Straus & Giroux.

Kalman, B. (1994). *Dirt movers*. New York: Crabapple Publishing Company.

Scarry, R. (1998). *Mr. Fixit's magnet machine*. New York: Simon & Schuster Children's Publishers.

Watson, M. (1997). "Facilitating the preschooler's exploration of his world by utilizing the constructivist approach to science." Paper prepared for the graduate course Trends and Issues in Science for Early Childhood Education, Kennesaw State University.

CHAPTER 14

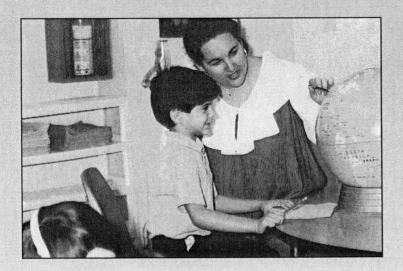

The Integrated Scientific Processes: Constructing Models

Constructing models is the scientific process we use to build visual or mathematical representations of objects or concepts we cannot see or measure directly. Models of dinosaurs, the solar system, the universe, the atom, human body organs, and other objects or concepts are constructed from inferences show to be generally true. Models are very powerful learning tools, and should be accurate.

To show the power of model building, we start with an activity that portrays the effect of animal camouflage.

What we experience of nature is in models, and all of nature's models are so beautiful.
Richard Buckminster Fuller, from *In the Outlaw Area*, profile by Calvin Tomkins in *The New Yorker* (January 8, 1966)

This is cause for celebration! A human with imagination!
Parry Heide, *Timothy Twinge* (New York: Lothrop, Lee & Shepard Books, 1993)

Constructing Your Ideas 14.1
Animal Camouflage

 Provide each group of students in your class with a bag of 50–60 toothpicks that includes 15–20 each of different colors (natural, red, green, blue, etc.). Go outdoors to a grassy area, and measure several squares of grass approximately one meter on each side, marking the square with string held in place by Popsicle sticks. Groups work together at each square. One student is designated as "It" and turns around while another student scatters the toothpicks about the square. At a signal, "It" turns around and picks up as many toothpicks as possible in, say, 20 seconds. Count the number of each color, and record this information. Repeat after retrieving all the remaining toothpicks until each group member has had a turn at being "It." Then add the numbers of each color all members of the group were able to pick up, and look at the data. Which color has the most number of toothpicks? Which color has the least?

The results of this activity represent a *model* of a major benefit of animal camouflage. You can now write a statement of this model.

Much of what we investigate scientifically we can work with directly. For example, we can actually experiment with the toy truck rolling down the inclined plane. We can actually dissolve sugar in water. Although we cannot see plant growth on a day-to-day basis, we can actually see the growth of plants over a period of time if we measure their heights each day and compare them.

However, there are many phenomena that we cannot see or measure. Recall, for example, the Mystery Box activity in Chapter 1. You subjected the box to much and varied exploration to try to identify what was inside. To increase your confidence level, you may have put together your own box with the same things in it you thought were in the Mystery Box, comparing the two boxes carefully to see whether they exhibited the same characteristics. The box you constructed was a *model* of the Mystery Box. In the activity "What's That Sound?" (Constructing Science in the Classroom 2.8) children put known items in plastic eggs to see whether they make the same sound as one of the eggs with an unknown item it in. They build *models* of the eggs.

Constructing models is the process by which an object or a phenomenon that we cannot see is represented as accurately as possible by something that we can see. For example, no one has seen a live dinosaur. Yet we have a pretty good idea of what they looked like through pictures and models. These representations have been crafted largely through the process of inferring what dinosaurs must have been like through close and detailed study of the fossil evidence.

Similarly, no one has seen an atom. Yet the atomic diagram is very familiar (see Figure 14.1). This diagram is a model of an atom, based on inferences made from detailed studies of how atoms behave under various circumstances.

Teachers often use models in their lessons. Examples include globes (which are models of the earth), dinosaur models, models of the moon, models of moon phases, models of the sun-earth-moon system, models of our planetary system, models of the human body such as plastic torsos, models of human organs such as eyes, the heart, and skin, and the like.

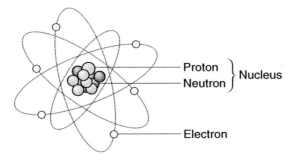

FIGURE 14.1   Typical diagram of an atom

Models are extremely powerful learning tools, presenting concrete visual representations that make lasting impressions. It is vitally important that the representations the models present are correct. It is far more difficult for people to replace erroneous models than it is for them to explore the correct model in the first place. Let us look how realistic some common models really are.

Constructing Your Ideas 14.2
Model of the Solar System

Our solar system often is portrayed as nine planets clustered closely together around the sun. In actuality, in a model that is scaled accurately, if the earth were 13½ inches from the sun, Pluto, the most distant planet in our solar system, would be over 44 feet from the sun. Try this in the hallway of your school.

Relative distances of all the planets from the sun are shown in Figure 14.2. To portray this in a dramatic fashion, line people up in the hallway at the planet distances. Select ten students, and give each of nine a paper cutout representing a planet; give the tenth student a paper sun. As you measure the planetary distances, the ten students hold up their planets and the sun so everyone can get a picture of the model.

Planet	Approximate Relative Distance from the Sun
Mercury	5¾ in.
Venus	10 in.
Earth	13 in.
Mars	1 ft. 9 in.
Jupiter	5 ft. 11 in.
Saturn	14 ft.
Uranus	19 ft. 4 in.
Neptune	34 ft. 1 in.
Pluto	44 ft. 8 in.

FIGURE 14.2   Approximate relative distances of planets from the sun

Constructing Your Ideas 14.3
How Thick Is the Earth's Atmosphere?

 The earth's atmosphere often is portrayed as very thick. Yet, the **stratosphere,** which is where passenger jetliners fly, is only about 30 miles above the earth. Compared with the 8,000-mile diameter of the earth, this represents a layer about 1 inch above the earth's surface if the earth were 13 feet in diameter. Pace out 13 feet in your classroom to get a true view. Then, to verify this proportion, look at a photograph of the earth taken from space. How thick is the atmosphere? (See Figure 14.3.)

THICKNESS OF THE EARTH'S ATMOSPHERE

CENTER OF EARTH

EDGE OF EARTH
TROPOSPHERE
STRATOSPHERE
MESOSPHERE
THERMOSPHERE
EXOSPHERE

The atmosphere is thought of as consisting of several layers. These layers do not have definite separations but intermingle with one another at their interfaces.

TABLE OF THICKNESSES OF LAYERS OF EARTH'S ATMOSPHERE

EXOSPHERE	250–625 miles
Beginning of Interplanetary Space	(400–1000 km)
THERMOSPHERE	50–250 miles
Contains Very Few Molecules	(80–400 km)
MESOSPHERE	30–50 miles
Contains electrically charged particles (ions) formed by collision of cosmic rays with air molecules. Ozone is found in lower levels of mesosphere and upper levels of stratosphere.	(50–80 km)
STRATOSPHERE	16–30 miles
	(25–50 km)
TROPOSPHERE	0–16 miles
Contains the weather	(0–25 km)

To show the relationship of the thickness of the earth's atmosphere to the diameter of the earth, use the following proportional equation:

$$\frac{\text{Atmospheric Thickness}}{\text{Earth's Diameter}} = \frac{1000 \text{ km}}{12,800 \text{ km}}$$

If we convert this to meters, the relationship is 1,000 meters: 12,800 meters.
Dividing by 100, the relationship becomes 10 meters:128 meters or 10 cm:128 cm

FIGURE 14.3   Thickness of the earth's atmosphere *(continued)*

This gives us the proportion that the earth's atmosphere is 10 cm above the earth's surface if the earth is represented by a circle 128 cm (or 1.28 m) in diameter. Proportions are as follows in the layers of the atmosphere (given an earth 1.28 m in diameter):

Top of Exosphere	10 cm
Top of Thermosphere	4 cm
Top of Mesosphere	.8 cm (8 mm)
Top of Stratosphere	.5 cm (5 mm)
Top of Troposphere	.25 cm (2.5 mm)

Cut a strip of adding machine tape about 2½ meters long. Place a dot at the center of the strip. This represents the center of the earth. Measure out from the dot 64 centimeters in each direction, and draw a line at the 64 cm mark. This represents the diameter of the earth. Now, draw lines at the proportional distances given above *from the surface of the earth* and label the atmospheric layers accordingly. The result is an accurate model of the thickness of the earth's atmosphere.

FIGURE 14.3 *(continued)*

Constructing Your Ideas 14.4
How Smooth Is the Earth?

Globes frequently show mountain ranges and plateaus as raised features on an otherwise flat surface. In actuality, the earth is smoother than a bowling ball. The tallest mountain is Mt. Everest, which stands at a height of 20,035[1] feet. If the earth's diameter were represented by a globe two feet in diameter, the height of Mt. Everest would be a bump approximately 5 ten-thousandths of an inch high. To show Mt. Everest as a bump an inch high, you would need a globe almost 2½ miles across to portray the proportionalities accurately.

You get the idea. How easy is it for you to believe these models? How do they make you feel? Is it easy or difficult for you to change your preconceived vision of the size of the solar system, the depth of the earth's atmosphere, or the height of Mt. Everest? If you have become accustomed to the standard (though instructional and economical) models, you probably are not very willing to accept these new conceptualizations. Such is the power of models.

A model commonly used in teaching is the dinosaur. Many schools encourage the study of dinosaurs at early childhood levels. Children are fascinated by them and love to learn their names and all kinds of information about different types. However, preoperational children are unable to make the cognitive leap necessary to abstract an actual size from the size of a model in proportional terms. You probably have heard about the child who studied dinosaurs in her kindergarten class using models of dinosaurs provided by the teacher. At home, her mother asks her how big

stratosphere—The layer of the earth's atmosphere where passenger jet planes fly; 16–30 miles above the earth's surface

FIGURE 14.4 Exploring dinosaurs

the dinosaurs were. "This big," replies the child, proudly holding her thumb and forefinger as far apart as they will go. Of course, the child is representing the size of the models, not the actual size of the dinosaurs. Preoperational children cannot visualize that a dinosaur is 100 or 1000 times as large as the model. They must experience real-life replicas of dinosaurs. Fortunately, this is not difficult (Figure 14.4).

Constructing Your Ideas 14.5
How Big Were the Dinosaurs?

Divide the class into groups, and ask each group to select a dinosaur they will make a model of. Obtain the dimensions of the dinosaurs. Sketch the dinosaurs out on large sheets of butcher paper and cut them out. Mount the finished models on the walls of a very large room.

Several activities to help children learn to construct models are suggested in Constructing Science in the Classroom 14.1–14.3. Some are appropriate for preschool children, and some are more appropriate for children in the early elementary grades.

Constructing Science in the Classroom 14.1
Hibernating Teddy Bears

AGE

AN ACTIVITY FOR CONSTRUCTING MODELS

8
7
6
5
4
3

Objective

The student will construct a model representing the hibernation of bears.

Provide each child or group of children several teddy bear cutouts prepared from newspaper. Fold the bears in half vertically and then in half again horizontally. Fill a pie pan with hot water, and gently place the folded bear on the surface of the water. What happens to the bear? (It unfolds.) Did your bear "wake up" from its "hibernation"? In this activity, children construct a model of hibernating bears waking up when the weather gets warm.

Ask children if they think the same thing would happen if the water were cold. Provide cold water and see what happens. Try the same thing with water of various temperatures to see whether temperature has an effect on the unfolding of the newspaper bears.

Literature Connection:

The Homeless Hibernating Bear by Kids Livin Life (1993). A hibernating bear is mistaken for a vagrant and is put in jail. However, several homeless children find a way to secure the bear's release.

Constructing Science in the Classroom 14.2
How Do Clouds Form?

AGE

AN ACTIVITY FOR CONSTRUCTING MODELS

8
7
6
5
4
3

Objective

The student will construct a model representing the formation of clouds.

Provide for each group the following materials: a large clear plastic cup, a baggie half filled with ice cubes, and a square of black paper as tall as the cups are. Explain to the class that they are going to investigate how clouds form. You might precede this activity with a trip outdoors to look at clouds.

Move from group to group and put a couple of inches of quite hot water (hot water from the tap will be fine) into their cups. Then move through the class again, and, for each group, light a match and drop it into the hot water in the cup. (Of course, the water will put out the match.) As an alternative to the match, ask children to scrape a little chalk dust from a chalkboard eraser into the cup instead of lighting the match. Immediately, the children cover the top of the cup with the baggie of ice cubes. They put the square of black paper behind the cup so they can see the cloud that forms.

(continued)

Now ask children how this model represents the formation of clouds. What do clouds need in order to form? What is the reason for the match or the chalk dust? Suggest they come up with variations on the model to see whether they can form clouds in a different way. Also suggest they do the activity *without* the match or chalk dust to see whether clouds form.

Teacher note: Clouds need a temperature differential and particles in the air in order to form. In nature, the temperature differential is achieved high in the atmosphere when warm air from the earth rises to meet cooler air higher in the atmosphere. The particles needed for the condensation of the water vapor may be tiny bits of dust or salt or other matter that is airborne. When the warm air that has water vapor in it meets the cooler air, the water vapor condenses onto the tiny particles forming clouds. (See Moore, 1992, pp. 23–27.)

Literature Connection:

The Cloud Book by Tomie dePaola (1985). In this book, common types of clouds are introduced along with myths that have been inspired by their shapes and ways they can be used to forecast weather.

Constructing Science in the Classroom 14.3
How Long Were the Dinosaurs?

AGE

8
7
6
5
4
3

AN ACTIVITY FOR CONSTRUCTING MODELS

Assign each child or group of children one dinosaur to investigate. Ask them to find out how long their dinosaur was. Also ask them to cut out a small silhouette model of their dinosaur, or provide them with an illustration or a model of the dinosaurs they have chosen.

In the hall, lay out a long strip of adding machine tape that has been marked into 1-foot increments. Each child, in turn, places his or her dinosaur cutout illustration, or model on the adding machine tape at the foot marker that represents how long the animal was. As an alternative, children can lie down on the adding machine tape, head-to-toe, until the entire length of the dinosaur has been filled with children. Then they count how many children it takes to make one of each kind of dinosaur.

Literature Connections:

An Alphabet of Dinosaurs by Peter Dodson (1995) is a book of information about familiar and newly discovered dinosaurs and the ways these creatures lived.

The Dinosaur Who Lived in My Back Yard by B. G. Hennessy (1988) compares the sizes of dinosaurs with things children are familiar with. "By the time he was 5, he was as big as our car."

Dinosaurs for Every Kid by Janice Van Cleave (1994) contains a wealth of information and activities for learning about dinosaurs.

The Magic School Bus in the Time of the Dinosaurs by Joanna Cole (1994). Children explore the age of dinosaurs and many life forms that thrived during that time. A geologic time scale shows the relative period involved.

Constructing Science in the Classroom 14.4
Why Does the Moon Shine?

AGE

AN ACTIVITY FOR CONSTRUCTING MODELS

8
7
6
5
4
3

Objective
The student will construct a model depicting why the moon "shines."

Ask children to look at the moon each evening for two or three days and to describe to the class the next day what they observe. Ask them why they think the moon shines.

Provide each group with an opaque paper cup into which you have placed a small Styrofoam ball. Seal the top with masking tape, and cut a small peephole into the side of the cup. Ask the children to shake the cup to demonstrate that there is something inside it. Then ask them to look through the peephole to see what they can see. (Because no light can get inside the cup, children should not be able to see the ball through the peephole.)

Now use a pencil to poke a small hole in the top of the cup through the masking tape. Shine a flashlight beam down into the cup through the hole on top, and again ask the children to look through the peephole to see what they can see. (This time, they should be able to see the Styrofoam ball.)

Ask children what the difference was between when they could not see the ball inside the cup and when they could see the ball.

This is a model of how the moon shines. The moon does not give off its own light. Instead, it reflects light from the sun.

To demonstrate this further, use a shoebox with a cover. Cut a peephole in the side of the box near one end, and cut a hole for a flashlight (which will represent the sun) in the end of the shoebox closest to the peephole. Hang a ping-pong ball (which will represent the moon) with a thread from the inside of the cover near the end opposite the flashlight hole. Hang a 2-inch Styrofoam ball (which will represent the earth) from the inside of the cover in a line between the "moon" and the "sun" using a thread. Attach this thread to a paperclip on the outside of the cover so you can lift the "earth" out of the path of the flashlight beam (see Figure 14.5). As the children look in the peephole, perform the following manipulations: (1) Ask them to tell what they see with the flashlight off. (2) Lift the "earth" out of the way of the flashlight beam, turn on the flashlight, and ask children what they see. (3) Drop the "earth" so it blocks the flashlight beam, placing the "moon"

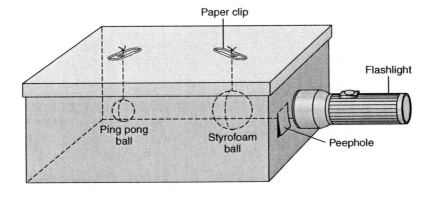

FIGURE 14.5 Shoebox model showing why the moon shines

in the earth's shadow, and ask the children what they see. This is a model that shows that the moon can be seen only because it reflects light from the sun. It also shows what happens during a lunar eclipse (when the earth blocks off the light from the sun causing the earth's shadow to fall on the moon).

Literature Connections:

The Berenstain Bears on the Moon by Stan and Jan Berenstain (1985). The Berenstain bears take a rocket trip to the moon where they cope with weightlessness, meteor showers, and moon dust.
Goodnight Moon by Margaret Wise Brown (1975). A little bunny says goodnight to each of the objects in his room, and, eventually, to the moon.

Constructing Your Ideas 14.5
An Activity For Constructing Models

Now it's your turn. Write a short activity that can be used to help children learn to construct a model. Specify age/grade level, and be sure the activity is appropriate to the children in the age/grade you specify. Cite a process-oriented objective for your lesson; the objective will read something like this: "The student will construct a model to demonstrate _____." Then get together in small groups and do the activities each member of your group has prepared.

Note

1. The height of Mt. Everest has been revised from the commonly accepted height of 29,028 feet to 29,035 feet as a result of measurements made in May 1999. The increase in height was caused by the continued movement of the Indian plate on which Mt. Everest stands toward China, pushing Mt. Everest up at a rate of about 2½ inches per year—"about as fast as fingernails grow" (Everest Tops Out, 1999).

References

Berenstain, S., & Berenstain, J. (1985). *The Berenstain Bears on the Moon.* New York: Random House.
Brown, M. W. (1975). *Goodnight moon.* Madison, WI: Demco Media.
Cole, J. (1994). *The magic school bus in the time of the dinosaurs.* New York: Scholastic.
dePaola, T. (1985). *The cloud book.* New York: Holiday House, Inc.
Dodson, P. (1995) *An alphabet of dinosaurs.* New York: Scholastic.
Everest tops out (1999). *U.S.A. Today,* November 2–14, 1999, 1.
Heide, F. P. (1993). *Timothy Twinge.* New York: Lothrop, Lee, & Shepard Books.
Hennessy, B. G. (1988). *The dinosaur who lived in my back yard.* New York: Puffin Books.
Kids Livin Life (1993). *The homeless hibernating bear.* Seattle: Gold Leaf Press.
Moore, K. W. (1992). *The weather classroom.* Atlanta: The Weather Channel.
Tomkins, C. (1966). In the outlaw area. *The New Yorker,* January 8, 1966.
Smith, M. W. (1975). *Goodnight moon.* Madison, WI: Demco Media.
Van Cleave, J. (1994). *Dinosaurs for every kid.* New York: John Wiley & Sons.

CHAPTER 15

Constructivism

In this text, you have been actively engaged in forming your ideas about the processes of science, the goals of science education, the nature of various science concepts, and ways of teaching science in early childhood education. You have been constructing these ideas in ways that make sense to you.

Everyone in your class has constructed different conceptualizations based on the backgrounds of experience and knowledge they bring to the class. New ideas presented have been assimilated in different ways by different students depending on their backgrounds.

The same is true of children. They attach meaning to new experiences based on the backgrounds of experience and knowledge they bring to the class. Suppose, for example, that the topic of the days is wild birds. Everyone loves birds, loves to see them feed at the feeder, loves to watch them flit around playing with each other and vying for dominant positions, and loves to see the baby birds waggle their wings as they learn to fly and feed

The single most important factor influencing teaching is what the learner already knows.
David Ausubel in D. P. Ausubel, J. D. Novak, and H. Hanesian, *Educational Psychology: A Cognitive View,* (2nd ed.) (New York: Holt, Rinehart and Winston, 1978), *iv*

Things are not untrue just because they never happened.
Dennis Hamley, *Hare's Choice* (New York: Doubleday, 1990)

themselves. Everyone, that is, except the child whose family believes that wild birds are a nuisance and uses a variety of methods to drive them away. As is the case of the child described in Chapter 1 who was afraid of dogs because he saw his brother get bitten by one, this child brings an entirely different experience to the class, including the absolutely certain knowledge that birds are bad.

There are different experiences and different prior understandings present among the children in an early childhood class concerning virtually every topic you choose to bring up, whether it deals with life science, physical science, earth and space science, or something else. Some of these prior experiences are known by the teacher, but most are not.

The notion that people build their own knowledge and their own representations from their own experience and thought is called *constructivism*. Each activity that has been suggested thus far and indeed the book itself is constructivist in orientation, for the idea is for you to make your own sense of the material.

It is the basic premise of this book that learning in science occurs best when approached from a constructivist point of view. In this chapter you will examine the nature of constructivism and ways of teaching science from a constructivist perspective.

Constructing Your Ideas 15.1
Defying Gravity

 Obtain the following materials:

Transparent plastic 8-ounce cups
Piece of cardboard slightly larger than the opening of the cup
Pitcher of water
Kitchen dishpan

Carefully fill the cup with water until it is overflowing. Slide the cardboard piece over the top until it completely covers the top of the cup. Be sure there are no air bubbles. Hold the cardboard in place with one hand, and, gently holding the cup with the other hand, turn the cup upside down. Hold the entire system over the dishpan, and let go of the cardboard (see Figure 15.1).

What happens? If you have followed directions carefully, the cardboard will stay on the cup holding the water inside—defying gravity!

Why do you suppose this happens?

(continued)

FIGURE 15.1   Defying gravity

The typical explanation offered for the cardboard holding the water in the cup when it is upside down is as follows: The external upward force on the cardboard due to air pressure is greater than the internal downward force of the water, thus holding the cardboard in place. Of course, one can infer that, if there were air bubbles in the cup, the downward pressure on the cardboard would equal the force of the water *plus* the force of the air. Thus, the total internal downward force on the cardboard would be greater than the external upward force, and the cardboard would fall.

To test this, try filling the cup to within a quarter of an inch from the top. Then slide the cardboard over the opening, turn the whole thing upside down as before, and let go of the cardboard. What happens? Can you explain why?

Try several variations as you seek to solve this problem—cups of different materials, covers of different materials (cardboard covered with plastic wrap, aluminum foil, and so on), different liquids inside the cup, liquids at different temperatures, and so on.

In all probability, the results of your activity were unexpected. (They certainly were when, by accident, some of the water leaked out of the cup when I was showing the "defying gravity" activity to a class of graduate students a couple of years ago!)

Having experienced an unexpected result, it now becomes necessary for you to find an explanation. You and the other members of your class may choose to tinker with the variables in this activity over several weeks' time until you are finally able to construct an understanding of what is happening in the system. You will know your construction is valid when it (a) offers a satisfactory explanation for what happens in all the cases you tried and (b) accurately predicts what will happen in each case.

In coming to an understanding of this unexpected series of events, you have constructed your own understanding. And much of what you constructed was based on your own personal prior conceptualizations and any prior experiences you may have had with this phenomenon.

NATURE OF CONSTRUCTIVISM

Constructivism suggests that "as we experience something new we internalize it through our past experience or knowledge constructs we have previously established" (Crowther, 1997, p. 3). Although constructivism has become highly popular in education circles in recent years, the ideas behind it have been around for a long time. Socrates, Plato, and Aristotle spoke of the formation of knowledge in the fifth and fourth centuries BC. John Locke (1623–1704) held that no one's knowledge can go beyond one's experience (ibid.). Giambattista Vico wrote in 1710:

1. "Epistemic agents [people who know] can know nothing but the cognitive structures they themselves have put together . . . the human knower can know only what the human knower has constructed."
2. "God alone can know the real world, because He knows how and of what He created it."
3. "In contrast, the human knower can know only what the human knower has constructed." (vonGlasersfeld, 1989)

Jean Piaget (1896–1980), considered by many to be the father of constructivism, provided the foundation for contemporary constructivism. He viewed knowledge as a process of organization and adaptation rather than a static state of being. He taught that knowledge is a relationship between the knower and the known in which the knower constructs his or her own representations of what is known. Piaget viewed the mind as a complex collection of cognitive structures called **schemata**. Schemata are opened, enlarged, divided, and connected in response to information that is taken into a person's mind. Taking new information into existing schemata is called **assimilation**, and opening new schemata is called **accommodation**. The mind works toward a state of self-satisfied understanding called **cognitive equilibration**. In order for new information to "make sense," it must either be assimilated into existing schemata or accommodated into new schemata that are connected to existing schemata in meaningful ways. In this manner, new information is connected with existing information. The result is construction of understandings that evolve or are reformulated in response to lack of fit between the new experiences and the previous understanding.

The schemata are linked to each other in ways that are unique to each individual, representing the individual's unique experiences and the unique

schema—(pl. **schemata**) A cognitive structure

assimilation—Enlarging schemata with new information

accommodation— Forming new schemata or splitting off new schemata from existing ones to accommodate new information

cognitive equilibration— A state of mental satisfaction

connections the person has made between and among those experiences. In a sense, schema theory is analogous to a well-organized filing system. Each file is labeled with its appropriate content. You might have separate files, for example, for addresses, finances, personal correspondence, business letters, homework, and so on. You would continue to file completed homework in the "homework" file until it becomes full. When it is full, you would need to open a new "homework" file. Similarly, you would need to open a new file if a new category of material, such as term papers, presented itself and had to be accommodated. These actions somewhat resemble the mental phenomena of accommodation and assimilation. You would assimilate new material into existing files where possible, and you would accommodate overloads or new categories with new files. You, alone, would know what the files contain, how the new files connect with the old files, and the rationale for opening new files. Your system would be unique to you!

The crux of Piaget's theory of cognitive development is the drive for cognitive equilibration, a state of mental equilibrium. Achieving mental equilibrium means an individual understands and is satisfied with the sense things make. Attaining mental equilibrium often is accompanied by the "light bulb" going off, or a phrase such as "Oh! Now I see!"

Mental equilibrium occurs as a result of your attempts to relate new experiences to understandings that already exist in your mind. Like the filing system just described, you assimilate new information by finding the existing schemata from your prior experiences in which the new material most appropriately belongs. When the existing schemata get too cumbersome for you to be able to work with, you split off part of one or more of them and start new ones. The new ones are connected in ways unique to your method of thinking and your prior experiences. If you encounter new material that cannot be readily assimilated into existing schemata, you accommodate this new material by forming new schemata that are connected in some fashion to existing schemata. You are achieving equilibrium; you are connecting new experiences with your prior thinking.

For example, suppose you are taking a course in early childhood science education methods. Some of the new information of the course makes immediate sense; this information is assimilated into existing schemata that deal with the same ideas and that cause the schemata to expand. This might be the case with the notion of doing hands-on activities with children. You may already have the understanding that hands-on activities are a meaningful way to involve children in science, and the new information reinforces and expands your understandings. However, some of the information is brand new to you, and you either assimilate it into existing schemata or you open new schemata that connect to existing schemata as you make sense of this new material. This might be the case with the notion of implementing technology in early childhood science activities. You may have some technological background in appropriate schemata, but you might never have thought of ways to use technology in early childhood science programs. You either assimilate the new information about technology into your schemata dealing with hands-on science or your schemata dealing with technology, or you create a new schema combining the two and linked to both.

Because the development of schemata begins as soon as the mind is capable of processing stimuli (perhaps even before birth), clearly it is to the child's advantage to acquire the richest and most widely varied experiential base possible. This gives children schemata that they can enlarge through assimilation and to which they can make new and meaningful connections as they open new schemata through accommodation. Thus, new learnings can be developed.

vonGlasersfeld wrote that teachers must abandon the notion that knowledge is a "commodity" that can be transferred to children, and they must replace that notion with an attempt to discover what actually goes on in children's minds as they learn.

> As long as the educator's objective was the generation of more or less specific behaviors in the student, the educator saw no need to ask what, if anything, might be going on in the student's head. Whenever the student could be got to "emit" the desired behaviors in the situations with which they had been associated, the instructional process was deemed successful. The student did not have to *see* why the particular actions led to a result that was considered "correct," nor did the educator have to worry about how the student achieved it; what mattered was the "performance," i.e. that he or she was able to produce such a result.
>
> If, in contrast, the objective is to lead the children or students to some form of *understanding*, the teacher must have some notion of how they think. That is to say, teachers must try to infer, from what they observe, what the students' concepts are and how they operate with them. Only on the basis of some such hypothesis can teachers devise ways and means to orient, direct, or modify the students' mental operating (vonGlasersfeld, 1991, p. 22).

According to the principles of constructivism, each learner must construct meaning for himself or herself. The only learning that can take place is that which is connected to knowledge, experience, and conceptualizations that already exist in the learner's mind. What a child learns is not a copy of what he observed in his surroundings but is the result of his or her own thinking and processing. As Tobin (1991) wrote, "Learners have no option but to use what they already know as a basis for making sense out of any experience they have."

In the experiences you have encountered thus far in this book, you have undoubtedly discovered that the same event can be interpreted differently by different people according to their prior experiences. *No two people internalize the same experience in the same way.* Thus, it follows that information a teacher attempts to "transmit" or "impart" to children is not necessarily learned in the manner that the teacher intended. It is incumbent on teachers to learn how each child is constructing information and then to help each one attach new experiences to prior experiences and knowledge in ways that are both meaningful and convincing to the child.

You have been asked to construct your own valid conceptualizations for the scientific processes, a number of scientific concepts, and science-teaching methodologies by exploring, thinking, tinkering, and resolving conflicts and questions in your own mind. In the same way, the constructivist teacher's primary job is to enable each child to find and make his or her own cognitive connections that result in valid internalized meanings unique to them. Validity is achieved in a child's mind when the child has resolved the mental disturbances under investigation.

The teacher does this by asking questions to see how the children may have previously constructed information related to the topic. The teacher then leads the children through exploratory activities that encourage them to investigate on their own and come to their own conclusions about what is happening. The teacher interacts with each child to see how he or she is constructing the new information and helps the child formulate sound conclusions by aiding in reconstructing information in ways that are both valid and meaningful *to the child*.

DISEQUILIBRATION

Exposure to new experiences often causes the phenomenon of **cognitive disequilibration.** Cognitive disequilibration comes from witnessing unexpected occurrences and is indicated by lack of understanding, or confusion, or sometimes surprise. It signifies that the new experience does not readily fit into existing schemata as the concept of *bear* could be assimilated into the schema dealing with *animals*.

When we see unexpected experiences in many movies, we explain them through "special effects," "computers," or some other reasonable explanation. We know that dinosaurs can't attack people today, and we find that they were added to the movie by computers. We know that the Empire State Building hasn't blown up, and we find that a model was built for the movies. We know that sharks haven't eaten the actors in the movie, and we find that a motorized model was used instead of live sharks. When we see unexpected effects in magic shows, and we explain these occurrences to ourselves on the basis of mirrors or transparent wires.

Unexpected occurrences are often called **discrepant events** and must be explained by our mind in some fashion. Discrepant events produce the dissatisfaction in our mind that Piaget called *cognitive disequilibration* and that others call *cognitive dissonance* (think of a sixth-grade band tuning up), *cognitive perturbation,* or *cognitive itch.* Cognitive disequilibration begs for a solution. Discrepant events are often used by constructivist teachers to spark children's curiosity about the validity of their prior beliefs.

In this course, you have encountered many discrepant events whose resulting cognitive disequilibrations have caused you to rethink your prior conceptualizations. This is because what happened was different from what you expected. For example, you found that water stays in an inverted cup with cardboard over the opening regardless of how much air is in the cup; you also found that some crayons float whereas others sink.

The "floating coffin" (Figure 15.2) presents another good example of a discrepant event. It can be purchased at novelty shops and consists of two

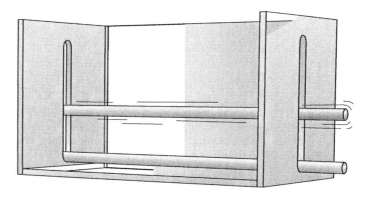

FIGURE 15.2   A "floating coffin"

round bars of steel in a frame. One of the bars (the "coffin") floats above the other. How can this be? Our experience tells us that steel bars do not float in mid air. However, our experience also tells us that there must be a reasonable explanation for what we observe. As we work to reconcile the difference between what we see and what we believe, we become satisfied that magnetism could explain this discrepant event.

The constructivist teacher seeks to induce cognitive disequilibration by setting up situations that encourage children to question their existing beliefs and ask what is going on. The constructivist teacher allows children themselves to encounter situations that run counter to their prior beliefs, thus encouraging the children to question their beliefs. Children attempt to make predictions based on prior understandings. When these predictions do not work, the children question their prior beliefs. This brings the existing beliefs to the surface, giving the teacher access to what is in the children's minds and thus the opportunity to help the children reconstruct their beliefs in valid ways that include the new information and that make more sense to them.

To aid children in their reconstruction of previously acquired beliefs, the teacher may encourage them to investigate on their own, or the teacher may introduce minimal understanding of the conceptualization as generally agreed upon by the scientific community. The result is that the child is compelled to relate the new phenomenon, new ideas, and new experiences and observations to existing knowledge in ways that are most appropriate *to the child.*

It is a fundamental principle of the constructivist approach to learning that cognitive disequilibration is a necessary precursor of learning—that learning will not take place unless one seeks explanations. If our existing understandings could explain everything, there would be no need for further understanding. As Dennett (1991) writes, "the only work that the brain must do is whatever it takes to *assuage epistemic hunger*—to satisfy curiosity in all its forms. If [a person] is passive or incurious about topic *x*, then no material about topic *x* needs to be prepared. (Where it doesn't itch, don't scratch.)" (p. 16)

vonGlasersfeld (1989) explained the phenomenon as follows:

> [C]ognitive change and *learning* take place when a scheme, instead of producing the expected result, leads to perturbation, and perturbation, in turn, leads to accommodation that establishes a new equilibrium. As a result, the human mind is a complex network of schemata which are intricately connected to each other in patterns completely unique to the individual. (p. 128)

PRIOR BELIEFS

Children come to school with beliefs about the natural world already in place. These beliefs are the result of what they have observed, what they have experienced, and, especially for young children, what they have been told. Some of these beliefs are congruent with accepted scientific principles. For example, children may be aware that animals such as bears hibernate in the winter, that water can make gullies, and that toy cars go down the track faster when the track is steep.

However, some of their beliefs may not be congruent with currently accepted scientific principles. For example, children may believe that camels store water in their humps (they store fat for energy, not water), that shadows are alive, and that heavy balls fall faster than light balls.

Constructing Your Ideas 15.2
Falling Balls

In this activity, we investigate the relationship between how much an object weighs and how fast it falls when dropped.

You will need several balls of different sizes and weights. Suggestions include tennis balls, ping-pong balls, large marbles, steel ball bearings, and so on.

Select two balls of differing weights and/or sizes. First predict what the relationship in speed between the two balls will be. Hold them several feet above the floor such that the bottoms of both balls are the same distance above the floor (see Figure 15.3).

Drop the balls at the same time, and listen for the sounds they make when they hit the floor. If your floor is carpeted, you may wish to find an uncarpeted floor or use a large aluminum roasting pan so you can hear when they hit.

From the sounds the balls make, you can tell when they land. This, in turn, enables you to infer how fast they fall.

Do this several times, and form your conclusions.

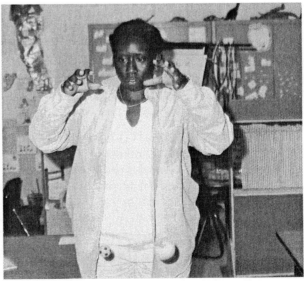

FIGURE 15.3 How fast do the balls fall?

What was your prediction? Many students predict that heavier balls will fall faster than lighter balls. This prediction is based on their prior experiences and an "intuitive" sense that it must be "true." (How could light balls fall as fast as heavy ones?) Yet, the activity showed that light balls and heavy balls hit the floor at the same time when dropped from the same height—regardless of the difference in their weights.

If you came into this activity with the prior belief that heavy balls fall faster than light balls, you are experiencing another cognitive disequilibration, and you find yourself having to reconstruct that prior conceptualization in light of new experiences. It is highly unlikely that you would attempt to reconstruct your prior conceptualization if someone had simply told you that weight doesn't matter.

CONCEPTUAL CHANGE

The process of learning is a continuous series of constructing and reconstructing one's understandings. The new understandings constructed represent conceptual changes. It is a fundamental tenet of the constructivist approach that conceptual changes occur only in response to dissatisfaction with existing conceptualizations. Conceptual change does *not* occur in response to being told something. For example, a child's belief that a plant can grow from a button is unlikely to change by telling the child otherwise. But, by planting buttons and seeds and observing the results, the child will see for himself that his prior conceptualization was faulty.

As adults, we often experience the phenomenon of prior beliefs being resistant to words. To test this, think about such volatile issues as the abortion controversy, the evolution vs. creationism debate, and capital punishment. Chances are that you have your own well-developed conceptualizations on these issues, and all the rhetoric in the world is not going to cause you to change your mind.

VALIDITY OF SELF-CONSTRUCTED CONCEPTUALIZATIONS

In your explorations with the upside-down cup of water, it was suggested that you continue to explore until you had developed a conceptualization that (a) offers a satisfactory explanation for what happens in all the cases you tried and (b) accurately predicts what will happen.

If a new conceptualization constructed by the child seems more plausible than the prior notion, it may be accepted tentatively as a replacement. For lasting acceptance, three factors must be achieved.

1. The new conceptualization must have explanatory power. It must provide a plausible explanation for each occurrence of the phenomenon. For example, prior to investigating what is and what is not magnetic, children may believe that coins are magnetic. They will need to try pennies, nickels,

dimes, quarters, half-dollars, and maybe even silver and gold-colored dollars to internalize a reconception that coins are not magnetic.

2. The new conceptualization must have *predictive power*. It must accurately predict what will happen in new and as yet untried occurrences of the phenomenon. For example, the new conceptualization that coins are not magnetic must accurately predict that even foreign coins are not attracted to magnets.

3. The new conceptualization must be convincing to other investigators. Children discuss their ideas with each other in small groups, providing their own input and listening to others as they formulate their own notions. They refine and revise their ideas as they hear other people (including their teacher) critique their ideas and ask penetrating questions the child may not have thought of. This phase is sometimes referred to as "social constructivism" and involves using input from other persons as new experiences to aid in the personal construction of new conceptualizations. For example, if someone else in the group or the class has encountered a coin that is magnetic, the child investigating magnetism will somehow have to deal with this information in forming the new conceptualization or explain the unanticipated occurrence in some manner. We must encourage children to share their conclusions and to demonstrate that the results of their investigation have both predictive and explanatory power. Having children work in groups helps promote this critical sharing. Different people investigate the same question in different ways, and when they share their information, the strengths and weaknesses of each person's thinking become apparent. The collective thinking of a group is more likely to be valid than the isolated thinking of any one individual. Children construct their own conceptualizations as individuals. But interaction with other children and the teacher in the class helps them expand their thinking and incorporate the thinking of others into their own thoughts. "Although children construct understandings for themselves—personal meaning—it does not occur in isolation of others" (Shepardson, 1997, p. 873).

If all three factors have been met (plausible explanation, accurate prediction, and group agreement), the conceptualization is very likely to be valid. At least it is held valid until a new experience induces a new cognitive disequilibration and the conceptualization must be revised or refined again to accommodate the new information.

RIGHT AND WRONG REVISITED

As we discussed in Chapter 1, in traditional science education, teachers present information for children to learn, and children are assessed to determine whether they have learned it. The assessment typically is in the form of questions. Sometimes children's responses to the questions are said to be "right," and sometimes they are said to be "wrong."

Let us revisit the question of whether there are "right" and "wrong" answers from the constructivist point of view.

Constructing Your Ideas 15.3
Naming the Poles of a Magnet

You will recall that magnets have two poles called North and South. Like poles repel each other, and unlike poles attract.

The mineral *lodestone* is a natural magnet obtained from mines that produce iron ore. Lodestone pieces behave just like magnets.

Obtain a lodestone and tie a string around it so it balances when it dangles from the string. Twist the string gently to rotate the lodestone as it dangles, and let it spin back and forth until it comes to rest (see Figure 15.4). Do this several times. You will notice that the same end of the lodestone consistently points toward the earth's magnetic north pole.

What name will you give the end of the lodestone that points north?

If you decide to call it "north" because it points toward the north pole, you are right. If you decide to call it "south" because opposites attract, you are right.

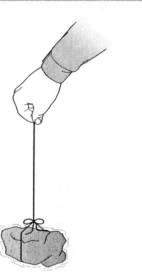

FIGURE 15.4 What will you name the end of the lodestone that points to the north?

This activity demonstrates that different people can construct the same phenomenon in two completely different ways, both of which are correct, and it illustrates the principle that was first suggested in Chapter 1 and which has permeated this book: *There are no right answers, and there are no wrong answers.* In the constructivist approach, we discover that it is far more important to ask children the reasons for their answers than it is to pronounce their answers either right or wrong. But, you may say, in science surely there are right answers and wrong answers. Yes, there are answers that are congruent with currently accepted scientific principles. But, to lead children to predetermined answers is to deny them the excitement of discovering things for themselves and to deny them the ownership of their own thinking (see Zahorik, 1997). If children are to learn, they must own and value what *they* do and *their* conceptualizations, not the teacher's. Our job as teachers is to lead children to their own sound thinking. We must send the signal in class to all children that their answers are at least as important as anyone else's—including the teacher's and the textbook's.

Thus, we seek validation and support for children's answers, not correctness. We judge children's conceptualizations on the basis of the principles of validity discussed earlier. We ask children for the reasons for their responses rather than declaring them right or wrong. In this way, children take ownership of their thinking and keep the excitement of discovery and wonder and inquiry.[1]

The next chapter discusses how to implement the constructivist approach in the science class.

SUMMARY

Constructivism is the notion that people build their own knowledge from their own experience and thought. Because all people have unique sets of experiences, different people have different conceptualizations about the same phenomenon. Piaget theorized that the construction of knowledge occurs through taking new information into existing schemata through assimilation, opening new schemata through accommodation, and achieving equilibration by connecting the schemata in ways that are sensible but unique to the individual.

To encourage extensive, rich, and valid constructions, teachers of early childhood science expose children to many new experiences. They also utilize discrepant events in their lessons to induce cognitive disequilibrations. Children are compelled to resolve these cognitive surprises by examining their prior beliefs and reconstructing their prior thoughts to form new understandings that satisfy the disturbances induced by the discrepant events. Teachers encourage children to construct their own understandings and their own valid meanings of scientific concepts. Validity of children's constructions occurs when their construction adequately explains an occurrence, accurately predicts the outcome of other similar occurrences, and is agreed to by others.

Note

1. The entire November 1999 issue of *Educational Leadership* 57 (3) is devoted to constructivism in education.

References

Ausubel, D. P., Novak, J. D., & Hanesian, H. (1978). *Educational psychology: A cognitive view* (2nd ed.). New York: Holt, Rinehart and Winston.

Crowther, D. T. (1997). The constructivist zone: Editorial. *Electronic Journal of Science Education* 2(2). On-line at http://unr.edu/homepage/jcannon/ejse/ejsev2n2ed.html.

Dennett, D. (1991). *Consciousness explained.* Boston: Little, Brown.

Hamley, D. (1990). *Hare's choice.* New York: Doubleday.

Shepardson, D. P. (1997). Of butterflies and beetles: First graders' ways of seeing and talking about insect life cycles. *Journal of Research in Science Teaching, 34* (9), 873–889.

Tobin, K. (1991). *Learning how to teach science.* Paper presented at the annual meeting of the Southeastern Association for the Education of Teachers in Science, Stone Mountain, Georgia, 1991.

Vico, G. (1710). *De antiquissima Italorum sapientia.*

vonGlasersfeld, E. (1989). Cognition, construction of knowledge, and teaching. *Synthese 80,* 121–140.

vonGlasersfeld, E. (1991). Knowing without Metaphysics: Aspects of the Radical Constructivist Position. In F. Steier, (Ed.), *Research and reflexivity.* London: SAGE Publications.

Zahorik, J. (1997). Encouraging—and challenging—students' understandings. *Educational Leadership, 54*(6), 30–32.

CHAPTER 16

Process-Oriented Inquiry

In Chapter 1, you explored the notion that it is better to teach children how to do science than it is to teach them about science. It was suggested that people do science by applying the processes of science by means of inquiry into the investigation of various phenomena. It was also suggested that in quality early childhood science education programs, teachers use the inquiry methodology in their teaching.

In Chapters 2–14, you investigated each of the twelve basic and integrated processes of science. You also investigated ways of teaching the processes, ways of facilitating the development of children's mastery of the processes, and ways of using the processes in science investigations. In Chapter 15 you investigated the nature of constructivism and its application to the early childhood education science classroom, and you explored ways of facilitating children's learning in a constructivist manner.

He who wishes to teach us a truth should not tell it to us, but simply suggest it with a brief gesture which starts an ideal trajectory in the air along which we glide until we find ourselves at the feet of the new truth.
José Ortega y Gasset, "Preliminary Meditation," *Meditations on Quixote* (New York: Norton, 1961), (Original work published 1914)

The answers aren't important really . . . . What's important is—knowing all the questions.
Zilpha Keatley Snyder, *Changeling* (Old Tappan, NJ: Simon & Schuster Children's, 1970)

It is now appropriate to pull all these experiences together by exploring actual science education methodologies so you can develop your conceptualizations of the most effective ways to teach science in the early childhood classroom.

Constructing Your Ideas 16.1
Batteries and Electricity

Obtain the following materials for each group of students in your class:

Two or three 1½-volt "D" batteries
Two or three 1½-volt flashlight bulbs
Some bell wire
(These materials can be procured at hardware stores.)

Also obtain battery holders, bulb holders, knife switches, and 1½-volt motors if they are available.

Using these materials, figure something out you didn't know before. Spend about half an hour in your explorations.

As you are fooling around with these materials, write down your responses to the following three questions:

1. What did you figure out that you didn't know before?
2. What questions do you have that you weren't able to resolve?
3. If you had sufficient funds, time, and equipment at your disposal, what would the next step in your investigation be?

Share your responses with the class.

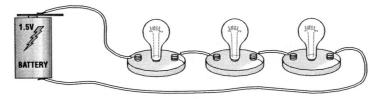

Three bulbs connected in series

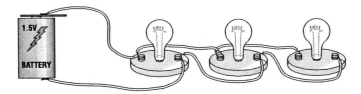

Three bulbs connected in parallel

FIGURE 16.1   Some ways of connecting light bulbs to batteries

What did the students in your class find out that they didn't know before? Students in classes similar to yours reported they found (1) if you connect the top and the bottom of a battery with a wire, the wire gets hot; (2) you don't get shocked if you touch the top and bottom of a 1½-volt battery with your fingers; (3) the bulbs light regardless of which way you connect them to the batteries; (4) if you connect the bulbs in series (one after another) and then disconnect one of them, they all go out; (5) if you connect the bulbs in parallel (each bulb having its own direct connection to the battery) and then disconnect one of them, the rest stay lit; (6) the more bulbs you connect in series, the dimmer each one lights; and (7) if you connect two or three batteries end-to-end, the light bulb gets brighter.

What unanswered questions do you still have? In other classes, students said they wanted to know where the electricity comes from, what a battery is made of, how a light bulb works, how houses are wired, what would happen if higher-voltage batteries were used, and a host of other questions.

What would you study further if you had the time and resources? In other classes, some students said they would want to investigate series and parallel circuits more completely. Some said they would want to investigate house wiring and ways to ensure safety. Some said they would want to learn enough about electricity so they could write a children's fiction book about it. Some said they would want to investigate what life would be like without electricity—how people's lives would change and how they would live. There have even been a few students who said (courageously and truthfully) that they would not like to study anything more about electricity at all!

THE EXPOSITORY-DISCOVERY CONTINUUM

Many teaching methodologies have been described by educators. Competent teachers develop a repertoire of methodologies. No *single* methodology meets the needs of all the students in a class all the time, so teachers select the approach most appropriate for the lesson to be taught and the children in their class.

Teaching methodologies can be arranged on the basis of relative amounts of teacher and learner contribution to the learning situation. Such an arrangement can be portrayed in the expository-discovery continuum shown in Figure 16.2.

Three points are highlighted on this continuum: the *expository* methodology, the *guided inquiry* methodology, and the *free discovery* methodology. The degree to which the teacher dominates the learning situation decreases as one moves from the left end of the continuum to the right end. Conversely, the

FIGURE 16.2 The expository-discovery continuum

degree to which children direct their own learning situation increases from the left end to the right end of the continuum. Where would you place the activity on batteries and electricity suggested in Constructing Your Ideas 16.1?

EXPOSITORY METHODOLOGY

In the expository methodology, material is presented to children. The teacher decides what is to be taught and what activities will be employed. The teacher is dominant. Typical activities include lecturing, explaining, reading books and stories, showing videos, doing science demonstrations, and doing other teacher-focused activities. The teacher is center-stage, and the children are expected to pay attention and absorb and learn whatever the teacher presents. Children may and may not be engaged, and it is difficult if not impossible for the teacher to know who is engaged and who is not. Certainly, if the story, lecture, video, or demonstration is skillfully and entertainingly crafted and presented, children are more likely to pay attention than if the material and presentation are dull and boring. But the only way the teacher can tell is to stop the lesson and ask questions; even then, teachers cannot be sure whether the children are internalizing what was intended. As Anderson and Lee (1997) put it, "[S]tudents always retain personal control over their attention and effort" (p. 724). I suspect that much (maybe even most) of your previous educational experiences have been expository in nature, so you can easily identify the advantages and disadvantages of this methodology.

Expository teaching is necessary in certain circumstances, which might include providing directions for a science activity, demonstrating how to do a science activity before setting children to work on their own, listing safety precautions to be taken in a science activity, citing rules for a field trip, giving directions for fire drills and other severe weather drills, and the like. The expository methodology also is useful for providing information on topics children cannot readily investigate on their own such as volcanoes and earthquakes, sounds made by the different instruments of an orchestra, and animals of Africa and the rainforest. These topics may best be presented through a carefully designed and interestingly presented expository approach.

But consistent use of the teacher-dominated expository approach has several serious disadvantages:

1. Uncertainty of the degree of mental involvement of the children
2. Inability to tailor lessons to meet the individual needs of *each* child
3. Inability to get all children to follow the flow of the lesson at the same pace
4. Uncertain relevance of the material to *each* child's life
5. Encouragement of children to be passive learners
6. Fostering of overdependence on the teacher as the source of knowledge
7. Reduced encouragement of children to think for themselves
8. Reduced encouragement of children to develop and test their own constructions of their own conceptualizations

(adapted from Eggen & Kauchak, 1994, p. 411)

FREE DISCOVERY METHODOLOGY

In the free discovery methodology, the children decide what is important for them to learn. Under the guidance of the teacher, children plan and set up their own learning activities to explore the topics they have chosen. They devise their own inquiry situations and develop their own activities. Often the topic is chosen as a result of some interest the child is motivated to explore more deeply. The teacher acts as resource, co-inquirer, and facilitator. Children are deeply involved cognitively, and so is the teacher.

The free discovery methodology is prevalent in Montessori and other specialized schools. In Montessori schools, children select topics and activities of interest to them; their learning is facilitated through the discovery approach and is tailored and paced according to the individual needs of each child.[1] In a different innovation, the renowned preschools for children age 3–6 in the town of Reggio Emilia, Italy, use a constructivist approach to teaching and learning wherein children are encouraged to create their own meanings as they explore complex situations through a free discovery approach. The Reggio Emilia program is based on the uniqueness of each individual child and rejects the " 'absoluteness' of methods . . . developmental stages, and cognitive processes that are [said to be] perfect, continuous, and irreversible" (Municipality of Reggio Emilia, 1996, p. 15). The belief is that children have their own timing and rhythm, and will learn through individualized facilitation by the teacher (ibid.).[2]

The activity on batteries and electricity suggested at the beginning of this chapter is free discovery in nature. The only factor keeping it from being at the extreme right end of the continuum is the preselected topic. In a true free discovery atmosphere, you would have been asked to select a topic of interest to you and to plan your own method of investigation under the facilitation of an instructor.

Constructing Your Ideas 16.2
Reactions to Free Discovery

 How did you feel when you were doing the free discovery activity? Excited? Interested? Empowered? Free? Frustrated? Confused? Uninterested? Directionless?
Discuss this as a class.

As you may have inferred, free discovery is the ideal vehicle for the constructivist approach to learning, for children *must* resolve cognitive disequilibrations by constructing new and valid conceptualizations as they move through their investigations. Free discovery places the responsibility for learning squarely in the learner's lap, thereby ensuring children's ownership of the knowledge.

However, the free discovery methodology presupposes that children are able and ready to take responsibility for their own learning, that they can identify specific topics worthy of study, that they can develop meaningful learning experiences that foster their own cognitive development, and that they can work somewhat independently. Children in early childhood classes normally do not possess the degree of maturity required for successful implementation of free discovery in the classroom.

There are other disadvantages to free discovery:

1. Lack of structure
2. Frustration by children over reduced dependence on the teacher
3. Possible increase of behavior-management problems (though there could be a decrease in behavior-management difficulties because children are interested and engaged)
4. Increased requirement for equipment and materials
5. Increased organizational and other managerial requirements
6. Decreased teacher control over the curriculum

GUIDED INQUIRY METHODOLOGY

In the guided inquiry methodology, the teacher selects the topic to be investigated, prepares the lesson, and provides the structure within which the investigations proceed. The children perform the activities, try additional variations and extensions not necessarily suggested by the teacher, and work with the materials to see what is happening and to make sense out of it. As in free discovery, the teacher serves as resource person, co-inquirer, and guide (not director). The teacher develops an initial activity and has a variety of additional activities and materials available to assist children in their extended investigations. The teacher helps the children in *their* endeavors (not the teacher's). The teacher asks questions and listens to the children's responses, seeking to understand how they are constructing the conceptualizations addressed in the lesson. She probes. She asks more questions, some of which are intended to help children focus their thinking, and some of which are intended to help her find out what the children are thinking. The classroom is hands-on and laboratory in focus and typically features small groups of children working together.

In the beginning of the lesson, the teacher may provide a high degree of guidance, which may include instructions for the initial investigation, constraints of time, group size, materials available, and so on. As the lesson proceeds, she works toward reducing the teacher-centered focus and increasing the student-centered focus. As children explore the activities prepared by the teacher and demonstrate valid construction of their conceptualizations, the teacher encourages them to move out to explore on their own. Indeed, the teacher may suggest different avenues of exploration for children who are experiencing difficulty with the activities already prepared or who express keen interest in a different, but related, topic.

The guided inquiry methodology encourages children to construct their own conceptualizations while at the same time exposing them to the content suggested for the grade or level. The *National Science Education Standards* (National Research Council, 1996) urges that teachers utilize inquiry teaching in their science education programs at all levels. Teaching Standard A addresses inquiry teaching directly:

> Teachers of science plan an inquiry-based science program for their students. In doing this, teachers . . . select science content and adapt and design curricula to meet the interests, knowledge, understandings, abilities, and experiences of students (ibid. p. 30).

Hagerott (1997) describes teaching physical science concepts to first-grade children while he was an engineering student. He decided that the best approach was "Curiosity, developed through active participation" (p. 718), and he employed the principles of guided inquiry by having the children start their investigations with experiencing principles of gravity, friction, inertia, and force for themselves. Activities included hanging from monkey bars with and without a heavy book bag to investigate forces; dropping from the monkey bars to investigate gravity; sliding down the slide with and without towels to investigate friction; making and propelling paper airplanes to investigate the combination of gravity, friction, inertia, and force. Each experience led to an analysis of the experience by the children, who ultimately sought to answer the question, "Why?" He concludes that "scientific education is dreadfully out of sync with the power of children's natural curiosity . . . We need to make science hands-on. It'll be more fun for all of us, and the kids will take care of the rest" (p. 720).

Guided inquiry utilizes an inquiry constructivist approach in which science content is used as a vehicle for mastery of the processes. Therefore, this methodology, applied to science education, can be termed the *process-oriented inquiry methodology.*

Education students (and, for that matter, all college students) have become accustomed to expository methods of instruction. Consequently, you need to move slowly from your beliefs in the merits of expository teaching to an understanding of the merits of guided inquiry. You may need to reconstruct your prior conceptualizations about teaching in general and teaching science in specific. You began doing this in your explorations of the processes of science. The next step is to try teaching in a guided inquiry manner. By testing this methodology and finding it safe, rewarding, and exciting, you will build the confidence that is prerequisite to successful constructivist approaches to teaching and learning science.

Figure 16.3 provides descriptors of constructivist teaching that uses the process-oriented guided inquiry methodology. Please use this list frequently to check your teaching, especially during your field experiences and the beginning stages of your professional career.

DESCRIPTORS OF PROCESS-ORIENTED GUIDED INQUIRY TEACHING
1. Plans thoroughly; identifies process-oriented objectives
2. Relates lesson to processes more than products
3. Shows logical development of processes and concepts in the planning
4. Provides for hands-on learning; students handle materials
5. Asks open-ended inquiry questions
6. Encourages children to ask questions
7. Encourages children to initiate ideas
8. Encourages children to investigate their own questions and ideas
9. Uses children's questions and responses to develop the topic
10. Encourages the use of many sources of information, including print material, multimedia, electronic communications, and people
11. Avoids supplying answers or explanations
12. Encourages children to suggest causes for what they observe
13. Encourages children to discuss and challenge each other's conceptualizations
14. Encourages children to reflect
15. Responds to individual needs
16. Relates topics to children's lives

FIGURE 16.3 Descriptors of process-oriented guided inquiry teaching
Adapted from Martin, 2000 and Yager, 1993.

PROCESS-ORIENTED GUIDED INQUIRY LESSON PLANNING

All well developed lessons, including lessons taught in the process-oriented inquiry methodology, require planning. In fact, constructivist lessons require more extensive planning than expository lessons because the teacher must plan for as-yet unknown questions, contingencies, and inquiry directions that emerge as the children develop their own personal constructions.

The first three components of planning process-oriented inquiry lessons (See Figure 16.4) are (1) the age or grade level of the children in your class; (2) the specific scientific process or processes addressed in the lesson; and (3) the science topic or topics addressed that will be the vehicle through which the children will gain experience in the processes. These three components are then used to write the objective. The appropriate content standard from the *National Science Education Standards* may be provided to show that the content selected for the lesson is consistent with that recommended by the *Standards*.

The objective sets the direction for the lesson. Recall the story of the seahorse in Chapter 8. The moral of the fable was "if you're not sure where you're going, you're liable to end up someplace else" (Mager, 1984). In the process-oriented inquiry lesson plan, the objective is process based and uses the scientific concept you identified to serve as the vehicle for exploring the process that is the focus of the lesson. You need to give considerable thought to how you will wed the process and the content as you prepare the objective.

Once you have prepared the objective, you can articulate what you want the children to discover. You are going to be encouraging children to figure things out for themselves, so you need to indicate what you want them to work at discovering. This, added to the objective, helps provide focus to the lesson. This is not to say that you will plan to lead the children to *your* conclusions but rather that you will plan to lead them to theirs.

You will want to describe your introduction to the lesson: books you will use, directions you will give, special instructions for behavior expectations and safety precautions, a cognitive disequilibration you will induce, a demonstration you might show, a video you might employ, and so on. Describe how you will open the conversation that introduces the lesson and how you will keep it going. The introductory activity should be described thoroughly, for this phase of the lesson will set the tone for the children's subsequent explorations.

The list of materials enables you to assemble all the necessary materials for the planned activities and, to the extent possible, for extensions and variations of the activity you expect children to explore. This way you won't leave anything out and have to suffer the pain of instructing children to take a recess while you obtain the material you were missing. The list of materials also enables you to assemble all necessary materials each time you do the lesson without having to search through the entire lesson plan to figure out what you need. Many teachers keep the materials in shoeboxes or other cartons suitably labeled so they don't have to start from "scratch" in assembling materials each time they do the activity.

Children's activities need to be described completely. Don't leave anything out; there is nothing worse than having to stop children in the middle of an activity and then start over again because something was left out. Children will do the planned activities to start with, but as they proceed with their inquiries, they will want to try other variations and perhaps pursue other avenues. Be sure to anticipate these detours as much as you can and be prepared to facilitate the children's inquiries.

You need to list typical discussion questions to help guide you as you guide children toward their own valid constructions. These questions should be inquiry in nature, should encourage children to do their own thinking, and should stimulate them to do their own investigating. Don't forget that a construction that is valid to the child has three components: (1) explanatory power; (2) predictive power; and (3) the utilization of input from other children and the teacher (see Chapter 15).

You also should plan how you will encourage children to investigate the phenomenon on their own—to expand their inquiries or to start new inquiries. Some children may be content simply to do the activities the teacher tells them to do. These children need to experience the thrill and satisfaction of original inquiry, and your plan should indicate what you will do to foster their independent investigations.

You need to forecast the types of conclusions you anticipate the children will reach. Again, this is not to say that you lead children to *your* conclusions. But you need to be able to assess whether the children and the lesson are successful. If the children come to expected conclusions or to unexpected conclusions that are valid, you will know that your lesson is "on the mark."

No science lesson is worth having children investigate unless it relates to their own lives in some way. This part of the lesson plan answers the question, "So what?" Many times, well-meaning teachers ask children to do activities that have little or no application to their daily lives. If an activity cannot be applied to children's lives, the lesson lacks meaning. Thus, ensuring relevance also ensures meaningfulness of the lesson to children's lives.

A recommended format for the process-oriented inquiry lesson plan is shown in Figure 16.4. You will notice that the lesson plan format closely parallels the descriptors of constructivist teaching found in Figure 16.3. Please become familiar with the components, and include them in every lesson you prepare.

Two lesson plans using the suggested format are shown in Figures 16.5 and 16.7.

LESSON PLAN FORMAT FOR PROCESS-ORIENTED INQUIRY EARLY CHILDHOOD SCIENCE LESSONS

1. Targeted grade or age level	1. Self-explanatory
2. Scientific processes addressed	2. One or more of the processes of science that serve as the focus of the lesson
3. Science topic addressed	3. The science topic that will be used as the vehicle for exploring the processes on which the lesson focuses (appropriate content standard from *National Science Education Standards* may be referenced).
4. Process-oriented objective	4. One or more objectives written in process form
5. What do I want children to discover?	5. The scientific information children should be able to articulate as a result of the lesson
6. Description of introductory activity and initial discussion	6. Details about how you will introduce the lesson
7. Materials needed	7. The list of materials needed, including equipment, materials, and available print, multimedia, electronic communications, and people resources together with materials needed for extensions and variations of the activity you anticipate children will want to explore
8. Description of activities	8. Details of what the children will do to explore the concept and what you will do to help them in their explorations
9. Typical discussion questions	9. Typical questions you will ask of groups to stimulate their thinking toward the objective
10. How children will be encouraged to investigate on their own in the classroom	10. What children might do to continue the investigation in greater depth and explore additional variations and related topics
11. Expected conclusions	11. The conclusions you anticipate children will formulate as a result of their investigations
12. Applications to real-life situations	12. Practical and life-based applications of the lesson.

FIGURE 16.4   Lesson plan format for process-oriented inquiry early childhood science lessons

MAKING MUD

1. *Targeted grade or age level:* 3–4 year-olds
2. *Scientific processes addressed:* Observing, communicating
3. *Science topic addressed:* Properties of earth materials (National Science Education Content Standard D)
4. *Process-oriented objective:* The student will observe what happens when water is added to dirt and will communicate the observations to each other.
5. *What do I want children to discover?* Water mixed with dirt makes mud.
6. *Description of introductory activity and discussion:*
   * First, read *Pigs in the Mud in the Middle of the Rud* by Lynn Plourde and John Schoenherr (1997). This is a story about animals that won't budge from the middle of the muddy road ("rud") during mud season in Maine.
   * In small groups, show children cups of several different kinds of dry dirt.
   * Ask children to describe what they observe: color, texture, materials in the dirt, sizes of particles, and so on.
   * Select one of the cups of dirt and add water to it, stirring until the water and dirt are thoroughly mixed.
   * Ask children what they observe in this cup.
   * Ask if they can remember the name for this material ("mud").
   * Provide directions for their activity.
     * Add water to the different cups of dirt, one at a time.
     * Stir gently.
     * Observe and describe what they observe.
     * Safety considerations: Pour the water carefully. Hold onto the cup when stirring.
7. *Materials needed*
   * Transparent plastic cups
   * Dirt samples (relatively dry)
   * Plastic spoon
   * Plastic pitcher of water
   * Magnifying glasses
   * Sand
   * Smocks for protecting children's clothing
8. *Description of activities*
   * Children will add water to one cup with dirt in it, stir it, and keep stirring in more water until they get mud. They will describe to the group what they observe.
   * Children will do the same thing with each different kind of dirt.
   * Then children to do the same thing with the sand and describe what they observe.
9. *Typical discussion questions:*
   * What does dirt look like?
   * How much water do you need to add before you get mud?
   * Do you need to add the same amount of water to each kind of dirt to get the same effect?
   * Does the mud look like the dirt? How are the mud and the dirt alike? How are they different?
   * Would the same thing happen with a different kind of dirt? Let's try it and see.
   * What happens when you add water to the sand?
   * Do you get the same results with the sand as you do when you add water to dirt? Why do you suppose that happens?
10. *How children will be encouraged to investigate on their own in the classroom:* Pails of different kinds of dirt, a pitcher of water, and cups, spoons, and magnifying glasses will be provided in the science center. Children will be encouraged to try all kinds of dirt, including mixtures of different kinds of dirt.
11. *Expected conclusions:* Mud comes from water mixing with dirt.
12. *Applications to real-life situations:* When it rains, the dirt becomes mud.

FIGURE 16.5 A process-oriented inquiry lesson plan on making mud

Adapted from a presentation made at the National Science Teachers Association Southeast Conference in 1996 by Julie Stacy, a graduate student in education at Kennesaw State University.

SPACE SNACKS

1. *Targeted age or grade level:* 4–6 year-olds

2. *Scientific processes addressed:* Observing, measuring, inferring

3. *Science topic addressed:* Properties of objects and materials (National Science Education Content Standard B)

4. *Process-oriented objective:* The student will observe and measure crumbs resulting from eating snacks and will infer characteristics most appropriate for food to be eaten in space.

5. *What do I want children to discover?*
   Children should discover that some snacks result in more crumbs than others and that the most appropriate foods for eating in space are those with the fewest crumbs and least waste.

6. *Description of introductory activity and discussion*
   a. Show a short video that portrays the gravity-free environment of a spaceship.
   b. Select small groups.
   c. Pose the question, "What do you suppose astronauts eat in space?"
   d. Would they eat cookies? Why do you think so? Ask the same questions about crackers, apples, bananas, and potato chips. Use children's responses and input to extend the conversation.
   e. Pose another question: "What would happen to the crumbs if astronauts were to eat a cracker?"

7. *Materials needed*
   • Snack foods (cookies, crackers, potato chips, marshmallows, and M&Ms)
   • White paper napkins

8. *Description of activities*
   First find out whether anyone is allergic to any of the snack foods being offered. (Check school records if necessary; allergies should be recorded for each child.) If someone is allergic, ask that child to omit that food from the activity and observe what others find out instead. Provide each child with one of each kind of snack. Children take a small bite of one snack over a white napkin. They use a different napkin for each snack, put the remainder of the snack piece on the napkin, and put it to one side while they taste each snack. They then examine each napkin and make a judgement as to the quantity of crumbs that fell. If desired, they can develop a system for measuring the amount of crumbs left behind, such as estimating the number of crumbs, counting them, comparing their sizes, or arranging the napkins in order of which ones have the most crumbs so children can determine the "crumbiness" of each snack. The specific method they use will emerge during the lesson. Finally, children infer which of these snacks is/are best for space travel, providing reasons for their responses.

9. *Typical discussion questions*
   • Which snacks made the most crumbs?
   • Which snacks made the fewest crumbs?
   • Which snacks would you recommend that astronauts take with them to space? Why?
   • What other foods could astronauts eat?
   • What foods should astronauts *not* take with them? Why?
   • Which snacks would make it uncomfortable in your bed if you were to eat it there?

10. *How will children be encouraged to investigate on their own in the classroom?* Napkins will be available, and children will be encouraged to make assessments of the "crumbiness" of different snacks they eat at school.

11. *Expected conclusions:* The potato chip will produce the most crumbs, followed by the cracker, the cookie, the M&Ms, and the marshmallow.

12. *Applications to real-life situations:* Some foods produce more crumbs than others. Although we on earth don't have to worry about crumbs floating in our air, we do have to be careful of making messes.

FIGURE 16.6 A process-oriented inquiry lesson plan on foods appropriate for space travel

Adapted from a presentation made at the National Science Teachers Association Southeast Conference in 1996 by Julie Stacy, a graduate student in education at Kennesaw State University.

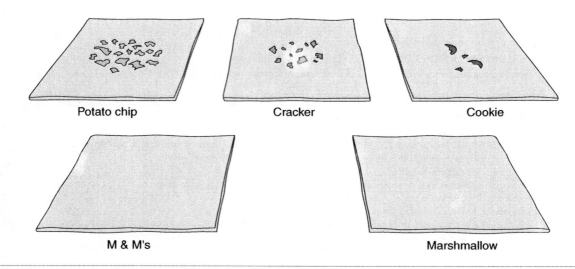

FIGURE 16.7   Which napkin has the most crumbs?

MICROTEACHING

You have spent time examining, constructing, and reconstructing your conceptualization of quality science teaching in early childhood levels. We have suggested that the process-oriented inquiry constructivist approach fulfills the goals of contemporary science education and meets the needs of all children.

The next step is for you to try this methodology so you experience it firsthand from the point of view of doing the teaching. You have experienced process-oriented inquiry in numerous activities thus far but from only the learner's point of view. Now is the time to do some teaching.

You will do this teaching in the form of "microteaching," which involves presenting a short lesson to a small group of colleagues. The "micro" in microteaching can refer to both the lesson, which is considerably reduced in scope and length, and to the size of the group you are teaching. Much has been written about the value of microteaching in preservice teacher preparation. Detractors argue that the teaching is not sufficiently similar to actual classroom teaching to be valuable. However, research shows that microteaching is "an effective way to have students in methods classes plan, teach, and evaluate a lesson presented to a small group of their peers" (Pauline, 1993, p. 9). Perhaps the most compelling argument in favor of microteaching is the consistently and overwhelmingly positive feedback that students report. Microteaching has been a key component of my science methods classes for many years, and students have been unanimously positive about the experience—even in their anonymous end-of-course evaluations.

Constructing Your Ideas 16.3
Microteaching

Prepare a process-oriented guided inquiry lesson that takes about 15 minutes to teach. Write a lesson plan for the lesson in accordance with the format given in Figure 16.4. The lesson will be presented to a small group of students in your class and should involve hands-on exploration by *all* members of the group. Materials and equipment should be easily available and should be inexpensive or free. Bring *all* materials needed for the group to participate fully in the lesson.

Teach this lesson to a group of your classmates. Videotape your teaching. After the lesson, ask your classmates to critique your lesson on the basis of the inquiry descriptors presented in Figure 16.3.

The videotaping is extremely useful for your self-assessment of your teaching. The peer critique also is very valuable, but only if every member of the peer group (a) agrees to be objective, frank, and constructive in their critiques *and* (b) agrees to never bring a critique up again after the critiquing session is finished (unless the student whose teaching was critiqued brings it up himself or herself and solicits additional input).

In private, look at and reflect on the videotape, the feedback from your group, and your own awareness of what went on during the lesson. From your reflections, write an honest critique of your lesson. (Remember that a critique contains strengths as well as areas that need additional work.) Finally, rewrite the lesson plan to reflect changes you would make as a result of the critique.

SUMMARY

There are many different teaching methodologies, and they can be arranged according to the relative amounts of teacher and learner input. In the expository methodology, the teacher presents material for children to absorb. The children have little or no input into the nature of the lesson. Although expository methodologies are required when the teacher wants to impart information efficiently, children may and may not be engaged in the learning process, and there is no real way to find out whether they are absorbing the material. In the free discovery methodology, children make the decisions about what they are going to study and how they are going to study it. The teacher acts as facilitator and co-inquirer. Although this methodology fosters children's constructions of their own ideas, younger children may have difficulties in assuming responsibility for their own learning. In the guided inquiry methodology, the teacher selects the topics to be investigated and outlines the basic procedures for inquiry. Children do the planned activities and then branch out on their own to investigate the topic in accordance with their interests and abilities. The teacher acts as facilitator and co-inquirer.

Process-oriented inquiry is a guided inquiry methodology in which children investigate phenomena the way scientists do. They apply the processes of science in an inquiry format to investigate questions, situations, and other scientific phenomena the teacher suggests and that they themselves pose as a result of the initial exposure planned by the teacher. The teacher acts as facilitator and co-inquirer.[3]

We never know for sure what children are learning. But, with the process-oriented inquiry methodology, we *do* know that children *are* learning—each in accordance with his or her needs, abilities, interests, learning strengths, and experiential bases. And the certainty of each child learning *something* is far preferable to the possibility of children not learning.

Notes

1. Information about Montessori schools is available on the World Wide Web at www.montessori.edu.
2. For more information on the Reggio Emilia approach to early childhood education, see Katz and Cesarone (1994).
3. The National Science Foundation has published a monograph entitled *Foundations, Vol. 2: Inquiry,* a resource for teachers and administrators interested in inquiry-based science education in elementary and middle schools. The book discusses the power of children's thinking and what children gain through inquiry; it also contains a section on assessment of science inquiry. For further information access the National Science Foundation Internet site as www.her.nsf.gov/HER/ESIE/index.html.

References

Anderson, C. W., & Lee, O. (1997). Will students take advantage of opportunities for meaningful science learning? *Phi Delta Kappan 78*(9), 720–724.

Eggen, P., & Kauchak, D. (1994). *Educational psychology: Classroom connections.* New York: Merrill.

Gasset, J. O. Y. (1961). *Meditations on Quixote.* New York: Norton.

Hagerott, S. G. (1997). Physics for first graders. *Phi Delta Kappan 78*(9), 717–720.

Katz, L. G., & Cesarone, B. (Eds.). (1994). *Reflections on the Reggio Emilia approach.* ERIC Document No. ED375986.

Mager, R. F. (1984). *Preparing instructional objectives* (rev. 2nd ed.). Center for Effective Performance, Inc., 2800 Peachford Road, Suite 2000, Atlanta, GA 30338.

Martin, D. J. (2000). *Elementary science methods: A constructivist approach* (2nd ed.). Belmont, CA: Wadsworth/Thompson Learning.

Municipality of Reggio Emilia (1996). *The municipal infant-toddler centers and preschools of Reggio Emilia: Historical notes and general information.* Reggio Emilia, Italy: Reggio Children Srl.

National Research Council (1996). *National science education standards.* Washington, DC: National Academy Press.

Pauline, R. F. (1993). Microteaching: An integral part of a science methods class. *Journal of Science Teacher Education 4*(1), 9–17.

Plourde, L., & Schoenherr, J. (1997). *Pigs in the mud in the middle of the rud.* New York: Blue Sky Press.

Second volume of NSF monograph series discusses inquiry (2000). *NSTA Reports! 11*(6), p. 17.

Snyder, Z. K. (1970). *Changeling.* Old Tappan, NJ: Simon & Schuster Children's.

Yager, R. E. (1993). The need for reform in science teacher education. *Journal of Science Teacher Education 4*(4), 144–148.

CHAPTER 17

Learner Differences

No two children are alike. Children vary in innumerable ways, ranging from physical differences, including gender and race, to cognitive differences, differences in socioeconomic background, cultural background, primary language, background of experiential exposure, and a host of other ways.

As you recall from Chapter 1, it is a major goal of science education that *all* children have equal opportunity to learn science and that *all* children achieve scientific literacy (National Research Council, 1996, p. *ix*). Furthermore, as you recall from your explorations of constructivism and inquiry, children learn by attaching new experiences to previous ones. These prior experiences vary enormously from individual to individual. Because no two children are alike, it is useful to consider some ways in which they are different that have an effect on how they learn science.

The most universal quality is diversity.

Michel Eyquem de Montaigne, "Of the Resemblance of Children to Their Fathers," *Essays* (New York: G. P. Putnam's Sons, 1907); (Original work published c. 1580–1588)

We see them come,
We see them go.
Some are fast.
And some are slow.
Some are high.
And some are low.
Not one of them
Is like another.
Don't ask us why.
Go ask your mother.

Dr. Seuss, *One Fish Two Fish Red Fish Blue Fish* (New York: Random House, 1993)

In groups, make a list of as many ways as you can think of in which children are different from each other. Spend about 5 minutes on this activity in your group. Then compile a master class list.

How many differences did you list? Students in classes like yours have compiled lists of as many as a hundred ways in which children are different from one another. All these individual differences affect how children learn.

Some of these differences have been shown to have an effect on science learning. In this chapter, you will explore several individual differences you should consider as you construct your early childhood science program.

LEARNING MODALITIES

People take in and process information in three basic ways that are termed modalities. The three learning modalities are visual (seeing), auditory (hearing), and kinesthetic (feeling or using any of the many senses included in the sense of touch described in Chapter 2). In any individual, one of these modalities is generally stronger than the others.

Try this. Sit with your hands folded for a moment or two. Then fold your hands the opposite way (so the other thumb is on top). Next, fold your arms in front. Then fold them the opposite way.
  Which is more comfortable? How do you feel when you fold your hands or your arms in the opposite way?

Folding your hands or your arms in the more comfortable way is analogous to utilizing your dominant or more comfortable learning modality. Folding your hands or your arms in the opposite way is analogous to being required to utilize your less dominant or less comfortable learning modality. You can function in the less dominant learning modality, but not as well. It just doesn't feel right.

Constructing Your Ideas 17.3
What Is Your Dominant Learning Modality?

To get an idea of what your dominant learning modality is, try this. Divide your class into pairs. (If there is an odd number of students in your class, you will need one group of three students.) Assign the number "1" to one of each pair and the number "2" to the other person (and also to the third person if there is a group of three). Ask the 1s to leave the room to get instructions. The 2s remain in the room. The instructions are as follows: The 1s are to ask a series of questions of the 2s, and, while pretending to write the responses of the 2s to the questions, they actually write how the eyes of the partner move: up, down, or to one side.

Now the 1s ask the following questions of the 2s and record the data.

1. What is the name of your favorite television program?
2. What is the name of the movie you saw recently that you liked the best?
3. Who is your favorite actor?
4. Who is your favorite actress?
5. Who is your favorite relative (not of your immediate family)?
6. What is your favorite song or piece of music?
7. What is your favorite model of car?
8. What is your favorite sport to watch?

a. Visual learner looks up.

b. Auditory learner looks to one side.

Finally, the 1s reveal the data they have been recording.

If your partner's eyes generally move upward when pondering the response to the questions, this may indicate a visual learner. If the eyes generally move sideways, this may indicate an auditory learner. If the eyes generally move down, this may indicate a kinesthetic learner[1] (see Figure 17.1).

Now select two or three students who exhibited the visual modality, two or three who exhibited the auditory modality, and two or three who exhibited the kinesthetic modality. Go through the questions one at a time, and ask them to describe in as much detail as possible what they recalled as they formulated their responses.

c. Kinesthetic learner looks down.

FIGURE 17.1 The direction a person looks when trying to recall information provides a clue as to predominant learning style.

Chances are that the visual learners will describe what they see–the television images, the theater marquee, people's faces, the jacket of the record or CD, the players playing the game. In all probability, the auditory learners will describe what they hear—the sounds and the theme music of the television show and the movie, the voices of the people, the song or musical theme itself, the sounds of the game. The kinesthetic people will probably describe what they feel—the emotions associated with the television program and the actor and actress, the seat cushion or the stickiness of the movie theater's floor, the physical impact of the relative, the feel of playing the game.

The data collected from your classmates may show that two or even all three modalities were operating at the same time. However, on close examination you will probably find that one of the three tends to be strongest for any individual.

One's dominant learning modality is as comfortable as handedness or, as we have seen, the way one folds hands or arms. Research has shown that children's achievement in general (Dunn, 1988, 1990) and in science (Kuerbis, N. D.) is fostered by being given the opportunity to learn in their more comfortable learning styles. Thus, teachers should prepare activities to include learning opportunities in all three modalities—visual, auditory, and kinesthetic.

Learning Experiences for Visual Learners

Visual learners learn best through visual stimuli. They remember and process information by seeing photographs, drawings, videos, movies, charts, models, actual materials, and so on. Activities comfortable to visual learners include observing and classifying pictures or drawings, describing characteristics of objects they see, preparing graphs or pictorial representations, setting up bulletin boards, setting up displays, and so on. Constructing Science in the Classroom 17.1 shows an activity that employs the visual learner's strengths.

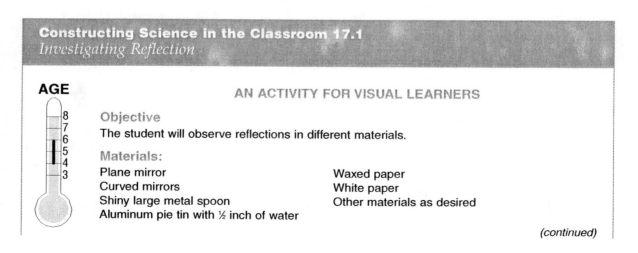

Constructing Science in the Classroom 17.1
Investigating Reflection

AGE

8
7
6
5
4
3

AN ACTIVITY FOR VISUAL LEARNERS

Objective
The student will observe reflections in different materials.

Materials:

Plane mirror   Waxed paper
Curved mirrors   White paper
Shiny large metal spoon   Other materials as desired
Aluminum pie tin with ½ inch of water

(continued)

Ask the children to look at the reflections of their faces in each of the items provided. For each, ask them to indicate whether their reflection was as they expected it to be or smaller, larger, distorted in some other way, or nonexistent.

Literature Connection:

Bouncing and Bending Light by Barbara Taylor (1990) suggests projects to demonstrate the effects of mirrors and lenses on light rays.

Learning Experiences for Auditory Learners

Auditory learners learn best through auditory stimuli. They remember and process information by listening to lectures, explanations, discussions, people's voices, sound tracks, musical jingles, sound effects, rhythmic effects, sounds of actual materials, and so on. Activities comfortable to auditory learners include experimenting with sound, listening to animals, listening to outdoor sounds, singing songs, composing songs, listening to what happens to materials in an investigation, and so on. Constructing Science in the Classroom 17.2 shows an activity that employs the strengths of the auditory learner.

Constructing Science in the Classroom 17.2
Sounds of Rubber Bands

AGE

8
7
6
5
4
3

AN ACTIVITY FOR AUDITORY LEARNERS

Objective

The student will predict the effect of changing the thickness or the tension of rubber bands on the pitch of the sound produced when plucked.

Materials:

An assortment of rubber bands
Small box without cover

First provide safety precautions to children: no snapping rubber bands, no slingshot activity, no stretching the rubber bands so tightly that they break, and others you feel appropriate. Also be sure children can distinguish higher pitches and lower pitches. To verify this, you can use a pitch pipe or a piano, or you can sing. Play or sing notes of different pitches, and ask children to identify whether each is higher or lower in pitch than the one that came before.

Now give each child a rubber band. Ask them to hold it between their two hands until it is just barely taut. Ask them to pluck it with one finger and remember the pitch of the sound it produces. (They will have to hold the rubber band close to their ears to hear its sound.) Ask them to stretch it a little bit more, pluck it again, and compare the pitch with that of the first try. Children should do this with different tensions and form their conclusions. Then ask them to do the same thing with rubber bands of different thicknesses and form conclusions concerning the relationship between thickness and pitch.

(continued)

Finally, if desired, children can construct and play a rubber band "guitar" using rubber bands of different thicknesses and tensions strung on a shoebox or other coverless box (see Figure 17.2).

Literature Connection:

Ty's One-Man Band by Mildred Pits Walter (1980). Ty utilizes several everyday objects (a washboard, a comb, wooden spoons, and a pail) as musical instruments.

FIGURE 17.2   A shoebox guitar

Learning Experiences for Kinesthetic Learners

Kinesthetic learners learn best through one or more of the many aspects of the sense of touch. They remember and process information by feeling things, hefting things, putting things into certain places, pantomiming, dancing, writing, drawing, and so on. Activities comfortable to the kinesthetic learner include balancing, investigating motion, investigating forces, investigating friction, classifying objects by texture, dramatizing the results of an activity, experimenting with sand, and so on. Constructing Science in the Classroom 17.3 shows an activity that employs the strengths of the kinesthetic learner.

Constructing Science in the Classroom 17.3
Exploring Gears

AGE

8
7
6
5
4
3

AN ACTIVITY FOR KINESTHETIC LEARNERS

Objective

The student will interpret data collected from exploring interconnected gears in terms of generalizations about gears.

Materials:

Gear set (such as those available from commercial science suppliers, toy stores, or Legos®)

First have children count the number of teeth on each gear to be used in the activity, and mark the number of teeth on each gear. Next, have children color one tooth so they can keep track of the number of times each gear turns through a revolution.

(continued)

Ask the children to select two gears and mount them so their teeth interlock. They then turn the larger gear through one complete turn and count the number of turns the smaller gear makes. Ask them to do this with different pairs of gears.

Now ask whether there is a relationship between the number of teeth on each of the gears in a pair and the number of turns the smaller gear makes when the larger gear is turned one turn. Younger children may conclude that the smaller gears turn more times than the larger gear. Older children may develop a "Law of Gears" that says the number of turns made by interlocking gears depends on the number of their teeth. (For example, a gear with 16 teeth will turn a gear with 8 teeth through two full revolutions when it is turned through one revolution.)

Also ask the children to observe the *direction* each gear turns.

Ask children to play around with the gears to see what they have to do to get a gear to move in the *same direction* as the gear being turned.

Literature Connection:

Bicycle Book by Gail Gibbons (1995) is a nonfiction book that provides information about bicycles, including basic mechanics, the different parts, functionality, maintenance, and more.

Learning Experiences for Visual, Auditory, and Kinesthetic Learners

Young children tend to be essentially kinesthetic in learning modality through kindergarten age. Activities for young children should tap into their kinesthetic strength and should include maximum hands-on experiences. In time, the visual modality develops strength, and so does the auditory modality (Dunn, 1988, p. 305). Teachers should be aware of their own strongest modalities and be on their guard against using this modality predominantly in their teaching. Research has shown that, when teachers teach in their own modalities to children with different dominant modalities, children exhibit lower achievement (Dunn, 1990, p. 18). Thus it is incumbent on teachers to know their most comfortable learning styles and utilize the strengths associated with them in their teaching while also making efforts to teach in their less dominant learning styles so all children have equal advantages.

Summary strategies for planning instruction that takes account of children's learning modalities are as follows:

- Guard against over-teaching in *your* preferred style or modality.

- Provide a variety of teaching approaches so all children have the opportunity to learn through their strongest modalities and are challenged to use other modalities as well.

- Incorporate a good mixture of learning modalities.

- Help children identify their preferred learning modalities.

- Include kinesthetic experiences in your teaching repertoire.

Now it's your turn. Select a process-oriented inquiry investigation, and write activities you can include specifically for the visual learner, the auditory learner, and the kinesthetic learner.

LOCUS OF CONTROL

Another individual difference that influences children's science learning is locus of control. Locus of control is a characteristic that describes "whether people attribute responsibility for their own failure or success to internal or to external factors" (Slavin, 1994, p. 355). People have either a predominantly *internal* locus of control or a predominantly *external* locus of control. People with an internal locus of control believe they control the outcomes of their actions, and people with an external locus of control believe the outcomes of their actions are controlled by external factors such as luck, other people, or their own helplessness.

Like other factors in education, locus of control can be thought of as a continuum with external locus of control on one end and internal locus of control on the other end (see Figure 17.3).

Most people exhibit characteristics of both the external and the internal locus of control and so can be placed somewhere along the continuum.

The presence of an internal locus of control is a powerful predictor of achievement (Brookover, et. al., 1979, p. 355). The internal locus of control has been shown to have a positive influence on the degree to which children seek to investigate on their own and are willing to make predictions (Rowe, 1978). This is attributed to the notion that children with an internal locus of control believe they have influence over what happens—that success (or failure) is due to their own efforts, investigations, and hard work.

On the other hand, children with an external locus of control believe they have little or no control over the outcomes of their efforts. They attribute their successes or failures to outside factors and adopt the attitude that there isn't much point in trying hard or in investigating things. They feel "What's the use?"

External Locus of Control   Internal Locus of Control

⟵——⟶

FIGURE 17.3 Locus of control continuum

As you can tell, children with an internal locus of control are more successful in scientific inquiries than children with an external locus of control because they believe that their investigations and experimental efforts do in fact influence the outcomes of their inquiries. Thus, teachers are encouraged to help children with an external locus of control develop a more internal locus of control. The technique essentially involves helping such children see where their efforts have made positive differences. Help children focus on how *their* efforts affected the outcomes of investigations. Ask "no risk" questions such as "Tell me about your investigation with gears." Avoid "correct response" questions such as "How many times should the smaller gear move around?" and questions that the child may perceive as threatening, such as "What did you do with these gears?" Encourage children with the external locus of control to verbalize, write, draw, or dramatize the results of their investigations (Rowe, 1978; Tomlinson, 1987).

Specific teaching strategies that can be employed to foster a more internal locus of control are shown in Figure 17.4.

FIELD DEPENDENCE/FIELD INDEPENDENCE

Field independence is the ability to recognize camouflaged information easily. You may have seen "hidden figures" puzzles in children's publications such as *Highlights for Children*. A number of objects are drawn into the picture so they blend in with their surroundings. The idea is to find each of the objects that are hidden in the picture.

CLASSROOM STRATEGIES THAT FOSTER THE DEVELOPMENT OF AN INTERNAL LOCUS OF CONTROL

1. Encourage children to evaluate the outcomes of investigations.
2. Encourage children to suggest ways of changing variables.
3. Encourage children to suggest additional or different ways of investigating a given phenomenon.
4. Encourage children to suggest topics for investigation and to set their own goals.
5. Encourage speculation by asking questions.
6. Teach children to ask questions.
7. Use sufficient wait time in questioning to allow children to formulate well thought-out responses.
8. Encourage children to evaluate their own progress.
9. Encourage cooperative inquiry.
10. Change cooperative groups when they are no longer functioning.

FIGURE 17.4 Classroom strategies that foster the development of an internal locus of control
(From Martin, 2000, p. 244)

Constructing Your Ideas 17.5
Hidden Figures

Just for fun, obtain a copy of *Highlights for Children* or other publication that contains a hidden figures puzzle. Allow each student in your class to find all the objects, and time how long it takes each person either to find them all or to give up.

People who can find the objects in the puzzle with relative ease are said to be *field independent*. People who have a difficult time finding the objects are said to be *field dependent*. Field independent individuals have the ability to ignore the surrounding camouflaging field; to them, the objects "pop out" of the picture quite readily. Field dependent individuals, on the other hand, look for the objects within the context of the camouflaging background, and find they have to search meticulously to discover the objects (see Figure 17.5).

Camouflaged information is not always visual in nature. Think, for example, of the TV quiz show, *Jeopardy*. Many of the "answers" contain far more information than is necessary to achieve the correct "question." For example, an item might be something like the following:

The coat of arms of this Swiss capital contains a prominent figure of a "bear."

What is the superfluous information? How easy or difficult is it for you to separate the essential information from the nonessential information? Field

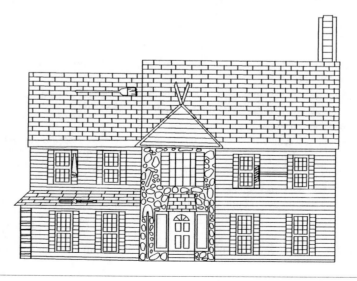

FIGURE 17.5 Find the following tools needed for home maintenance: broom, hammer, two ladders, pliers, saw, screwdriver, shovel, rake.

independent individuals are able to discard the nonessential information readily and bore directly to the problem: "What is the capital of Switzerland?" Field dependent individuals may picture the coat of arms with the bear and try to put this information together with a city in Switzerland. As they try to put everything together, they get so overloaded with extraneous information that they have a difficult time seeing the central problem.

Studies have shown that field independent students consistently exhibit higher achievement in science than field dependent students (Lawson, 1985). This is attributed to the greater ability of field independent students to master the processes of science and think independently. Thus, it is desirable to foster the development of field independence in children. Collings (1985) showed that, although field independence and field dependence seem to be inherited traits, field dependent children can learn to think more field independently with training and education. This is corroborated by studies that show that children in affluent families exhibit more field independent characteristics than children from lower socioeconomic backgrounds (Bertini et. al., 1986). The explanation offered is that children in affluent families are given more opportunities to solve puzzles and play games, are more likely to have access to children's magazines, and have more opportunities to discuss their experiences with knowledgeable adults. From these studies, we can conclude that providing children opportunities to solve puzzles, make up and answer riddles, draw pictures for others' interpretations, and the like help foster field independent thinking.

Frequent activities using the processes of science also help children grow in field independence. For example, observing is a process skill that can be practiced with increasing refinement. When children are first asked to observe an object such as a rock or a feather, the field dependent children may focus on the entire object, describing its overall look, its beauty, its form, and so on. With a little encouragement, children will begin to look for the details that make up the whole: the texture, grains, particles, and layers that make up the rock, or the quills, individual parts, and subtle differences in color that make up the feather. Classifying is a process skill that requires attention to detail. For example, if children collect leaves from the school yard, they must observe the differences among them in order to sort them into groups. The process skill of identifying variables requires that children identify the various factors that affect something that happens. For example, in order to investigate what makes plants grow best, children must isolate each factor that might influence the growth.

In addition to providing practice in the process skills, employing inquiry-oriented learning methodologies helps field dependent children move toward a more field independent mode by encouraging them to see how each person's contributions to an investigation influenced the outcome.

Specific suggestions for fostering the development of field independence among all children are provided in Figure 17.6.

STRATEGIES FOR FOSTERING FIELD INDEPENDENCE IN YOUNG CHILDREN
- Encourage children to work age-appropriate jigsaw puzzles.
- Play games such as "20 Questions" and "What's in the Bag?" with children.
- Provide age-appropriate board games for children to play with.
- Ask children to make up riddles.
- Ask children to make up stories with hidden meanings.
- Read detective stories and ask children to solve them before the end.
- Provide advance overviews of lessons.
- Encourage children to work with computers.
- Employ constructivist teaching techniques.
- Stress the processes of science.
- Utilize inquiry-based methodologies.

FIGURE 17.6 Strategies for fostering field independence in young children

GENDER BIAS

Constructing Your Ideas 17.6
What Is a Scientist?

Take a few moments and draw a picture of a scientist. Then share all the pictures with the class.

What characteristics were predominant in the drawings? Which gender was more frequently portrayed? Was it male? Or was it female?[2]

The scientist is typically portrayed as an older man with unkempt hair who is immersed in a laboratory with test tubes, burners, and all kinds of scientific paraphernalia. This stereotypical image has been reinforced by the media who seek action shots of male scientists in their laboratories and by science textbooks that, until recently, have included far more pictures of male scientists than females (see Figure 17.7).

Armed with the male stereotype of the scientist and their own feelings that science is a "male thing," female teachers tend to involve boys more than girls in science activities. They ask more science questions of boys than girls. They look to the boys to help solve science-related problems. They ask the boys to take the lead in group science inquiries.

These behaviors have resulted in boys receiving a significantly better science education than girls, even in the same classroom (Baker, 1989, Becker, 1989).

You will recall that we have repeatedly asserted that science education must give equal opportunity for *all* children to learn science. This means girls

What are your beliefs about women in science?

FIGURE 17.7   A view of science

must have the same opportunity to learn science as boys. There are two important factors you must consider in this connection. The first is your own preconceived notion about the "maleness" of science. Teachers who believe science is more appropriate for boys than for girls convey that message in both overt and subtle ways. Examine your own thoughts carefully, and bring your bias, if any, to the surface. If you find you have a "maleness of science" bias, work toward constructing a bias-free attitude. Suggestions for undertaking this construction include the following:

- Read about women in science.
- Study the women Nobel Prize winners on the Nobel Prize Internet Archive on the Internet at http://nobelprizes.com/.

**TEACHING STRATEGIES TO AVOID GENDER BIAS
IN EARLY CHILDHOOD SCIENCE EDUCATION**

- Call on girls as often as boys.
- Ask girls as many questions as boys.
- Give girls the same amount of wait time as boys.
- Give the same kind of feedback to girls that you give to boys.
- Give nonverbal affirmations such as smiles and head nods to girls as often as to boys.
- Ask both girls and boys questions with the same degree of difficulty.
- Form single-gender groups.
- In mixed groups, be sure the girls are as active in actually doing science as the boys.
- In mixed groups, avoid having girls act as "secretary."
- Engage girls as much as boys in hands-on activities.
- Share the roles of women in science with the class.
- Refer to scientists as "he or she."

FIGURE 17.8   Teaching strategies to avoid gender bias in early childhood science education

- Contact the Association for Women in Science (AWIS) for materials on women in science. Write to AWIS, 1522 K Street, N.W., Suite 820, Washington, DC 20005.

- Increase your awareness of the roles women play in current scientific discoveries and inquiries.

The second factor to consider in providing girls the same opportunity as boys to learn science is teaching technique. Specific strategies are suggested in Figure 17.8.

CULTURAL DIFFERENCES

The United States is undergoing significant demographic changes. Statistics from the 1990 U.S. census show that in the decade 1980–1990, the population of African Americans in the United States increased by 13.2 percent, the population of Native Americans increased by 37.8 percent, the population of Hispanics increased by 53 percent, and the population of Asians increased by almost 108 percent (see Figure 17.9). Shirley Malcolm (1990) reports, "By the year 2010, one in every three 18-year-olds will be black or Hispanic, in comparison with one in five in 1985" (p. 112).

PERCENT OF POPULATION INCREASE OF MAJOR ETHNIC GROUPS IN THE UNITED STATES 1980–1990	
Ethnic Group	Percent Increase 1980–1990
White	6.0
Black	13.2
Native American	37.9
Hispanic	53.0
Asian	107.8

FIGURE 17.9 Demographic changes in the United States, 1980–1990 (compiled from *The World Almanac,* 1994)

Constructing Your Ideas 17.7
Local Demographic Changes

 Investigate how the population make-up in your local area is changing. Sources of this information would include the U.S. Census Bureau, the local chambers of commerce, public school records, libraries, court records, and others. Report back to the class.

The rapid change in demographics is causing the racial, ethnic, and cultural mix in today's schools to be substantially different from what it was even a few years ago. Ethnic and cultural factors exert powerful influences on the way children learn. It is clear that differing cultural backgrounds lead to differing prior experiences and that children from different cultures bring different perceptions and understandings to the classroom. In addition, it has been demonstrated that children from given cultural or ethnic backgrounds have developed culture-specific ways of learning that may not always be congruent with the teacher's way of teaching. Thus, it is useful to explore multiculturalism as it applies to science teaching and learning.

This book is about teaching in a constructivist approach, utilizing the process-oriented inquiry methodology to enable *all* children to learn science. As we have demonstrated, children differ from each other in numerous ways, including race, ethnicity, and culture. Thus, from a constructivist perspective, multiculturalism can be considered a special case of individual learning differences.

Perhaps the greatest factor in facilitating multicultural education is attitude. Successful multicultural teachers recognize, respect, and value cultures different from their own. The best way to develop a sense of valuing culture is to find your own biases. Examine your own racial, ethnic, and cultural beliefs. Honestly disclose to yourself any bias you uncover. Talk with others about the biases you find. You may even find it helpful to hold frank discussions with colleagues and others who are in cultural groups for which you have a bias. These discussions will lead to increased understanding on the part of both individuals. And increased understanding is a major step on the road to respecting and valuing cultures other than your own. It is absolutely essential that you uncover, recognize, and reconcile your cultural biases if you are to be an effective teacher. As Hilliard (1994) wrote, educators must give positive notice of the natural diversity that is present in every classroom and must avoid *not* noticing diversity as much as they avoid giving negative notice.

In a constructivist-oriented multicultural approach to teaching and learning, teachers employ a variety of teaching styles consistent with the learning styles of the children in the class. As was indicated earlier, children of different cultures have different ways of approaching learning. Representative learning needs associated with general cultural patterns of learning are shown in the following box. Though by no means exhaustive, these generalizations may enable you to gain basic sensitivity to the culture-based learning needs of the children in your classes.

Hispanic students tend to learn best when they have a personal relationship with the teacher and can interact with peers in small groups (Willis, 1993, p. 7; National Council for the Social Studies, 1992).

African American students respond best to collaborative, hands-on approaches (Willis, 1993, p. 7) that center around natural topics of life and prefer to use analogies to familiar phenomena to help make unfamiliar information more meaningful (Anderson, 1994, p. 99).

In Asian cultures, learning tends to be more "circular" than "linear" (Willis, 1993, p. 7). In "circular reasoning," many new ideas around a central topic lead to understanding of the central topic; this is in sharp contrast to the logico-syllogistic reasoning ("if-then" arguments and deductive analyses) inherent in European and American cultures. Asian children tend to defer to the intellectual authority of their parents and the teacher and hesitate to argue with these authorities even on an intellectual basis.

Native American children learn by observing and imitating the actions of their parents, elders, older siblings, and the teacher and are raised to be careful observers and thoughtful listeners. Native American children are better at processing visual information than verbal information and acquire new information best through observation. They work well in group settings but are reluctant to volunteer information or "recite" in front of the class, preferring to withdraw into "purposeful silence" (Deyhle & Swisher, 1997, p. 141).

General characteristics of effective multicultural teaching are essentially the same as general characteristics of constructivist inquiry teaching. They include the following:

- Encouraging children to share their experiences with each other

- Providing activities that meet the needs of individual children

- Ensuring the lessons and units are relevant to children's lives

- Utilizing hands-on activities

- Encouraging children to verbalize their reasoning processes

- Guiding children in how to ask questions

- Helping children make connections of new information with information they already possess

Many classes will include children who have recently arrived from foreign countries. Their English may be poor or even nonexistent, and their cultural assimilation of American ways may have not yet occurred. They often feel out of place. Experience has shown that applying the general principles of multicultural education helps these children find their place and learn at the same time. Particularly effective strategies for helping these students include the following:

- Provide a homework folder with clear directions.

- Assign a "buddy."

- Ask the child to write his or her name on the desk in the native language.

- Prepare bulletin boards with "Hello" and other common phrases written in the native languages of children in the classroom or school.

- Display flags of native countries represented.

- Mark native countries represented on world maps.

- Ask children to decorate their science folders or portfolios with drawings of their native country.

- Invite parents to class to discuss their native country.

- Highlight and discuss scientific contributions made by individuals who come from the child's native country or whose heritage is the child's native country or region.

Teachers must consider cultural and ethnic differences when planning instruction. Units and lessons must reflect the learning styles of all children in the classroom, including those from diverse ethnic and cultural groups. Topics selected for study can include those for which scientists from diverse cultures and countries have made significant contributions or discoveries. Cultural differences must be celebrated, not ignored or tolerated. Most importantly, we must "stop seeing cultural differences as developmental disturbances . . . Our thinking about the education of . . . minority children needs to begin not from an assumption of deficiency but from a recognition of cultural competence" (Bowman, 1994, p. 224).

MULTIPLE INTELLIGENCES

Research in intelligence has led investigators to the conclusion that "Intelligence is a multi-dimensional phenomenon that occurs at multiple levels of our brain/mind/body system. There are many ways by which we know, perceive, learn, and process information" (Lazear, 1992, p. 9). Howard Gardner's widely acclaimed theory of multiple intelligences suggests that individuals have eight or more basic intelligences. The traditionally accepted logical-mathematical and linguistic intelligences measured by IQ tests are but two of the wide array of talents available to people that they use to make sense out of new information. In any one person, one or more of these basic intelligences is stronger than the others (Gardner, 1983, 1995). Thus, in early childhood science education, good teachers encourage children to use their predominant intelligences to guide their constructions and reconstructions; they reject the notion that children learn predominantly through employing the logical, deductive, mathematical, and linguistic brain power traditionally referred to as intelligence. The eight intelligences are described as follows:

> *Spatial:* The ability to perceive spatial dimensions of the world accurately. Well developed in architects, artists, sculptors, cartographers, anatomists, and hunters.
> *Bodily-Kinesthetic:* The ability to use one's body or body parts such as hands and fingers to solve problems and express ideas. Well developed in athletes, dancers, and actors.
> *Musical:* The ability to think in music, hear music almost continuously, and remember musical patterns. Well developed in musical performers, people who play musical instruments or sing, and people who enjoy listening to music.
> *Linguistic:* The ability to use language effectively to express ideas to others. Well developed in writers, poets, storytellers, lawyers, editors, journalists, and (hopefully) college textbook authors.
> *Logical-Mathematical:* The ability to use mathematical operations and to reason logically. Well developed in mathematicians, accountants, statisticians, scientists, and computer programmers.
> *Interpersonal:* The ability to understand and interact sensitively with other people. Well developed in teachers, clergy, sales people, and politicians.
> *Intrapersonal:* The ability to understand oneself and act in accordance with this self-knowledge. Well developed in people who exhibit self-discipline and independence.
> *Naturalist:* The ability to exhibit sensitivity to one's natural surroundings. Well developed in botanists, zoologists, ecologists, explorers, and farmers.

Constructing Your Ideas 17.8
Your Strongest Intelligences

To get an idea of the strongest intelligences of the people in your class, pretend you are going to develop a unit on dinosaurs. Ask each student in the class to write down the first one or two activities that first come to mind; use an abbreviated, one- or two-sentence form. Share these with the class.

Because teachers tend to plan their lessons in ways that are comfortable to the teacher, your first response to being asked to suggest activities may be a good indicator of your own stronger intelligences. Students with a strong *linguistic* intelligence may have listed a book or two they would like to read to the children. Students with a strong *spatial* intelligence may have suggested an activity in which children put together dinosaur skeleton models from pre-cut parts. Students with a strong *logical-mathematical* intelligence may have suggested an activity in which children dig up small dinosaur models previously buried in sand and match each model with its line drawing on a hand-out. Students with a strong *musical* intelligence may have listed a song about dinosaurs, such as "My Name Is Stegosaurus."

Students with a strong *interpersonal* intelligence may have suggested group work to research and construct "My Dinosaur" books. Students with a strong *bodily-kinesthetic* intelligence may have suggested that children dance a dinosaur dance. Students with a strong *intrapersonal* intelligence may have suggested assigning each child to research a different dinosaur and present the results to the class. Students with a strong *naturalistic* intelligence may have suggested that children go on a pretend dinosaur hunt outdoors (see Figure 17.10).

FIGURE 17.10 Studying dinosaurs

You will observe that each activity just portrayed contains elements of several intelligences but that the intelligence identified seems to be the strongest.

The idea behind the theory of multiple intelligences is for teachers to be aware that there are many paths available to children as they construct and reconstruct their conceptualizations. With this knowledge, teachers can provide a variety of activities in their efforts to respond to the needs of all children. It is neither necessary nor desirable to provide eight different ways to explore every topic. Nor is it necessary or desirable to ensure that every child develop every intelligence. Rather, the teacher's goal is to develop a repertoire of learning activities and approaches that capitalize upon the eight intelligences in order to help children "use their combination of intelligences to be successful in school" (Checkley, 1997, p. 10).[3]

Strategies for teaching science in each of the eight intelligences are suggested in Figure 17.11.[4]

STRATEGIES FOR FOSTERING SCIENTIFIC INQUIRY UTILIZING THE EIGHT INTELLIGENCES

SPATIAL	Make models Draw pictures
BODILY-KINESTHETIC	Dance Pantomime Play-act such concepts as movement of heavenly bodies and movement of clock hands
MUSICAL	Sing songs Learn tunes Play classical music in background ("Mozart Effect") Invent and sing songs about scientific concepts
LINGUISTIC	Read Write Send e-mail Describe to others what you did in an investigation
LOGICAL-MATHEMATICAL	Search the World Wide Web Draw and interpret graphs Express conclusions in mathematical formats
INTERPERSONAL	Lead discussions Participate in discussions Ask clarifying questions Work on scientific investigations in teams
INTRAPERSONAL	Organize games Direct play activities Function well in cooperative groups Keep a science journal
NATURALISTIC	Classify according to natural surroundings Find origins

FIGURE 17.11   Strategies for fostering scientific inquiry utilizing the eight intelligences

SCIENCE EDUCATION FOR CHILDREN WITH DISABILITIES

The Individuals with Disabilities Education Act (IDEA) was signed into law in 1990 and was renewed in 1997. The Act mandates that all children with disabilities are to be provided a free and appropriate education in the least restrictive environment. This means that children with disabilities are entitled to be educated in general classrooms to the extent possible, given the child's handicapping condition.

The process-oriented inquiry approach to science education encourages the qualities that have been identified as necessary for teaching children with disabilities. These qualities include (a) providing concrete, hands-on learning experiences, (b) reducing the emphasis on reading and writing as the primary mode of learning, (c) encouraging high levels of group interaction and group participation, (d) providing for individual differences, (e) encouraging inquisitiveness, (f) encouraging children to investigate phenomena of interest to them (Caseau & Norman, 1997).

Dalton, Morocco, & Tivnan (1997) suggest utilizing a Supported Inquiry Science (SIS) approach when teaching children with disabilities. The SIS technique includes (a) providing a safe environment for expressing new, different, or innovative thoughts, (b) designing units around unifying topics, (c) eliciting children's prior conceptions and encouraging them to construct new conceptualizations in light of new experiences, (d) using whole-class instruction and discussion to help children develop their constructions, (e) using individual, small-group, and whole-class instructional formats, (f) using multiple modalities, and (g) embedding assessment within the instruction.

Does this sound familiar? It should. The research on teaching science to children with disabilities suggests using techniques that are embodied within the constructivist, process-oriented inquiry methodology that is the subject of this book. From the constructivist viewpoint, teaching children with disabilities is not seen as a special problem requiring a special methodology. Rather, teaching children with disabilities is seen as a special case of teaching *all* children.

SUMMARY

One of the primary goals of education is to provide equitable opportunities for *all* children to learn. There are endless individual differences that influence the way children learn science. One of these differences is modality. Children exhibit strength in the visual, the auditory, or the kinesthetic learning modality, and teachers plan different activities that favor each modality. Because young children tend to be kinesthetic, hands-on science experiences allow them to utilize this learning style in their investigations while concurrently helping them strengthen their other modalities. Another learner difference that affects science learning is locus of control. Children with an internal locus of control are more successful in devising and executing personally constructed science investigations than children with an external locus of control, so teachers work with children with an external locus of control to help them strengthen the internal component of this learning style. Field dependence/field independence is another learner difference that affects science learning. Field independent children are more successful in science activities than field dependent children, so teachers work to move field dependent children toward a more field independent mode.

Gender bias is a factor in teaching and learning science, and the teacher ensures that both boys and girls have equal opportunities to demonstrate success in science. Cultural differences inherent among children of different backgrounds strongly affect their prior experiences and the ways they learn. Teachers recognize the learning competence of all cultures and tailor their teaching to accommodate cultural diversity. The theory of multiple intelligences suggests that children have at least eight different intelligences, the strengths of which vary from child to child. Science teachers recognize these differences and provide separate learning experiences to favor each intelligence. The learning needs of children with disabilities are accommodated best through the instruction inherent in the process-oriented, inquiry-based, constructivist methodology.

No teacher can possibly know every individual difference that characterizes each individual child. It is hoped that the learning characteristic descriptions and strategies for fostering positive achievement in science suggested in this chapter will aid teachers in providing for the unique needs of all individuals in their classrooms and in personalizing the teaching.[5]

Notes

1. Dunn, Dunn, & Price (1975, 1977, 1981, 1988, 1989) have developed and validated a *Learning Style Inventory (LSI)*. This inventory can be used with children grades three and above. If you want to find out more about your own personal learning modalities and learning styles, you may want to take and interpret the *LSI*.
2. Many "draw a scientist" studies involving both children and adults have been conducted over the years. For details on the nature of the studies and their results, visit the "draw a scientist" websites that can be accessed from http://www.storyline.com/sl/tsdraw2e.html.
3. The entire September 1997 issue of *Educational Leadership* is devoted to an exploration of many aspects of Gardner's Theory of Multiple Intelligences.
4. For a more complete discussion on ways of using the theory of multiple intelligences in the classroom, see Lazear (1992). Refer especially to the "Multiple Intelligences Lesson Idea Matrix" on pp. 28–29.
5. The entire September 1999 (Volume 57, No. 1) issue of *Educational Leadership* is devoted to the topic of "personalized learning."

References

Anderson, J. A. (1994). Examining teaching styles and student learning styles in science and math classrooms. In M. M. Atwater, K. Radzik-Marsh, & M. Strutchens (Eds.). *Multicultural education: Inclusion of all.* The University of Georgia, Department of Science Education, 212 Aderhold Hall, Athens, GA 30602-7126. P. 99.

Baker, D. (1989). Teaching for gender differences. *Research Matters . . . to the science teacher.* In *The Georgia Science Teacher, 29*(7), 7–8, 141–169.

Becker, B. J. (1989). Gender and science achievement: A reanalysis of studies from two meta-analyses. *Journal of Research in Science Teaching, 26*(2), 141–169.

Bertini, M., Pizzamiglio, L., & Wapner, S. (Eds.). (1986). *Field dependence in, psychological theory, research, and application.* Hillsdale, NJ: Lawrence Erlbaum Associates.

Bowman, B. T. (1994). The challenge of diversity. *Phi Delta Kappan 76*(3), 218–224.

Brookover, W., Beady, C., Flood, P., Schweister, J., & Wisenbaker, J. (1979). *School social systems and student achievement.* New York: Praeger. Cited in Slavin, 1994. *Educational psychology: Theory and practice.* Boston: Allyn and Bacon.

Caseau, D., & Norman, K. (1997). Special education teachers use science-technology-society (STS) themes to teach science to students with learning disabilities. *Journal of Science Teacher Education, 8*(1) 55–68.

Checkley, K. (1997). The first seven . . . and the eighth: A conversation with Howard Gardner. *Educational Leadership, 55*(1), 8–13.

Collings, J. (1985). Scientific thinking through the development of formal operations: Training in the cognitive restructuring aspect of field-independence. *Research in Science & Technological Education, 3*(2), 148–152.

Dalton, B., Morocco, C. C., & Tivnan, T. (1997). Supported inquiry science: Teaching for conceptual change in urban and suburban classrooms. *Journal of Learning Disabilities, 30*(6), 670–684.

Deyhle, D., & Swisher, K. (1997). Research in American Indian and Alaska Native Education: From assimilation to self-determination. In M. W. Apple (Ed.). *Review of Research in Education 22.* American Educational Research Association, 1230 Seventeenth Street, Washington, DC 20036-3078.

Dunn, R. (1988). Teaching students through their perceptual strengths or preferences. *Journal of Reading, 31*(4) 304–308.

Dunn, R. (1990). Rita Dunn answers questions on learning styles. *Educational Leadership, 48*(2), 15–19

Dunn, R., Dunn, K., & Price, G. E. (1975, 1979, 1981, 1985, 1989). *Learning style inventory.* Lawrence, KS: Price Systems.

Gardner, H. (1983). *Frames of mind: The theory of multiple intelligences.* New York: Bantam Books.

Gardner, H. (1995). Reflections on multiple intelligences: Myths and messages. *Phi Delta Kappan, 77*(3), 202–203, 206–209.

Gibbons, G. (1995). *Bicycle book.* New York: Holiday House.

Hilliard, A. G. (1994). Foreword to E.W. King, M. Chipman, and M. Cruz-Janzen. *Educating young children in a diverse society.* Boston: Allyn and Bacon.

Kuerbis, P. (n.d.). Learning styles and science teaching. *Research matters . . . to the science teacher.* National Association for Research in Science Teaching.

Lawson, A. L. (1985). A review of research on formal reasoning and science teaching. *Journal of Research in Science Teaching, 19*(3), 233–248.

Lazear, D. G. (1992). *Teaching for multiple intelligences.* Bloomington, IN: Phi Delta Kappa Educational Foundation. (*Fastback* No. 342).

Malcolm, S. (1990). Who will do science in the next century? *Scientific American,* February, 1990.

Martin, D. J. (2000). *Elementary science methods: A constructivist approach* (2nd ed.). Belmont, CA: Wadsworth/Thompson Learning.

de Montaigne, M. E. (1907). *Essays.* New York: G. P. Putnam's Sons. (Original work published *c.* 1580–1588).

National Council for the Social Studies (NCSS) Task Force on Ethnic Studies Curriculum. (1992). Curriculum guidelines for multicultural education. *Social Education,* September, 1992, 274–292.

National Research Council. (1996). *National science education standards.* Washington, DC: National Academy Press.

Rowe, M. B. (1978). *Teaching science as continuous inquiry: A basic* (2nd ed.). New York: McGraw-Hill Book Company.

Seuss, Dr. [pseud. For Geissel, T. S.] (1993). *One fish two fish red fish blue fish.* New York: Random House.

Slavin, R. E. (1994). *Educational psychology: Theory and practice.* Boston: Allyn and Bacon.

Taylor, B. (1990). *Bouncing and bending light.* New York: Watts.

Tomlinson, L. M. (1987). Locus of control and its effect on achievement. ERIC Document Number ED 276 965.

Walter, M. P. (1980). *Ty's one-man band.* New York: Scholastic.

Willis, S. (1993). Multicultural teaching: Meeting the challenges that arise in practice. *ASCD Curriculum Update,* September, 1993. Association for Supervision and Curriculum Development, 1250 N. Pitt Street, Alexandra, VA 22314-1453, pp. 1–8.

CHAPTER 18

Assessment

In this text we have emphasized that it is better for children to learn how to do science than it is for them to learn about science. We have suggested that the most effective way for children to learn how to do science is through the process-oriented inquiry methodology.

We also have suggested that it is better for children to construct their own understandings than to repeat the teacher's understandings. We have proposed that the validity of child-constructed conceptualizations can be ascertained by the explanatory and predictive power of their conceptualizations. We have indicated that, through the constructive approach, different children are very likely to construct different conceptualizations which, given the limited range of children's experiences and the limitations to their inquiries imposed by age, availability of time, and availability of resources, may all be equally valid.

It ain't over till it's over.
Yogi Berra, *The Yogi Book: "I Really Didn't Say Everything I Said"* (New York: Workman Publishing, 1998), 121

And half the fun of nearly everything, you know, is thinking about it beforehand, or afterward.
Howard R. Garis, *Uncle Wiggily's Storybook* (New York: Putnam Publishing Group, 1972), (Original work published in 1921)

It must seem to the perceptive student that assessing science achievement in this milieu may be somewhat akin to shooting at the proverbial moving target or perhaps even like trying to capture a cloud. Assessment in constructivist settings need not be mercurial. In this chapter you will consider ways in which process-oriented inquiry teachers can construct authentic assessments of the accomplishments of children in their classes.

Constructing Your Ideas 18.1
Assessment Ideas

To set the stage for our investigations into assessment, take a few minutes in small groups and discuss what you think you should assess in your early childhood science education programs. For each, list one or more ways of assessing that item. List the group's collective ideas, and then share all the groups' ideas with the whole class. Extract from the various group lists the assessment notions that were common to all or most of the groups.

In this activity, you undoubtedly had to ask yourselves some difficult questions, for assessment not only provides an indication of the achievement of individual children, but often also provides an indication of the achievement of your entire class, and, by extension, of your teaching. Assessment is the primary interface between what your children do in your class on a day-to-day basis and their parents, the school community, and the public.

WHAT IS ASSESSED IN EARLY CHILDHOOD SCIENCE EDUCATION?

It is an educational axiom that children should be assessed on what they are expected to have achieved. If you have come to believe that it is better to teach children how to do science than it is to teach them about science, then you will want to assess their progress in doing science. This means you will want to assess their facility in the processes of science and their facility in inquiry. Furthermore, because a major goal of science education is for children to understand how science contributes to society and culture (National Research Council, 1996, p. 2), you also will want to assess your children's attitudes toward science.

What about content? The National Science Education Standards indicate that "An essential part of scientific literacy is greater knowledge and understanding of science subject matter" (ibid.). Because your process-oriented inquiry lessons focus on children's explorations of specific science topics, you may also want to assess their understandings of the content.

Finally, you doubtless will want to assess your own teaching and the effectiveness of your early childhood science education program.

The *National Science Education Standards* (National Research Council, 1996) includes five standards dealing with assessment. These standards urge that the assessments be consistent with the science teaching and program, be fair, provide opportunity for *all* children to demonstrate achievement in science, and be interpreted carefully and soundly (see inside front and back covers for the full listing of the *National Science Education Standards*).

ASSESSING PROCESS SKILLS

A primary goal of early childhood science education is for children to become increasingly proficient in their use of the scientific process skills. For each process skill, a set of indicators can be developed to show children's proficiency in that skill. Process proficiency indicators are suggested in Figure 18.1. Note that these indicators are provided only as a guide. You will need to construct your own indicators that take into consideration the specific process goals you have established for your class of children and their unique characteristics.

SOME INDICATORS OF PROFICIENCY IN THE SCIENTIFIC PROCESSES

Observing	Identifies objects
	Utilizes more than one sense
	Utilizes all appropriate senses
	Describes properties accurately
	Provides qualitative observations
	Provides quantitative observations
	Describes changes in objects
	Describes differences in similar objects
Classifying	Identifies major properties on which objects can be sorted
	Identifies properties common to all objects in a collection
	Sorts accurately into two groups
	Sorts accurately in multiple ways
	Forms subgroups
	Establishes own sorting criteria
	Provides sound rationale for classifications
Communicating	Describes objects accurately
	Provides descriptions such that others can identify unknown objects
	Transmits information to others accurately in oral and written formats
	Verbalizes thinking
	Describes events accurately and completely
	Provides sound rationale for conclusions
	Describes own ideas in a rational and understandable way

FIGURE 18.1 Some indicators of proficiency in the scientific processes
(Adapted from Martin, 2000)

(continued)

Measuring	Selects appropriate type of measurement (length, volume, weight, time)
	Selects appropriate unit of measurement
	Uses measurement instruments properly
	Applies measurement techniques appropriately
	Uses standard and non-standard units appropriately
	Seeks to quantify differences among objects through appropriate measurements
Predicting	Forms patterns of similar events
	Extends patterns of similar events
	Predicts prior to investigation
	Performs simple predictions
	Applies the process of prediction in appropriate situations
	Exhibits rational reasoning for predictions
	Suggests tests to check for accuracy of predictions
Inferring	Utilizes all information in making inferences
	Avoids inventing information to support inferences
	Describes relationships among objects and events observed
	Separates appropriate from non-appropriate information
	Exhibits sound reasoning in explaining inferences
	Applies the process of inferring in appropriate situations
	Interprets graphs and charts correctly
Identifying and Controlling Variables	Identifies factors that might affect the outcome of an investigation
	Identifies variables that can be manipulated
	Identifies variables that cannot be manipulated easily
	Describes procedures for keeping non-manipulated variables constant
Formulating Hypotheses	Constructs a hypothesis when given a problem or question
	Formulates own hypothesis from own problem
	Verbalizes sound reasoning when explaining hypotheses
Defining Operationally	Tells whether a variable can be measured conveniently
	Recognizes the need for operational definitions
	Decides how to measure variables in operational terms
	Expresses logical connection between the variable to be measured and the operational definition
Interpreting Data	Identifies data needed
	Identifies ways of measuring needed data
	Collects usable data
	Utilizes data tables
	Constructs own data tables
	Constructs and interprets graphs
	Makes valid interpretations of data
Experimenting	Follows directions for an experiment
	Develops alternative ways to investigate questions
	Manipulates science materials appropriately
	Performs trial-and-error investigations
	Identifies own experimental procedure
	Formulates valid conclusions
Constructing Models	Differentiates between a model and the real thing
	Identifies appropriate needs for models
	Interprets models in terms of the real thing
	Develops appropriate models

FIGURE 18.1 *(continued)*

There are several ways of assessing children's proficiency in the process skills. The first is observing. When you circulate among the groups, you watch children doing the activities, you interact with them, and you suggest ways they can strengthen or improve their skills. This is the kind of assessment that is built into the teaching. It is the kind of assessment music teachers and coaches use when working with individual students or teams. It is the kind of assessment that is designed to foster increased achievement rather than measure after-the-fact retention. Make some notes during or after the activity concerning how well each child progressed toward skill mastery; these notes become part of the child's class science records.

If you want a more formal process skill observational assessment, prepare a list of specific indicators you feel would show children's progress. You could use the indicators in Figure 18.1 to help you get started. Prepare a copy of the list for each child, and check off indicators that they exhibit as you circulate around the room. A somewhat structured approach to assessing process skills using indicators is illustrated in Constructing Science in the Classroom 18.1.

Constructing Science in the Classroom 18.1
Sinking and Floating Fruits

AGE

8
7
6
5
4
3

AN ACTIVITY TO SHOW PROCESS ASSESSMENT

Objective
The student will predict whether given fruits will sink or float in a pan of water.

Materials

Six to eight different kinds of fruits (orange, grapefruit, apple, banana, grape, strawberry, and other fruits in season)
Pan filled with water

The teacher provides a variety of fruits, a pan of water, and a chart with two columns labeled "SINK" and "FLOAT" on which each fruit is pictured. Ask the children first to select a fruit and predict whether it will float or sink. Then ask them to test their predictions by placing the fruit in the water; then they place the fruit in the proper column of the chart.

Indicators of proficiency in predicting selected for this activity:

a. _____ Makes a prediction before trying it out
b. _____ Records prediction on chart
c. _____ Offers reasons for predictions based on a pattern (e.g., "Large fruits will sink and small fruits will float.")
d. _____ Reconciles actual happening with prediction
e. _____ Records actual happening on chart
f. _____ Changes predictions based on test results of previous predictions
g. _____ Seeks clarification on the meaning of "sink" for fruits that come to rest in the middle of the water

Finally, you may wish to have periodic formal task-oriented assessments of children's proficiency in the process skills. On the appointed day, set up several "stations," each of which requires the students to perform a process activity that will indicate proficiency. Children rotate from station to station and do the activity while you record their performance on a checklist specifically prepared for this hands-on assessment. You may use the list to check off that each child either did or did not accomplish the task. Or you may wish to assign "quality" ratings, say from 1 to 4 to indicate level or proficiency, with a "1" indicating "not observed," a "2" indicating minimum proficiency, a "3" indicating satisfactory proficiency, and a "4" indicating greatest proficiency. Figures 18.2, 18.3, and 18.4 show examples of the hands-on station method of assessing children's performance in process skills.

**SAMPLE PRACTICAL PROCESS SKILLS ASSESSMENT
FOR EARLY CHILDHOOD SCIENCE EDUCATION PROGRAMS**

Station 1: Two different vegetables
  Activity: Describe the characteristics of each vegetable. Tell what senses you used.
  Process skill assessed: Observing

Station 2: A collection of 5–10 different kinds of seeds
  Activity: Sort the seeds into two groups and name each group.
  Process skill assessed: Classifying

Station 3: An object in a paper bag
  Activity: Describe the object to a partner such that the partner can identify it correctly.
  Process skill assessed: Communicating

Station 4: A wooden block and some pennies
  Activity: Find how many pennies long the block is.
  Process skill assessed: Measuring

Station 5: A tub of water with several objects beside it
  Activity: Predict whether each object will sink or float.
  Process skill assessed: Predicting

**Station 6: Three opaque canisters with different things in them and a tray with
the same things and one or two additional things next to the canisters**
  Activity: Tell what's in the canisters by shaking them.
  Process skill assessed: Inferring

Station 7: Three different rocks
  Activity: Describe each rock's characteristics. Tell how the rocks are alike and how they are different.
  Process skill assessed: Observing

Station 8: Collection of 10–12 shells
  Activity: Sort the shells into groups and name each group.
  Process skill assessed: Classifying

Station 9: Two wooden blocks and a simple two-pan balance
  Activity: Tell which is heavier and how you know.
  Process skill assessed: Measuring

Station 10: Picture of an outdoor scene with long shadows
  Activity: Tell where the sun is.
  Process skill assessed: Inferring

FIGURE 18.2 Sample practical process skills assessment for early childhood science education programs

A station where children demonstrate proficiency in the skill of observation

**SCORING SYSTEM FOR PRACTICAL PROCESS SKILLS ASSESSMENT
FOR EARLY CHILDHOOD SCIENCE EDUCATION PROGRAMS**

Score	Criterion
1	Not seen
2	Performed at minimum levels
3	Performed well
4	Performed in an outstanding and advanced manner

Station	Process Skill	Score
1	Observing	_____
2	Classifying	_____
3	Communicating	_____
4	Measuring	_____
5	Predicting	_____
6	Inferring	_____
7	Observing	_____
8	Classifying	_____
9	Measuring	_____
10	Inferring	_____
	TOTAL	_____

Divide by maximum total of 40 = PERCENTAGE   _____

FIGURE 18.3 Scoring system for practical process skills assessment for early childhood science education programs

SAMPLE SCORING FOR A CHILD DOING THE PRACTICAL PROCESS SKILLS ASSESSMENT SHOWN IN FIGURES 18.2 AND 18.3

Station	Process	Score	Reason for score
1	Observing	2	Child did not use sense of smell.
2	Classifying	4	Child formed two mutually exclusive groups.
3	Communicating	1	Child was able only to identify object—not describe it.
4	Measuring	3	Child measured whole units; did not round increments to nearest whole.
5	Predicting	4	Child made accurate predictions and tested each.
6	Inferring	2	Child used limited investigation.
7	Observing	3	Child described properties; did not tell similarities and differences.
8	Classifying	3	Child formed only two groups, but they were mutually exclusive.
9	Measuring	4	Child operated balance properly.
10	Inferring	2	Child said "sun is in the sky"; did not give location.
	Total Score	28	
	Percentage	$28 \div 40 = 70\%$	

FIGURE 18.4 Sample scoring for a child doing the practical process skills assessment shown in Figures 18.2 and 18.3

ASSESSING INQUIRY

In process-oriented inquiry, children use the processes to inquire into scientific phenomena. In doing this, they bring prior conceptions to the surface in response to new experiences. They construct and reconstruct new conceptualizations in such a way that the new conceptualization resolves the internal cognitive dissonance and is shown to be valid at the time of construction through its power to explain the phenomenon and accurately predict related occurrences that have not yet been tried.

To assess children's facility with inquiry, let us return to Chapter 16. Figure 16.3 shows descriptors of teacher performance in inquiry teaching. Using these indicators, we can construct an Inquiry Assessment Activity checklist similar to those we constructed for assessment of the scientific processes. Such a checklist is shown in Figure 18.5. As with the process skills indicators, this is provided only as a guide. You will need to construct your own sets of indicators that are tailored to meet your objectives and those of the children in your classes.

The list of inquiry indicators can be used in informal and formal ways. The most informal use involves casual observation. A somewhat structured approach to assessing inquiry using indicators is illustrated in Constructing Science in the Classroom 18.2.

**SOME INDICATORS OF PROFICIENCY IN INQUIRY
FOR EARLY CHILDHOOD SCIENCE EDUCATION**

- Selects and applies processes appropriately
- Asks appropriate questions about phenomena under investigation
- Initiates own ideas for investigation
- Investigates own questions and ideas
- Utilizes a variety of information resources, including printed material, multimedia, and people
- Relates investigations to prior experiences
- Suggests causes for what is observed
- Explains thought process in a rational and understandable way
- Seeks input of others about own ideas and conceptualizations
- Discusses and critiques the conceptualizations of others
- Reformulates conceptualizations in light of new evidence, new experiences, and input from others
- Subjects conclusions to tests of explanatory power and predictive power
- Seeks opportunities to continue explorations
- Exhibits realistic self-appraisal
- Relates learning to out-of-school situations

FIGURE 18.5   Some indicators of proficiency in inquiry for early childhood science education

Constructing Science in the Classroom 18.2
Investigating the Reaction of Vinegar with Materials

AGE

AN ACTIVITY TO SHOW INQUIRY ASSESSMENT

Objective

The student will predict whether vinegar will react with given materials.

Materials:

Vinegar
Eyedroppers
Plastic plates
Limestone, sandstone, marble rock chips, chalk, baking soda, baking powder, salt, flour, sugar, and other materials that do or do not react with vinegar

Safety precautions: No tasting of the materials, including the vinegar; wear goggles.

First, put on your safety goggles and demonstrate the activity for the class. Put a mound of baking soda on a plastic plate in front of the class. Add 2–3 tablespoons of vinegar. Ask children to watch it fizz as the vinegar reacts with the baking soda. The reaction will continue until either the vinegar or the baking soda is used up. (Teacher information: The reaction produces the gas carbon dioxide [CO_2]. As this gas escapes from the mixture, it causes the fizzing.)

Now ask children to don their goggles. Ask them to place a small amount of the first substance on the plastic plate, and predict whether it will fizz. Ask them to provide reasons for their predictions. Then they fill the eyedropper with vinegar and drop two to three drops of vinegar on the material to test their predictions.

(continued)

Inquiry questions might include the following:

• What can you conclude about the kinds of materials vinegar reacts with?
• What minerals or rocks can be identified using vinegar?
• How else are chemical reactions applied in our daily lives?
• Could you invent a toy that uses the principles you explored in this activity?

Literature Connection:

The Magic School Bus Gets Baked in a Cake: A Book about Kitchen Chemistry based on an episode from the animated TV series (Cole, 1995) portrays children exploring the chemistry involved in baking, especially the production of gas from baking soda mixed with vinegar.

Indicators of Proficiency in Inquiry

Score	Criterion
1	Not seen
2	Performed at minimum levels
3	Performed well
4	Performed in an outstanding and advanced manner

Criterion	Score
a. Makes accurate observations of the interaction between vinegar and other materials	_____
b. Asks questions about what is happening when the mixture fizzes	_____
c. Asks questions about what is different when the mixture does not fizz	_____
d. Asks to try materials not supplied	_____
e. Suggests using water or other liquids to see what happens	_____
f. Shares previous experiences with chemical reactions	_____
g. Formulates tentative generalizations about what reacts and what does not react with vinegar	_____

Total   _____
Maximum Score = 28
Divide earned score by 28 to obtain percentage

ASSESSING ATTITUDE

Attitude is a person's dispositions or feelings toward something. It is formed from an accumulation of feelings about similar experiences. If the experiences are largely pleasant, exciting, successful, and rewarding, the individual can be expected to develop a positive attitude. If the experiences are unpleasant, dull, boring, unsuccessful, and pointless, the individual can be expected to develop a negative attitude.

Because science permeates virtually all aspects of modern society and technology, it is important for children to develop positive attitudes toward science and toward doing science. Children reveal their attitudes toward science in many indirect ways. For example, children with positive attitudes toward sci-

---

SOME INDICATORS OF A POSITIVE ATTITUDE TOWARD SCIENCE
- Uses extra time for science investigations
- Indicates that science is fun, exciting, and interesting
- Verbalizes curiosity
- Extends in-school science activities outside school
- Voluntarily participates in out-of-school science activities
- Visits museums, botanical gardens, and other public attractions with a science orientation
- Seeks additional work in science
- Takes an active role in maintaining the class science center and live plants and animals in the classroom
- Chooses science-related television programs to watch
- Plays science-related board games and/or computer games
- Reads science-related books and other print material
- Participates in science-related activities at home

FIGURE 18.6   Some indicators of a positive attitude toward science

ence may ask questions related to their out-of-school science-related experiences. They may ask to do science more often than has been planned. They may ask their parents to take them to science-related activities. They may talk about watching science-related television shows or playing science-related games. They may bring to school science-related projects or share science-related experiences they have had at home. All these are indicators of positive attitudes toward science.

Determining attitude is, at best, a subjective activity. But a list of indicators can be prepared that show positive attitudes toward science. Such a list is suggested in Figure 18.6. You may wish to prepare such a basic list for each child in your class. The list should reflect the situation of the school and community and should include blanks at the bottom for indicators the children exhibit that are not on the prepared list. For each indicator, put a check mark (or a date) next to it each time the child exhibits the behavior. In this way, you will gain an idea of attitude and changing attitude toward science.

ASSESSING CONTENT

In the process-oriented inquiry approach to science education, the teacher selects topics from the world of science for children to investigate. As the children inquire, they construct and reconstruct their conceptualizations about the topics.

The goal of science education is for children to learn how to do science rather than to learn about science. Nonetheless, there is a public sentiment favoring the acquisition of science content by children. Because educators are accountable to the public, you will probably be requested to assess children's achievement in science content. This assessment can be done through verbal questioning or through paper-and-pencil tests. Content assessment items are often provided by textbook publishers and can be used in your classes. These assessments can be used to show that children have acquired understandings of the science topics studied and can be used to highlight concepts that children need to investigate more thoroughly.

To satisfy public demands, schools, school districts, and even states often require that certain content be "covered" in certain grades. If this is the case, you can use the content required by the district as the basis for the process and inquiry activities, thus enabling children to learn both process and the required content. For example, if the district requires that kindergarten children learn about magnets, you can use magnets and magnetism as the vehicle by which children observe, classify, communicate, measure, predict, and infer. You can develop inquiry activities that use magnets and magnetism. However, bear in mind that in inquiry it is desirable to let children explore in directions their own thinking takes them. To restrict the content used for process and inquiry vehicles is to limit their explorations.

School districts often require that children take specific standardized achievement tests to assess achievement, highlight areas of strength, and diagnose specific weaknesses. The science sections of the standardized tests are primarily content in nature (although recent efforts have focused on ways to include process and inquiry items) and normally do not assess the processes and inquiry skills or the specific items of content that have been explored in a particular classroom. But they are here to stay. As Haladyna, Hass, & Allison (1998) remind us, we must recognize that "The public continues to support [standardized] testing because it perceives that test scores are valid indicators of children's learning" (p. 264).

To help children do their best on standardized achievement tests, it is suggested that you devote a small amount of time reviewing, reinforcing, and presenting areas of content that are prescribed for the tests. Assist children in developing their test-taking skills such as how to bubble in chosen responses, how to eliminate unlikely responses in multiple-choice questions, how to use other test items to help in answering more difficult items, and how to manage time. Have children take one or two practice tests in the same format as the standardized test to identify test-taking difficulties that need attention. Helping children develop sound test-taking skills helps ensure that test results reflect competence in subject matter and not lack of test-taking skills.

One of the basic premises of the process-oriented inquiry approach to early childhood science is that children will learn the content that is the focus of their inquiries and will retain it longer than through other methodologies because children are constructing their own meanings. If you believe this, then student acquisition of content should pose no particular concern. Assessment of content achievement should be considered simply another aspect of the total assessment program rather than its focus; the focus is on processes and inquiry and how well children are learning how to *do* science.

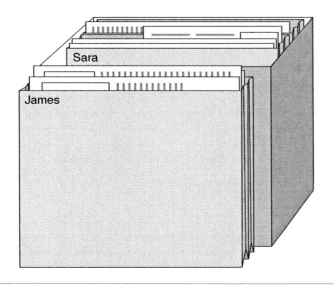

FIGURE 18.7 An early childhood education science portfolio

THE EARLY CHILDHOOD EDUCATION SCIENCE PORTFOLIO

Having considered methods of assessing children's achievement in process skills, inquiry, and content, and their attitudes regarding science, it is prudent to investigate ways of putting all this information together.

The portfolio has emerged as the primary method of authentic assessment (Collins, 1992; Hart, 1994). Simply put, the early childhood education science portfolio is a personalized collection of artifacts that shows each child's development in science. Through the portfolio, a picture of the whole child is shown, including skill with the processes of science, facility in inquiry, and achievement in content, as well as attitudes, interests, ideas, learning styles, cognitive development, and a host of other factors.[1]

Evidence of achievement appropriate for the early childhood education science portfolio may include the following:

- Teacher assessments of process skills—qualitative and quantitative

- Teacher assessments of inquiry—qualitative and quantitative

- Assessments of content achievement

- Samples of child's work in science investigations such as

  - Observations made

  - Classification systems devised

  - Descriptions of investigations

- Completed data tables

- Graphs and charts prepared

- Samples of completed class work

- Evidence of out-of-class science activities

- Evidence of the child's recognition and application of science in daily life

- Anecdotal records

- Records of individual discussions held with children

- Photographs of children at work

- Science journals

You will want to formulate your own list tailored to the school situation and the children in your class. It is a good idea to solicit the input of parents because the portfolios ultimately are shared with them. Parents can help in deciding what is most helpful and meaningful to them as they help their children. This practice also has the advantage that the parents know what to look for and praise when the portfolio comes home.

What does a portfolio look like? The product should be carefully planned. What you do not want is a huge folder filled with a potpourri of children's work that you have to sift through and try to make sense out of when the term ends. Experienced portfolio users suggest having a "working" portfolio and a "permanent" portfolio (Lambdin & Walker, 1994, p. 319). The working portfolio is an easily accessible accordion-style folder into which you drop items you may want eventually to include in the permanent portfolio. Much of this material will be discarded or taken home as the term progresses.

The permanent portfolio is also an accordion-style folder but of a different color and is kept in a secure place. It includes items from the working portfolio that prove to be most representative of the child's progress and achievement. This is the portfolio that is used for preparing end-of-term reports and is made available for parents to inspect during open-house or parent conferences.

The portfolio system of assessment provides the opportunity for information to be presented that best shows each child's abilities, understandings, achievement, and progress.

REPORTING TO PARENTS

The most authentic reporting system is the narrative and/or parent conference. The information in the portfolios provides everything needed for reporting progress while also providing real examples, documents, and data to illustrate and substantiate the written report and parent conference. In preparing for the conference, single out one or two specific positive comments for the parent to "take home." Try not to overload the parents with information;

they won't remember what you say if you say too much. Instead, focus on the one or two accomplishments you want the parent to remember. Parent conferences also present ideal opportunities for you to suggest activities the parents can do at home with their children to strengthen, reinforce, and extend the science experiences you provide in school.

Whereas many school districts are getting away from report cards for children at the early childhood grade levels, many districts still require that report card marks be given periodically as a measure of children's progress. Thus, the question arises as to how to translate the assessment data you have collected in the portfolio into marks.

The school's marking system may be broad (such as E for "excellent," S for "satisfactory," and N for "needs improvement"). In this case, qualitative assessments will enable you to determine term marks that are fair and that accurately represent each child's progress and achievement.

However, the school's marking system may be quantitative in nature (A, B, C, D, and F, or percentages). In this case, you will need to calculate marks. The first task is to establish the factors that go into the mark and the percentage or weight of each factor. *All* factors that go into determination of the mark for science should deal with science achievement and not such factors as behavior or performance in other areas such as reading, writing, spelling, and mathematics except as they play significant roles in the science program. Factors you might consider when calculating the science mark could include the following:

- Scores on process checklists

- Scores on practical tests

- Scores on inquiry checklists

- Scores on tests of content

- Class work

- Extra activities done by the child

- Homework

The final mark should be calculated in accordance with a weighted system that has been preestablished and shared with the children and their parents. A typical plan for establishing marks might look like this:

Process skill achievement	30%
Inquiry achievement	30%
Other activities	30%
Content achievement	10%

You will notice that the provision for content achievement is relatively modest. Considering its secondary place in the scheme of early childhood science education, the content achievement factor, if included at all in the marking system, should be small.

As you doubtless have inferred, the establishment of numerical, letter, or other symbolic marks is artificial, for marks cannot represent the totality of what a child has achieved. In addition, marks are difficult to assign in process-oriented inquiry science, for it is difficult to establish measurable criteria that can be administered uniformly with all children. However, the suggestions provided in this chapter for assessing children's science achievement and preparing marks should help you grade your children fairly and consistently.

Constructing Your Ideas 18.2
A Plan for Assessment

Now it's your turn. Construct a system for assessing children's achievement in science in the early childhood school setting and for reporting their achievement to parents. Share your system with the other students in your class and your instructor, seeking their input and critiques to help you refine your constructions.

ASSESSING THE EARLY CHILDHOOD EDUCATION SCIENCE TEACHER AND PROGRAM

No lesson, unit, or school term is complete until the teacher has examined the class's response and her own performance and has reflected upon both in order to construct for herself increasingly accurate understanding of her effectiveness as a teacher.

Competent teachers continuously evaluate their teaching effectiveness while they are teaching in the classroom. Competent teachers engage in reflection, sometimes alone and sometimes with other professionals, to identify strengths of previous work and areas that need improvement. Competent teachers also reflect on the appropriateness of the curriculum for the children in their classes and on their own changing attitudes toward science and science teaching.

Introspective reflection is supported in the literature (e.g., Sparks-Langer & Colton, 1991) and is a powerful vehicle for enabling teachers to create science lessons that are meaningful to children and that better reflect the individual differences and varying prior constructions children bring to the class. Introspective reflection enables teachers to check their own skill in urging children to inquire, to come up with their own ideas, and to develop their own plans to investigate their own ideas.

It is suggested that teachers keep their own reflective journals and portfolios.[2] Journals and portfolios together with participation in learning cohorts and attendance at professional seminars all assist the teacher in introspective reflection. You commenced this practice of self-appraisal when you critiqued your microteaching lessons. You are urged to continue this vital reflection process throughout your teaching careers to reconcile your actions with your beliefs, your teaching practices with your education, and the outcomes of your teaching with your intents.

SUMMARY

Assessment must measure what is taught. Accordingly, assessment in constructivist early childhood science classrooms measures facility with scientific processes, facility with inquiry, attitudes toward science, and, to a lesser extent, achievement of content.

Teachers assess children's proficiency in the scientific process skills and in inquiry by observing their work. The assessments can be general and informal or can address specific rubrics that indicate degree of proficiency, and they can be qualitative or quantitative in nature. Teachers assess children's attitudes toward science by looking at ways in which they express interest in science in school and at home. Teachers assess children's acquisition of content through occasional content-related tests. They prepare children for standardized achievement tests by ensuring the science concepts to be tested are included in the science program. The science portfolio and the parent conference are the most authentic ways of reporting progress and achievement, although periodic marks can be calculated from the various assessments. Teachers are vigilant in their continuous assessment of their teaching and the science program.

In this chapter, you have begun to design your own authentic assessment programs that are congruent with your conceptualization of process-oriented inquiry science teaching. Your constructions and conceptualizations of assessment will become more solidified with time and experience. However, you must continue to search for new ideas and ways of assessment that truly indicate what children have gained in their science education, and you must continuously evaluate your science program and your teaching to highlight strengths and uncover weaknesses in your regular efforts at refining your program and your teaching.

Notes

1. Ways of having preschool children develop reflective science portfolios are provided in Smith (2000). Through the use of their portfolios, preschool children hold conversations about their accomplishments, growth, plans, and goals.

2. Details about preparing preservice teacher portfolios and using the *National Science Education Standards* to provide a framework for teacher assessment of past actions, current situations, and intended outcomes are found in Moseley, C. (2000).

References

Berra, Y. (1998). *The Yogi book: "I really didn't say everything I said."* New York: Workman Publishing.

Cole, J. (1995). *The magic school bus gets baked in a cake: A book about kitchen chemistry.* New York: Scholastic.

Collins, A. (1992, March). Portfolios: Questions for design. *Science Scope,* 25–27.

Garis, H. R. (1972). *Uncle Wiggily's storybook.* New York: Putnam Publishing Group.

Haladyna, T., Haas, N., & Allison, J. (1998). Continuing tensions in standardized testing. *Childhood Education, 74*(5), 262–273.

Hart, D. (1994). *Authentic assessment: A handbook for educators.* Menlo Park, CA: Addison-Wesley Publishing Company.

Lambdin, D. A., and Walker, V. L. (1994, February). Planning for classroom portfolio assessment. *Arithmetic Teacher,* 318–324.

Martin, D. J. (2000). *Elementary science methods: A constructivist approach* (2nd ed.) Belmont, CA: Wadsworth/Thompson Learning.

Moseley, C. (2000). *Standards* direct preservice teacher portfolios. *Science and Children, 37*(5), 39–43.

National Research Council. (1996). *National science education standards.* Washington, DC: National Academy Press.

Smith, A. (2000). Reflective portfolios: Preschool possibilities. *Childhood Education, 76*(4), 204–208.

Sparks-Langer, G., and Colton, A. (1991). Synthesis of research on teachers' reflective thinking. *Educational Leadership, 48,* 37–44.

CHAPTER 19

The Early Childhood Science Classroom

You have been exploring process-oriented, activity-based, constructivist science teaching—science teaching in which children inquire into problems generated from their own interests and curiosities and that engage them in activities that may expand into areas of inquiry that had not been planned in advance and over which the teacher may have little or no curricular control.

The constructivist preschool and early childhood education classroom is buzzing with activity. During science time, children are busy investigating, exploring, trying out new ideas, discussing observations with others in their group, and, in general, expressing the excitement they feel about their inquiries and discoveries. During other times of the day such as centers time, children may be involved in many different activities—reading, drawing, exploring science things, studying bulletin boards, putting puzzles together, and engaging in creative play as well as continuing to

It is in fact nothing short of a miracle that the modern methods of instruction have not yet entirely strangled the holy curiosity of inquiry . . . . It is a very grave mistake to think that the enjoyment of seeing and searching can be promoted by means of coercion and a sense of duty.

Albert Einstein (1952), *Ideas and Opinions* **(New York: Crown)**

"The time has come," the Walrus said, "To talk of many things."

Lewis Carroll, *The Walrus and the Carpenter* **(Berkeley: Archetype Press, 1938), st. II**

explore the science ideas—all at the same time. To manage such a classroom requires careful planning and painstaking organization.

The constructivist classroom, at first glance, may appear disorderly. This is especially true to the observer who believes that, in orderly classrooms, children are quiet, are seated at their desks or tables, and do the same thing at the same time. The constructivist classroom is orderly but in a different sense from what is commonly associated with keeping "good order."

In this chapter, we will look at some practical suggestions that may help you develop an orderly classroom in which children are free to inquire, explore, and construct their own meaningful conceptualizations.

ORGANIZING THE CLASSROOM

One requirement for successful and meaningful involvement of children is that the classroom be arranged and organized to be inviting, safe, and conducive to children's involvement in their own learning. There is no "best" way of organizing the constructivist classroom. The key is flexibility. Move tables and/or desks to accommodate the needs of each lesson. For small-group activities, arrange the furniture so groups of four or five children can work cooperatively. For project work involving larger groups, move it into larger clusters. For activities that require utilization of a large area of the floor, move furniture to the edges of the room. For large-group instruction, have children assemble on the floor near the chart, bulletin board, chalk board, science center, or other center of instruction.

Reserve an area for a science center where you put interesting things children can investigate and where children can continue their investigations of activities begun in class, share investigations they have done at home, display collections, or show things they have brought from home (see Figure 19.1). The science center can be as simple as a small table at one side of the room devoted to science materials or as extensive as a large area of the room devoted to science. The size and location of the science center depends on the nature of the activities and materials selected for it. The area it occupies may vary from week to week or from month to month, depending on the topics under investigation, children's interests, and your own interest. It is best if children help set up, change, and maintain the science center; after all, it is *their* area for exploration. Encourage children to choose to utilize the science center when they have free time.

FIGURE 19.1   At the science center

ORGANIZING BULLETIN BOARDS

The most engaging bulletin board is interactive. Interactive bulletin boards are designed so children can do something with them. Examples include the following:

Hang small plastic bags into which children have placed damp paper towels on which they have placed seeds. Label each with the child's name, and watch the seeds sprout and grow (see Figure 19.2).

Draw a map of the United States onto which children plot areas where endangered species are protected, regions where different crops are grown, the localities of volcanoes, and the like.

Hang manila envelopes decorated with pictures of fish, farm animals, domestic pets, plants, and the like. Children drop pictures they have cut out of magazines into the envelopes during their centers time. After a week or so, empty each of the envelopes and discuss how children classified the pictures.

Prepare a "Seed Museum" bulletin board. Children bring in seeds found at home, in stores, or outdoors. Children put them in transparent envelopes or paste them to small cards and place them on the bulletin board in classification groups that develop as the children bring in more seeds.

FIGURE 19.2   A science bulletin board

Make a "rainforest" out of crepe paper, with a rainforest floor, understory, and canopy. Children cut pictures of rainforest animals and plants and place them in the appropriate layers on the bulletin board.

Children should be free to work with the classroom bulletin board just as they would with any other center, for the interactive bulletin board *is* a center.

ORGANIZING MATERIALS AND EQUIPMENT

Keep materials and equipment in boxes clearly labeled with their contents. When you assemble materials for an activity, put them in a small box such as a shoebox or plastic garment box, and label it with the activity's name. Replenish the nonperishable expendable materials after completing the activity, and put the box away; you won't have to start from scratch the next time you decide to utilize that activity. Some teachers call this approach "shoebox science." You will have to purchase duplicates if the same materials are used in different activities, but it may be worth the slight additional expense to have activities ready to use. Note that most of the activities suggested in this book use inexpensive materials that can be purchased at grocery stores and hardware stores.

Keep the materials you used for interactive bulletin boards, special centers, and displays in boxes labeled appropriately. Many teachers find it useful to take pictures of bulletin boards and displays and keep them together with the materials to help guide them when they want to re-create the presentation.

The more expensive materials and equipment, such as microscopes, thermometers, pan balances, binoculars, and the like, should be stored in labeled containers that are easily accessible to the teacher.

ORGANIZING TIME

Because science is often lower on the list of academic priorities than some other subjects, you may have to plan carefully to get enough time to implement your constructivist science plan. Flexibility is the key to efficient time organization. Many lessons can be accomplished in 20–30 minutes, and you can probably find the time to do one of these every day by programming science into the daily schedule. Other activities require more time, and for these, you can allocate the required time two or three times a week. To preserve continuity and encourage in-depth explorations, you can plan to have more extensive science explorations every day for a week or so, and then skip science the following week to make up for the extra time used in science.

Because preparing for science activities often requires a substantial investment of time in planning and in assembling materials and equipment, consider coteaching with a colleague. Select lessons or units of particular interest to you. You plan and present your lessons twice—once to your class and once to your colleague's class. Your colleague does the same with other lessons. Also, consider bringing two or more classes together for some lessons. Each teacher assumes a role in the lesson in a cooperative teaching endeavor. For activities that require specialized equipment such as microscopes, set up the lesson in one classroom, and rotate all the classes through that room for the lesson. You either can do the lesson yourself for all classes, or you and your colleagues can collaborate on it.

To select the most efficient scheduling scheme, you need to know how long it will take the children to do the planned activities. Timing the activities is both an art and a skill. Try each activity yourself first to see how long it takes. Assemble the materials needed for each group ahead of time, and package complete sets in plastic bags, ready to be handed out to groups when it is time for children to start their investigations. *Never* give children the materials until you are ready for them to begin their inquiries—you won't be able to compete successfully with the materials for their attention once you pass the materials out.

Give complete instructions including safety precautions *before* you allow children to start an activity. Introduce the activity in a large-group setting, and hold preliminary conversations and question-discussion sessions during this large-group time. Also show them how to do the initial activity. After you give the directions, ask one or two children to repeat them to be sure the class understands them. Then break the class into groups and give out the materials. Have one or two children pass out the materials to save you time. After the activity is finished, have children clean up their work stations, put the materials back into the packages, and bring them back to you. Close the activity with a large-group discussion in which you and the children summarize findings, engage in more discussion, and set directions for follow-up activities if appropriate.

ORGANIZING FOR SAFETY

"Safety first," goes the slogan. This slogan is as appropriate to the early childhood education science program as it is to any other situation. Always put the safety of the children in your classes uppermost in your mind. No teacher wants to see children get injured. And no teacher wants the liability that could come from injuries or illnesses attributable to classroom activities.

At the beginning of the year, talk with children about the importance of safety in science. Stress that, in the interest of safety as well as the orderly exploration of scientific concepts, children should follow four basic rules:

1. Cooperate with each other and with you to ensure a safe science atmosphere;
2. Behave in an orderly and responsible manner during science activities;
3. Listen for your voice as they do their science activities so they can hear additional instructions you might want to give; and
4. Use common sense at all times during science activities.

Then, to demonstrate that you have discussed safety issues with the children and that they understand the importance of safety, have them sign a safety contract such as the one shown in Figure 19.3. For very young children, you can insert names in the contracts when you are satisfied the children understand what they are agreeing to.

SCIENCE ACTIVITIES SAFETY CONTRACT

I will:

- Follow all instructions given by the teacher.
- Protect my eyes and my body during science activities by wearing safety goggles and lab smocks.
- Carry out good safety practices.
- Conduct myself in a responsible manner at all times.

I, (name)_____, have read and agree to obey the science activities rules listed above. I also agree to obey any additional instructions given by the school or given by the teacher in class.

_____   _____
Date   Signature

FIGURE 19.3   Science activities safety contract

Adapted from materials provided by the National Science Teachers Association

Have each child bring in an old oversized shirt to use as a science smock. The smocks can be decorated with science themes so the children will be encouraged to limit their use to science activities.

The children should wear safety goggles during all science activities that have any potential for liquids or solids accidentally getting into the eyes. This includes activities involving water, vinegar, fruits, fruit juices, rocks, minerals, and the like. It is a good idea to have children wear their safety goggles for every science activity so they get into the habit of doing so. Of course, it is expected that the teacher will don goggles as well. Safety goggles that fit young children can be purchased through school science supply companies; they normally are large enough to fit over glasses comfortably.

To the extent possible, use plastic instead of glass. Virtually all the materials you will use in early childhood science education that normally are made of glass also come in plastic. This includes jars, beakers, vessels, and even thermometers.

Most rocks and minerals are safe. However, a few are poisonous and should not be used. These include galena (lead sulfide), cinnabar (mercury sulfide), asbestos, and arsenopyrite, realgar, and orpiment (all minerals of arsenic). If you have these minerals in a classroom collection, dispose of them.

Anticipate safety problems each time you plan an activity, and include appropriate safety instructions in the introduction of each activity. Many of the activities in this text have safety considerations addressed. Safety tips are also offered throughout in the text where appropriate.

Be sensitive to children's allergies. Many children are allergic to certain foods and odors and even certain animals. Check for allergies before having them do activities that involve manipulating materials that might produce allergic reactions. Ask the school nurse whether allergy records are kept on the children in your class. If they are not, send a letter to parents at the beginning of the school year asking them to identify their children's allergies. Plan alternative but equivalent activities for the children with the allergies. Be sure to tell children *never* to taste or eat anything unless you specifically tell them otherwise.

ORGANIZING LIVING LABORATORIES

Many early childhood education classrooms have living things that become living laboratories fostering continued development of the process skills, especially observation. Living laboratories teach responsibility and are excellent vehicles to teach respect for life.

Pets

Many animals can be used as classroom pets. Figure 19.4 shows a sampling of classroom pets that have been used successfully in early childhood education classrooms.

Provide appropriate cages for your pets; they should have areas for adequate exercise. Be sure the animals get enough water and the proper food. Ask

**PETS COMMONLY FOUND IN EARLY CHILDHOOD SCIENCE
EDUCATION CLASSROOMS**

Birds	Hamsters
Chameleons	Lizards
Gerbils	Rabbits
Guinea pigs	Salamanders

FIGURE 19.4   Pets commonly found in early childhood science education classrooms

FIGURE 19.5   Look at our pet!

in a pet store for specific guidance concerning the care of your pets and the kind of food to provide. Assign children the responsibilities of keeping the food and water containers filled, cleaning cages, and doing other chores to care for the pets. Also plan how the class will provide for the care of the pets over weekends, holidays, and summer vacations (Figure 19.5).

Aquariums

Aquariums are a delight to have in the classroom. Limit yourself to fresh-water aquariums unless you have previously had successful experience with salt-water aquariums. Fresh-water aquariums require much less maintenance than salt-water aquariums and are much easier to establish. Aquariums can range from a simple goldfish bowl with two or three fish and a few plants to help aerate the water to a large aquarium with filters and motorized aerators. Be careful not to have more fish in the aquarium than the recommended number, for they will all die if there are too many. Clerks in pet stores and aquarium stores can advise you the maximum and optimum numbers of each kind of fish to put in your particular size of aquarium. Feed the fish very sparingly. Young children do not yet have the small muscle coordination needed to feed fish sparingly, but if you have older children in your class, teach them how to feed the fish so they can assume the responsibility. Scrape the inside walls of the aquarium with a "widget" when green algae starts to build up on the inside of the glass or plastic walls. Keep a few snails in the aquarium to help keep the bottom clean; they are scavengers and will help keep the entire aquarium clean by feeding on material the fish won't eat.

Note that federal regulations prohibit experimenting with vertebrate animals. This means that fish, hamsters, lizards, and other classroom animals should not be subjected to experimental procedures. For example, this federal regulation would not permit an activity in which children add ice cubes to a jar with goldfish to see how the goldfish react. Not only are such experimental procedures illegal, but they also show children a lack of respect for life.

Plants

Plants in the classroom provide the same living laboratory benefits as other living things. Plants can range from seedlings in paper cups or small pots that children are experimenting with to potted plants for decorative purposes. It is important that the plants receive plenty of direct sunlight. Locate the plants as close to a window as possible. Assign children the responsibility of watering the plants, but have them check the dampness of the soil first to be sure they don't overwater them. The soil should be kept damp but not soaked. From time to time, give the plants a little fertilizer, either mixed with the water or in the form of a solid sprinkled on the surface or imbedded in the soil.

Terrariums

A terrarium is a collection of small plants growing in soil in an open container. Any container will work. Sometimes aquariums are used as terrariums, especially aquariums that have begun to leak or are otherwise unsuitable for their originally intended function. Put a layer of fine gravel on the bottom of the container; this helps keep the soil from becoming too wet and radiates humidity that helps the health of the terrarium. Follow this with a layer of activated charcoal (available at most plant and gardening stores). The charcoal absorbs undesirable materials and odors and helps keep the terrarium "sweet." Next, place a piece of discarded curtain, nylon stocking, or other porous fabric to keep the soil from mixing with the gravel and charcoal. Finally, put a layer of potting soil two or three inches deep on top (see Figure 19.6).

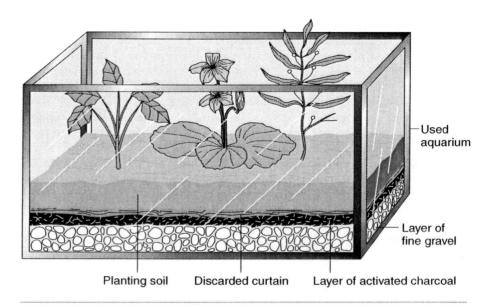

Used
aquarium

Layer of
fine gravel

Planting soil   Discarded curtain   Layer of activated charcoal

FIGURE 19.6 A terrarium

FIGURE 19.7 Watering the classroom terrarium

Plants typically include mosses, small ferns, and perennials that stay green year-round. The care of a terrarium is simple: Place it in a well lit location, preferably by a window, and water it *gently and sparingly* every few weeks. The plants will grow, and children can watch the terrarium's progress through the school year. It is especially meaningful to have children help decide what to include in the terrarium and to prepare the terrarium and plant the plants (Figure 19.7).

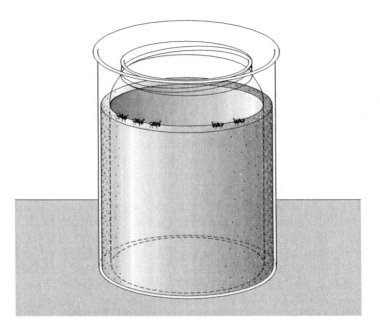

FIGURE 19.8 A homemade ant farm

Ant Farms

One of the more fascinating living laboratories is the ant farm. Constructed properly, they form an ideal exhibit of insect behavior. The easiest way to set up an ant farm is to buy a ready-made kit; they are available at pet stores and toy stores and come with a coupon that you send to the supplier who, in turn, sends you a supply of live ants to put in your ant farm. Alternatively, you can construct your own ant farm as follows: Obtain a transparent, wide-mouth plastic container and a smaller plastic cup or jar that fits inside the container so that there is about a half inch between the large container and the smaller container all the way around. Fill the space between the two containers with damp sand, and tamp it into the space (see Figure 19.8). Collect a few ants from the school yard, put them on top of the sand, and watch them work. Tunneling activity should start in a few days. Provide food for the ants on the top of the sand; food can consist of anything you might have at a picnic— bread crumbs, tiny pieces of lettuce, cookie crumbs, and so on. Be careful not to overfeed or overwater your ants; a tiny bit of food and a tiny bit of water once a week should be fine.

The book *Ant Cities,* written and illustrated by Arthur Dorros (1987), describes the organization of ant communities, the specialization of ant roles within the community, and some of the characteristics of ant life. The book includes instructions for making an ant farm.

ORGANIZING GROUPS

It has been shown that cooperative learning fosters achievement.[1] This principle is abundantly clear in the constructivist approach to science education where children discuss their observations, thoughts, and findings with each other in their attempts to seek clarification and establish validity. The traditional cooperative learning model suggests that children in each group be assigned specific roles such as materials manager, recorder, and communicator. However, in process-oriented inquiry science, we encourage *all* children to manipulate materials, discuss their ideas with each other and with the teacher, and pursue their own lines of investigation. Thus, it is recommended that, in science, children work in groups that are cooperative in the broader sense—wherein children work with each other on all aspects of an investigation rather than being assigned specialized roles. All children do all the activities, record their own observations, and discuss their own notions and ideas with other children and with the teacher. In this way, all children are given the opportunity to construct their own unique conceptualizations and refine them until they resolve their own unique mental disequilibrations.

ORGANIZING CHILDREN'S BEHAVIOR DURING SCIENCE ACTIVITIES

In the constructivist approach to science teaching, children talk with each other, try out different things, argue, and squeal with excitement. They often appear to be "off task" as they attempt to reconcile the new experiences with what they already know and explore the activities in tangential directions.

Behavior management in the constructivist classroom is governed by a primary principle: Every child has the right to learn, and the teacher has the right to facilitate this learning. How can the constructivist teacher keep order in the classroom in the face of what seems to be an open invitation to chaos?

First and foremost, the teacher must be *present* with the groups as they pursue their activities. The teacher is a co-inquirer. The teacher facilitates the children's inquiries, helps them focus on the questions at hand, and helps them organize their explorations. The constructivist teacher is very busy, moving from group to group to clarify, discuss, ask questions, answer questions, and, in general, assist each group and each child. The time children are working in groups is not a time for the teacher to catch up on paperwork or put things away or get things ready for the next lesson. This is the crucial time when the teacher interacts with the children, helps them in their explorations, helps them figure out how to investigate questions that have arisen as a result of the activities, and, especially, sees how the children are constructing information. This is the time to facilitate.

Second, the teacher must establish behavior expectations prior to each activity. There may be different behavior regulations for each of the several modes of teaching employed. Rules of behavior appropriate for large-group instruction are different from those appropriate for small-group work. In large-group instruction, expectations include children raising their hands to be recognized, not talking when someone else (including the teacher) is talking, listening to everyone's contributions (including other children's), not wandering around, and honoring other rules typical for large-group instruction. Rules of behavior appropriate for small-group activities include using "inside voices" and staying in their group's assigned area for the duration of the activity. If children in one group need help while the teacher is working with another group, they can quietly raise their hands. Some teachers provide "help" cards for each group that one person can raise to alert the teacher of their group's need.

For very young children and for those activities that require detailed teacher direction or equipment or materials difficult for children to use without supervision, the teacher can hold the activity in the style of a center. The teacher assembles the materials on one table and calls small groups to this table one at a time to do the activity under her direction. The rest of the children work on other activities or in other centers during this period of time.

Constructivist teachers effectively eliminate the reward-punishment system of classroom management. If children want to "play" instead of work, teachers can use the principle of self-referencing behavior. In this system of behavior management, the teacher calls the child's attention to improvement in undesirable demonstrations of behavior so the child can see the progress being made: "You are doing a great job today . . . much less fooling around than yesterday!" This is contrasted with rule-referencing behavior management in which the teacher reprimands the child for infractions of rules and metes out the accompanying consequence: "You broke the rule, and now you have to pay the price." Teachers also can use the 1-2-3 system of behavior management: (1) Name the individual; (2) state the specific action to be stopped or to be done; and (3) state the reason. ("James, raise your hand when you want to talk so everyone gets a chance to share." "Elizabeth, stop talking out of turn; children cannot hear what others are saying.") Say this quietly and in close proximity to the offending child so as not to call widespread attention to the child or the problem. This encourages self-referencing behavior, eliminates confusion and ambiguities, and treats each individual with dignity. While children are working on their own activities, a high degree of interaction exists between teacher and individuals and small groups. Opportunities continually exist for private encouragement of students to exhibit appropriate behavior and for private correction of inappropriate behavior. Others have written that treating children with dignity is key to successful classroom management (Glasser, 1990, 1996). I have found this to be true.

Because the concept still exists that good teaching is reflected by exemplary children's behavior, it is important to let your building administrators know how you manage your classroom during science activities. Take a few minutes to describe to them what you are doing in your science program, what your goals are, and what to look for in your classroom. This will keep them informed and may help you achieve your goals through their input. Invite your administrators to your class when children are doing an activity.

Support for the child-centered constructivist approach to teaching and learning must come from within the school; inviting parents, colleagues, and administrators to your classroom to observe children at work helps secure the needed support.

It has been demonstrated over and over that behavior problems are minimal in constructivist classrooms. This is because children are active, are cognitively engaged, are interested, and are treated with dignity and respect. Their explorations and constructions are valued. They have a say as to what they do during the science class. They are building positive self-concepts while they are performing the activities. And they have power to work out their own activities in the ways they best see fit.

If we want to teach in a constructivist mode, we ourselves must recognize that we also are constructing information out of our own new experiences. The only way we can change a preexisting rules-based discipline "road map" is to try a different approach, begin developing different teacher-child interactions, and evaluate the results. Success in these new interactions will aid in our construction of the more complete constructivist classroom. Changing our expectations that children conform to a set of rules and changing our concept of how children solve problems and construct their own information are good first steps. Most important, we must change the outlook that effective teaching is synonymous with keeping children quiet.

ORGANIZING PARENT RESOURCES

meta-analysis—Analysis of a group of similar studies previously published

In many school districts, increasing parents' involvement with their children's education has emerged as a top priority. Research has suggested that "a high level of parental involvement [in children's education] appears to have a direct impact on student achievement" (Rosenthal & Sawyers, 1996, p. 195). A **meta-analysis** of 66 studies reported by Henderson and Berla (1994) documented numerous positive effects for students whose parents were involved in some way in their children's education. These effects include the following:

- Higher grades

- Higher standardized achievement test scores

- Better attendance

- Regularly completed homework

- Fewer placements in remedial classes

- More positive attitudes at school

- More positive behavior

- Higher graduation rates

- Greater enrollment in postsecondary education programs

Jonson (1999) writes, "Parental participation impacts a student's level of success more than any curriculum reform, self-esteem-building activity, computer technology, or other innovation" (p. 121). The Early Childhood Longitudinal Study, Kindergarten Classs of 1998–99 conducted by the U.S. Department of Education indicates that family characteristics and home experiences are two of the factors that determine children's knowledge and skill development (Research links, 2000, p. 4).[2]

The National Science Teachers Association has published a position paper entitled "Parent Involvement in Science Education" in which it is affirmed that "parents play an essential role in the success of students in schools" (1994, p. 5). In the *National Science Education Standards* (National Research Council, 1996), Program Standard D urges that "The K-12 science program must give students access to appropriate and sufficient resources, including quality teachers, time, materials and equipment, adequate and safe space, and the community" (p. 218). Program Standard F urges that "Schools must work as communities that encourage, support, and sustain teachers as they implement an effective science program" (p. 222). (See inside front and back covers for the complete listing of the *National Science Education Standards*.)

Involving parents in the science program not only provides much needed assistance but also gives them the opportunity to experience for themselves what the process-oriented inquiry constructivist science program is all about. This first-hand experience is the best way of developing support for your program and for children's experiences in school.

Drake (1995) summarizes categories suggested by James P. Comer for successful fostering of parent involvement in schools:

1. Information exchange: Keeping parents informed and welcomed through newsletters, information packages, and school conferences
2. School-based support: Involving parents as tutors and resource persons
3. Home-based instruction: Providing activities to support and reinforce what is taught in the classroom
4. School governance: Involving parents in school councils and committees

With the current emphasis on parent involvement in their children's education, parents, guardians, and care givers are becoming increasingly comfortable in working with schools to achieve goals common to both the school and the parents.

Parent Involvement in Exchanging Information about the Science Program

Parents can become involved in the exchange of information between the classroom and home. If parents are to become involved in their children's science education, they need to know what their children are doing at school. One way of keeping parents informed is through newsletters sent home periodically. Parent volunteers can be asked to aid in preparing these newsletters. In the newsletters, describe the topic(s) being explored, the method and activities being used in the explorations, the overall goals and purposes of the explorations, and the expected outcomes. Also suggest enrichment and follow-up activities parents can do with their children at home such as extensions, home-based activities, suitable books, computer activities, Internet resources, television shows, and other applicable resources that may help parents get involved with their children's inquiries. (Specific ways parents can engage their children in science activities at home are suggested in Chapter 20.)

An excerpt from a newsletter to parents of a first-grade class beginning a study of oceans is shown in Figure 19.9.

The newsletter is a good place to ask for donations of materials, help at school, volunteers for field-trip chaperones, and other assistance you would find useful. In requesting donations, be sure to include requests for materials that can be obtained for little or no cost. Parents can be asked to assist in preparing the newsletter. Try to obtain translations for parents not fluent in English.

Parents can also help prepare monthly calendars for parents that highlight all special activities forecast for the class, including those related to science. (See Chapter 20 for a more complete exploration of parent assistance in the early childhood science education program.)

EXCERPT FROM A FIRST-GRADE NEWSLETTER

This week our class is going to start a unit on oceans. We will investigate several concepts about oceans, including:

- Differences between ocean water and lake water
- Differences between salt water and fresh water
- Names and locations of oceans
- Animals and plants found in oceans
- How people study oceans
- The beach
- Shells and crabs
- Water sports
- Water safety

We will do many hands-on activities, read books, write poems and stories, look at pictures, watch videos, and play computer games dealing with ocean topics. We will establish e-mail communication with a first-grade class in Miami, Florida, to exchange information and ideas and to ask questions. We will make life-sized cut-outs of fish, and we will construct a bulletin board to show ocean habitats.

You can help your child by reading books with your child about oceans and fish and marine life, telling stories about your own experiences with oceans and beaches and fishing, and asking your child to describe and explain the activities done at school.

We would love to have some help. If you could spare an hour or two sometime during the next month, please let me know.

FIGURE 19.9 Excerpt about upcoming science activities from a first-grade newsletter

Parent Nights

Parent nights are excellent vehicles for familiarizing parents, administrators, and colleagues with the nature of your science program and the goals and objectives you have established for science learning in your class. Many teachers hold parent evenings once a semester or even once a month.

Prepare activities similar to those you use with the children for parents to do. Divide them into groups as you would the children in your class, and handle the activity as you would any other process-oriented inquiry activity. Call the adults' attention to the wonderment they feel when they make new discoveries. Help them see how they use the processes in their inquires and how the activity relates to everyday events. Show them that they are experiencing *doing* science—a learning strategy that may be quite different from the way they were taught science. You may have everyone in attendance do the same activity, paralleling the way you approach science education in your class. Or, because they are adults, you may choose to have an adult orientation to the activities. Prepare several different activities and place them around the room in stations or centers. Ask the adults to move through the different stations until they have investigated them all. Have all equipment and materials set up at each station, and provide laminated sheets with directions and questions similar to the directions provided for children in their activities. Circulate among the groups to facilitate inquiry, answer questions, and help individuals focus on their efforts.

At the end of the evening, discuss with parents the goals and objectives you have established for your science program, and discuss ways in which parents can get involved with their children's science education through home activities.

Parent Involvement in Classroom Science Activities

Parents can be of tremendous assistance for your science program. They can serve as lab assistants who obtain, prepare, and organize materials for science activities. They can participate in facilitating children's inquiries during science. Parents with particular interests or expertise can make presentations to the class or can set up exhibits, explain them to the children, and guide children through them. Parent assistance can be solicited for preparing take-home science kits (see Chapter 20). Parents can organize material donations campaigns (but be sure to specify the materials you need so you don't end up with materials you can't use). Parents can spearhead special projects such as garden-building Saturdays and can contact local merchants for contributions.

Parent Involvement in Establishing Science Assessment Procedures

Parents can contribute to classroom-based school governance by serving on committees that help determine criteria for science assessment and for science portfolio construction. They can also participate in committees that help

FIGURE 19.10   Parents cut open a fish to show to the first grade class.

establish general or science-specific guidelines for authentic systems of reporting children's achievement and progress.

Getting Parent Involvement Started

Research and the professional literature have shown that schools and teachers must take the first steps in forming partnerships with the parents. As Epstein and Sanders (1998) put it, [I]f schools reach out, *then* parents will become partners in their children's education regardless of income level, education level, where they live, how many adults are at home, or any other factor" (p. 392). It is hoped that every teacher will take the steps needed to involve parents and the community in enriching the children's education. It is not difficult to get started. Simply "ask parents how they want to become involved . . . Listening to parents will help all educators; in turn, all students can benefit" (Peña, p. 169).

ORGANIZING COMMUNITY RESOURCES

In addition to parents, guardians, and primary care givers, numerous community resources can be tapped to enrich your science program. Stores, markets, and other local facilities can be asked to host field trips (see Chapter 20). Doctors, nurses, dentists, dental hygienists, veterinarians, engineers, architects, and other local professionals can be asked to make presentations, lead discussions, and provide inquiry-based activities for your class.

Local scientists are often willing to provide inquiry experiences related to their own specialties. However, they typically are concerned about how to relate their professional specialties to young children and how to behave as the "teacher-in-charge," challenging children to become involved in meaningful ways. In addition, teachers are typically concerned that material presented by visiting scientists will be way over the heads of the children. However, these concerns need not impede your willingness to accept these volunteer services.

In one town, a senior scientist in a local laboratory provided materials and equipment for a second-grade class's study of bacteria and was the major facilitator of this topic for the class (Kesselheim, Graves, Sprague, & Young, 1998). Prior to the scientist's first visit, the teacher and the scientist discussed the plan, the activities, the expectations, and the roles of the teacher and the scientist in the teaching/learning experience. As a result of this highly successful experience, Kesselheim et al (ibid.) recommend that the visiting scientist and the teacher engage in this type of careful and selective planning in advance of each visit of a scientist to the classroom.

Involving scientists in the early childhood science program not only provides much-needed program enrichment and assistance but also gives the scientists the opportunity to experience for themselves what the process-oriented inquiry constructivist science program is all about. This first-hand experience is the best way of developing their support for your program and for children's experiences in school.

SUMMARY

Effective early childhood science educators arrange their classrooms for maximum involvement of children in science explorations, thereby fostering children's ability to do science. The classroom has plants, animals, other interesting living laboratories, interactive bulletin boards, and a science center for fostering children's independent investigations and observations. Teachers prepare science lessons with clear directions for the initial activities, and they focus on safety precautions. Their classroom management is firm but positive and conducive to children's independent explorations. They solicit and use the services of parents, scientists, and other community resources.

The process-oriented inquiry classroom is efficient and orderly, encourages children to construct their own conceptualizations, and provides ownership of knowledge and thinking to the children. It is a constructivist classroom that stems from a deeply held belief that children can use the processes to do science, that the science children do is valuable, and that flexible and efficient classroom arrangements foster children's personal inquiries in science.

Notes

1. For a discussion of cooperative learning techniques see Graves (1990).
2. A copy of the Early Childhood Longitudinal Study, Kindergarten Class of 1998–99 can be downloaded from the Internet site http://nces.ed.gov.

References

Carroll, L. (1938). *The walrus and the carpenter.* Berkeley: Archetype Press.

Dorros, A. (1987). *Ant cities.* Madison, WI: Demco Media.

Drake, D. (1995). Using the Comer model for home-school connections. *The Clearing House, 68,* 313–316.

Einstein, A. (1954). *Ideas and opinions.* New York: Crown.

Epstein, J., and Sanders, M. G. (1998). What we learned from international studies of school-family-community partnerships. *Childhood Education, 74*(6), 392–394.

Glasser, W. (1990). The quality school. *Phi Delta Kappan 71*(6), 424–435.

Glasser, W. (1996). Then and now: The theory of choice. *Learning 25*(3), 20–22.

Graves, T. (1990). Cooperative learning and academic achievement: A tribute to David and Roger Johnson, Robert Slavin, and Shlomo Sharan. *Cooperative Learning 10*(4), 13–16.

Henderson, A., and Berla, N. (1994). *A new generation of evidence: The family is critical to student achievement.* Columbia, MD: National Committee for Citizens in Education.

Jonson, K. F. (1999). Parents are partners: Building positive home-school relationships. *The Educational Forum, 63*(2), 121–126.

Kesselheim, C., Graves, R., Sprague, R., & Young, M. A. (1998). Teacher and scientist: A collaboration of experts. *Science and Children 35*(8), 38–41.

National Research Council. (1996). *National Science Education Standards.* Washington, DC: National Academy Press.

National Science Teachers Association. (1994, October/November). An NSTA position statement: Parent involvement in science education. *NSTA Reports!* Arlington, VA: National Science Teachers Association.

Peña, D. (1999). Mexican-American family involvement. *Kappa Delta Pi Record, 35*(4), 166–169.

Research links parent involvement to kindergartens' success (2000, April). *Community Update, 76*(4). Washington, DC: U.S. Department of Education, 4.

Rosenthal, D. M., and Sawyers, J. Y. (1996). Building successful home/school partnerships: Strategies for parent support and involvement. *Childhood Education 72*(4), 194–200.

CHAPTER 20

Science beyond the Classroom

In this text, we have tried to make the point that the only learning that can take place is that which results from connecting new experiences with existing knowledge. We have suggested that one of the main goals of early childhood science education is to broaden and deepen children's experiential bases, enabling them to develop an ever expanding and widening store of information from which they can construct new conceptualizations.

Science exists all around us—in schoolyards, on sidewalks, in gardens, in grocery stores, hardware stores, and banks, in ponds and lakes and streams, in museums, botanical gardens, and zoos, and at home. The school classroom is the center for systematic development of process and inquiry skills. But there are limitations to what a teacher can expose children to in the classroom setting. The constructivist science program takes advantage of multiple opportunities for children to experience and do science both in and outside the classroom.

The art of raising challenging questions is easily as important as the art of giving clear answers . . . The art of cultivating such questions, of keeping good questions alive, is as important as either of these.
Jerome Bruner Telling Stories to Make Science: Karplus Lecture Excerpts. NSTA Reports! (April/May, 1990)

"And now," cried Max, "let the wild rumpus start!"
Maurice Sendak, *Where the Wild Things Are* (New York: HarperCollins Children's Books, 1988), (Original work published 1963)

In this chapter, you will explore ways to incorporate outdoor learning centers and field trips into your science program and ways to encourage parent involvement in their children's science education.

OUTDOOR LEARNING CENTERS

Outdoor learning centers can range in complexity from an area of the schoolyard where the teacher and the children gather simply for a change of scenery, to gardens, ponds, butterfly gardens, and even elaborate nature trails and amphitheaters. Outdoor learning centers provide areas where children can observe and investigate their natural surroundings. They are ideal sites for explorations into weather, clouds, bugs, animals, plants, erosion, rocks, and other natural phenomena. Studies in outdoor settings promote development of the naturalist intelligence (Checkley, 1997; Meyer, 1997) and positive attitudes toward science (Stone & Glascott, 1997–1998) in addition to development of process and inquiry skills.

cumulus cloud—Massive puffy cloud with a flat base

Children can engage in many activities using the environment around the school building. A few are suggested in Constructing Science in the Classroom 20.1–20.5.

Constructing Science in the Classroom 20.1
Daytime Sky Watching

AGE

8
7
6
5
4
3

AN OUTDOOR LEARNING ACTIVITY

Objective
The student will observe the daytime sky.

Bring children outdoors on a partly cloudy day, and ask them to describe what they see. (See page 275 for a safety precaution.) Ask them to describe the shapes of **cumulus clouds** (cumulus clouds are puffy white clouds). What do they see? Do the clouds change shape? What are the new shapes? Does everyone see the same things in each cloud? Or do different people see different things? While still outside, read *Little Cloud* by Eric Carle (1996a). In this book, Little Cloud has fun changing into different shapes and playing make-believe until it finally does what clouds are supposed to do. Ask children to compare what they see in the clouds with what is described in *Little Cloud*.

Ask children to describe other things they see (or what they have seen before) in addition to clouds in the sky: birds, butterflies, planes, kites, and so on. What color is the sky? Read *The Sky* by Ariane Dewey (1993). This book suggests that, by using one's powers of observation and imagination, many wonderful things can be found in the seemingly empty sky—meteorological, astronomical, mythological, and more, from flying saucers to Santa Claus. Pause after each page to ask children to compare what they observed in the sky with what was described on that page in the book.

If desired, older children can culminate the sky-watching activity by writing Haiku poems about what they observed in the sky. Younger children can make cloud panoramas out of cotton balls and construction paper.

Safety precaution: Never allow children to look directly at the sun. The lens in the human eye acts as a magnifying glass, concentrating the sun's rays on the retina and burning the retina much as a magnifying glass can be focused to burn a leaf. However, the retina does not contain nerves sensitive to pain, so people cannot feel the burn. In addition to the visible light, the sun's ultraviolet rays can cause serious damage to eyes. Because children want to look at the sun, it is necessary to provide them with an alternative to looking at it directly. Smoked glass, overexposed film, and other filters that used to be considered safe are now known *not* to be safe for looking at the sun. Two safe ways are suggested; in both, the sun is behind the children so they cannot look at it directly. One way is to use a pinhole projector. Pinhole projectors work on the same principle as the pinhole camera and are relatively easy to make. Obtain a large shoebox. Cut a hole about an inch square in one end of the shoebox, and cover it with a piece of aluminum foil taped to the outside. Use a pin or a thin nail (such as a thin brad) to poke a hole in the aluminum foil. Cut a viewing hole in the side of the box near the opposite end. With the cover placed on the box to keep the inside dark, aim the end of the box with the pinhole toward the sun. The sun's image will be projected onto the inside of the opposite end of the box. Children look at the sun's image through the viewing hole. You may have to experiment with the size of the pinhole to get a sharp image; the longer the box, the larger the pinhole needs to be (see Figure 20.1).

The other safe way to look at the sun's image is to focus the sun through binoculars onto a piece of paper. Hold the binoculars so that the wide lens (objective) is facing the sun and the eyepiece is aimed toward a piece of white

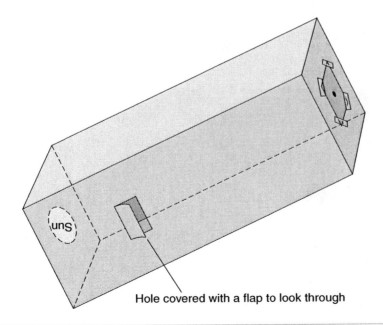

Hole covered with a flap to look through

FIGURE 20.1 A sun viewer

paper. Move the binoculars around until you see the sun's image on the paper. Use the focus knob to bring the sun's image into clear focus. The binoculars will not become hot because they reflect all the sun's energy through mirrors or prisms from the objective lens to the ocular (see Figure 20.2). Of course, you should *never* look directly at the sun through the binoculars.

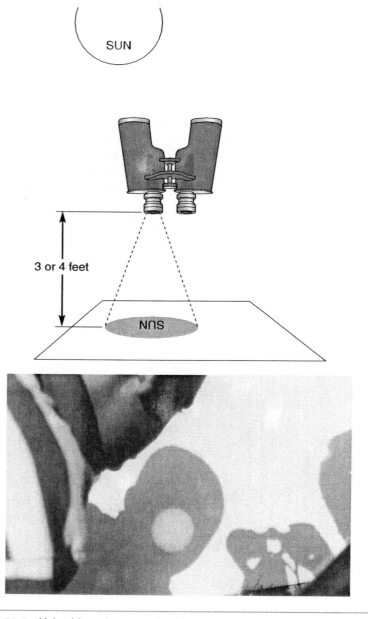

FIGURE 20.2   Using binoculars to project the sun's image

Use either of the preceding methods for children to view the sun and especially to see eclipses of the sun by the moon when the moon passes between the earth and the sun.

Constructing Science in the Classroom 20.2
Sidewalk Ecology

AN OUTDOOR LEARNING CENTER ACTIVITY

AGE

8
7
6
5
4
3

Objective
The student will observe living things in the environment of a sidewalk.

Take the children outdoors and ask them what they can see in the general area of the sidewalk. They may see grass and other plants poking up through the sidewalk cracks. Ask why plants grow like this and what this shows about how plants grow and what they need to grow. They may see ants. Ask them to observe the ants carefully. Do all ants follow the same path? How do the ants know what path to follow? Are any of the ants carrying anything? What? What is it for? What do they use to carry things? Are there any groups of ants helping each other carry something? Why is more than one ant needed to carry it? Are there any ant hills

FIGURE 20.3   Observing the ecology of a sidewalk

nearby? How do the ants go in and out of their hill? (Connect this experience with the ant farm if you have one. If you don't have one, this would be a good time to get one started.)

Ask similar questions about other insects and other living things children may notice.

Can children see the edges of the sidewalk? If so, maybe they can see what the sidewalk is made of. Is there evidence of erosion near the sidewalk? If so, ask children what they think might have caused the erosion.

Back in the classroom, have books with pictures of living things seen on the excursion for children to explore.

Safety note: Do not let the children touch any insects or get so close to them that they crawl onto the children. Children may be allergic to insects, and many ants, especially fire ants, can and do bite. Also be on the lookout for bees, wasps, and hornets. If you see them, *quietly* coax the children to a different area. In addition, don't let the children touch unfamiliar plants; many are poisonous, and children may be allergic to some.

Literature Connection:
Two Bad Ants by Chris Van Allsburg (1988) is a tale of two ants that linger in a house instead of returning home. They encounter numerous misfortunes during their stay. The nature of each misfortune has to be inferred from the text and the illustrations.

Constructing Science in the Classroom 20.3
Schoolyard Ecology

AGE

8
7
6
5
4
3

AN OUTDOOR LEARNING CENTER ACTIVITY

Objective

The student will observe plants and animals in the schoolyard.

Take the children for walks in the schoolyard several times during the year. Ask them to look for plants, trees, insects, birds, and other animals.

What kind of plants do they see? Do they have flowers? Are more plants found in areas of full sun or in areas of full or partial shade? Are the plants that are found in full sun different from those found in the shade? Are all the plants green? Or are there some brown or white plants such as mushrooms?

What kinds of trees are there? How tall are the trees? How big around are the tree trunks? Can children wrap two hands around the trunk? Or can they wrap their arms around the trunk like they are hugging the tree? Or does it take more than one child to wrap arms completely around the trunk? What does the bark look like? Try making a bark rubbing using a soft lead pencil and a sheet of paper.

Look for insects. What kinds do children see? Are any of them camouflaged? How do they move? Do they walk? Crawl? Fly? Is there any evidence of what they eat?

Look for other animals and evidence of other animals such as squirrels and chipmunks. Where do they live? How do you know?

Look for birds. What kinds of birds do children see? How high do they fly? What sounds do they make?

Safety note: Take the walk yourself first to be sure there is no poison ivy or poison oak and to be sure the area is free of undesirable animals such as snakes, mosquitoes, and wasps. Tell children they *must* stay together in a single group so everyone can see what everyone else finds.

Back in the classroom, suggest that children look in illustrated books to find examples of what they observed on the walk.

Take this walk several times during the school year. Each time, ask children to point out what has changed since the last time, and ask them to infer reasons for these changes.

Literature Connection:

The Grouchy Ladybug by Eric Carle (1996b). A grouchy ladybug, looking for a fight, challenges everyone she meets regardless of their size. After she meets her match, she becomes a much nicer ladybug.

Constructing Science in the Classroom 20.4
A Walk around the School

AGE

8
7
6
5
4
3

AN OUTDOOR LEARNING CENTER ACTIVITY

Objective

The student will observe natural habitats near the school building.

Take children for a walk around the school building. Ask them to focus on plants, animals, and evidence of erosion they see within, say, 10 feet of the building walls. Facilitate their observations by asking questions as suggested in Constructing Science in the Classroom 20.1 and 20.2 (see also Constructing Science in the Classroom 7.10).

Erosion is likely to be evident wherever drainpipes empty onto the ground. Ask children to look for areas where the water has caused a change in the ground. How are these areas

(continued)

different from the rest of the ground? Are there gullies? How much grass and how many other plants grow in these areas? Why is this area different from the rest of the yard?

Have people done anything to slow down or prevent extensive erosion? Are there beds of stone or pebbles or wide drainage areas at the ends of the drainpipes? Why are these there? What do they do?

Safety note: Be sure to tell children to stay together as a single group as you walk around the building.

Back in the classroom, engage the children in an activity in which they investigate erosion, such as Constructing Science in the Classroom 20.5.

Literature Connection:

Roxaboxen by Alice McLerran (1992). A hill covered with rocks and wooden boxes becomes an imaginary town.

Constructing Science in the Classroom 20.5
Investigating Erosion

AGE

8
7
6
5
4
3

AN ACTIVITY FOR CONSTRUCTING MODELS

Objective
The student will construct a model of erosion by water.

As a follow-up to the walk around the school where children observed the effects of erosion (Constructing Science in the Classroom 20.4), ask them to construct a model that they can use to investigate the effects of water erosion on sand.

Provide a dishpan and some sand. Wet the sand, and have children build a hill out of the wet sand. Use sticks to represent trees and pebbles to represent large rocks in the hill. Select children one at a time to be the rain-pourer. Provide the pourer with a fine-holed watering can filled with water. Have the pourer hold the spout over the top of the hill and slowly, but steadily, pour the water onto the hill until the can is empty. This simulates a gentle rain (see Figure 20.4).

Ask children to observe what happens to the sand. Are any gullies formed? What happens to the sand that is washed away from the hill? Does it form any kind of pattern at the base of the hill? What is the effect of the sticks and the pebbles?

FIGURE 20.4 Investigating forces that cause erosion

(continued)

Next, use a sprinkling can with larger holes. Rebuild the hill, and ask a child to simulate a heavy rain in the same way the light rain was simulated. Ask the same kinds of questions.

Ask children to tell the differences in the effects between light rain and heavy rain on the erosion of the sand from the hill. Ask children whether they think erosion is good or whether it should be prevented. Ask their reasons for their responses. What can people do to prevent erosion?

Finally, ask the children to develop erosion-preventing techniques that could be used on the sand hill, and then try the light and heavy rain simulations to find the effect their techniques have on erosion.

Literature Connection:

The Sun, the Wind, and the Rain by Lisa W. Peters (1988) is the story of a girl who builds a sand mountain on a beach. She compares her mountain to a mountain she sees in the distance. The story describes the rapid shaping of the sand mountain by wind and rain, the same forces that took thousands of years to shape the real mountain.

GARDENS

The primary requirements for successful gardens are good soil, good drainage, and lots of direct sunlight. Your school may have one or more gardens already established. If not, there may be an area in the schoolyard that could be turned into a garden. Invite parents and children to participate in a garden construction day. Dig out the grass and weeds, frame the area with rocks or garden bed timbers, and fill it back up with a mixture of native dirt and commercially available garden soil. If you ask, maybe your local hardware, lumber, and garden stores would be willing to donate materials and supplies.

Once you have prepared the garden beds, decide with the children what to plant. I suggest you select fast-growing plants such as zinnias, marigolds, radishes, and the like so children can see results in a week or so. You will have to teach younger and inexperienced children how to plant the seeds one at a time; otherwise they may be inclined to dump the entire package of seed into a single hole.

Have children measure the heights of the plants every day and chart the rate of growth on chart paper in the classroom. They can use rulers, or they can put pencil marks on strips of paper to indicate how tall the plants are. If they use the latter method of measuring, cut the strips at the marked height, and mount them on a chart side-by-side for each day's measurements.

Assign tasks of daily watering and weeding. Take the class outside to inspect the fruits of their labors every day or two. Assign different children to thin the seedlings to make room for plant growth. Ask them why thinning is necessary. Also ask them what they should look for in deciding which seedlings to pull out.

You can have an actively growing garden during normal growing seasons in your area. Local nurseries can provide tips on what grows best for your purposes and may even be willing to donate seeds and seedlings.

Some teachers develop garden areas specifically to attract butterflies or hummingbirds. These gardens need to be large enough for children to walk into and require considerable planning and construction efforts. Plantings include fragrant and colorful flowering perennials and annuals. Because different species of butterflies have different color and taste preferences, the butterfly garden should have a variety of plants to attract the most butterflies. Planting clusters of the same plant makes the plant more noticeable to the insects. Keep a bucket of water buried to its rim in the garden to attract water-loving species; add juices or sweet drinks to the water to make the liquid especially attractive. If the butterflies lay eggs that hatch into caterpillars, children can study the life cycle and metamorphosis of butterflies. But use gloves when handling the caterpillars because some caterpillars can sting or cause a rash. It is better to be safe than sorry.

FIELD TRIPS

In addition to classrooms, outdoor learning centers, the schoolyard, and gardens, there are many other places where children can observe and explore science. These nontraditional settings include ponds, farms, plant nurseries, grocery stores, hardware stores, banks, zoos, botanical gardens, museums, and many other places where science abounds.[1] By venturing into the community and into nature through field trips, teachers and children reap the benefits of authentic learning, and children become actively engaged in their own learning by interacting with the world around them (Willis, 1997).

Museums are particularly attractive destinations for field trips. There are some 11,700 museums across the United States. They focus on all kinds of topics, and they include all types, sizes, budgets, and rural and urban geographic locations. A 1998 survey showed that the vast majority of museums have committed staff and resources to serve school children in their areas and to develop programs and materials that meet the local school curriculum standards and guidelines (New Survey, 1999).[2]

Field trips require planning, and in the constructivist classroom, much of this planning is done in conjunction with the children. The first step is to decide where to go. A field trip possibility can be suggested by the teacher to supplement the topic under study, or it can arise from the children's own ideas as they pursue their investigations. Once the decision to take the field trip has been finalized, you should take the trip yourself to work out logistics. Obtain the necessary approvals from the field trip site, determine entrance fees, and list specific activities available for children to pursue at the site. Determine how long the trip will take, scout out lunch and rest room facilities, and plan what kind of clothing the children will need to wear. Also scout out features that are likely to engage children's interest along the way.

Then, back at school, establish the date, the method of funding, the mode of transportation, and the number of chaperones needed. (A ratio of one chaperone for every four or five children is suggested for early childhood education field trips.)

Once all this is done, describe the trip to the children and engage them in a discussion of what they would like to learn and what they would like to do during the trip. Plan the details in conjunction with them. Keep a running list of trip objectives they offer to use in helping them stay focused during the trip and to use in the posttrip discussion. Using the children's input, write a letter to parents explaining the trip, the trip's goals, and what the children will do. Attach the permission blank required by the school.

Figure 20.5 shows an example of a letter to parents announcing a kindergarten trip to a plant nursery. For legal reasons, the permission form used should be the one prescribed by the school.

If you have children in your class whose parents do not read English, ask whether the parents have friends who could translate the letter for them. If not, attach a translation of the letter and permission blank in the parent's native language. Local chambers of commerce, courthouses, and universities often employ bilingual people who would be willing to do the translation for you.

Because there may be one or more children who, for one reason or another, will not be able to go on the trip, plan equally interesting activities for them to do while the rest of the class is away. Note, however, that in most states, the law requires that *all* children be able to go on field trips regardless of whether they can pay.

Dear Parents:

    Our class has decided to go on a field trip to the Sekip Nurseries and Garden Store. This field trip will enrich our understanding of the different kinds of plants that grow in our area. We will learn how plants grow, how they are started, what they need in order to grow, which plants grow best in shade and which grow best in full sun, and the answers to many other questions we have asked about plants.

    The trip is scheduled for Friday, April 12th. We will leave the school at 8:30 AM and will travel by school bus to the nursery. The trip to the nursery will take about 30 minutes. The managers of the nursery have agreed to show the children the facilities and to answer their questions. We plan to stay at the nursery for about 2 hours, and we will be back at school by 11:30 AM in time for lunch.

    Please indicate your permission for your child to participate in this field trip by filling in and signing the attached blank. Return the permission slip with your child by April 5th. Keep this letter for your records.

    We look forward to having a wonderful time and to learning lots of new things about plants.

Sincerely,
(teacher)

FIGURE 20.5   Letter to parents announcing a field trip to a plant nursery

On the day of the trip, remind the children of the learning objectives and goals they decided upon. Establish behavior expectations and discuss safety regulations. During the trip, interact with the children as you would in a classroom science inquiry activity. Help them crystallize their questions and thoughts. Help them figure out answers to their questions in an inquiry manner. Point out interesting features seen during the trip that the children may have missed. In general, act as a facilitator for their personal constructions of new ideas.

When the trip is over, ask the children to identify the most important or significant things they learned on the trip. Suggest follow-up activities as appropriate based on the demonstrated interests of the children, questions that remain unanswered, and concepts that remain unexplained.

A summary of the elements of planning and going on field trips is shown in Figure 20.6.

Figure 20.7 shows a variety of field trip sites together with some of the learning opportunities available at each. The list is provided to give you some ideas. You are sure to be able to refine the list to reflect facilities available in your local area. The learning opportunities are related to science and are suggested to help you facilitate children's discussions of what they would like to accomplish. They range in appropriateness from age 3 to 7 or 8. Of course, each teacher will tailor the trips planned to meet the local situations and the needs of the children in the class.

SCIENCE AT HOME

In Chapter 19, you explored ways in which parents can become involved in classroom activities. In this section, suggestions are offered for ways in which parents can become involved in their children's science inquiries at home.

There is much science to be experienced at home. Electricity, water, plumbing, heating, air conditioning, telephones, televisions, radios, computers, the Internet, e-mail, the postal service, garbage and trash collection and disposal, and a host of other daily encounters are experienced at home. All are potential sources for children's development of the scientific processes and for their inquiries.

Parents can encourage children to observe carefully using all their senses, predict what might happen, test different explanations, and think about how and where they could obtain more information. For example, in letting children help bake a cake, parents can foster the process of measuring by letting children measure out the ingredients; they can foster the process of observing through encouraging children to examine crystals of sugar and salt; and they can foster the process of hypothesizing through asking them to speculate why the cake rises in the oven.

Take-home science kits are an excellent way for teachers of young children to encourage parents, guardians, and other primary care givers to help their children continue their science explorations at home. Take-home science activity kits contain materials and directions for science activities children can

ELEMENTS OF PLANNING AND GOING ON FIELD TRIPS

What to Do	*Source*
1. Decide where to go	Teacher and children
2. Take the trip in advance	Teacher
▌ Establish route	Teacher
▌ Obtain site permission	Site representative
▌ Find out entrance fees	Site representative
▌ List activities available	Site representative and teacher
▌ Determine time for trip	Teacher
▌ Find lunch facilities	Teacher
▌ Find rest room facilities	Teacher
▌ Determine clothing requirements	Teacher
3. Establish date of trip	Teacher and administration
4. Arrange transportation	Teacher and administration
5. Determine cost	Teacher
6. Establish funding	Teacher and administration
7. Arrange chaperones	Teacher and parents
8. Discuss trip with children	Teacher and children
▌ Ask what children would like to learn and record their responses	
▌ Ask what children would like to do and record their responses	
9. Write parent letter	Teacher and children
10. Secure parent permission	Teacher and parents
11. Plan for children unable to go on trip	Teacher
12. Collect money	Teacher
13. Plan for medical emergencies	Teacher
14. Provide first-aid kit	Teacher
15. Establish behavior expectations	Teacher and chaperones
16. Establish groups for each chaperone	Teacher and chaperones
17. Reconfirm with the site	Teacher and site representative
18. Go on trip	Teacher, children, chaperones
▌ Facilitate inquiries	Teacher and chaperones
▌ Point out interesting features	Teacher and chaperones
▌ Help children focus on their goals	Teacher and chaperones
19. Hold posttrip discussion	Teacher and children
▌ Ask most significant thing each child learned	
▌ Arrange for follow-up activities as appropriate	

FIGURE 20.6   Elements of planning and going on field trips

SOME FIELD TRIPS AND THEIR LEARNING OPPORTUNITIES

Destination	Some Learning Opportunities
Pond	Observe plants and animals, plant and animal habitats, and ecosystems. Collect insects. Collect leaves.
Lake shore	Observe plants and animals, plant and animal habitats, shoreline features, and sand and rocks. Identify water sports.
Ocean beach	Observe plants and animals, plant and animal habitats, and shoreline features. Observe intertidal area, effects of tides, waves and wave motion. Observe dunes and dune shapes. Watch crabs. Collect shells.
Desert	Observe plants and animals, desert ecology, kinds of sand, and sand dunes and dune shapes. Identify adaptations of plants and animals to desert environment. Infer dune movement. Observe windblown sand.
Grocery store	Study organization of merchandise. Observe methods of refrigeration. Observe food preparation. Identify methods of ensuring food safety. Identify uses of technology. Observe what individual workers do.
Hardware store	Study organization of merchandise. Identify uses of different kinds of hardware. Observe materials and supplies found in hardware stores. Identify uses of technology. Observe what individual workers do. (Note that some hardware stores have project-building events for children.)
Bank	Observe security systems. Observe money handling and money sorting. Identify uses of technology. Observe what individual workers do.
Zoo	Many activities are available. Check with educational coordinator. Children also may be able to see what animal scientists do.
Museums	Many activities are available. Check with educational coordinator. Children also may be able to see scientists at work.
Botanical gardens	Observe plants, plant varieties, and exotic plants. Observe plant care. Observe ways in which different plants grow. Observe what plant scientists do.
Plant nurseries	Observe plant varieties. Observe plant germination, growth, and care. Identify best plants for the local area and regions in local yards where plants grow best. Compare outside and inside plants. Observe what individual workers do.
Planetarium	Observe images of constellations, the sun, the moon, stars, planets, comets, and eclipses. Observe apparent movement of the night sky. Observe apparent movement of the daytime sky. Identify uses of technology. Children also may be able to interact with scientists.
Commercial dairy	Observe dairy-product processing, manufacturing, and packaging. Identify kinds of dairy products. Observe pasteurization. Identify methods of ensuring food safety and cleanliness. Observe what individual workers do.

FIGURE 20.7 Some field trips and their learning opportunities

(continued)

Ice cream plant	Identify ingredients and the sources of ingredients. Identify flavors. Observe manufacturing and preparation techniques.
Farmer's market	Observe organization of products, kinds of foods, and methods of food preservation and food safety. Observe exotic foods. Infer sources of foods. Observe what individual workers do.
Factories and assembly plants	Observe manufacturing process, assembly, final product, and inspection. Identify raw materials and parts. Observe procedures to ensure plant safety. Observe what individual workers do.
Television station	Observe equipment. Interact with personalities. Observe broadcast booths. Identify responsibilities of director, cameraperson, producer, and others. Identify uses of computers. Observe use of blue backgrounds for superimposed computer images. Interact with different specialists.
Radio station	Observe equipment. Interact with personalities. Observe broadcast booths. Identify responsibilities of director, cameraperson, producer, and others. Identify uses of computers. Interact with different specialists.
Weather station	Observe instruments and identify what they tell. Identify responsibilities of meteorologists. Identify uses of technology. Observe method used for forecasting. Observe production of weather maps. Identify severe weather warnings and the role of the U.S. Weather Service.
State and national parks	Many activities are available. Check with educational coordinator. Children may be able to interact with different specialists.
Fire station	Identify duties of fire fighters. Observe fire trucks and how the equipment works. Identify methods of fire prevention. Observe alarm and response systems.
A vegetable garden	Observe plants. Identify parts of plants eaten. Observe how vegetables grow. Observe planting, cultivating, caring, and harvesting.
A flower garden	Observe plants and flowers and how the different flowers are grown. Observe planting, cultivating, and caring.
Symphony or band rehearsal or concert	Identify instruments of the orchestra and band and the sounds they make. Identify characteristics of sound: pitch, volume, and quality.
Farm	Observe plants and animals, care of animals, how vegetables are grown, cultivated, cared for, harvested, and prepared for selling. Observe farming equipment. Identify uses of technology.
Dairy farm	Observe cows. Identify the food cows eat. Observe milking machines and milk storage facilities. Trace the dairy process from cows feeding to milk storage and shipment. Observe sanitation, cleanliness, and cleanliness tests.
Fisherman's wharf	Observe whole fish. Identify kinds of fish. Smell the odors. Observe fishermen unloading the catch. Identify ways seafood is preserved and how seafood is distributed to markets.

FIGURE 20.7   *(continued)*

do at home with their parents, guardians, primary care givers, older siblings, or other adults. The materials and directions are packaged in easily transported containers such as sturdy paper bags. Materials are inexpensive and easy to obtain from grocery stores, drug stores, and hardware stores. Directions are written so as to be easy to follow. They should include a brief explanation of what the activity is intended to accomplish, a list of the materials included and the materials needed to be supplied at home, step-by-step directions, and typical questions parents can ask their children to promote inquiry. You may also wish to include references to books and other sources of information parents may want to use to further engage their children. The kit may also include a data sheet for parents to use to help their children keep track of the results and a quick evaluation and feedback form for parents and children to complete together.

Send the kits home with the children and let them have them for up to a week to give parents time to do the activity with their children. Keep track of who takes which kit home so you can call for their return if necessary.

Each kit should contain most of the materials needed to do the activity so the materials parents have to supply themselves are minimal. Some teachers make up several kits of the same activity and send them home on a rotating basis. Some teachers make up kits of different activities and rotate them until all children have brought each kit home. It would be useful if the kits pertain to the science topic currently under study, but this is not necessary. Remember that the primary goals of early childhood science education are exposure to as many different experiences as possible, as the development of positive attitudes toward science, and the development of process and inquiry skills.

A number of grant sources provide funding (on a competitive basis) for home-school partnership arrangements. You may be able to secure grant funding for the materials and supplies for the take-home kits. (See Chapter 24 for information on grant writing.)

Many of the activities in this text can be used as take-home science activities. Additional take-home activities are suggested below.

RAISIN DANCE

In this activity, children try to figure out why raisins rise to the top of a glass of water when vinegar and baking soda are added.

Materials provided in kit:	Raisins
	Tall transparent plastic cup
	Baking soda
Materials to be provided at home:	Vinegar

Directions: Fill the plastic cup nearly to the top with tap water. Put a few raisins in the water and observe what happens. (They sink to the bottom.)

(continued)

Add one tablespoon of baking soda and dissolve it in the water. Now add two tablespoons of vinegar and stir it into the water. What happens to the raisins? (They rise to the top of the water and then sink; they "dance.")

Explanation for parents: The vinegar and baking soda react to form carbon dioxide gas. Tiny bubbles of the gas adhere to the wrinkled skin of the raisins and allow them to rise in the water. When the raisins reach the top, the gas escapes into the atmosphere, and the raisins sink. This continues until the reaction between the vinegar and the baking soda is complete.

Variations: Try using different amounts of vinegar and baking soda.
Try using club soda or other highly carbonated beverage instead of the baking soda and vinegar.
Try different temperatures of water.
Try other variations you and your child may think of.

Other resources:
Literature: *The Magic School Bus Gets Baked in a Cake: A Book about Kitchen Chemistry* by Joanna Cole (1995). The class winds up inside the cake they are trying to bake and learns about mixtures and reactions that occur when different ingredients are put together.
Television program: The Magic School Bus
Computer activities: The Magic School Bus

Optional Data Sheet

My raisins danced when I

(1) _____

(2) _____

(3) _____

(4) _____

(5) _____

Evaluation by Parent

When did you do this activity with your child? _____

Do you feel this activity was meaningful to you and your child?_____

_____

Were the directions easy to follow? _____

Do you have any suggestions as to how we can improve this activity?

_____

What did you and your child learn from this take-home kit _____

_____

Please suggest other science topics you would like to have us put in a take-home kit. _____

FREEZING WATER
In this activity, children explore factors involved in water freezing.

Materials provided in kit: Six plastic cups
                                          Magic marker

Materials to be provided at home: Water
                                          Salt
                                          Sugar
                                          Cola with sugar
                                          Diet drink
                                          Other liquids

Directions: Fill the cup about two-thirds full with water.
               Mark the level of the water in the cup with the magic marker.
               Put the cup in the freezer.
               Check the state of the water in the cup every 20 minutes or so until it is completely frozen.
               What happens to the water?
               Compare the level of the water in the cup with the level when it turns to ice.
               How long did it take to freeze completely?

Explanation for parents: When water freezes, tiny crystals of ice form. These ice crystals arrange themselves in a complex pattern where individual crystals are linked to each other at their edges. This takes up more room than the water molecules, and thus water expands when it freezes.

Try other variations such as those in the following suggestions. Be sure you fill the cup to the same mark as the original water experiment each time so you will have the same volume. Be sure to use plastic cups, not glass ones, to avoid breakage.

▮ Add a few tablespoons of salt to a cup of water and see how long it takes to freeze.
▮ Add a different amount of salt to a cup of water to see how long it takes to freeze.
▮ Do the same things using sugar.
▮ Open a bottle or can of regular soda with sugar, pour some into a cup, and see how long it takes to freeze. (Don't try to freeze an unopened can of soda; the expansion may cause the can to burst.)
▮ Do the same thing with diet soda.
▮ Do the same thing with fruit juices or drink mixes. Fill the cup about two-thirds full with the liquid, add a Popsicle stick, and freeze it. Children can eat their lesson.
▮ Try other variations you and your child can think of.

(continued)

Optional Data Table
How long it took to freeze different liquids

Liquid	How long it took to freeze
Water	
Water with _____ spoons of salt	
Water with _____ spoons of salt	
Water with _____ spoons of salt	
Water with _____ spoons of sugar	
Water with _____ spoons of sugar	
Water with _____ spoons of sugar	
Regular soda	
Diet soda	
(Other)	

Evaluation by Parent

When did you do this activity with your child? _____

Do you feel this activity was meaningful to you and your child?_____

_____

Were the directions easy to follow? _____

Do you have any suggestions as to how we can improve this activity?

_____

What did you and your child learn from this take-home kit _____

_____

Please suggest other science topics you would like to have us put in a take-home kit. _____

NIGHTTIME SKY WATCH
In this activity, children and their families observe the night sky.

Materials provided in kit: Flashlight with two or three layers of red cellophane over lens to avoid being blinded after eyes get used to the dark
Ideas for nighttime sky watch
Drawing of where to look for planets
Sky chart

Materials to be provided at home: Binoculars (if available)
                                     Monocular (if available)
                                     Telescope (if available)

Directions: The best time of year to hold a nighttime sky watching session in the Northern Hemisphere is late fall or early winter. Hold it after dark. Allow about an hour after sunset for the sky to get dark. Then, while outdoors, allow 20 minutes for eyes to get used to the dark. Avoid holding the session when the full moon is high in the sky.

Hold it in a place that is dark—away from buildings and tall trees and away from streetlights. Be sure trees and building walls don't get in the way of viewing the lower portion of the sky.

Be sure everyone wears warm clothing—it gets cold out there at night!

What to Look for

1.   If the moon is out, you can see its phase, brightness, and color. You can also see craters and other features very well through binoculars.
2.   You may be able to see planets. [The teacher may wish to include a drawing of where to find planets with this package.] Planets you are most likely to be able to see are Mars, Jupiter, and Saturn. (Venus is visible in the early mornings when it is out.) You can see the moons around Jupiter with binoculars; there may be two, three, or four moons lined up around the planet. The rings of Saturn are visible with low-powered telescopes.

     How can you tell a planet from a star? (1) Planets are brighter than the stars in the area. (2) Planets tend to "glow" rather than "twinkle." (3) Planets are on an imaginary line that connects the position of the moon with the position where the sun set.
3.   Notice the differences in brightness and colors of the stars. Stars may be white, blue-white, blue, yellow, green, or red.
4.   Prominent constellations in the northern sky.

     Big Dipper   This is an open cluster of five stars. The two stars in the bowl of the Big Dipper point toward the North Star. *Mizar* (second star in the handle) is a double star. You can see two stars instead of one if you look slightly *away* from the star.

     Little Dipper   The last star in its handle is the North Star (also called "Polaris").

     Cassiopeia   This constellation is shaped like a *W* or an *M.*

     Cepheus   This constellation is shaped like a hat.
5.   Prominent constellations in the late autumn and early winter.

     Orion   Orion, the Hunter, is a very prominent constellation. Look for three bright stars lined up in a row, fairly far apart from each other and somewhat inclined to the horizon. These are Orion's "belt." One of the shoulders is a red star named Betelgeuse (pronounced "beetlejuice") and is a red giant. Orion contains the Great Nebula of Orion, a cloud of gas in the process of coming together to form a new star. This is the middle "star" in Orion's sword—but this middle "star" isn't a star at all—it is the Nebula. It is dramatic to look at it with binoculars or a small telescope.

(continued)

Big Dog   This constellation follows Orion around the sky. It is low on the horizon. The dog's nose is represented by the star named Sirius, which is the brightest star in the sky.

6. Prominent constellations visible during spring and summer.

Spring: Leo   Bootes
               Virgo   Corona Borealis
               Cancer

Summer: Cygnus   Lyra
               Sagitta   Scorpius
               Hercules

7. What I saw:

8. Comments and questions:

_____

_____

_____

_____

_____

Evaluation by Parent

When did you do this activity with your child? _____

Do you feel this activity was meaningful to you and your child?_____

_____

Were the directions easy to follow? _____

Do you have any suggestions as to how we can improve this activity?

_____

What did you and your child learn from this take-home kit _____

_____

Please suggest other science topics you would like to have us put in a take-home kit. _____

SUMMARY

The constructivist early childhood science education teacher takes advantage of the variety of science inquiry opportunities available outside of the school building in addition to those devised for more traditional classroom use. Outdoor learning centers provide natural environments in which children can inquire into phenomena of nature; they can be as simple as the school grounds or as complex as specially constructed facilities for specialty studies of nature. Field trip opportunities abound, and the constructivist teacher includes visits to local facilities and establishments as part of the normal curriculum to enlarge children's experiential base, to foster growth in inquiry, and to provide for development of increasingly positive attitudes toward science. Because parents are children's "first and most influential teacher" (Rillero, 1994, p. 1), today's early childhood science program seeks to involve parents in helping children continue their scientific inquiries by encouraging parents to inquire with their children at home and sending home science kits for children to do with their parents. By building out-of-school experiences into their programs, early childhood science educators promote each child's interest in science and desire and ability to do science.

Note

1. See Melber (2000) for descriptions of uses of non-traditional science activities in science programs.
2. You can obtain additional information about educational opportunities at museums, and you can download a summary publication and a case study workbook of museum education entitled *True Needs, True Partners* from the Institute of Library and Museum Services website at http://www.imls/gov.

References

Bruner, J. (1990, April/May). Telling stories to make science: Karplus lecture excerpts. *NSTA Reports!*

Carle, E. (1996a). *Little cloud.* New York: Philomel Books.

Carle, E. (1996b). *The grouchy ladybug.* New York: Harper Collins.

Checkley, K. (1997). The first seven . . . and the eighth. *Educational Leadership 55*(1), 8–13.

Cole, J. (1995). *The magic school bus gets baked in a cake: A book about kitchen chemistry.* New York: Scholastic.

Dewey, A. (1993). *The sky.* New York: Green Tiger Press.

McLerran, A. (1992). *Roxaboxen.* New York: Puffin Books.

Melber, L.M. (2000). Tap into informal science learning. *Science Scope, 23* (b), 28–29

Meyer, M. (1997). The greening of learning: Using the eighth intelligence. *Educational Leadership 55*(1), 32–34.

New survey shows increase in museum education programs. (1999, July/August). *Community Update, 69.* Washington, DC: U.S. Department of Education, 2.

Peters, L. W. (1988). *The sun, the wind, and the rain.* New York: Henry Holt.

Rillero, P. (1994). Doing science with your children. Eric Document No. ED 372 952.

Sendak, M. (1988). *Where the wild things are.* New York: HarperCollins Children's Books.

Stone, S. J., and Glascott, K. (1997–1998, Winter). The affective side of science instruction. *Childhood Education.*

Van Allsburg, C. (1988). *Two bad ants.* Boston: Houghton Mifflin.

Willis, S. (1997, Winter). Field trip studies: Learning thrives beyond the classroom. *Curriculum Update.* Alexandria, VA: Association for Supervision and Curriculum Development.

CHAPTER 21

Technology in Early Childhood Science Education

We live in an age of technology in which young children often know more about technology than their teachers. Technology has become part of children's everyday lives. They talk on cellular telephones, play videos and video games, surf television channels, operate camcorders, play with talking and moving toys that function through computer chips, and learn letters, words, songs, and patterns using computer-based consoles. Many preschool and early-elementary-grade children also surf the Internet, send and receive e-mail, expand their information bases through CD-ROM information sources, and use computer-based games and learning programs at home.

People tend to think of educational technology in terms of computers. But schools have used educational technologies for years. When the chalkboard was introduced to schools, it was

Technology . . . . the knack of so arranging the world that we don't have to experience it.
Max Frisch, *Homo Faber* (Frankfurt: Suhrkamp Verlag, 1957)

Man is still the most extraordinary computer of all.
John F. Kennedy (1963)

The whole world had changed. Only the fairy tales remained the same.
Lois Lowry, *Number the Stars* (New York: Houghton Mifflin, 1990)

considered revolutionary. Films, filmstrips, movies, videos, models, and charts have become integral components of teaching and learning. Audiotapes continue to be used for song and dance. Calculators are used to help children in mathematics and science. The overhead projector, originally developed for business, has found numerous applications in education for showing transparencies, mathematics manipulatives, money, clocks, color tiles, pattern blocks, magnetic fields, and a host of other uses.

However, the emergence of the personal computer, the subsequent development of cost-effective desktop and laptop computers and user-friendly software, and the expansion of the Internet to public access have had the most profound impact on technology in the classroom. Educational uses of computers include word processing, spreadsheets, databases, graphing, presentation software, electronic mail, the World Wide Web, and a multitude of increasingly sophisticated applications. Computers can provide practice, create realistic simulations, act as tutors, provide instant access to huge amounts of information, and enable children and their teachers to communicate with peers throughout the world.

There is more to educational technology than computers. But computers and their applications dominate the educational technology scene. It is imperative that teachers become sufficiently familiar with computer-based technology so that they can use technology comfortably in the classroom. In this chapter, you will examine a variety of computer applications and ways you can use them to foster the process-oriented inquiry early childhood science education program.

A TECHNOLOGY INVENTORY

To get started, a technology inventory is presented to help you assess your skills in the technology arena. Complete this inventory as a self-assessment.

Constructing Your Ideas 21.1
A Technology Inventory

 What is your "ETQ" (Educational Technology Quotient)? To find out, place an *x* on the blank that represents your level of proficiency in each of the following technologies commonly used in schools today. Then calculate your ETQ using the scoring guide at the end.

TECHNOLOGY	MY PROFICIENCY			
	I Don't Know the First Thing about It	I Can Use It Somewhat	I Can Use It Well	Know It So Well I Can't Do without It
Chalkboard	1	2	3	4
White board	1	2	3	4
Overhead projector	1	2	3	4
Typewriter	1	2	3	4
Camera	1	2	3	4
Tape recorder	1	2	3	4
CD player	1	2	3	4
Filmstrip projector	1	2	3	4
TV set	1	2	3	4
Video player	1	2	3	4
Camcorder	1	2	3	4
Basic calculator	1	2	3	4
Word processing program	1	2	3	4
Database program	1	2	3	4
Spreadsheet program	1	2	3	4
Graphing program	1	2	3	4
Presentation software	1	2	3	4
Video games	1	2	3	4
Computer games	1	2	3	4

(continued)

TECHNOLOGY	MY PROFICIENCY			
	I Don't Know the First Thing about It	I Can Use It Somewhat	I Can Use It Well	Know It So Well I Can't Do without It
Desktop publishing program	1	2	3	4
Sign and banner programs	1	2	3	4
E-mail	1	2	3	4
The Internet	1	2	3	4
CD-ROMs	1	2	3	4
LCD projector panel	1	2	3	4
Laserdisks	1	2	3	4
Science laboratory probes	1	2	3	4
Digital camera	1	2	3	4
Digital scanner	1	2	3	4
Cell phone	1	2	3	4

Scoring: Add your points and divide by 120. This is your ETQ or Educational Technology Quotient.

What did you score? 85 is about average. If you scored in this range, you will want to improve the technologies you don't know very well (the 1s and 2s), and the motivation for doing so will come through need. If you scored below 60, you might want to give serious consideration to improving your technological skills. If you scored 100 or above—you're practically home!

Reproduced with permission from Martin, D. J. (2000). *Elementary Science Methods: A Constructivist Approach*. Belmont, CA: Wadsworth/Thompson Learning.

WHY USE COMPUTER-BASED TECHNOLOGY IN EARLY CHILDHOOD SCIENCE EDUCATION?

In 1990, 97.3 percent of the public elementary schools in the United States reported using computers; this is contrasted with 11.1 percent that reported using computers in 1981 (World Almanac, 1994, 196). In 1994–1995, there was one computer for every 79.3 students in public elementary schools; by 1997–1998, there were almost 16 times as many computers in public elementary schools, with one computer for every 6.9 students (Brunner, 1999, 882). In 1996, 13 percent of elementary schools in the United States had access to the Internet, and 85 percent of elementary schools without Internet access had plans to connect to it by the year 2000 (ibid., 883). The United States Department of Education launched a nationwide educational technology initiative in 1999 entitled "Preparing Tomorrow's Teachers to Use Technology" to "help ensure that tomorrow's teachers can integrate technology effectively into the curriculum and can understand the new styles of teaching and learning enabled by technology" (U.S. Department of Education, 1999). The thrust is toward enabling teachers to learn to use technology, learn to teach the use of technology to the children in their classes, and learn how to incorporate technology into their curriculum and daily teaching.

There are numerous reasons for teachers and children to use computer-based technology in the early childhood classroom, many of which directly affect science education.

One reason is that technology is used everywhere. Computers are used in virtually every business from fast-food restaurants to brokerage firms, banks, grocery stores, auto repair shops, hospitals, warehouses, factories, and airlines. Computers are used in school districts for many purposes, including attendance, scheduling, cafeteria meal planning and preparation, and many other functions. School secretaries prepare correspondence using word-processing programs and prepare individualized mailings using the mail-merge function of word processors. Postage can even be printed on the envelopes after purchasing quantities over the Internet. Teachers' paychecks are generated by computer. Accounting and inventory functions are computerized. The list of ways in which computers are used is endless. Because computers play such an integral role in every aspect of every person's life, it seems logical that they should play an integral role in children's education. With adequate teacher training and investment in **hardware** and **software,** computer-based technology will become as much a part of the classroom as it is in other aspects of the school and children's lives.

hardware—The computer and its accessories

software—Programs that are operated by a computer

A second reason for using computer-based technology in the classroom is that many children are accustomed to using it. Just as the use of educational videos seeks to teach children through familiar media, the use of computer-based technology seeks to provide a comfortable learning atmosphere for children familiar with using technology. At the end of 1998, over 40 percent of U.S. households had computers, and one-quarter of U.S. households had access to the Internet (National Telecommunications and Information Administration, 1999). In 1997, 14 percent of children age 2–4 and 25 percent of children age 5–9 used e-mail and the Internet, and these percentages are expected to increase to 24 percent and 43 percent respectively by the year 2002 (Quick Facts, 1998). As Craig (1999b) put it, today's children are the "Net Generation" (28).

Third, in keeping with the goal of schools to provide equal learning opportunities for *all* children, using technology in the classroom helps bridge a widening "digital divide." U.S. Census Bureau data for 1998 show the following:

▌ Adults with college degrees were more than 8 times as likely to have a computer at home as those with elementary education and were nearly 16 times as likely to have access to the Internet at home.

▪ High-income households in urban areas were more than 20 times as likely as low-income households to have access to the Internet at home.

▪ Children in low-income white families were more than three times as likely to have access to the Internet at home as children in comparable black families and four times as likely as children in comparable Hispanic families.

▪ Children in two-parent white households were nearly twice as likely to have access to the Internet at home as children in single-parent white households; children in dual-parent black households were almost four times as likely to have access to the Internet at home as children in single-parent black households.

▪ Among families in the $15,000 to $35,000 annual income bracket, more than 32 percent of white families owned computers, compared to 19 percent of blacks and Hispanics (*New York Times,* 1999).

The list goes on. It is evident that there is a technology usage and access gap defined by factors such as race, income, and family structure. As in other aspects of education, it is the schools' responsibility to play a role in narrowing this digital deficit.

A fourth reason for using computer-based technology in early childhood classrooms is to enable children and teachers to gain access to types and amounts of information otherwise unavailable, thus providing expanded resources for children's use in their inquiries and enabling them to widen their experiential bases. Using laserdiscs, children can see photographs, view videos of action scenes, and hear explanations on a multitude of topics ranging from animal habitats to earthquakes, volcanoes, whales, bubbles, and just about anything else. Entire encyclopedias are available on CD-ROM discs. The Internet can provide up-to-the minute information on just about any topic. Children can use it as an information resource. Teachers can use it to obtain background information for lesson-planning ideas. The store of information available through technology is virtually unlimited.

A fifth reason for incorporating technology in the classroom is to foster increased communications skills. In developing a class website, children employ refined communications skills. Through the use of e-mail, children can communicate with children in other locations. With the use of Power-Point and Hypermedia software, children can develop their own presentations for other children, other classes, and parents. These presentations may include video and audio clips that the children themselves have produced, photographs that they have taken with digital cameras, and text—all in the same presentation. To use these programs requires communications skills.

Another reason is to enable children to strengthen learning styles that have been shown to be related to science achievement (see Chapter 17). Technology can foster the internal locus of control by providing situations that require children to pursue their own strategies to solving problems, thus demonstrating that they are in control of their own learning (Steinberg, 1989). Technology has been used to expand the degree of field independent cognitive operations on the part of field dependent children. Computer programs were created to help children recognize differences in paired pictures and rows of shapes to help decrease their dependence on surrounding details for figure recognition (Collings, 1985). The operation of computer programs is itself an aid for developing a more field independent style, for children must focus on the details of the programmed material rather than on the program's global aspects. The use of computers can also be an invaluable aid to children with learning disabilities, children whose primary language is not English, and children with physical handicaps.

Finally, perhaps the most compelling reason for using advanced technology in early childhood science education is that *scientists use it*. One of the premises underlying early childhood science education is that children should *do* science, not just read about science, and that children should do science the way scientists do it. This means using technology.

The National Science Teachers Association adopted this posture in their position statement, "The Use of Computers in Science Education":

> Just as computers play a central role in developing and applying scientific knowledge, they can also facilitate the learning of science. It is, therefore, the position of the National Science Teachers Association that computers should have a major role in the teaching and learning of science. (1993)

In the *National Science Education Standards* (National Research Council, 1996), Content Standard E urges that science programs give attention to technology and its use in scientific inquiry and in society (see inside front and back covers).

TUTORIAL AND CD INFORMATION PROGRAMS

Computer tutorial programs are designed to teach and reinforce one or more concepts. Typically a tutorial program presents a question or a situation and asks the user to key a response. If the response is correct, a reward of some sort is displayed, such as points, distance up a mountain, smiley faces, applause, trumpet fanfares, and the like. The student is then presented with the next question or situation, which may be a continuation of the same scenario or may be an incremental level higher in difficulty. If the response to the initial situation is incorrect, an appropriate message appears, and the student is asked either to try again or to open the instructional portion of the program to study the concept and then try the same or a similar question again. In some tutorial programs, the instruction comes first and is followed by mastery questions.

Tutorial programs provide immediate reinforcement of children's responses and are similar to the programmed texts of the 1960s and 1970s.

They often contain the basic elements of quality expository teaching, including gaining attention, overviewing the lesson, providing objectives, reviewing prerequisite information, delivering new information, offering mastery guidance, and providing formative and summative evaluations with feedback.

Tutorial programs are useful in the classroom for several situations. They can be used as adjuncts or enrichment for material the class is studying so children will gain exposure to additional perspectives and examples. They can be used to enable children who have been absent from school to study the material they missed. They can be used to permit children to study topics that have captured their interest but that will not be included in the curriculum. They can be used to encourage children to pursue given topics at more advanced levels. Tutorials are also a useful means for teachers to study the background science of topics they are planning to teach.

Computerized teaching has been shown to exert a small but positive effect on learning (Hancock & Betts, 1994). However, tutorials are clearly expository in nature and thus have limited value in inquiry-oriented science programs. Perhaps the best application of tutorials is as a resource available for children whose inquiries lead them to the desire to investigate content not covered in the program.

The current generation of tutorial software is delivered in compact disk (CD) format, is much more interactive, and offers many more options for study than the earlier programs.

The *JumpStart* Learning System series (Knowledge Adventure, Inc.) and the *Reader Rabbit* series (The Learning Company) offer tutorial programs on CDs appropriate for a range of ages, including preschool and very young children. The programs for preschool children focus on patterns, shapes, colors, music, and number and language development skills. Children color pictures, match shapes, count objects, identify letters, and do other engaging activities with the mouse. Rewards are provided for success, and encouragement is provided for children who need to try again. The patterns and shapes sections are particularly useful for practice in the process skill of classification. Children must first learn how to use the mouse, but the programs are easy for children to operate independently once they have mastered the mouse. The programs provide the option of keeping the scores of individual children so the teacher or parent—and the children themselves—can track progress. *JumpStart* provides science sections in the programs designed for grades 1–5.

Many of the *Magic School Bus* topics, popular in book form and in cartoon form on public television, are available in computerized form on CD (Microsoft). Children click on pictures on the richly illustrated screens to see and hear explanations about examples of the main topic. The *Animals* program (for children ages 6–10), typical of the series, includes information about animals from desert, swamp, arctic tundra, mountain, island, savanna, and rainforest environments. Children can do games, puzzles, reports, and "experiments" and can construct posters.

The Dinosaur Hunter (DK Interactive Learning) is an interactive CD that presents detailed facts about dinosaurs, their habitats, and their living styles,

FIGURE 21.1   Preschoolers at the computer

and the opportunity to search for buried dinosaur bones. The CD also contains several videos and 3-D dinosaur images that can be manipulated.

There are informational CDs on just about any topic, for just about any age level from child to adult, and at just about any level of sophistication. Most of those intended for use by children include pictures, sound, and videos in addition to print material. Typically, an index of specific topics is provided. The investigator selects the desired topic and then selects the desired presentation: photographs, essays, sound bytes, videos, and others that may be available. Often the photos and essays can be printed.

The National Geographic Society has prepared many informational CDs on a variety of natural history topics. One, entitled *Mammals* (National Geographic Society), contains information about hundreds of the world's mammals. The information is in the form of pictures showing the adult and baby animals in a variety of natural settings, sound clips so children can hear what sounds the animals make, and videos of some mammals showing how they move and how they interact with the environment. An option is available to listen to the printed explanations accompanying many of the pictures being read out loud.

Other examples of CD information bases include encyclopedias, talking dictionaries, atlases, catalogs, telephone books, and the like. Library catalogs and the ERIC, PSYCHLIT, and other reference databases in your college or university library are probably provided on CDs.

Constructing Your Ideas 21.2
Exploring Tutorial and Interactive Computer Programs

The goal of this activity is for you to make a thorough exploration of a tutorial or an interactive CD program.

Obtain a copy of a program you might want to use in your classroom. Be sure the program is compatible with the operating system of the computer you will be using. If the program you choose is on CD, be sure your computer has a CD drive and has the memory and other specifications cited on the program package.

Follow the directions for loading the program. Parts of it may be loaded onto the hard drive of the desktop computer you will be using, but you can delete it from the hard drive if necessary when you are finished. If the program comes with operating suggestions, follow them to explore the entire program. Actually do the computerized activities yourself, taking on the role of a child who might work the program. If the program allows printing of scores, certificates, or student work, print representative samples.

Then prepare either a short written or oral presentation for your class so others can benefit from your explorations.

WORD PROCESSING AND DESKTOP PUBLISHING

Most computers come with word-processing programs already installed on them. Word-processing programs are used for typing written reports, essays, manuscripts, and the like. Unlike the typewriter, they have formatting options built in so you can manipulate the text in multiple ways, such as varying the

number of spaces between lines, the margins, and the indentations,

centering text or aligning it to the left or the right or both, and under-

lining text or putting it in *italics* or **boldface**. Most programs provide

a choice of type fonts and sizes that are compatible with the

capabilities of the accompanying printer. Type sizes typically vary

from small to regular and very large.

In many schools, children are encouraged to do some of their written work through the use of word processors. It has been shown that children who regularly use word processors for their writing exhibit higher quality and greater quantity of writing (Hancock & Betts, 1994). The spell-check feature enables children to focus on content without being overly concerned about correct spelling. Most spell checkers offer a selection of correctly spelled words as replacements for incorrectly spelled words; this requires children to select the correct spelling, thus fostering spelling skills.

Have children prepare some of their science reports using a word processor. Children also can use word-processing programs to construct labels for pictures and drawings they include in booklets they make, construct labels for bulletin board pictures and items on display, make signs, make posters, and do any of a number of other written activities where neatness and quality of presentation are factors.

Desktop publishing programs allow children or the teacher to create newsletters, pamphlets, brochures, signs, banners, flash cards, calendars, and even big books—all with a professional look. Many word-processing programs have desktop publishing capabilities, including the capability to include pictures, manipulate text and pictures, and do many other fancy things. Use the desktop publishing application to prepare the newsletters about your science program described in Chapter 19 (see Figure 21.2). Also

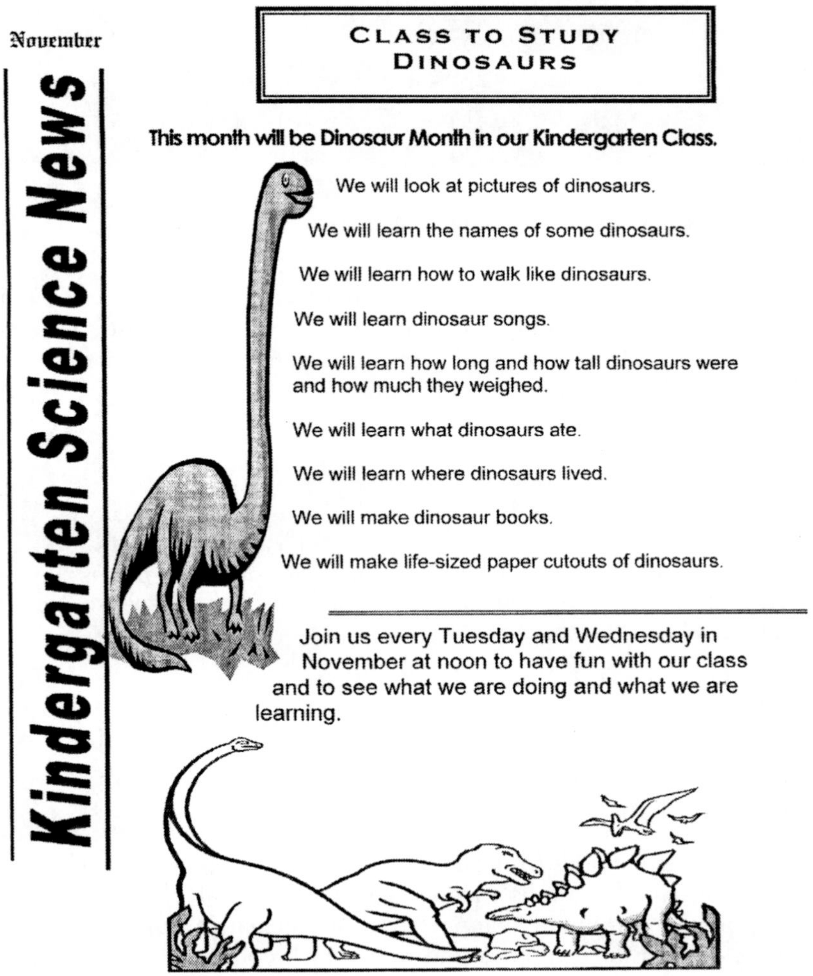

November

Kindergarten Science News

CLASS TO STUDY DINOSAURS

This month will be Dinosaur Month in our Kindergarten Class.

We will look at pictures of dinosaurs.

We will learn the names of some dinosaurs.

We will learn how to walk like dinosaurs.

We will learn dinosaur songs.

We will learn how long and how tall dinosaurs were and how much they weighed.

We will learn what dinosaurs ate.

We will learn where dinosaurs lived.

We will make dinosaur books.

We will make life-sized paper cutouts of dinosaurs.

Join us every Tuesday and Wednesday in November at noon to have fun with our class and to see what we are doing and what we are learning.

FIGURE 21.2 A science announcement prepared using desktop publishing (Microsoft Word 97 application)

FIGURE 21.3   Doing a class announcement on a computer

use this application to create banners and signs advertising special classroom events such as Science Day and special activities welcoming guest speakers (Figure 21.3). Turn children's original work into big books. The uses of desktop publishing applications are virtually unlimited.

Constructing Your Ideas 21.3
Using Desktop Publishing

Use a desktop publishing program or the desktop publishing capabilities of a word-processing program to create a one-page illustrated flyer to distribute to parents and other classes, inviting them to participate in "Whale Day" in your classroom.

SPREADSHEETS AND GRAPHING APPLICATIONS

Spreadsheets (the term comes from the field of accounting) are used to organize quantitative data so graphs can be generated and calculations can be made by applying automatic computerized mathematical operations. A spreadsheet is divided into columns and rows. Each column contains a specific kind of data, and each row contains the data for a specific case. For example, a spreadsheet created for household expenditures might contain columns for rent, food, gas, electricity, water, telephone, gasoline, and entertainment. There might be a row for each day. You would enter the expenditures in the cell created by the intersection of the appropriate column with the row of the day on which the expenditure occurred. Through applying mathematical operations built into the spreadsheet, you could find total daily, weekly, and monthly expenditures, and total expenditures for each category such as food, or for a combination of categories such as utilities including gas, electricity, and water. You also could find average expenditures and other summary information that might help you with your budgeting efforts.

Most spreadsheets have graphing functions built in, and you can use this application to create pie charts, columnar graphs, line graphs, and graphs in other formats that portray the information. For example, you might want to create a pie chart that shows the percentage of total expenditures for a month by category of expense.

As a teacher, you can take advantage of the power of spreadsheets in several ways. You can use spreadsheets to keep track of personal school and professional expenses, to chart children's progress in mastering given skills, and to create grade books that automatically calculate term or final grades according to percentage weights of the various grading components that the teacher builds into the program. One example of teacher use of spreadsheets for classroom operations involves charting student progress in process skill mastery. In Chapter 18 we suggested a quantitative method of assessing mastery in process skills, where each skill is assessed on a scale of 1 to 4, with a score of 1 representing the lowest and a score of 4 representing the highest degree of skill mastery. A spreadsheet can be used to record each assessment. Each student will be entered in a row, and the results of each process skill assessment will be entered in a different column. From this data, the teacher can find totals and averages of the assessments as the school year progresses and can create charts or graphs for a visual portrayal of the progress of each student or the class as a whole. If the assessment of each process skill were to be entered in separate columns, the teacher could discover student progress in the mastery of each skill as well as in the general development of the process skills. Figure 21.4 shows a spreadsheet in which overall process skill assessments for nine children are recorded each week for two months. Figure 21.5 shows a graph of one of the student's progress in process skills, and Figure 21.6 shows a summary graph displaying progress made by the class as a whole during the two-month period.

Perhaps the most useful application of spreadsheets in early childhood science education lies in its graphing capabilities. When children engage in inquiries that result in numerical data, the teacher can enter the children's data in the spreadsheet and use the graphing function to generate graphs that portray the data. As was indicated in Chapter 12, graphs portray data visually, making it easier for children to interpret the data. Many of the activities described in this text result in outcomes that can be portrayed graphically. For example, the plant growth graphing activity shown in Constructing Science in the Classroom 5.5 can be done by inputting the data on a computer

OVERALL PROCESS SKILLS ASSESSMENTS								
Name	Week 1	Week 2	Week 3	Week 4	Week 5	Week 6	Week 7	Week 8
Amy	26	32	33	30	36	36	33	36
Andrew	26	30	30	30	32	29	32	35
Donetta	28	31	35	35	36	33	37	38
Elizabeth	30	32	36	33	35	40	38	41
Katie	24	23	29	34	33	38	35	39
James	26	27	29	35	35	38	40	41
Julie	29	35	35	39	41	42	40	40
Miguel	30	35	35	36	32	41	40	38
Saleem	27	28	38	35	38	41	40	40
AVERAGE	**27**	**30**	**33**	**34**	**35**	**38**	**37**	**39**

FIGURE 21.4　Overall process skills assessment data table (Microsoft Excel application)

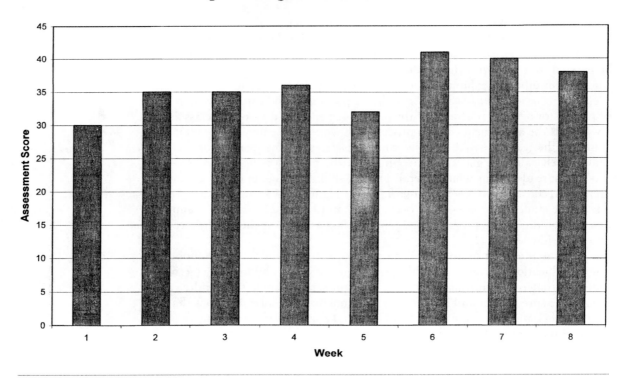

FIGURE 21.5　Graph of one child's overall process skills assessment (Microsoft Excel application)

Class Performance on Process Skills Assessments

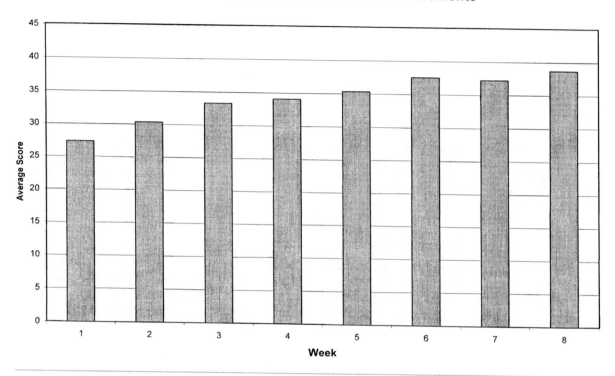

FIGURE 21.6   Graph of overall class performance on process skills assessment (Microsoft Excel application)

spreadsheet. The graph showing the relationship between length of peapods and number of peas in Constructing Science in the Classroom 12.3 was done using the graphing function of a spreadsheet.

There are numerous uses for spreadsheets. As you explore the capabilities and power of spreadsheet and graphing applications, you are sure to find additional ways these programs can help make life easier for you, enrich and expand the learning environments of children, and help children in their constructions of science.

Constructing Your Ideas 21.4
Using Spreadsheets and Graphing Programs

Using spreadsheet and graphing programs, create a visual portrayal of the noonday outdoor temperatures every school day for one month.

First, create a hypothetical data set showing outdoor noonday temperatures each day school is in session (Monday through Friday) for a month. The data table would be formatted similar to the following one.

(continued)

Day	Temperature
Monday	73
Tuesday	71
Wednesday	68
Thursday	66
Friday	70

Enter all the data into the spreadsheet, and print a copy of the spreadsheet for review. Then use the graphing function to construct a graph that visually displays the data in an appropriate manner. Be sure to have labels where needed so the graph can be interpreted. Print a copy of your graph to share with other members of the class.

DATABASES

Databases are computer programs that are used to organize, sort, and analyze descriptive and other qualitative data. Modern software such as *Microsoft Office* and *ClarisWorks* combine database, spreadsheet, and graphing functions with other powerful programs that can be linked together and used to produce rich arrays of information manipulation and presentation.

Databases are organized much like spreadsheets; columns typically are used for different kinds of information and rows typically are used for specific cases. For example, you might want to keep a database of pertinent information about the children in your class. This information might include the address, telephone number, mother's name, father's name, bus assignment, allergies, and names and ages of siblings. You would have a column for each specific kind of information, and you would have a row for each child. As in the spreadsheet, the information pertaining to a child is entered in the cell formed by the intersection of the appropriate columns with the row designated by the child's name (see Figure 21.7).

Through the search and sort mechanism provided in the database program, you can obtain many different summaries of the data, such as who rides each bus, who has certain allergies, and who has younger or older siblings (Figure 21.8).

KINDERGARTEN CLASS ROSTER

Name	Address	Telephone	Mother's Name	Father's Name	Bus	Allergies	Sibling 1 Name	Sibling 1 Age	Sibling 2 Name	Sibling 2 Age	Sibling 3 Name	Sibling 3 Age
Amy	317 Elm St	378-4259	Clarissa	David	15	Pollen	Kyle	4	Joshua	7		
Andrew	21 Church St	378-9177	Sherri	Steven	10		Steven	4	Merilee	9		
Donetta	54 Elm St	378-7359	Lucretia	Jeremy	15	Pollen	Lucinda	3	LaWanda	3	Aiesha	2
Elizabeth	228 Oak Dr	378-5591	Deborah	George	10	Wheat	Robert	2	Emily	2	Michael	7
Katie	73 Maple St	378-9225	Mary	James	15	Chocolate, Pollen	Ashley	3	Joshua	4		
James	73 Maple St	378-9225	Mary	James	15	Chocolate, Pollen	Ashley	3	Joshua	4		
Julie	437 Birch St	378-9367	Linda	Randy	10	Wheat	Jennifer	1	Jacob	3		
Miguel	96 Elm St	378-2188	Maria	Pedro	15	Pollen	Gabriel	7	Teresa	9		
Saleem	215 East Place	378-1178	Miriam	Ali	12	Milk	Talal	3	Jasmeen	4		

FIGURE 21.7 Kindergarten class roster (Microsoft Excel application)

Database programs are useful in helping children continue their development of the process skills, especially classifying and interpreting data. Databases are also useful in helping children broaden their inquiries. The teacher can develop databases for just about any topic the children are studying for use in discovering new information. For example, a teacher could develop a database of characteristics of birds seen in the local area. The characteristics might include length, male-female resemblance, habitat, song, and nesting habits (see Figure 21.9). The teacher prepares the database, and the children operate the sorting function to discover commonalties among local birds such as which birds can be found in certain areas, in which birds the male and female look alike, most common nesting habits, and so on (Figure 21.10). To involve children more completely in this activity, have each child look up the agreed-upon information on four or five birds. Then enter this information into the database, and make it available for children to explore through the sorting technique.

Similarly, homemade databases can be developed for dinosaurs (including characteristics, locations, food preferences, and the like), planets (including size, distance from earth, temperature, number of moons, atmosphere, and so on), and other topics children are exploring.

Bus	Name
10	Andrew
10	Elizabeth
10	Julie
12	Saleem
15	Amy
15	Donetta
15	James
15	Katie
15	Miguel

Name	Allergies
James	Chocolate, Pollen
Katie	Chocolate, Pollen
Saleem	Milk
Amy	Pollen
Donetta	Pollen
Miguel	Pollen
Elizabeth	Wheat
Julie	Wheat
Andrew	

Name	Sibling 1 Name	Sibling 1 Age	Sibling 2 Name	Sibling 2 Age	Sibling 3 Name	Sibling 3 Age
Amy	Kyle	4	Joshua	7		
Andrew	Steven	4	Merilee	9		
Miguel	Gabriel	7	Teresa	9		

FIGURE 21.8 Lists of kindergarten children who ride each bus, have certain allergies, and who have older brothers and sisters (from database in Figure 21.7, Microsoft Excel application)

Name	Length (inches)	Male-Female Resemblance	Habitat	Song	Nest
Red Head Woodpecker	21-24	Similar	Groves	Churr	Hollows in Trees
Bluebird	18	Sl Different	Open Country	Musical	Natural Cavities
Oriole	18-20	Similar	Open Woods	Whistle	Lower Tree Branches
Starling	19-21	Similar	Cities	Whistles; Clicks	Builds Nests
Sparrow	15	Different	Cities	Chirps	Builds Nests
Nuthatch	11	Similar	Open Pine Woods	Twitter	Nests in Cavities
Chickadee	11	Similar	Woods	Whistle	Nests in Cavities
Cardinal	19-23	Different	Woodland Edges	Whistle; Chirp	Shrubbery
Titmouse	15	Similar	Woodlands	Whistle	Nests
Red-Winged Blackbird	18-24	Different	Marshes	Gurgle	Nests; Water Shrubs
Robin	23-28	Different	Cities	Caroling	Lower Tree Branches

FIGURE 21.9   Birds database (Microsoft Works application)

NAMES OF BIRDS IN WHICH MALE AND FEMALE LOOK ALIKE

Name	Length	Habitat	Song	Nest
Red Head Woodpecker	21–24	Groves	Churr	Hollows in Trees
Oriole	18–20	Open Woods	Whistle	Lower Tree Branches
Starling	19–21	Cities	Whistles; Clicks	Builds Nest
Nuthatch	11	Open Pine Woods	Twitter	Nests in Cavities
Chickadee	11	Woods	Whistle	Nests in Cavities
Titmouse	15	Woodlands	Whistle	Nests

FIGURE 21.10   Names of birds in which male and female look alike (Microsoft Works application)

As was discussed earlier in this chapter, many commercial databases are available, most of which are in CD format and include pictures, sound, videos, and games, puzzles, and other activities children can do. But the database constructed in the classroom with the help of the children provides maximum learning benefits as well as a sense of ownership.

ELECTRONIC MAIL

Electronic mail, better known as *e-mail,* involves typing messages on a computer and sending them through designated telephone or Internet lines to recipients anywhere in the world. E-mail capabilities generally accompany subscriptions to Internet providers. Each subscriber has a unique e-mail address. Many colleges and universities provide e-mail access to students through the institution's servers.

To use e-mail, type the address of the recipient in the address box, type the message, and click "send." Your message will be received in a matter of moments.

E-mail has wide application in the early childhood education inquiry science program. Under the teacher's direction, the class can communicate with children in other classes in the United States and around the world. This communication can be general in the form of developing partnerships with other classes. Or it could ask a class to dupicate an activity the children have done to see what happens in different locations, such as at sea level, at high altitudes, or in a different hemisphere.

E-mail can be used to communicate with scientists or other experts about areas the children are investigating. They can ask for input and expert advice about their investigations from people who know. Many scientists include their e-mail addresses on their Internet home pages or with articles and other materials they have published on the Internet. Universities frequently include the e-mail addresses of faculty. Most scientists and other experts are willing (if not eager) to help young scientists in their quest for resolution to their inquiries.

Constructing Your Ideas 21.5
Sending E-mail

Send an e-mail message to your instructor. Simply let your instructor know what your e-mail address is. Ask that your instructor return an e-mail with the message that yours was received.

THE INTERNET AND THE WORLD WIDE WEB

The development and growth of the Internet and the World Wide Web is the largest factor contributing to the explosive growth in accessibility to information we are experiencing today.

The Internet is a complex network of electronic communications that loosely connects millions of information sites worldwide. It was developed in 1969 as a military application to ensure that communications would continue uninterrupted even if global conditions were to become catastrophic. The World Wide Web was developed in 1991 to permit the inclusion of nonmilitary sites worldwide.

Every Internet site has its own unique address that starts with http://, which stands for *HyperText Transfer Protocol*. The address is called the *URL* (Uniform Resource Locator) and contains several elements separated by dots or forward slashes. Of particular interest are the three-letter designations at the end of the URL that tell the nature of the site: "edu" means the site is an educational institution; "gov" indicates a government site; "com" indicates a commercial site; "mil" indicates a military site; and "org" indicates the site is an organization. Web browsers such as *Netscape Navigator, Microsoft Internet Explorer, America OnLine (AOL),* and others enable your computer to connect to the websites.

There are essentially two ways of finding a site on the Internet: (1) Enter the URL in the address box of the web browser, and click "enter." The web browser will find the site and replace the browser screen with the site screen on your monitor. (2) Utilize a search tool such as *Yahoo, Excite, Infoseek, Lycos,* or any of a number of other search tools. Type key words in the "search for" window and click on the "submit" button. A list of websites matching your description will be displayed; there usually are more than you can possibly examine, necessitating you to narrow your search. Each item in the list is linked to the website it describes. Click on promising websites until you find what you are looking for.

Many Internet sites have built-in links to related internal and external sites. These linkages may be indicated with different-colored type than the rest of the text or with icons known as "buttons," or often, with both. A single click on the link will take you to the new site. The links may transfer you to a different section of a large document (like turning to a new chapter) or to a related local site (like a different department in a college, a listing of faculty, or the current schedule of class offerings), or to an external site such as the Educational Testing Services site where you can find current information on ETS tests. Some sites permit you to interact with the computers at the home site, such as applying to a college electronically, registering for courses over the Internet, or ordering books from a commercial book-selling site. The main site from which primary links are provided is called the *home page.* Finding sites and exploring the links these sites provide is called "surfing the net."

There are tens of thousands of Internet sites useful for early childhood science education. Some are geared toward children, and some are aimed at teachers and provide information background, lesson plans, references, suggested literature, video and multimedia titles, and other information valuable to teachers.

FIGURE 21.11 Surfing the net

Constructing Your Ideas 21.6
The Weather According to the Internet

The home page of The Weather Channel can be accessed at http://www.weather.com. Type this URL in the address window of your web browser, and look at The Weather Channel's home page.

What features do you observe?
What is today's weather forecast for your local area?
Find the current weather and the weather forecast for another area in the United States.
Find the current weather and the weather forecast for a foreign location.

Now click on the link to "Education." Then click on various links on the "Education" page to see what The Weather Channel can offer to children who have an interest in learning about weather and to teachers who are developing weather teaching/learning units.
Share what you find from this site with your class.

Constructing Your Ideas 21.7
Exploring NASA

The address of NASA's home page is http://www.nasa.gov. Type this URL in the address window of your web browser, and look at the enormous array of information available for students and teachers that can be accessed through the NASA web pages. Select one link and follow it through, link after link, page after page, and summarize what you find. Share your findings with your class.

Constructing Your Ideas 21.8
Surfing the Web for Science Sites

Use your web browser to access a web search tool such as *Yahoo, Lycos, Excite, Infoseek,* and so on. Type a few descriptive words such as "early childhood science education," "elementary science activities," or "early childhood science teaching" in the "search" box. Or you may wish to enter specific topics such as "weather," "dinosaurs," "gears," and the like, perhaps combined with limiting terms such as "children," "elementary school," "activities," "elementary school activities," "teaching," "lesson plans," and other similar terms.
Explore some of the promising sites your search produced.
When you come across a site you feel would be useful to you and other members of your class, write a brief two- or three-sentence summary together with the site's URL and distribute it to other class members; make a class list or booklet for use by all class members. If your class has its own web page, post your discoveries for others to access.

This text includes URLs of home page websites of professional organizations and a few other sites unlikely to experience address changes in the near future. However, URL addresses are undergoing a period of fluidity, resulting in numerous changes. Thus, it is suggested that you keep an ongoing list of sites you find useful and that you enter address corrections as they occur. To address this problem, the National Science Teachers Association (1999) has launched a *sci*LINKS project in which science textbook publishers can elect to include internet icons and codes in the margins at key subject areas. To search for Internet information, students and teachers access the *sci*LINKS website and enter the code that guides them to several of the best websites dealing with that topic. The website links are selected and maintained by teachers to ensure appropriateness and recency.

There are numerous ways the Internet can be incorporated into your early childhood science curriculum. Craig (1999) suggests asking children to create a list of topics they would like to learn about, perhaps relating to the subject being studied; the top choices become the focus of class investigations and, hence, the subjects for Internet browsing. Children can explore the Internet either individually or in groups. Of course, children must first learn how to explore the Internet; the technology or media specialist in the school often fulfills that requirement, frequently in technology lab settings.

There is growing concern over the appropriateness and safety of Internet sites for use by children.[1] Craig (1999) provides guidelines for children's use of the net; these guidelines are presented in adapted form in Figure 21.12.

In addition to using the Internet to find information, you and the children in your classes can use it to participate in scientific research efforts. In one such application, the *National Geographic Kids Network* provides hands-on net-based science units. The school buys the software package, which includes the needed software, a teacher's guide, student activity sheets, and the equipment needed to perform the suggested activities. Each classroom is part of a

---

NETIQUETTE

- Obtain approval for your topic from your teacher before you use the Internet.
- Use *only* your topic bank selections in exploring the Internet resources.
- Check for correct spelling.
- Read the description of the search results *carefully* before you click on the site.
- When selecting a site, be sure the title is related to your topic.
- Skim and scan the site for information related to your topic.
- Take notes.
- Record the addresses (URLs) of useful sites.
- *Chat Rooms are OFF LIMITS!*
- Never give out your name or the name of your school or your teacher!

FIGURE 21.12 Rules for children exploring the Internet (adapted from Craig, 1999)

research team composed of 9–15 other classes. Students use the computer to record data, create graphs, plot data on maps, report their findings, and exchange information with their global partners. The information from the team's schools is sent to a scientist, who analyzes the children's own data and provides feedback to each school site.

In New Hampshire, elementary schools connected through the Internet participate in projects in which children input data about bats, birds, and trees to develop regional ecological profiles (Lonergan, 1997).

Using the Internet, children can "travel" with bald eagles, monarch butterflies, sea turtles, songbirds, peregrine falcons, caribou, and loons during their annual migrations. Migrations of certain species are tracked by satellite from transmitters affixed to the animals; data can be transmitted to classrooms via Internet (Internet Project, 1995).

K–12 science teachers can access a 24-inch research-grade telescope located in the California mountains for astronomy projects. After the teacher reserves a block of time, the telescope can be controlled by the computer in the teacher's classroom and directed to move across the sky to a certain object. The object is photographed, and the image is sent back to the computer, where it is downloaded. Children can repeat the process to obtain additional images and thus study change (Classes View, 1995).

Children can communicate with astronauts in orbit via e-mail and closed-circuit television transmitted by satellite to ascertain the current status of experiments they themselves designed to be carried out in space.

Teachers should keep on the lookout for promising Internet and other computer-based activities that can be worked into the curriculum. Owston (1997) reports, "When computers are introduced into classrooms, teachers inevitably report that they change their teaching style to allow students greater autonomy in their learning. They tend to shift their style of teaching from a didactic to a more project-based approach" (30). The overriding questions about how to incorporate Internet technology into the curriculum are "Does this application help children *do* science?" and "Does this application help children assume ownership of their inquiries?"

VIDEO IN THE EARLY CHILDHOOD SCIENCE EDUCATION CLASSROOM

Many advances have been made in the field of video. Commercial and public television stations air instructional videos at times schools are in session so schools can pipe them into the classrooms. PBS (Public Broadcasting System) regularly broadcasts programs on science and nature. The Learning Channel and the Discovery Channel air programs on scientific topics suitable for young children. The Weather Channel broadcasts daily 10-minute explanations of weather phenomena and offers documentary videos for use in schools.

Children can produce their own videos. All it takes is a little know-how (or the assistance of the media specialist) and a desire to let children expand their horizons.

Laser videodiscs contain huge amounts of information about given topics; the information is presented in the form of text material, photos, frame-freezable videos, maps, and the like, and includes discussions, interviews, demonstrations, explanations, experimental procedures, minidocumentaries, computer animations, and so on. Many laserdiscs offer a choice of English or Spanish as the primary language. Laserdiscs can be used to illustrate or supplement lessons, and they can serve as resources for children who are investigating phenomena on their own.

A laserdisc requires a special disc player and a barcode reader that, when used with the manual accompanying the laserdisc, instantly locates the desired segment. Commercial laserdiscs come with directories that include the barcodes to provide ready access to the desired segments. Many textbook publishers now provide laserdiscs as supplemental material; barcodes in the teacher's editions enable teachers to select segments appropriate for their lessons.

EVALUATING COMPUTER SOFTWARE

As you have seen, a tremendous amount of computer software is available. Some is free; some costs only the price of the disk plus postage; some is expensive. Some require additional items of apparatus. As you have also seen, computer programs vary enormously as to the degree of children's inquiry they can support.

Many journals and magazines such as *Educational Technology* and *Journal of Computers in Mathematics and Science Teaching* contain software review columns; these will keep you apprised of new software and will aid in the evaluation process. *NSTA Reports!* (published by the National Science Teachers Association) contains periodic listings of computer software that has been reviewed and assessed. Specialized journals such as *Science and Children* and *Childhood Education* also contain reviews of software. The Association for Supervision and Curriculum Development (ASCD) publishes annual reviews of computer software. In addition, catalogs of educational software such as the *Educational Resources Catalog* are available.

In all cases, you should give special consideration to the degree to which a particular technology or technological application supports the process-oriented inquiry method of science instruction and the degree to which it enables children to explore on their own.[2]

Before investing in computer software for use by children, it is essential that you know what you are getting. Does it foster inquiry? It is user friendly? Has it been debugged? Is the content appropriate? Is it appropriate for the ages of the children in your class? Can it be networked so many children can use it simultaneously in a computer lab? Is it affordable?

The Software Evaluation Profile shown in Figure 21.13 is provided to help you evaluate software. The profile asks for *boilerplate* information above a double line; this information is obtainable from distributors. The essence of the evaluation is contained in the items below the double line that require you to preview the program. The rating score system suggested is subjective; the Overall Recommendation is the result of the review as a whole.

SOFTWARE EVALUATION PROFILE

Evaluator _____

Title and Version _____

Subject area _____

Cost _____   Cost for Site License _____

                                  Cost for Network Version _____

Grade Level   **Type**

High School   _____   Informational   _____

Middle School   _____   Drill and Practice   _____

Upper Elementary   _____   Tutorial   _____

Lower Elementary   _____   Game   _____

Kindergarten   _____   Word Processing   _____

Preschool   _____   Desktop Publishing   _____

                                        Spreadsheet   _____

                                        Graphical   _____

                                        Teacher support   _____

                                        Teacher organizational   _____

                                        Teacher utility   _____

                                        Teacher information   _____

                                        Other _____

Amount of effort/supervision required for children and/or teacher to learn program

Much _____   Some _____   Little _____

Hardware requirements   Type of computer _____

                              Hard disk? Capacity _____

                              Black & white or color monitor _____

                              Game card _____

                              Sound card _____

                              Video card _____

                              Mouse _____

                              Printer type _____

                              Other special hardware _____

Rating Scores (10 points each)   **OVERALL RECOMMENDATION**

Documentation & Instructions   _____   Strongly recommended   _____

General design   _____   Recommended   _____

Content   _____   Questionable   _____

Technical quality   _____   Not recommended   _____

Ease of program use   _____

Ease of installation   _____

TOTAL (60 MAX)   _____

Comments

_____

_____

FIGURE 21.13   Software evaluation profile

GETTING STARTED

The array of technology available to support process-oriented inquiry science programs is dazzling. Terminology often seems indecipherable, choices are seemingly infinite, and hardware can be expensive.

The question arises, "How do I get started?"

If you are already familiar with computers and other technological techniques, you may feel ready to jump right in and enrich your classes with computer applications. However, if you are uncomfortable with technology, it is suggested that you start slowly.

It is strongly urged that every teacher learn how to use at least a word-processing program, a spreadsheet program, a database program, a graphic application, e-mail, and the Internet. Consider signing up for a computer course or two; many are offered at colleges and universities, at local school districts in the form of in-service training, and through commercial firms. Courses range from entry level (starting with how to turn a computer on) to advanced training on specific programs and applications. The short time invested in becoming familiar with basic programs will save you countless hours in your professional role and will enable you to utilize computer technology effectively in your classroom.

In your classroom, try one or two applications that seem to have some merit, such as using a word-processing program to write letters, a spreadsheet to keep track of children's progress, and a desktop-publishing program to create signs and banners. Also try searching the Internet to find ideas for a unit or lesson you are planning. Do not be dismayed by initial difficulties; we all experience them. Keep working with the programs you choose, and you will be amazed at how rapidly you achieve proficiency.

Then try a scientific application, perhaps a tutorial program that presents a unit you are teaching. Children can run through this program as an additional activity or as a review activity. Many teachers allow children to include computer work in their free-time choices. Perhaps a game or two might be appropriate or a program on some topic that is interesting to your children but that you will not be able to include in your curriculum.

When you decide it is time to use e-mail or the Internet, demonstrate the technique first using a computer projector or an LCD panel. This is a panel that fits on top of the overhead projector which, when connected to the computer, projects whatever is on the computer monitor onto the projection screen.

When the time comes for you to provide input into the district's or the school's budget, be prepared to discuss the virtues of technology; your voice and your expertise may help put your school on the cybernetic highway. You can serve on your local school committee for software evaluation, and you can help develop a five-year plan for technology in your school. You can request that your school subscribe to technology magazines.

As you progress in your quest to use modern technology in your classroom, your excitement will mount from day to day. Keep adding to your store of information, expertise, and software, and you will find you are helping your children open doors to inquiry never before available. With technology, there is no limit to children's inquiries.

SUMMARY

Computer technology is rapidly becoming available to all schools, and there are many reasons for early childhood teachers to incorporate computer applications in their science programs. Tutorial and informational CD programs help children review, reinforce, and extend their science inquiries and provide enormous amounts of relevant and appropriate science information. Word-processing and desktop-publishing programs are used by children and teachers to prepare written material including reports, newsletters, signs, banners, and the like. Spreadsheets are used for analysis and graphical portrayal of experimental data. Commercial and homemade databases are used to help children broaden their inquiries. E-mail enables rapid worldwide communication, and the Internet enables children and teachers to access virtually unlimited stores of information.

As an early childhood science educator, you are urged to consider the extent to which given programs and technologies can aid children in investigating their own questions. The future is here, and advances in technology provide unlimited access for learning opportunities never before imagined. It is worth the effort it takes to become technologically proficient.

Notes

1. Additional suggestions for ensuring the safety of children while they are on the Internet are provided by Pittman and McLaughlin (2000).
2. The International Society for Technology in Education (ISTE), a very large teacher-based organization in educational technology, has published the *National Educational Technology Standards.* The *Standards* are the result of the collaboration of many professionals from education, mathematics, the sciences, and other professional fields. Full information about the *Standards,* their implementation, and accompanying books can be accessed at *www.iteawww.org* or the ISTE website at *www.iste.org* (Technology Standards, 2000).

SOURCES OF SOFTWARE

DK Interactive Learning, 95 Madison Avenue, New York, NY 10016.
Educational Resources, P.O. Box 1900, Elgin, IL 60121-1900; telephone 800-624-2926; Internet site: http://www.edresources.com
Knowledge Adventure, Inc., 1311 Grand Central Avenue, Glendale, CA 91201; telephone 800-542-4240
The Learning Channel: Internet site: http://tlc.discovery.com

Microsoft (Available at retail outlets throughout the world)

National Geographic Kids Network, P.O. Box 98018, Washington, DC 20090-8018; E-mail address: NGSHOTLINE@aol.com.

National Geographic Society, Washington, DC, 20036; telephone 800-368-2728; Internet site: www.nationalgeographic.com

Public Broadcasting System: Internet site: http://www.pbs.org

Reader Rabbit: The Learning Company Inc., One Athenium Street, Cambridge, MA 02142; telephone 800-227-5609

References

Brunner, B. (Ed.). (1999). *The Time almanac.* Boston: Information Please LLC.

Classes view telescope via computer. (1995, February/March). *NSTA Reports!*

Collings, J. N. (1985). Scientific thinking through the development of formal operations: Training in the cognitive restructuring aspect of field independence. *Research in Science & Technology Education, 3*(2), 145–152.

Craig, D. V. (1999). Science and technology: A great combination. *Science and Children 36*(4), 28–32.

Frisch, M. (1957). *Homo faber.* Frankfurt: Suhrkamp Verlag.

Hancock, V., and Betts, F. (1994). From the lagging to the leading edge. *Educational Leadership, 51*(7), 24–29.

Internet project lets students migrate north with wildlife. (1995, February/March). *NSTA Reports!*

Lonergan, D. (1997). Network science: Bats, birds, and trees. *Educational Leadership 55*(3), 34–36.

Lowry, L. (1989). *Number the stars.* New York: Houghton Mifflin.

Martin, D. J. (2000). *Elementary science methods: A Constructivist Approach.* (2nd Ed.). Belmont, CA: Wadsworth/Thompson Learning.

National Research Council. (1996). *National Science Education Standards.* Washington, DC: National Academy Press.

National Science Teachers Association. (December 1992/January 1993). An NSTA position statement on computers in science education. *NSTA Reports!* National Science Teachers Association, 1742 Connecticut Ave, NW, Washington, DC 20009.

National Science Teachers Association. (1999). NSTA launches *Sci*LINKS. *NSTA Reports! 10*(5), 1.

National Telecommunications and Information Administration. (1999). *Falling through the net: Defining the digital divide.* [On line]. Available: http://ntiant1.ntia.doc.gov/ntiahome/fttn99/execsummary.html.

Owston, R. D. (1997). The world wide web: A technology to enhance teaching and learning? *Educational Researcher 26*(2), 27–33.

Quick facts: Computer and Internet usage. (1998, August 11). *CNN.* [On line]. Available: http://www.media-awareness.ca/eng/ISSUES/STATS/usenet.htm

Pittman, J. and McLaughlin B. (2000). Making cyberspace safe for children. *Educational Leadership, 57*(6), 68–71.

Steinberg, E. R. (1989). Cognition and learner control: A literature review, 1977–1988. *Journal of Computer-Based Instruction, 16*(4), 117–121.

Technology standards publications released. (2000, March/April). *NSTA Reports!, 11* (5), 20.

U.S. Department of Education. (1999). Educational technology: Preparing America for the 21st Century. [On line]. Available: http://www.ed.gov/inits/FY99/1-tech.html.

World Almanac. (1994). Mahwah, NJ: Funk and Wagnall's Corporation.

CHAPTER 22

Reading, Writing, and Science

You have been constructing your conceptualization of quality science education. Hopefully there is congruence between your constructions and the notion that it is more important for children to do science than it is for them to learn about science. Yet, this notion of learning science by *doing* it seems to fly contrary to tradition. Many of us learned about science by reading textbooks and studying the illustrations and by watching the teacher do an occasional demonstration—that is if we had science at all.

One of the goals of education is literacy. And one of the primary goals of early childhood education is for children to learn to read and write. The written word in the form of stories, articles, explanations, references, and so on provides a tremendously powerful source of support for children's inquiries. When children write their findings, they crystallize their own thinking, often discovering strengths as well as weaknesses in their constructions. In addition, children's written word serves as a vehicle

The sole substitute for an experience which we have not ourselves lived through is art and literature.

Alexander Isayevich Solzhenitsyn, Nobel lecture, 1972

It is not often that someone comes along who is a true friend and a good writer. Charlotte was both.

E. B. White, Charlotte's Web (New York: Harper-Collins Children's Books, 1952)

for communicating the results of their inquiries to others—a precept at the very core of science.

In this chapter, you will investigate ways in which reading and writing can be incorporated into the process-oriented inquiry science program to foster children's inquiries and help them construct personal and valid conceptualizations of scientific concepts.

CHILDREN'S LITERATURE

Much children's literature has been cited in this text in the form of "literature connections" to activities. In addition to their value in fostering literacy, what purposes do stories serve in science programs?

Constructing Your Ideas 22.1
Goldilocks and the Three Bears

Obtain a copy of *Goldilocks and the Three Bears* such as the one told by Jan Brett (1996), and ask someone to read it aloud to the class.

In the story, Goldilocks samples each of three bowls of porridge left to cool. Papa Bear's bowl is the largest, Mama Bear's is medium-sized, and Baby Bear's is the smallest. Goldilocks finds that Papa Bear's porridge is too hot, Mama Bear's is too cold, and Baby Bear's is just right. Ask the question, "Does this make sense?" and survey the class for their responses.

Now obtain three bowls made of the same kind of pottery—a large one, a medium-sized one, and a small one. Prepare a batch of oatmeal (to simulate porridge). Pour the cooked oatmeal to the same relative level in each bowl. Record the temperature of the oatmeal in each bowl. Then let the bowls of oatmeal cool for about 10 minutes, and record the temperatures again. In which bowl does the oatmeal have the highest temperature? In which does the oatmeal have the coolest temperature? In which does the oatmeal have a temperature between the hottest and the coolest?

Is the story scientifically correct? Cite reasons for your response.

(Note: This activity is based on research reported by McClelland & Krockover, 1996.)

Introducing Cognitive Disequilibration

The *Goldilocks* porridge activity demonstrates one way children's literature can be used to foster science inquiries: introducing cognitive disequilibration. As was pointed out in Chapter 1, children bring much understanding of science with them to school. Many of their preconceived scientific understandings are the result of their experiences and their interactions with their environment. And some are the result of their experiences with fictional literature. Children (and, indeed, adults) tend to accept the written word at face value. (If it's in a book, it must be true.) Yet, children's fiction abounds with scientific conceptions that cannot be reconciled with experimental data.

FIGURE 22.1   Crystals of sugar

Goldilocks and the Three Bears is one example. Investigation shows that Baby Bear's bowl of porridge is the one that is too cold, and Mama Bear's bowl is the one that would be just right. Another example is found in *Two Bad Ants* by Chris Van Allsburg (1988). Through a process of inferring, the reader is led to believe that the crystals sought by the ants are sugar crystals. However, the crystals portrayed in the illustrations do not resemble actual sugar crystals as seen in magnified form (see Figure 22.1).

This is not to say that all children's literature should be subjected to scientific scrutiny. What better way to stimulate the imagination than through engaging stories? What better way of personifying characters than through talking animals? What better way of providing vicarious experiences than through excursions taken by bugs and dinosaurs? Certainly, we must let literature accomplish its intended purposes.

But introducing discrepant events is one of the foremost ways of stimulating children's need for reconstruction of previously held conceptualizations. Certain pieces of children's literature are excellent vehicles for inducing the disequilibrations that discrepant events cause.

Introducing Lessons

advance organizer—An introduction to a lesson that foretells the lesson's nature and objective and stimulates interest

Children's literature is often used to set the stage for a discussion and subsequent investigation. In this sense, it is used as the **advance organizer** for the lesson. An engaging story can capture children's interest and help focus their attention on the topic of the lesson. For example, the poem, "What's in the Sack?" in *Where the Sidewalk Ends* by Shel Silverstein (1974) can be used as an introduction to the activity, "What's in the Bag?" (Constructing Science in the Classroom 4.7). The teacher sets the stage by reading this poem and asking the children to guess what's in the man's sack, giving reasons for each guess.

SOME PROCESS-ORIENTED ACTIVITIES USING
***THE POPCORN BOOK* BY TOMIE DEPAOLA AS THE INTRODUCTION**

▪ Measure the time that elapses before the first kernel pops. Use different brands of popcorn to see whether there is a difference among brands.
  Processes: Communicating, Measuring, Predicting, Interpreting Data
▪ Describe how popcorn looks, feels, smells, tastes, and sounds before and after popping.
  Processes: Observing, Communicating
▪ Compare the volume of popcorn before and after popping.
  Processes: Measuring, Predicting, Interpreting Data
▪ Find whether unpopped and popped popcorn sinks or floats in water.
  Processes: Observing, Communicating, Predicting
▪ Predict and measure how far kernels pop out of an uncovered pan.
  Processes: Predicting, Measuring
▪ Compare the weights of popcorn before and after popping.
  Processes: Measuring, Predicting, Interpreting Data

FIGURE 22.2 Some process-oriented activities using *The Popcorn Book* by Tomie dePaola as the introduction

Based on the work of Melanie Aofiyebi, Virginia Billings, and Jennifer Winnerman, graduate students in education at Kennesaw State University

Jack and the Beanstalk as told by L.B. Cauley (1983) can be used to introduce children to investigations of plants, seed germination, requirements for plant growth, and conditions that would promote the tallest and most rapid growth of bean plants. *The Pumpkin Book* by Gail Gibbons (1999) is a story about a pumpkin that starts as a seed that grows into a vine that produces flowers that grow into pumpkins. It can be used in conjunction with investigations into plant growth, the nature and functions of stems and flowers, estimating and counting the number of seeds in a pumpkin, and interdisciplinary investigations centering on pumpkins. (Chapter 23 deals with interdisciplinary aspects of early childhood science education.)

Tiedt (1999) writes about integrating science and literature in a unit on ecology (often called "stewardship.") She utilized many children's literature titles in developing a meaningful interdisciplinary exploration that also drew upon children's experiences with taking care of their own belongings. The introductory piece of literature was *Stuartship* by Ryan Collay and Joanne Dubrow (1998). In this story, an old apple tree that Stuart feels belongs to him is about to be cut down. With the help of others, Stuart solves the problem. The unit also utilized a number of locally meaningful non-fiction descriptive and explanatory books.

The Popcorn Book by Tomie dePaola (1978) can be used to introduce a number of process-oriented activities such as those shown in Figure 22.2.

Validating Conclusions

Literature can be used to help children validate the conclusions they have reached. After completing an investigation, children compare their findings with the science presented in the book. Because the science in children's literature is often inaccurate and exaggerated, children are asked to *compare* rather than verify conclusions using the book. Who is right? The book? Or the children? To answer this question, they need to compare the accuracy of the ideas in the book with their own conclusions. If they are the same, the fact that the conclusion the children came up with is also in print is very empowering. If they are different, a powerful reason is provided for continuing the investigation to see who is right.

For example, *From Seed to Plant* by Gail Gibbons (1991), which explains how seeds grow into plants and illustrates the parts of both seeds and plants, can be used after children explore the nature of seeds to verify their findings (see Constructing Science in the Classroom 2.10). As an alternative to the suggested activity, provide children with two or three lima bean seeds that have been softened by letting them soak in water for an hour or two. Children first observe the outsides of the seeds and discuss how they look and feel. They guess what they will find on the inside of the seed and then cut one open with a plastic knife and observe. They compare their guesses with what they see and also with what the book depicts.

Mouse Paint by Ellen Stoll Walsh (1989) can be used to help children verify what they discover when they mix red, yellow, and blue icing. The

FIGURE 22.3 Mixing colors

teacher provides each child with a small amount of each of red, yellow, and blue icing and a Popsicle stick, instructing them to mix the icings together, two at a time on a paper plate. They leave the mixture on the plate and identify the colors that result. After all the children have completed the activity, the teacher reads *Mouse Paint*. In this story, mice walk into red, yellow, and blue paint. As they walk from color to color, they mix the paints, forming new colors. This story may help children validate the conclusions they made as a result of their own investigations, or it may stimulate them to pursue further investigations if their conclusions are not the same as those shown in the story.

Presenting Factual Information

Some children's literature presents factual information and is used to stimulate interest and verify findings. Books by Eric Carle such as *The Very Hungry Caterpillar (1987)*, *The Very Quiet Cricket (1990)*, *The Very Busy Spider (1985)*, *The Very Lonely Firefly (1995)*, and *The Grouchy Ladybug (1986)* use personification to demonstrate important characteristics of the creatures. The alphabet book series by Jerry Pallotta is a treasure trove of facts about birds, butterflies, deserts, dinosaurs, freshwater animals, bugs, frogs, oceans, reptiles, and other topics. In *The Magic School Bus* series by Joanna Cole, Mrs. Frizzle, the teacher, takes her class on impossible field trips where children discover factual information on many different topics.

Providing Practice in the Processes

Children's literature can be used to provide practice in the scientific processes.[1] The process of observing is sharpened as children study the illustrations in children's books. Understanding the process of measuring is enhanced through such classics as *How Big is a Foot?* by Rolf Myller (1962), a story about building a bed for a queen using the builder's foot as the unit of measurement instead of the king's, and *Inch by Inch* by Leo Lionni (1995), a story about an inchworm proud of his ability to measure anything under the sun.

The process of inferring is required to decide what the crystals are in *Two Bad Ants* by Chris Van Allsburg (1988) and to decide what animal is lurking behind the bushes in *Who Is the Beast?* by Keith Baker (1990). Young children are encouraged to solve the mystery of what lies behind the cut-out holes in *Look Book* by Tana Hoban (1997).

Sources of Children's Literature

There are many sources in which children's fiction and nonfiction titles are cited and summarized. There also are many sources in which newly published titles are reviewed. Some sources you might want to consider are listed in Figure 22.4.

SELECTED SOURCES OF CHILDREN'S LITERATURE TITLES APPROPRIATE FOR EARLY CHILDHOOD SCIENCE

Brainard, A., & Wrubel, D. H. (1993). *Literature-based science activities: An integrated approach, grades K–3.* New York: Scholastic Professional Books.

Butzow, C. M., & Butzow, J. W. (1989). *Science through children's literature: An integrated approach.* Englewood, CO: Teacher Ideas Press.

Butzow, C. M., & Butzow, J. W. (1998). *More science through children's literature: An integrated approach.* Englewood, CO: Libraries Unlimited.

Lima, C. W., & Lima, J. A. (1998). *A to zoo: Subject access to children's picture books* (5th edition). New Providence, NJ: R. R. Bowker.

Moore, J. E., & Evans, J. (1991a). *Exploring science through literature: Level A, grades K–1.* Monterey, CA: Evan-Moor Corp.

Moore, J. E., & Evans, J. (1991b). *Exploring science through literature: Level B, grades 2–3.* Monterey, CA: Evan-Moor Corp.

Raines, S., & Canady, R. J. (1989). *Story s-t-r-e-t-c-h-e-r-s: Activities to expand children's favorite books.* Beltsville, MD: Gryphon House.

Raines, S., & Canady, R. J. (1992). *Story s-t-r-e-t-c-h-e-r-s: Activities to expand children's favorite books.* Beltsville, MD: Gryphon House.

Ramirez, G. Jr., & Ramirez, J. L. (1994). *Multiethnic children's literature.* Albany, NY: Delmar Publishers, Inc.

Terrific Science Press Staff. (1996). *Teaching physical science through children's literature: Twenty complete lessons for elementary grades.* New York: McGraw-Hill Professional Publishing.

Each year, the March issue of *Science and Children,* published by the National Science Teachers Association, includes an annotated bibliography of children's nonfiction books dealing with scientific information. The list is compiled in conjunction with the Children's Book Council and includes all science fields and biography. This issue also lists books in Spanish.

The Association of Childhood Education International (ACEI) in Washington, DC publishes a *Bibliography of Books for Children,* which is revised every three years. New titles in both English and Spanish are reviewed in *Childhood Education,* the journal of ACEI.

The website of the Center for the Study of Books in Spanish for Children and Adolescents at California State University in San Marcos lists thousands of titles in Spanish. Subject headings, full bibliographic references, suggested grade levels, and brief descriptions are given in both English and Spanish. The website is updated each week. You can access this website at http://www.csusm.edu/campus_centers/csb/.

Many public libraries have extensive collections of children's literature—both fiction and nonfiction.

FIGURE 22.4 Selected sources of children's literature titles appropriate for early childhood science

---

SUGGESTED CRITERIA FOR EVALUATING CHILDREN'S LITERATURE FOR USE IN THE EARLY CHILDHOOD SCIENCE PROGRAM

1. Does the book foster the development of processes?
2. Does the book provide the opportunity for children to ask and answer their own questions?
3. Does the book encourage children to think for themselves?
4. Is the science topic addressed appropriate to the lesson?
5. Is the content based on sound scientific principles? Is it accurate?
6. Are the illustrations clear? Are they accurate?
7. Is the book written at the level of the children in your class?
8. Is there a multicultural component? Is this component free of stereotyping?
9. Is the book free of gender bias?
10. Does the story help foster positive attitudes toward science?
11. Does the book show the close association between science and other disciplines?

FIGURE 22.5   Suggested criteria for evaluating children's literature for use in the early childhood science program

Evaluating Children's Literature for the Early Childhood Science Program

Before selecting a piece of literature for use in the early childhood science class, you need to determine whether it is appropriate. It goes without saying that you should read the book yourself first. Ask yourself whether the book is appropriate for its intended purpose. Are the illustrations clear? Is the story line easy to follow? Is the science accurate? Some suggested criteria useful for evaluating children's literature for early childhood science classes are shown in Figure 22.5.

Multicultural Children's Literature

When selecting literature for use in your science classes, don't overlook the multicultural element. Much of the literature cited in this text is multicultural in nature. There are many additional fine titles written from Afrocentric, Hispanic, Native American, and other ethnic and cultural perspectives. For example, *Whistle for Willie* by Ezra Jack Keats (1977) is African-American in ethnicity. This book deals with sound and is ideal to use in conjunction with lessons dealing with sound such as those suggested in Constructing Science in the Classroom 2.1, 2.3, 2.8, and 17.2. *The Egyptian Cinderella* by Shirley Climo (1989) can help children sharpen their observation skills by asking them to compare this book with the traditional *Cinderella*. *Bringing the Rain to Kapiti Plain: A Nandi Tale* by Verna Aardema (1981), Native-American in ethnicity, is a book about clouds as the source of rain and is an excellent accompaniment to a lesson or a unit dealing with the observation of weather phenomena. The delightful book *8000 Stones: A Chinese Folktale* by Diane Wolkstein (1972), eastern in culture, portrays the use of nontraditional units of measure and describes how to weigh something very large. It is an excellent story for helping children understand the concept of measuring weight. *Moon Rope* by Lois Ehlert (1996), a Peruvian folktale in which Fox and Mole try to climb to the moon on a rope woven of grass, can be used in conjunction with a lesson or a unit on the solar system or the moon.

Children's Magazines

A well-equipped early childhood classroom has magazines available. There are several magazines that help promote children's experiential base and their skills in the scientific processes and in inquiry. A list of some science-related magazines suitable for young children is given in Figure 22.6.

SCIENCE TEXTBOOKS

Many school districts adopt textbooks that teachers are expected to use in their teaching of science. Some teachers are tempted to let the text determine the science program. There are several reasons for this. Teachers may feel unprepared to teach science and want the guidance the textbook provides. Teachers may prefer to have a structured program of the sort that textbooks offer. Teachers may look to texts for instructional resources, avenues of questioning and discussion, and directions for demonstrations and children's activities (Armbruster, 1993).

In the extreme, some teachers may limit their science program to the textbook. Their typical lesson begins with the children reading out of the text or discussing the pictures. The teacher then may do a demonstration, show a video, or hold a question-and-answer discussion in an effort to get children involved and to increase meaningfulness. Occasionally the children may participate in an activity. The text is then used to close the lesson, and the questions at the end of the chapter or section serve as class work or homework. It should be obvious that this type of textbook use replaces inquiry with knowledge acquisition and verification activities. Children read about science instead of doing science. They do not have the opportunity to make and test predictions, and they do not have the opportunity to verify their conclusions because the investigations and the expected results are written out in the text. They do not have the opportunity to develop facility in the processes of science or in inquiry, and they are not likely to construct positive attitudes about science. The text provides all the needed information, and children are discouraged from "actively making meaningful connections to their existing knowledge" (Ulerick, 1989). This is the antithesis of constructivism.

Textbooks, by their very nature, ignore the individual needs of individual children and assume all children have the same prior knowledge. Given this characterization of science textbooks, some teachers employing constructivist

**SOME CHILDREN'S MAGAZINES SUITABLE FOR EARLY
CHILDHOOD SCIENCE EDUCATION**

Click

The mission of this magazine is to show young learners the world around them and to lead them on a variety of adventures, most of which focus on science topics. Suitable for children ages 3–7.

> Click
> P.O. Box 7499
> Red Oak, IA, 59591
> Telephone 800-827-0227

Dragonfly

Published by the National Science Teachers Association, *Dragonfly* is a science investigation magazine that inspires children to become researchers in their own inquiries and links children and scientists in the investigations. The principle objectives are to involve children in the creative process of science, to help them see how science relates to their lives, to engage minority and at-risk children in science, and to help teachers and parents guide active, experiential learning more confidently. The magazine comes with guides for teachers and guides for parents. Suitable for children ages 8 to 14.

> *Dragonfly* - NSTA
> P.O. Box 90477
> Washington, DC 20090-0477
> Telephone 800-722-NSTA

Ranger Rick

Published by the National Wildlife Federation, this magazine has full-color photos, presentations on many different animals, and puzzles, games, riddles, and more. The magazine is designed for children ages 7–12.

> National Wildlife Federation
> 8925 Leesburg Pike
> Vienna, VA 22184
> Telephone 703-790-4000

World

Published by the National Geographic Society, *World's* features encourage its readers to protect the planet's resources and to learn more about geography, adventure, wildlife, science, and youngsters of special distinction from around the world. Suitable for children ages 8 to 14.

> National Geographic *World*
> P.O. Box 63007
> Tampa, FL 33663-3007
> Telephone 800-647-5463

Your Big Backyard

Published by the National Wildlife Federation, this magazine introduces young children to nature with picture stories, games, and special sections for parents. Suitable for children ages 3 to 6.

> National Wildlife Federation
> 8925 Leesburg Pike
> Vienna, VA 22184
> Telephone 703-790-4000

FIGURE 22.6   Some children's magazines suitable for early childhood science education

techniques have felt like throwing the texts away. However, textbooks have several advantages:

1. Textbooks are excellent sources of information for children.
2. Teacher's guides are excellent resources for teachers.
3. A textbook series provides a scope and sequence that ensures continuity from grade to grade and consistency within grade levels.
4. Topics included in textbooks are generally appropriate for the children's ages and grade levels.
5. Topics in textbooks are generally developed thoroughly, with prerequisite information introduced in proper sequence.

Traditional Science Textbooks

Standard textbooks normally are provided in a series, typically for grades K–6 in the elementary school. Much as we constructivists like to argue in favor of getting rid of basic texts in early childhood education, we need to explore ways we can use them to foster the process-oriented inquiry science program.

Traditional science texts are divided into major units of study, each with chapters on different aspects of the unit. For example, a text may have a unit on plants. The unit may have individual chapters on leaves, roots, stems, and flowers. Higher grade-level texts in the series treat the same broad units in increasingly sophisticated ways. The idea is that the text becomes the basis for study. The teacher is expected to cover the text, and the children are expected to master the concepts presented. The text provides structure and continuity, and the teacher's manual provides lesson plans or suggestions for lesson plans, background information, and sources of helpful ancillary material.

The chapters in traditional texts typically provide an introduction to a concept, followed by a discussion and explanation of the concept and the principles involved and then activities children can do to verify the material. The constructivist teacher can use this type of textbook to good advantage by using the textbook in reverse so children do the activities first and then use the text for validation (Barnam, 1992). For example, suppose the text presents material on leaves. Different kinds of leaves are shown, their characteristics are identified, and examples of many different kinds of leaves are pictured and described. Observation and grouping activities are outlined for children to do to become familiar with the different kinds of leaves. However, the constructivist teacher who is required to use this text can have the children explore leaves using the process-oriented inquiry approach *before* the children are given the text. Then, after the children have had the opportunity to construct their own conceptualizations about the nature and variety of leaves, the teacher can ask them to refer to the text (which now serves in a validation and extension role)—confirming what the children have already found out for themselves and perhaps answering some of the questions they asked during their explorations. In fact, it may be desirable to have several copies of each of a number of different texts available in the classroom to aid the children in their investigations.

In addition, textbooks are an especially useful aid for the study of concepts that would not lend themselves well to children's original explanations. For example, the names, order, and properties of the planets probably won't be discovered by children through inquiry activities. This is just where the textbook comes in—to show the needed information in an interesting and exciting manner.

Activity-Oriented Science Series

A newer generation of the science textbook is the activity-oriented series. While maintaining a structured scope and sequence and providing ancillary teacher materials, the focus is on student inquiry. Many omit traditional textual material and provide, instead, inquiry-based activity sheets, multiple reference materials on the specific topics included in the particular grade level and even, in some cases, the materials required to do the activities. The activity-oriented series attempts to foster hands-on science and, in the hands of constructivist-oriented teachers, can serve as excellent guides for student constructions of concepts.

There are also a number of published investigative science programs that focus on hands-on inquiry science and that have been tested through use in actual classrooms and have been revised to reflect difficulties and concerns. The programs are based on certain orientations in science education such as the learning cycle (Chapter 1), hands-on learning, and inquiry learning. Program materials include student investigation guides, ancillary materials appropriate for the age/grade of the children, detailed teacher's manuals that explain the philosophy and goals of the program and provide specific lesson plans, additional implementation suggestions, overhead transparencies, appropriate handouts, lists of appropriate materials, and lists of useful supplementary materials. Some programs are sold complete with all materials required for the hands-on activities for given grade levels, minus the common items such as sugar and vinegar that are to be purchased as they are needed.

Several hands-on investigative science programs are described in Figure 22.7. Though some have elementary grade designations, the materials can be adapted for use in preschool.

Textbook Review

Deciding which science text or program to use is one of the most important and most difficult professional judgements a teacher can make (Gibbs & Fox, 1999). It is vital that teachers become involved in the selection of materials they will use in the classroom. As a professional, you will have the opportunity to serve on textbook selection committees. In this capacity, you can ensure that materials are selected with the input of the teachers who will use them, that the materials that are adopted are understood by teachers, and that teachers are given both time and resources to implement the new materials. Consider advantages and disadvantages of using traditional texts, activity-oriented textlike materials, science programs, or none at all.

SELECTED EARLY CHILDHOOD SCIENCE EDUCATION PROGRAMS THAT UTILIZE CONSTRUCTIVIST APPROACHES

AIMS (Activities for Integrating Mathematics and Science) uses a hands-on, inquiry-oriented interdisciplinary approach that integrates mathematics, science, and other disciplines. *AIMS* materials include over 40 volumes of guided-inquiry student investigations involving a wide variety of topics. Materials appropriate for kindergarten through 12th grade are available. *AIMS* also has available complete laboratory kits, manipulatives, equipment, data organizers and charts, a newsletter, and a magazine showing new activities and evaluation results. The activities are inquiry in orientation and constructivist in nature. Some investigations can be adapted for use in preschool. For information contact:

AIMS Education Foundation
P.O. Box 8120
Fresno, CA 93747-8120
On the web at http://www.aimsedu.org/

ESS (Elementary Science Study) is one of the original discovery approaches to elementary science education. Its developers came from both the scientific and the teaching fields. Units are described in teachers' guides and are designed to help children develop the fundamental skills necessary for organized scientific thought. Over 40 units deal with common scientific phenomena from ant farms to sand. Each unit suggests many open-ended, hands-on, inquiry-oriented activities children can investigate as they form and validate personal constructions of the phenomena. Some of the units can be adapted for use in preschool. Equipment kits are available. For details, contact:

Delta Education, Inc.
P.O. Box 3000
Nashua, NH 03061-3000
Telephone (800) 442-5444
On the web at http://www.delta-ed.com/

GEMS (Great Explorations in Math and Science) is an extensive set of inquiry activities for children in preschool through 10th grade. There are more than 60 teacher's guides and handbooks dealing with a multitude of subjects from animals and their defenses, ants, butterflies, opossums, ladybugs, penguins, and trees to physical science and earth and space science topics. The teacher's guides and handbooks feature clear step-by-step instructions, complete background information, and literature connections. GEMS can be used either as an independent curriculum by grouping units together or as a supplement to the existing curriculum. The *GEMS Network News* is a free newsletter that contains valuable information about science education and news about uses of existing units and the development of new units. PEACHES

FIGURE 22.7 Selected early childhood science education programs that utilize constructivist approaches

is an arm of GEMS that deals exclusively with science for very young children. Many of the PEACHES activities are incorporated into the GEMS units. GEMS and PEACHES were developed at the Lawrence Hall of Science, which continues to be its headquarters. For more information, contact:

University of California, Berkeley
GEMS
Lawrence Hall of Science #5200
Berkeley, CA 94720-5200
Telephone (510) 642-7771
On the web at http://www.lhs.berkeley.edu/GEMS/GEMS.html

Insights is a hands-on inquiry-based elementary science curriculum designed to meet the needs of children in urban classrooms, grades K–6. The program integrates science with language arts and mathematics in a science-technology-society setting. (See Chapter 23 for a discussion of the Science-Technology-Society approach to interdisciplinary science education.) Seventeen 6–8 week modules are available, each including a comprehensive teacher's guide and a set of materials. For further information contact:

Education Development Center, Inc.
55 Chapel street
Newton, MA 02160
On the web at http://www.edc.org/CSE/imd/insights3.html

Optical Data Corporation offers many videodisc-based science units suitable for young children in the "Windows on Science" and "KinderVentures" programs. Units are available on a wide variety of topics from the life sciences, the physical sciences, and the earth and space sciences. The videodiscs contain age-appropriate information on each topic, ranging from videos of scenes from sites throughout the world to demonstrations of activities, scenes of children performing the activities, illustrated explanations, microscopic illustrations, and the like. Videodiscs come with teacher manuals and student activity booklets and can be tailored to meet the needs of children in any particular class through the use of the barcodes and a barcode reader that permit instant access to any segment on the videodisc. For further information, contact:

Optical Data Corporation
A Division of the McGraw-Hill Companies
1221 Avenue of the Americas
New York, NY 10020
Telephone (800) 524-2481
On the web at http://www.opticaldata.com/

A science textbook evaluation form that you may find useful as a point of departure is shown in Figure 22.8. Many districts have developed their own review forms that reflect the educational philosophy and educational needs of children in the district. But in many cases, it is the review committee's job first to come up with the criteria for selection. Your input will be sought and valued. In fact, participation of teachers such as preschool teachers who may not actually be using all the materials reviewed will help ensure that the full program is suitable.

WRITING IN THE EARLY CHILDHOOD SCIENCE PROGRAM

One of the primary responsibilities of the early childhood educator is to teach children to write. Though science is an area in which children can accomplish much without being required to do a great deal of writing, it is an ideal vehicle to provide meaningful reasons for writing. Science lessons can help young children gain familiarity and skill in the abstracts of the written language as well the understanding that writing is both convenient and necessary. There are a number of specific ways in which writing can be incorporated in early childhood science education programs. Many of these ways presuppose that the children are ready and able to write.

Recording Children's Responses

When the teacher is asking questions in whole-group settings, children's responses can be written on chart paper to form a record of class ideas that is referred to from time to time. Writing the child's first name next to his or her response helps reinforce the written response and also promotes personal ownership of the response. Conclusions discussed during whole-group sessions can be recorded on chart paper, together with reasons why each conclusion was made. Again, each child's name is recorded by the appropriate conclusion, and the discussion continues until all children have provided their input.

In the Constructing Science in the Classroom activities, it is suggested that many of the data tables include both pictures and words for the objects to be investigated together with blanks for the additional objects children might want to include. To encourage reading, the teacher adds either the full name or the first letter of the object in the picture. To encourage writing, the teacher asks the children to write the words or the first letters of the objects they want to try but which are not on the data table. They first identify the object they want to try and then write its name or initial on the data table—with the help of the teacher if required (Figure 22.9).

Science Journals

Many early childhood teachers encourage children to keep science journals. One kind of science journal is a notebook in which children write about science. The entries may include brief descriptions of what they found out in their investigations, summaries of special science events that occurred in the

SCIENCE TEXT EVALUATION REVIEW FORM

TITLE _____

AUTHOR(S) _____

PUBLISHER _____

COPYRIGHT DATE _____ LEVEL(S) _____

Rate each of the following from 1 (lowest) to 10 (highest)

_____ Process oriented

_____ Fosters inquiry

_____ Suggests inquiry activities

_____ Inductive in presentation

_____ Encourages children to explore on their own

_____ Suggests extension activities

_____ Suggests remedial activities

_____ Contains appropriate content

_____ Content information accurate

_____ Illustrations clear and accurate

_____ Reading level appropriate

_____ Free from gender bias

_____ Contains multicultural component without stereotyping

_____ Reflects interdisciplinary approaches

_____ Interdisciplinary problems are relevant and issue oriented

_____ Suggests literature connections

_____ Suggests special treatments for children with special needs

_____ Contains information on scientific careers

_____ Includes technology

_____ Attractive

_____ Material well organized

_____ Ancillary materials available from publisher

_____ Physical characteristics of student text

_____ Cost value

_____ Teacher's edition contains background information, additional activities, and print, video, and electronic resources

_____ Teacher's edition rich in supplemental materials

_____ **TOTAL POINTS**

Comments _____

_____

_____

_____

_____

Overall Recommendation:	Strongly Recommend	_____
	Recommend	_____
	Questionable	_____
	Do Not Recommend	_____

Reviewer's name _____ Date _____

FIGURE 22.8 Science text evaluation review form

FIGURE 22.9 Using a data table

class, descriptions of science-related activities they did on their own, summaries of science-related trips they took with their families, and anything else relating to science they want to write—or draw—about and keep in their journals.

Another kind of science journal is a folder in which children keep their written responses to specific tasks provided by the teacher, their completed class sheets and data tables, creative writing pieces, and other written materials assigned by the teacher. The folder science journal is also a place where children keep written records of unassigned science-related activities they have experienced, such as trips, science-related television programs, videos, and movies, and the like.

The science journal can be made available along with the portfolios for parents during conferences; the journals show personal dimensions of activity and progress in science that are not necessarily evidenced in the portfolios.

Creative Writing

Creative writing activities in the science program often provide an avenue through which children can express ideas that demonstrate their understanding. For example, children may be asked to write and illustrate a story about finding a dinosaur in the school playground. What does the dinosaur do? How big is it? What do the children do? How do they feel? Or children may write and illustrate short stories about what it would be like to be an animal so well camouflaged that it cannot be seen in its natural environment but which accidentally strays into a different environment. What happens to the animal? What does it do? How does it feel? Many of the topics children study in early childhood science lend themselves to the creative writing efforts of children.

Preparing Written Material on the Computer

Children's writing skills are put to good use in making signs and posters, in writing invitations to special events and thank-you notes to guest presenters, and in preparing (with the teacher's help, of course) articles and other material for inclusion in the Science Newsletter (see Chapter 21 on Technology).

CONFLICTING VIEWS ON READING AND WRITING IN SCIENCE

There are opposing views to incorporating reading and writing in the early childhood science program. Most assuredly, reading and writing skills are essential areas of development for children. On the other hand, science is one area that children can investigate successfully independent of reading and writing. This gives rise to the question of the role of reading and writing in quality science education and the extent to which reading and writing should be an integral part of the science program.

One argument suggests that reading and writing should have a *limited* role in early childhood science. Some children learn to read and write faster than others, some have greater facility than others, and some enjoy reading and writing more than others. Science is a field that can be studied *without* having to read or write. Children who experience difficulty with language can succeed in science by doing activities, investigating, and discussing with others. For example, children can classify shells without having to read about their characteristics; the teacher can assess their success by asking them to talk about their classification system rather than through written descriptions. In another example, it is entirely possible to experiment successfully with the effects of different surfaces on the force needed to move a block of wood without reading about the concept of friction or writing one's findings.

An opposing argument suggests that reading and writing must be an integral part of every aspect of the early childhood curriculum, including science. All children are capable of recording their observations by picture or by writing statements in journals. Children's literature and writing activities can enhance science learning by improving vocabulary, refining auditory and visual skills, and fostering creativity. Reading can also foster development of process skills such as observing, formulating hypotheses, inferring, predicting, and interpreting data. Reading requires children to engage prior knowledge. "Because of the reciprocal relationship between science and reading, teaching them together can be mutually beneficial" (Armbruster, 1993).

Children's success in the science arena can serve as a catalyst to develop the self-confidence needed for more successful language experiences. The most powerful reading strategy teachers can implement is to enable children to provide themselves with meaningful purposes for reading. Science can provide purposes for reading and writing through children's own desire to pursue interesting areas of science inquiry in greater depth. Children will come to want to read to obtain background information or explanatory information, to find out what has already been discovered, to challenge their ideas with new viewpoints, and to confirm or validate their conclusions. Reading and writing may also stimulate greater interest in science on the part of children who are not interested in science.

There are pros and cons to using reading and writing in the early childhood science program, each valid in its own right. The solution lies in compromise and in the judicial use of your "bag of tricks." As usual, you will have to make up your own mind. We do not take sides on this issue. However, we stress once again that children must learn science by *doing* science, not by reading *about* science.

SUMMARY

Learning to read and write and to enjoy reading and writing are among the most important goals of early childhood education. Reading and writing and scientific investigations can complement each other, and there are many ways reading and writing can be incorporated into the early childhood science programs. Children's literature may serve to pique children's interest in a lesson or a unit when it is used as introductory material. Children's literature can be used for reference, for exploratory expansion, for inquiry validation, for practice in the scientific processes, and for any of a number of other purposes in the science program. Children can experience the value of writing when the teacher records their responses for the whole class to see. They put their writing skills to good use in writing about their investigations, helping with the class newsletters, writing creative pieces, and in doing many other writing activities that logically accompany, enable, expand, and enrich the science program.

However, although reading and writing are of paramount importance, children's scientific inquiries do not necessarily depend on reading and writing for success. Science is learned by *doing* science, and teachers must exercise judicious judgement about the incorporation of reading and writing in the early childhood science program.

Note

1. For more detailed information, references, and suggestions for lessons that relate children's literature to the basic scientific processes, see Barclay, Benelli & Shoon (1999).

References

Aardema, V. (1981). *Bringing the rain to Kapiti Plain: A Nandi tale.* New York: Dial.

Armbruster, B. B. (1993). Reading to learn. *The Reading Teacher, 46*(4), 346–347.

Baker, K. (1990). *Who Is the beast?* San Diego: Harcourt Brace Jovanovich.

Barcley, K., Benelli, C., & Shoon, S. (1999). Making the connection! Science & literacy. *Childhood Education, 75*(3), 146–152.

Barnam, C. R. (1992). An evaluation of the use of a technique designed to assist prospective elementary teachers use the learning cycle with science textbooks. *School Science and Mathematics 92*(2), 59–63.

Brainard, A., & Wrubel, D. H. (1993). *Literature-based science activities: An integrated approach, Grades K–3.* New York: Scholastic Professional Books.

Brett, J. (1996). *Goldilocks and the three bears.* Madison, WI: Demco Media

Butzow, C. M., & Butzow, J. W. (1989). *Science through children's literature: An integrated approach.* Englewood, CO: Teacher Idea Press.

Butzow, C. M., & Butzow, J. W. (1998). *More science through children's literature: An integrated approach.* Englewood, CO: Teacher Idea Press.

Carle, E. (1985). *The very busy spider.* New York: Philomel.

Carle, E. (1986). *The grouchy ladybug.* New York: HarperCollins Publishers.

Carle, E. (1987). *The very hungry caterpillar.* New York: Philomel.

Carle, E. (1990). *The very quiet cricket.* New York: Philomel.

Carle, E. (1995). *The very lonely firefly.* New York: Philomel.

Cauley, L. B. (1983). *Jack and the beanstalk.* New York: Putnam.

Climo, S. (1989). *The Egyptian Cinderella.* New York: HarperCollins Children's Books.

Collay, R., & Dubrow, J. (1998). *Stuartship.* Eugene, OR: Flower Press & Creative Hands.

dePaola, T. (1978). *The popcorn book.* New York: Holiday House.

Ehlert, L. (1996). *Moon rope.* San Diego: Harcourt Brace.

Gibbons, G. (1991). *From seed to plant.* New York: Holiday House.

Gibbons, G. (1999). *The pumpkin book.* New York: Holiday House.

Gibbs, W. W., and Fox, D. (1999). The false crisis in science education. *Scientific American, 281*(4), 87–93.

Hoban, T. (1997). *Look book.* New York: Greenwillow.

Keats, E. J. (1977). *Whistle for Willie.* Madison, MI: Demco Media.

Lima, C. W., & Lima, J. A. (1998). *A to zoo—Subject access to children's picture books* (7th edition). New Providence, NJ: Bowker.

Lionni, L. (1995). *Inch by inch.* Madison, WI: Demco Media.

McClelland, A. K., & Krockover, G. H. (1996). Children's understandings of science: *Goldilocks and the Three Bears* revisited. *Journal of Elementary Science Education, 8*(2), 32–65.

Moore, J. E., & Evans, J. (1991a). *Exploring science through literature, level A, grades K–1*. Monterey, CA: Evan-Moor Corp.

Moore, J. E., & Evans, J. (1991b). *Exploring science through literature, level B, grades 2–3*. Monterey, CA: Evan-Moor Corp.

Myller, R. (1962). *How big is a foot?* New York: Atheneum.

Raines, S., & Canady, R. J. (1989). *Story s-t-r-e-t-c-h-e-r-s: Activities to expand children's favorite literature*. Beltsville, MD: Gryphon House.

Raines, S., & Canady, R. J. (1992). *Story s-t-r-e-t-c-h-e-r-s: Activities to expand children's favorite books*. Beltsville, MD: Gryphon House.

Ramirez, G., & Ramirez, J. L. (1994). *Multiethnic children's literature*. Albany, NY: Delmar Publishers, Inc.

Silverstein, S. (1974). *Where the sidewalk ends*. New York: Harper and Row.

Solzhenitsyn, A. I. (1979). Nobel lecture.

Terrific Science Press Staff. (1996). *Teaching school science through children's literature: 20 complete lessons for elementary grades*. New York: McGraw Hill.

Tiedt, I. M. (1999). Library of conservation. *Science and Children, 37*(3), 18–21.

Ulerick, S. L. (1989, April). Using textbooks for meaningful learning in science. *Research Matters . . . to the Science Teacher*. National Association for Research in Science Teaching *Newsletter*.

Van Allsburg, C. (1988). *Two bad ants*. Boston: Houghton Mifflin.

Walsh, E. S. (1989). *Mouse paint*. San Diego: Harcourt Brace.

White, E. B. (1952). *Charlotte's web*. New York: HarperCollins Children's Books.

Wolkstein, D. (1972). *8000 stones: A Chinese folktale*. New York: Doubleday.

CHAPTER 23

Interdisciplinary Integration

You doubtless have inferred that science is interdisciplinary in nature. You have observed that science draws extensively on mathematics for measurement and interpretation of data, that it requires language skills for communication, and that it is closely interlaced with technology and social issues.

Not only is science interdisciplinary relative to other subjects, it is interdisciplinary relative to itself. Traditionally, science is divided into three large areas—the life sciences, the physical sciences, and the earth and space sciences. Yet, these areas are interdependent among themselves. For example, one cannot investigate the interactions of living things in a playground habitat (a life science topic) without also investigating the effects of weather on the habitat (an earth and space science topic). One would not investigate rockets and space travel (a physical science topic) without including investigations about how space travel affects the human body (a life science topic). One cannot investigate the

The means by which we live have outdistanced the ends for which we live. Our scientific power has outrun our spiritual power. We have guided missiles and misguided men.
Martin Luther King Jr. *The Strength to Love* **(Cleveland Fount Books, 1963), 73**

They dined on mince, and slices of quince,
Which they ate with a runcible spoon;
And hand in hand, on the edge of the sand,
They danced by the light of the moon.
Edward Lear, *The Owl and the Pussycat* **(New York: HarperCollins Children's Books, 1998). (Original work published 1845)**

nature of rocks and minerals (earth science topics) without also investigating how they change through physical and chemical interactions with the environment (physical science topics).

Science is a social study, and, as we have noted before, there is little point in studying science without also investigating how it is applied in our daily lives, how it has contributed to and influenced our social condition, and how science and technology drive each other. We must be able to help children construct an understanding of how the science topics they study are applicable to their daily lives. This, in fact, is one of the twelve headings in the extended lesson plan format suggested. If we can't answer the question, "So what?" we had better ask why we want children to study that topic in the first place.

You have been engaged in constructing your personal conceptualizations (somewhat independent of other disciplines) about the goals, objectives, and methodologies of quality science education. But, in actual practice, the early childhood teacher integrates all traditional subjects in an interdisciplinary approach to ensure meaningfulness of the topics being studied without separating the components artificially into separate and seemingly unrelated disciplines. In this chapter, you will explore ways you can approach early childhood science education from an integrated interdisciplinary approach.

TOWARD THE INTERDISCIPLINARY CURRICULUM

The standard approach to curriculum involves separating learning into individual subjects, each with its own time slot, its own text, and its own program of study. This fractionalized approach sends a powerful message to children that each subject has its own domain and is independent of the others. However, constructivist teachers are shifting from the compartmentalized approach to an integrated, holistic approach to learning. This approach is known as integrated curriculum, or interdisciplinarianism. Interdisciplinarianism involves the inclusion of more than one discipline in an area of study. The integration of reading and writing within the science program that you investigated in Chapter 22 is just one aspect of interdisciplinarianism.

As we have previously observed, no subject can be studied in isolation. To attempt to do so is futile—it simply cannot be done. For example, it is impossible to teach science without some use of language. Mathematics is essential for obtaining measurements, charting data trends, constructing graphs, and interpreting experimental results. Social studies provides the essential link between science concepts and principles and their usefulness to society; indeed, science derives its meaning, in large measure, from social contexts.

Barab and Landa (1997) write that

> Children learn by mobilizing their innate capacities to meet everyday challenges they perceive as meaningful. Skills and concepts are most often learned as tools to meet present demands rather than as facts to be memorized today in hopes of application tomorrow. Further, daily life is not separated into academic disciplines or divided into discrete time units; instead, the environment presents problems that one must address in an interdisciplinary, free-flowing way, usually in collaboration with peers and mentors. These lines of reasoning point toward curriculum units that are problem-centered; interdisciplinary; presented in an interactive, cooperative format; and appeal to a multitude of students. (52)

Interdisciplinary learning is the natural way people learn. In addition to their instructional responsibilities, teachers regularly integrate such areas as psychology, sociology, mathematics, economics, nutrition, safety, communication, drama, music, and scientific processes and principles of inquiry into their daily work. The occupations of police officer, fire fighter, doctor, and engineer—all interesting to young children—are interdisciplinary in nature. The police officer writes tickets, reads reports, uses the scientific processes in inferring solutions to crimes, calculates how much faster than the speed limit vehicles were traveling, and participates in neighborhood protection programs. The fire fighter locates emergencies on maps, drives trucks skillfully, maintains the equipment, decides on the best methods to extinguish fires, keeps up with recent fire-fighting techniques, and files reports. The doctor and the engineer are well versed in all subject matter areas and in how they work together.

THE DAISY INTERDISCIPLINARY MODEL

Constructing Your Ideas 23.1
A Multidisciplinary Unit

As a group, select a topic of study that would be appropriate for children in the age or grade level of class you plan to teach. The topic should be related to science, such as "Animals," "Melting Ice," "Environmental Camouflage," "Shifting Sand," and the like.

Write the name of the topic on chart paper or the board, and, beneath it, prepare spaces for the following subjects: reading, writing, science, mathematics, social studies, art, music,

(continued)

physical education, and other subjects children are typically required to study. In each space, list one or more activities relating to the main topic than can be used to teach concepts in that discipline.

For example, if your topic were "Birds" and your hypothetical class were first grade, you might cite the following activities:

Reading	Read *Make Way for Ducklings* by Robert McCloskey (Puffin Books, 1999)
Writing	Write a short story of what you could see if you could fly like a bird.
Science	Classify pictures of birds.
Mathematics	Count the number of birds that come to the bird feeder each day.
Social studies	Show on a map the routes hummingbirds take on their annual migrations.
Art	Construct and name a bird you make out of a paper plate and decorative paper.
Music	Learn and sing the song, *The Sparrow*, written by Grace Budd. (Refer to www.kididdles.com)
Physical education	Create and do a dance that represents birds.

In this activity, you constructed a skeletal course of study around a central topic. Each discipline was represented through activities and learnings that fit in with the central theme. This approach to interdisciplinary studies can be characterized by a *daisy model* (Figure 23.1). In the daisy model, the major area of study is represented by the center of the flower, and the other areas of study are added as the daisy's petals. Each subject retains its own distinctive characteristics, and each subject is readily identified by teacher and

THE DAISY MODEL Main subject is in the center; other subjects are attached as petals.

FIGURE 23.1   The daisy model of interdisciplinary integration

children alike. Each subject is treated independently, although it is related to the central topic. Mathematics is still taught as mathematics; reading is still taught as reading; and writing is still taught as writing. The primary difference between this approach and the discipline-centered approach is the thematic nature of the material.

Early childhood classroom centers often follow the daisy model or a variation of it. The following description of one approach to centers was written by a kindergarten teacher.

Science-Based Interdisciplinary Kindergarten Classroom Centers

Science objectives are met through discovery at all centers, including science-specific centers. Children learn about mixing colors at the Art Center. At the Block Center, basic physics principles such as rolling or catapulting are daily experiments. The Library Center includes magazines and books. Children get to see how pressure and/or heat can change the shape of objects at the Cooking Center. Children investigate funnels and volume at the Rice Center. At the Sand Center and Water Table, they make comparisons and observe how various substances react to water. I have a Pulley Center where children hoist classroom materials, and we are adopting a class pet, a rabbit. Parents help out with the centers daily, and I send suggestions for activities children can do at home.

FIGURE 23.2 In the science center

Jones (1999) describes another approach to centers in early childhood science education that she calls the "workshop" approach. In this approach, the teacher sets up several centers, all based on the same topic, such as "plants" or "magnets," in which children explore several aspects of the topic. Each day, children choose one center at which to work, providing they have not been at that center before. Children explore a different center each day until all children have experienced each center. The centers are level-appropriate and contain everything children need to work somewhat independently once the teacher has described each center to the class and given directions. The teacher observes, records, and assesses the children and the groups, and she bases subsequent instruction on the information she gains from experiences at the centers. Jones writes that the workshop approach "add[s] to the richness of the classroom and provide[s] flexibility for both students and teachers to pursue meaningful activities"(55).

Although the daisy model approach falls short of a truly interdisciplinary approach where the lines separating the subjects cease to exist, it nonetheless is a good beginning. You can start by combining one other content area with science as you did when you investigated ways of integrating literature and writing with science. With experience, you can integrate more completely.

However, as Barab and Landa (1997) note, "In striving for an interdisciplinary approach, the question is not how many disciplines one can integrate but rather 'Will the unit provide a diversity of learners opportunities to try difficult tasks and learn new skills in a motivating and rewarding context?' " (54).

THE ROSE INTERDISCIPLINARY MODEL

In the rose model of interdisciplinary studies, the subject areas lose their distinctive delineations (Figure 23.3). Unlike the daisy, where each petal is separate and distinctly visible, in the rose, all the petals are closely intertwined, and one sees the whole flower without regard to individual petals. In the rose model, learning focuses on a particular problem or situation meaningful and

THE ROSE MODEL All subjects are intertwined.

FIGURE 23.3 The rose model of interdisciplinary integration

of interest to children, and the children study whatever is necessary to bring about personal understanding.

Zais uses the term "problem-centered," referring to the organization of studies around "problems of living, both individual and social" (Zais, 1976, 43). He cites Hilda Taba, who wrote, "organizing the curriculum around the activities of mankind will not only bring about a needed unification of knowledge but will also permit such a curriculum to be of maximum value to students' day-by-day life, as well as to prepare them for participation in a culture" (Taba, 1962, 396).

The following account of a student teacher whose second-grade class produced a video about their school is a good example of the rose model of interdisciplinary studies.

The Video

I once supervised a student teacher who was assigned to second grade. This student had previously studied the communications field and had mastered the technique of producing documentary videos. When the principal learned this, she asked the student teacher to engage his second-grade class in producing a 10-minute video about their school to be used to familiarize new faculty, staff, and parents with the school. The student teacher discussed the project with his class, and together they decided on the contents of the video. He divided the children into several groups, each with responsibility for one or more distinct phases of the video. In groups, children drew the story boards and wrote the script for each segment. The student teacher taught the children how to operate the camcorder, and the children shot the video footage. When this was done, the children refined the script and read it into a tape recorder. The only thing the student teacher did by himself was combine the script with the video footage and edit the production.

During the course of this project, which lasted several weeks, the student teacher lamented that, although he was perfectly willing to engage the children in this project, and although he was certain they were having a lot of fun, he was becoming increasingly frustrated over the time spent when "no teaching was going on." He felt the prescribed curriculum had been set aside during this production, and he was not fulfilling his responsibilities as a teacher, for he had not covered the topics required for this period of time. I suggested that he list the topics that were supposed to be covered and indicate those that the children had learned through the video project. He did so and returned the list to me, dumbfounded that the children had in fact covered more of the prescribed curriculum than they would have if he had taught it in the traditional manner. The video production had enabled the children to learn more than they otherwise would have learned.

This student teacher was engaging in a totally integrated rose model approach to learning.

To develop a rose model integrated program, the teacher starts by engaging children in a conversation that results in identifying a topic about which the children have expressed interest in learning more. Let us say, for example, that the children have indicated a strong desire to learn about soft drinks. In the large group setting, the teacher asks the children what they need to learn in order to find out what they want to know about the topic—in this case, soft drinks. A brainstorming session follows during which the teacher records the children's responses. A sampling of first-graders' responses to learning about soft drinks is shown in Figure 23.4.

After the children have completed the "What We Need to Know" list, the teacher groups the subtopics in a sensible and efficient way and forms study groups based on interest in finding information on the subtopics. The groups may be discrete with each group investigating a different subtopic, and they may be overlapping to accommodate those with several inquiry interests. In addition, the teacher may turn one or more of the questions into class activities such as that shown in Constructing Science in the Classroom 23.1.

The teacher provides time and resources for the groups of children to pursue their investigations. Children have their own ideas of what to do, and the teacher has her own ideas of what the children ought to do as they pursue their investigations. She guides them accordingly. Activities might include reading, doing computer work, exploring the Internet, studying drawings, models, videos, and filmstrips, examining materials brought from home, and

---

WHAT DO WE NEED TO LEARN IN ORDER TO FIND OUT WHAT WE WANT TO KNOW ABOUT SOFT DRINKS?

A Sample of First-Graders' Responses

What kinds there are
Which kinds the kids think taste the best
Why they come in glass and plastic bottles and in cans
What kinds of cans they come in
Why they explode when we shake them and then open them
Regions of the country and the world where they are sold
What's in them
How they are made
How they get their fizz
How much they cost to make
How much they cost to bottle and ship to the stores
Why they cost so much
What the profit is
How popular different kinds are
How different kinds are advertised
How they got their names

FIGURE 23.4 What do we have to learn in order to find out what we want to know about soft drinks?

a host of other relevant activities. In a well laid-out classroom, children know where the resources are, and they work with what they need.

The teacher facilitates the children's inquiries by helping them identify sources of information, find the information they seek, consolidate this information, and make sense out of what they are discovering. The teacher is very busy, moving from group to group, helping children with resources, listening to the children, asking questions, probing for understandings, and challenging new understandings. The room is noisy, but everyone soon gets used to the din as they focus on their own activities. Children are busy figuring things out for themselves.

The time spent on the projects varies with the ages, grades, maturities, and interests of the children. Kindergartners might spend only a few days investigating a topic of their selection, whereas first and second graders might choose to make the study a longer effort.

In the end, all groups are brought together to report on their findings. This culminates with a large-group class discussion in which closure is brought to as many items on the original list as possible.

Constructing Science in the Classroom 23.1
Why Do Cans of Soft Drinks "Explode" When They Are Opened?

AGE

8
7
6
5
4
3

Objective

The student will define soft drink can "explosion" in operational terms. The student will isolate the variables that could cause a can of soft drink to "explode" on being opened. The student will devise and execute experiments to investigate the effect of each variable on the amount of explosion upon opening a can of soft drink.

First, ask the children what factors they think cause cans of soft drink to explode when being opened. Suggestions include heating the can and shaking the can, in addition to others they may think of. Because one of the variables may be can size, the class should agree to investigate only cans of the same size. Because other variables may include the kind of soft drink and regular versus diet types, the class should agree on a constant to be investigated. Try using standard-sized cans of soft drink to provide constancy; use diet soft drinks to avoid stickiness.

Provide several cans of soft drink. One at a time, implement each variable and open the cans. Teach the children to pull on the tab slowly so they can gauge the intensity of the explosion. From this introductory exercise, the children will (1) define *explosion intensity* in operational terms and (2) identify the variables to be investigated.

FIGURE 23.5 Listening for the sound of soft drink cans being opened

(continued)

Ask the children to develop experiments that will allow them to measure the effect of changing given variables—such as temperature or number of times shaken—on the intensity of the explosion experienced when the can is opened. Note that the temperature of the soft drink inside the can will have to be defined operationally.

Have the children do their experiments and record the data. You may wish to help them develop data sheets for their use.

Finally, ask the children to share their conclusions with the class. To provide concrete evidence of the explanatory and predictive power of their constructions, you might want to provide plastic bottles of the same kind of soft drink or cans of a different kind of soft drink. Ask children to apply their findings to these soft drinks to see whether they hold true for different kinds of containers and different kinds of soft drinks.

Literature Connection:

Soda Science: Designing and Testing Soft Drinks by Bernie Zubrowski (1997). This Boston Children's Museum activity book contains a collection of activities that focus on soft drinks.

Grace (1999) reports taking the interdisciplinary problem-centered program to its ultimate implementation by asking individual groups of children to create their own curriculum. Preservice teachers are assigned under her supervision to first, second, and other elementary grades. They form groups of two or three children and ask them what they want to study. The preservice teachers meet with each group to establish goals and activities. They assemble available materials and function as co-inquirers with each group, one at a time. The result is that

> The [children] themselves made the important decisions about what to study, how to study it, and how to demonstrate to others what they had learned. They were not merely engaged in a student-centered curriculum; they were engaged in a student-generated curriculum (50).

The ultimate goal of the rose model of interdisciplinary teaching and learning is the "production of an informed citizenry capable of making crucial decisions about current problems and issues and taking personal actions as a result of these decisions" (Yager, 1991, 94). The start children get in the formative years of the early childhood years paves the way. The early childhood science educator can begin by selecting thematic approaches similar to those investigated above. A sampling of interdisciplinary themes appropriate for early childhood science education is shown in Figure 23.6. You are certain to add to this list as you develop interdisciplinary lessons and units appropriate for the unique situation of your school and community and the children in your class.

The rose model represents true interdisciplinarianism in curriculum development. Topics are selected because of their intrinsic interest to children. Activities are undertaken and performed thoroughly by the children because of their desires to formulate a knowledgeable whole out of the various parts. Scientific inquiries, although potentially lengthy, are taken from the children's own questions and ideas and thus are meaningful. And the whole unit helps children fill in voids, construct new and missing information, and, perhaps most important, helps them learn how to learn.

**A SAMPLING OF INTERDISCIPLINARY THEMATIC APPROACHES
APPROPRIATE FOR EARLY CHILDHOOD SCIENCE PROGRAMS**

Apples	Nature studies
Authors (Tomie dePaola, Eric Carle, Jerry Pollata, and others who have written several children's books)	Oceans
	Pumpkins
	Regions of the United States (Wild West, Deep South, etc.)
Environment	
Families	Safety
Flowers	Seasonal activities
Harvest	Seasons
Health	Seeds
Holidays	Senses
Machines	Shadows
Music	Shamrocks
Native Americans	Trees

FIGURE 23.6 A sampling of interdisciplinary thematic approaches appropriate for early childhood science programs

SCIENCE, TECHNOLOGY, AND SOCIETY

Science-Technology-Society (STS) is a project-centered approach to science education that involves teaching and learning science in the context of human experience and that concurrently embodies the interdisciplinary goals inherent in the rose model. The experiences selected for investigation are identified by the children who are "full partners in planning and carrying out their own science lessons" (Yager, 1994, 34).

STS Approaches

In the STS approach, as in the rose model of interdisciplinary studies, children identify problems, questions, or unknowns, and participate in deciding what they need to do and need to know as they research answers and explanations. STS projects can involve any science-based problem children care to investigate. Problems can be global (such as animals in other countries, volcano eruptions, and earthquakes), national (such as health care issues, land use, and endangered species), local (such as waste disposal, recycling, and parks), or personal (such as trips to the dentist, stopped-up toilets, fires, and meal planning). STS projects center on real issues that children bring up. Local problems such as recycling and trash removal are often used as the basis for STS projects. Projects may begin with a situation at school, such as cleaning up a playground and keeping it clean. Teacher and children collaborate in deciding what to study, how to proceed, and how children will get involved. Many new questions and problems are encountered along the way that suggest new inquiries and new avenues of investigation. Teacher and children are co-inquirers into investigations that are inquiry in orientation.

STS is grounded in the constructivist learning model. Children learn to do science because they are doing investigations into their own inquiries. They come to understand the scientific concepts and processes because they surface from their daily living situations and can be applied to their own lives. STS gives children an understanding of what science and technology are and what the roles are that they play in our lives. Children learn through their involvement with real-world problems and issues. As Yager (1991) writes:

> Suddenly the program's major objectives are realized—merely by allowing students to identify questions, propose solutions and explanations, and employ tests for the validity of these items. Such basic ingredients of science are rarely experienced in traditional science education. (94)

The incorporation of children's literature into the science program is one of the easiest ways to embark on an STS approach. In the book, *Mike Mulligan and His Steam Shovel* by Virginia Lee Burton (1939), an old-fashioned steam shovel becomes outdated by more modern equipment. Children can explore this problem of adapting to technological change from a variety of viewpoints, including the nature of machines, building novel machines, providing directions for their operation, citing reasons why people should buy them, building their own unique and novel machines, and exploring the societal issues of equipment aging and obsolescence. Children will develop their own questions, problems, and avenues of exploration.

Environmental issues are of concern. Thus, STS problems can center on how to live in a constantly changing environment, how to change personal habits to be more environmentally friendly, how to keep the environment clean, and so on.

Recycling, conservation, and landfill problems are all appropriate STS topics. Waste management is an issue that directly affects children's lives. As an introductory activity, children can collect trash for one day, put it in a paper bag, and bury it in the schoolyard (Figure 23.7). If this is done at the beginning of the school year, it can be dug up every two or three months to see what is happening. Variations on this activity abound, and children are sure to come up with their own.

A listing of some topics that can be used for STS investigations is shown in Figure 23.8.

Personal Bias in STS Projects

To what extent should teachers introduce their personal biases when a class is pursuing a project? We all have personal (and sometimes emotional) feelings about many of the STS topics children bring up, from conservation issues to recycling and preservation of endangered species. A major goal of education is for children to learn to think for themselves. This means children must build their own informed constructions based on their own evaluation and validation of evidence.

There are many reasons for teachers to encourage children to come to their own conclusions. One involves promoting children's ownership of their

FIGURE 23.7 How long will it take these things to decay?

SOME STS TOPICS APPROPRIATE FOR EARLY CHILDHOOD SCIENCE EDUCATION

Air pollution
Amusement parks
Animals
Computers
Conservation
Drunk driving
Endangered plants and animals
Fingerprints
Food and food groups
Health
The Internet
Newsworthy happenings (including current newspaper articles dealing with science)

Plants
Playing
The rainforest
Recycling
Seat belt laws
Space travel
Substance abuse
Water pollution
Weather
Work

FIGURE 23.8 Some STS topics appropriate for early childhood science education
Adapted, in part, from Thirunarayanan, 1998

own thinking. When teachers allow their personal biases to set the direction of an investigation, children are denied the opportunity to think freely for themselves. For example, a teacher may slant a study of recycling in such a way that children get the idea that they are supposed to come up with evidence that supports recycling. However, in an investigation that is open ended, children would be asked to consider both positive and negative factors influencing recycling and come to their *own* informed decisions on whether recycling is useful. There is a story of a teacher who tried to get her first-grade children to embrace the principles of recycling. She asked all the children to come to class with descriptions of how their parents recycle materials. Several of the children's parents did not recycle and, in fact, thought recycling a waste of time. This put the children in the uncomfortable position of choosing between parents and teacher.

Another reason for keeping teachers' personal biases out of STS investigations involves the constantly changing nature of scientific knowledge. Facts that were once considered supportive of certain STS positions may be shown to be erroneous later on. For example, people are concerned about atmospheric warming. However, data show that, on the average, actual global warming from 1979 to 1994 was less than one-third the forecast rise.[1]

Still another reason involves the tendency of investigators to slant data to support given positions. It is incumbent on us as teachers to require children to interpret data objectively and to search for hidden variables. For example, the notion that recycling is good is based, in part, on conservation of energy resources. Community recycling efforts may involve curbside waste management programs that require more collection trucks, which means more fuel consumption and increased air pollution. Some recycling programs require considerable resources just to transport the materials to the recycling plants. These factors are part of the overall situation and should be considered by children as they study recycling. Looking at another example, most varieties of the spotted owl are on the extinction list, and steps are being taken to preserve this species. However, these steps often cause considerable financial and personal difficulties for citizens on whose land individual birds have nested. Children should consider all facets of animal and plant extinction and protection issues in their investigations.

STS represents an ultimate amalgamation of constructivism, science, and interdisciplinary investigations. It is to be hoped that every early childhood science teacher will explore STS possibilities for their own classes.

SIGNIFICANCE OF INTERDISCIPLINARY INTEGRATION IN EARLY CHILDHOOD SCIENCE PROGRAMS

Children can learn only what is meaningful to them. In science, there are so many topics to choose from that every child can find topics that are meaningful. Yet, science educators persist in covering certain prescribed content out of fear that, if children are not exposed to every science topic in a systematic manner, their science education will be lacking and the United States will continue to plummet on the international science report card.

Leaders in education and business for many years have urged moving from content-oriented science programs toward a science education that teaches "less so it can be taught better" (American Association for the Advancement of Science, 1989); that teaches science not as a body of knowledge but as a way of thinking (Sagan, 1989); and that focuses on children rather than teachers (Glasser, 1990). Interdisciplinary instructional techniques designed to engage children more actively in the learning process promote integration of science with other subject matter and the natural blending of topics in science, technology, and society. It is this integrated, interest-based, child-centered approach to teaching and learning that fosters the highest achievement in science as well as other subjects and that fosters children's positive attitudes toward school, learning, and science. Let us hope that these goals are set firmly in place for children during their early childhood science education experiences.

SUMMARY

All learning is interdisciplinary. Science draws upon many disciplines for meaning, application, and answers to inquiries. These disciplines include mathematics, communications skills, the social studies, and many others. Furthermore, the investigation of topics in any one branch of science draws upon understandings in the other branches.

There are several ways teachers can provide interdisciplinary learning experiences in early childhood education. One way involves selecting a science topic and providing experiences from the other disciplines that relate to or reinforce the central science topic. This procedure can be referred to as the daisy model. A second way involves the thematic approach, wherein the objectives and activities of all disciplines, including science, are interwoven in such a way that the study is congruent with the natural way children can be expected to explore that theme. This procedure can be referred to as the rose model.

A third way of providing interdisciplinary experiences is termed Science-Technology-Society, or STS for short. STS is similar to the rose model, but topics selected for investigation are those that deal with science, their interaction with technology, and their interdependence with social issues.

Natural learning does not occur in discrete, discipline-based segments. To the extent possible, early childhood science educators should adopt an interdisciplinary approach that parallels the natural approach children take in their learning. The constructivist teacher will understand this and implement interdisciplinary approaches in the entire teaching/learning opportunity.

Note

1. Source: World Climate review, University of Virginia. Forecast figures are based on a computer model developed at Geophysical Fluid Dynamics Laboratory, Princeton, NJ. Actual figures are taken from those measured by NASA satellites.

References

American Association for the Advancement of Science. (1989). *Project 2061: Science for all Americans.* Washington, DC: American Association for the Advancement of Science.

Barab, S. A., & Landa, L. (1997). Designing effective interdisciplinary anchors. *Educational Leadership 54*(6), 52–55.

Burton, V. L. (1939). *Mike Mulligan and his steam shovel.* Boston: Houghton Mifflin.

Glasser, W. (1990, February). The quality school. *Phi Delta Kappan,* 52–62.

Grace, M. (1999). When students create curriculum. *Educational Leadership 57*(3), 49–52.

Jones, W. (1999). A workshop approach. *Science and Children, 37*(3), 26–55.

King, M. L. Jr. (1963). *The strength to love.* Cleveland: Fount Books.

Lear, E. (1998). *The owl and the pussycat.* New York: HarperCollins Children's Books.

Sagan, C. (1989, September 10). Why we need to understand science. *Parade Magazine.*

Taba, H. (1962). *Curriculum development: Theory and practice.* New York: Harcourt Brace & World, Inc.

Thirunarayanan, M. O. (1998). An exploratory study of the relationships among science, technology and society (STS) issues as conceived by fifth-grade students. *Journal of Elementary Science Education 10*(1), 60–75.

Yager, R. E. (1991). Science/Technology/Society as a major reform in science education: Its importance for teacher education. *Teaching Education 3*(2), 91–100.

Yager, R. E. (1994). Assessment results with the science/technology/society approach. *Science and Children 32*(2).

Zais, R. S. (1976). *Curriculum: Principles and foundations.* New York: Harper & Row, Publishers, Inc.

Zubrowski, B. (1997). *Soda science: Designing and testing soft drinks.* New York: William Morrow & Company.

CHAPTER 24

The Early Childhood Science Education Professional

As a teaching professional, you have tremendous opportunities to share successes, contribute to discussions on open issues with other professionals, and exert your professional influence on the direction education takes. As a teaching professional, you also have responsibilities for providing the best possible education for each individual child, for meeting the educational needs of the school, the community it serves, and the nation, and for keeping up with new curricular materials, new ideas about pedagogy, and current developments in your profession.

The classroom teacher makes numerous decisions including what to teach and how to teach it. You have been continuously developing your ideas of the nature of quality early childhood science education, so your decisions about teaching science will be based on your personal constructions of informed notions

And gladly woulde he lerne, and gladly teche.
Geoffrey Chaucer, *The Canterbury Tales* (San Marino, CA: Huntington Library Press, 1995), 1.308 (Original work published c. 1387)

To teach is to learn twice over.
Joseph Joubert, *Pensées* (Paris: Union Général d'Editions, 1966), (Original work published 1842)

Let us not worry about the future. Those who do what is right are always rewarded.
Beatrice Schenk de Regniers, *The Enchanted Forest* (Atheneum, 1974 out-of-print)

obtained through this text, your own experiences in doing science, and, hopefully, your actual work with children.

Your work in this text is but the beginning of a lifetime of learning. Science changes, and you will want to know about major new developments and significant revisions in science content as they occur. Methodologies change, and you will want to be able to keep up with new ideas and new developments in **pedagogy.** You will want to reap the benefits of ideas shown by others to work in their classes, and you will want to contribute your own valuable experience and insights to your profession so others can reap the ideas you have constructed and have shown to be valid—or perhaps not valid—in your classes.

pedagogy—The science, art, and profession of teaching

The days when the teacher went to college to learn how to teach and then taught the same basic material in the same basic way for the next 20 or 30 years are over. Teachers are not automatons. Teachers are thinking, doing, and constructing human beings. Education is a learned profession, and you, the teacher, are a professional among professionals. This means that your learning is lifelong, that it never ends, and that it is constantly put to use as you help your profession mature in the 21st century.

In this chapter, you will explore ways you can promote excellence in your science program and take advantage of opportunities to influence education through making and justifying curriculum and methodology decisions, ways you can keep up with new developments in both content and pedagogy, and ways you can contribute to your personal professional growth as an early childhood science educator and to the growth of science education.

DECISIONS ABOUT CURRICULUM AND CONTENT

Throughout this text, you have been encouraged to construct your own conceptualizations about teaching early childhood science. You have given much consideration to the notion that it is better for children to learn how to do science than it is for children to learn about science. Your increasingly sophisticated constructions about teaching children to do science have come about by doing process-oriented inquiry activities yourself, by searching for explanatory and predictive reliability for your constructions, and by discussing your experiences and ideas with each other, your instructor, and other early childhood education professionals.

We have tried to make the point that it is the doing of science that matters—not the learning of specific facts, principles, and theories of science. We have tried to make the point that science education in early childhood settings must be developmentally appropriate, culturally sensitive and diverse, and integrated with other subjects in problem-centered and situation-focused inquiries.

Nowhere have we stipulated content. The fundamental premise of this text is that when children learn how to *do* science, they are also learning *about* science. They use scientific content as the vehicle for developing mastery in applying the scientific processes. And as they investigate science concepts through process-oriented inquiry, they are also constructing personal, valid, and firm conceptualizations about the science content that serve as the vehicle.

This is the essence of constructivist science education.

Nonetheless, in spite of decades of persuasive argument and agreement on the part of educators and scientists, many early childhood science programs remain focused on content. This is caused by a variety of factors, including a basic reluctance of teachers to construct process-oriented inquiry approaches for themselves; requirements of the school administration that teachers cover a prescribed scope and sequence; public reaction to reports of standardized achievement tests and the role these tests have in driving the science program; the unwillingness of policy makers and legislators to take the leap of faith to something new; and other equally important factors.

The National Science Foundation, the American Association for the Advancement of Science, and the National Science Teachers Association have addressed the content issue in the *National Science Education Standards* (National Academy of Sciences, 1996). (See also Chapter 1.) Though the *Standards* do not address early childhood science education explicitly, they suggest that, in early childhood science education programs, children should develop understandings and abilities aligned with the scientific processes and with inquiry and that early childhood science education programs should use topics from all the sciences as vehicles for inquiries. These topics include physical science, life science, earth and space science, science and technology, science in personal and social perspectives, and the history and nature of science. In addition, it is abundantly clear in the *Standards* that teachers should plan inquiry-based programs (NSES Teaching Standard A), guide and facilitate children's learning (NSES Teaching Standard B), implement programs that are developmentally appropriate, interesting, and relevant to children's lives (NSES Program Standard B), and provide programs that are interdisciplinary in nature (NSES Program Standard B) and that are coordinated with the mathematics program (NSES Program Standard C). (See inside front and back covers for the complete listing of the *National Science Education Standards*.)

Today's early childhood science teachers are faced with a curriculum dilemma. On one hand, the force of science education reform insists that science education focus on process-oriented inquiry and learning to *do* science rather than learning about science. On the other hand, powerful forces insist that science education focus on teaching the content of science.

Contemporary science education seeks to achieve three overarching goals:

1. Science as a process of inquiry and problem solving
2. Sufficient working knowledge of science to deal effectively with societal and technical issues
3. Preparation of the next generation of scientists

To accomplish these goals, contemporary science curriculum development must be guided by several broad considerations:

1. Process is more important than content.
2. Discipline boundaries among the sciences are softened.
3. Science is integrated with the rest of the curriculum.
4. Science is attached meaningfully to life.
5. Science content is based on fundamental scientific principles and concepts.

Exploring the properties of fluids

In your professional capacity as an early childhood teacher, you may be asked to cover certain science content. Because teaching prescribed science content seems to oppose our constructivist point of view, it is well to give consideration to this apparent dichotomy. How can you teach prescribed content and still maintain the constructivist approach? Many questions emerge that you will need to answer to your satisfaction. A few are suggested here; you are sure to be able to add more. Answers are suggested that may help you establish congruency between a requirement to cover certain prescribed content and principles of constructivist science education.

1. Q: What content should I use?
   A: If you are faced with an imposed curriculum or scope and sequence, use the content that is prescribed. Separate this content into two categories: (1) the content that lends itself well to inquiry investigation, such as magnetism, animal camouflage, nature of rocks and minerals, and the like; and (2) the content that does not lend itself well to inquiry, such as names of planets, names of dinosaurs, nature of ecological principles, and the like. Spend as much as two-thirds of the time available for science on inquiry activities using the principles in List #1 as the vehicles, and spend the remainder of the time available for science "imparting" the science information in List #2.

2. Q: How can I tell what content lends itself to inquiry as opposed to content that has to be imparted?
   A: If children have requested or are truly interested in a topic or if a topic involves manipulation of actual materials such as ice cubes, balls, rocks, toothpicks, and the like, then the topic can be approached from an inquiry perspective. However, if a topic involves learning something others have found out that children are not likely to be able to discover for themselves, such as the relative temperatures of planets, living habits of dinosaurs, method by which batteries work, and the like, then the topic probably lends itself better to a **didactic** approach than an inquiry approach. But, even with these topics, a truly constructivist environment promotes individual broadening and deepening of inquiries.

   didactic—An approach to teaching in which material is presented for students to learn

3. Q: Where can I get the background for the science content I must use?
   A: If your school requires the use of a text or other basic commercial material, the teacher's manual may include the basic background you will need. The Internet has lots of information. This text has some information. Fundamental principles of science can be found in many reference materials, such as *The Science Education Standards* (National Academy of Sciences, 1996), *NSTA Pathways to the Science Standards, Elementary School Edition* (Lowery, 1997), *Early Childhood and Science* (McIntyre, 1984), *Resources for Teaching Elementary School Science* (National Science Resources Center, 1996), *Benchmarks for Science Literacy* (American Association for the Advancement of Science, 1994), *Resources for Science Literacy* (American Association for the Advancement of Science, 1997), *Elementary Science Methods: A Constructivist Approach* (Martin,

2000), other college and elementary school science texts, and many other resource materials. There are two words of caution: (1) Be sure the science described is accurate; remember the principle that says, "Just because it's in a book doesn't make it right"; and (2) if you truly are emphasizing the constructivist, process-oriented inquiry methodology, the children's answers are far more important than answers that come out of a book. It is far better to lead children to their *own* valid constructions than it is to lead them to some preconceived "correct" concept. If you know the "correct" answer, you are more likely to lead children to it than you are if you don't know it.

4. Q: How do I accommodate children's interests when the science content is prescribed?

    A: Employ the project-centered rose model of teaching and learning. Focus the project on the required subject material, and engage children in a discussion of their questions about the topic. The questions chosen for investigation represent the children's common interests. If you are required to introduce concepts that, in your opinion, may be of questionable interest to the children in your class, develop dramatic introductions and dynamic lessons and utilize all the interest-grabbing devices at your disposal to try to make the material as interesting as possible. Remember that material is interesting to children just to the extent that it involves their own activities and is applicable to their lives.

5. Q: How close do I keep to a prescribed scope and sequence or curriculum?

    A: This varies from school to school and from district to district. If you have latitude, use it judiciously. If you do not have latitude, you need to follow the prescribed curriculum, alternating between inquiry and didactic styles of teaching and learning as appropriate to the prescribed content. See Question #1.

Now it's your turn to wrestle with the curriculum and content issues.

Constructing Your Ideas 24.1
Teaching the Content of Science

Continue the preceding list of questions as appropriate for your individual situation. Write the questions, and, for each, suggest answers and alternative solutions. Discuss each in your whole class setting, and record ideas you may not have thought of that are valid according to your current conceptualization of quality early childhood science education.

As a professional educator, you will have the opportunity to participate in the continuing professional dialogue about early childhood science curriculum and to make informed decisions about what to teach in your program. You will ultimately have to make the decisions about the curriculum and content to be included in the program. The constructions you made as a result of this text will help you make these very difficult (and sometimes controversial) decisions. As always, you will have to make up your own mind. And please remember what Glasser (1992) wrote:

> We should never forget that people, not curriculum, are the desired outcomes of schooling. What we want to develop are students who have the skills to become active contributors to society, who are enthusiastic about what they have learned, and who are aware of how learning can be of use to them in the future. (694)

DECISIONS ABOUT METHODOLOGY

In addition to decisions you make about curriculum, you also will make decisions about methodology. Far from being separate from each other, curriculum and methodology are inextricably intertwined, and the teaching decisions you make affect both.

The *National Science Education Standards* (National Academy of Sciences, 1996) urge schools and science teachers to adopt an inquiry approach. As you have learned, the inquiry methodology allows children to investigate problems thoroughly by applying the processes of science, thereby encouraging the construction and reconstruction of children's own valid conceptualizations. These constructions remain valid in children's minds until the next related discrepant event causes them once again to wonder about what is going on. This, in turn, leads them to investigate the phenomenon from the new perspective and to construct new conceptualizations that are more detailed and more thorough, yet equally valid.

For example, a 3-year-old child may construct a conceptualization about magnetism that says, essentially, that all things made of metal are magnetic. When the child is exposed to magnets in kindergarten or the first

Even batteries are attracted to magnets!

grade, she may observe that her original construction (that all things made of metal are magnetic) does not explain that brass paper fasteners are not magnetic. She will be compelled, cognitively, to explore this discrepancy, after which she may well come to the conclusion that only those metallic things that contain iron are magnetic and that metallic things without iron are not magnetic. This is a new, more sophisticated and detailed conceptualization that has both explanatory and predictive power relative to the recently observed discrepancies.

As you can infer, the inquiry approach is time consuming. Far less science content can be explored through inquiry than through other methodologies. Thus, one main factor to consider when making decisions about methodology is the amount of time available for science. The use of constructivist interdisciplinary approaches maximizes the use of the time available for children to gain skill in inquiry and the processes of doing science. The actual science content that will be introduced during the year will have to be weighed relative to the time available and decisions made that incorporate the notions you explored in the previous section.

CONSOLIDATING CURRICULUM AND METHODOLOGY DECISIONS

In this text, many issues have been raised about effective early childhood science teaching, such as the following:

▮ Doing science vs learning about science

▮ Teaching science to *all* children

▮ Deciding on goals of early childhood science education

▮ Instructing from a constructivist perspective vs imparting information

▮ Teaching in an inquiry vs an expository mode

▮ Identifying and accommodating individual learner differences

▮ Utilizing multicultural approaches

▮ Assessing children's accomplishments authentically

▮ Developing interdisciplinary studies vs using a discipline-centered approach

▮ Including reading and writing in science

▮ Considering the influence of state and federal goals and state and district mandates

▮ Considering the role of standardized tests

▮ Keeping classroom order

We have urged you to weigh all sides of each issue with open minds and to formulate your own ideas concerning each issue.

Now the time has come for you to put everything together. You now (or shortly will) have the opportunity to explain your early childhood science education program and approach to colleagues, parents, administrators, interested and concerned citizens, and other professionals. It is hoped that every teacher will be able to explain and defend his or her curriculum and methodology decisions based on personal constructions of the research, personal experiences, and the various positions, arguments, and situations encountered in this text and elsewhere. To help you crystallize your ideas, please complete Constructing Your Ideas 24.2 and Constructing Your Ideas 24.3.

Constructing Your Ideas 24.2
Explaining Your Science Program

This exercise enables you to refine the philosophy of early childhood science education you have been developing since the beginning of this text and to state it in operational as well as theoretical terms, thus giving you a committed and firm foundation for the successful implementation of your early childhood science program.

Divide the members of your class into groups: pairs, small groups, or halves. One group takes the role of the new teacher in a school who has decided to implement a science teaching methodology developed as a result of this course. The other group takes the role of an administrator. The opening question of the administrator is, "Tell me what you plan to do with your science program and why." Role play this for a while, and then reverse roles. Critique the discussions.

Did the teacher have a sound methodology in place? Was she able to justify it? Did she cite experts in the field? Professional societies? Research? Was she cognizant of opposing views? Was she sensitive to the needs of the local school and community? Had she considered all aspects, both pro and con? Was she thoroughly prepared? Was she able to provide satisfactory answers to the "administrator's" questions?

Constructing Your Ideas 24.3
The Metaphor Revisited

In this activity, you will return to the concept of the metaphor. In Chapter 1 you were asked to select a metaphor for your role as an early childhood education science teacher. Look at it. Is it still valid? Or do you want to change it? Rethink this metaphor now, and decide what it is to be. Remember that metaphors have been shown to be strong internal referents for teacher behavior and that the metaphor chosen subtly but powerfully drives teachers' professional actions and decisions. Talk about the metaphor you now choose, trying to isolate all its implications. Then make your final decision.

PROFESSIONAL ORGANIZATIONS

As you have been able to tell, teachers of early childhood grades are given an impossible task. They are expected to know about all subjects and to teach all things well. No one can possibly keep up with everything! So, in this age of specialization, it is suggested you single out one area that has become of particular interest to you on which to focus your continued professional development. Become an expert in that area. Others will look to you for expertise in your area, and you will find yourself assuming a leadership role in that field.

The area may deal with a specific subject such as science, mathematics, language arts, reading, social studies, music, physical education, or some other discipline. Or it may focus more on general issues in teaching, such as teaching preschool children or children whose first language and home language is other than English, or children with learning disabilities or children with special needs. Or it may focus on general issues in education such as multiculturalism or interdisciplinarianism. You have the opportunity to assume an active role in the field where your interest lies. Join the professional societies, subscribe to their publications, submit manuscripts for publication, attend their national, regional, and state conferences, and present the results of your work at their conferences.

This section describes the professional organizations that early childhood teachers interested in science might wish to consider. Websites for professional organizations discussed in this chapter are given at the end of the chapter.

National Science Teachers Association

The National Science Teachers Association (NSTA) is the largest science teacher organization in the nation. Its purpose is to stimulate, improve, and coordinate science teaching and learning.

NSTA publishes four journals, all of which welcome teachers' classroom ideas and reports of teachers' action research. *Science and Children* is devoted to science teaching in preschool through middle school. Articles include descriptions of innovative projects and programs, descriptions of hands-on activities, reports of new developments in science and research in science education, informational pieces, and helpful hints. *Science and Children* is the ideal publication to help early childhood science educators keep up with their profession.

NSTA also publishes *Science Scope,* which focuses on the unique needs and characteristics of children of middle and junior high school age; *The Science Teacher,* which focuses on high school science; and the *Journal of College Science Teaching,* which focuses on teaching and learning science in college. In addition, NSTA publishes *Quantum,* a magazine that contains brain teasers and challenging problems for students in high school through college.

NSTA publishes a bimonthly newsletter, *NSTA Reports!* which contains articles of current interest and importance to all science educators. *NSTA Reports!* also includes listings and descriptions of websites, children's literature, videos, professional literature, and other ancillary materials appropriate for high-quality science education.

NSTA holds an annual national conference attended by thousands of teachers from all grade levels, at which hundreds of presentations are made, many by classroom teachers who present new and innovative classroom teaching ideas and the results of individual research projects. NSTA also holds several regional conferences each year similar in format to the national conference. Each state has one or more state science associations affiliated with NSTA concerned with helping classroom teachers at all levels improve their teaching of science and children's learning of science. Most states have annual association meetings at which classroom ideas, papers on current paradigms and issues in science education, classroom ideas, and results of action research projects are presented.

National Association for Research in Science Teaching

The National Association for Research in Science Teaching (NARST) promotes scholarly research and discussion of issues in the field of science education. The association publishes a monthly scholarly journal, the *Journal of Research in Science Teaching,* containing manuscripts of research on science teaching. The articles, which seek to affect science-teaching practice, are thoroughly researched by the authors and are thoroughly reviewed by peers. NARST hosts an annual conference where panel discussions, position papers, and research papers dealing with science education are presented.

Association for the Education of Teachers in Science

The Association for the Education of Teachers in Science (AETS) focuses on research in science education teaching and learning and the application of research in the classroom. AETS publishes two journals. *Science Education* contains descriptive articles and research reports dealing with curriculum, instruction, assessment, science teacher education, children's learning, current issues and trends, and international science education. The *Journal of Science Teacher Education* contains articles on methodology, instructional design, current issues in science education, position statements, new ideas, consolidated research findings, and critical reviews of literature pertaining to professional development in science teaching. Both journals publish results of action research reported by teachers. A third journal, the *Journal of Elementary Science Education,* is published in collaboration with AETS and contains articles dealing with elementary science teacher education and elementary science teaching and learning.

AETS holds an annual meeting at which papers about new developments in science education are presented. There are several regional associations affiliated with AETS, and each of those holds its own annual conference; these conferences provide excellent forums for classroom teachers to present the results of their action research.

Academies of Science

Each state or region of a state has an Academy of Science that provides a forum for interaction among professors, teachers, and college students on a variety of scientific topics; many have sections devoted to science education. The individual academies of science are normally affiliated with the National Association of Academies of Science. Each state or region of a state also has a Junior Academy of Science that promotes science among elementary, middle grades, and secondary students. Each junior academy of science is affiliated with the corresponding Academy of Science and with the American Junior Academy of Science. Both the National Association of Academies of Science and the American Junior Academy of Science are affiliated with the American Association for the Advancement of Science (AAAS).

Other Science-Related Professional Organizations

There are dozens of additional science-oriented organizations, some with specialized focus such as the Sierra Club and the Audubon Society. The early childhood science teacher desiring to get involved with science will not have a difficult time finding the organization that best suits his or her needs and interests.

Early Childhood Education Organizations

Two organizations devoted to principles, developments, and trends and issues in early childhood education are the Association for Childhood Education International (ACEI) and the National Association for the Education of Young Children (NAEYC). ACEI focuses on the education and development of children from birth to adolescence; NAEYC focuses on the growth and development of children from birth through age 8. Both hold annual national conferences. Both publish journals. ACEI publishes *Childhood Education* and the *Journal of Research in Childhood*, and NAEYC publishes *Young Children*. All these journals are peer reviewed and contain articles dealing with early childhood education including teaching methodology, curriculum, and instructional design, as well as position statements, teacher-prepared materials, and new ideas. The journals also include listings and reviews of children's literature, websites, videos, professional literature, and teacher and student materials appropriate for early childhood education settings. Although neither of these organizations specializes in science education, both address current early childhood science education trends and issues in the journals and at the annual conferences.

PROFESSIONAL WORKSHOPS AND SEMINARS

Another way early childhood education teachers can keep up with developments in science and science education is by participating in science workshops. Schools, school districts, colleges, universities, and professional science organizations often offer inservice programs on various topics lasting from an hour or two to a week or two. These topics may range from an overview of a newly developed curriculum to in-depth, constructivist, process-oriented inquiry-based explorations of any of a variety of science topics. The content- and methodology-based workshops generally encourage participant participation in the constructivist manner that you have become used to in this text. Often the workshop participants can earn credits that can be used for periodic teaching license renewal requirements or for college graduate credit.

FIGURE 24.1 At a science workshop

If your interest in early childhood education is science, you are urged to become an active participant in and contributor to the professional science education organizations and the inservice offerings. If your interest lies elsewhere, you are urged to participate in at least one science-based refresher program every few years. Schoenfeld (1999) laments that teachers in today's schools do not have significant professional lives. He says,

> Teaching is an extraordinarily difficult and demanding profession. To do it "right" demands very high levels of knowledge, skill, and dedication . . . Once teachers are hired, their workdays are structured in ways that provide negligible opportunities for interacting with colleagues in meaningful ways. Beyond that, almost no teachers have opportunities on the job, or outside it, for sustained and well-conceived professional development . . . One of the most important issues that we need to confront in the coming decades is how to change that state of affairs. (13)

Regardless of your primary interests, it is imperative that you keep up to date in science education, science content, and constructivist methodology through active participation in professional organizations, conferences, and workshops, and through regular review of professional publications.[1]

GRANTS

There is money out there for science education! You can get some of it for your science program in the form of grants. Grants can range in monetary value from $100 or less to several million dollars and are available from governmental agencies, public foundations, private foundations, colleges and universities, large and small companies, public and private school districts, and even parent-teacher associations and individuals.

Granting agencies typically stipulate the kinds of projects they will consider. For example, communications companies are typically interested in grant proposals dealing with technological advances at all levels. However, medical foundations are more interested in awarding grants for medical research than they are in awarding grants for improving early childhood science education.

Individual early childhood science teachers should focus on smaller grants in the $100 to $1000 range that will be used to purchase equipment, materials, and services to expand or enrich the early childhood science education program. Grants have been funded for constructing butterfly gardens, preparing planting areas, building outdoor amphitheaters and nature trails, purchasing basic calculators for children's use, purchasing software and texts for special projects, and the like. Grants will probably *not* be funded if they request money for snacks, giveaways, additional supplies normally provided by the school, materials and supplies traditionally supplied by the teacher, or uses that do not have definite and unique end products. To find sources of grant money, check the Internet and ask your school administrator, school district personnel, local colleges and universities, and others "in the know."

The first rule of "grantsmanship" is to be sure your proposed use of the grant money is consistent with the granting agency's purposes. For example, you would not propose to build an outdoor garden for grant funding designated for improvement of public television programming. Instead, you would look for a grant source that offers money for projects that include outdoor gardening. It is not only permissible but it also is a good idea to contact the granting agency for examples of projects that have been funded in the past and how much the projects were awarded.

The second rule of grantsmanship is to make your proposal succinct, direct, and to the point. Follow the guidelines provided by the granting agency in writing the proposal. Supply *all* the information they require. In describing your proposal, be sure it is very clear. Avoid the temptation to ramble or to assume the reviewers know what you are writing about. (Many of the reviewers come from the world of business and professional service, *not* education.) Be sure the words you write describe your project vividly. Ask a colleague or a friend who doesn't know anything about your situation or your idea to read your proposal to see whether it is understandable. Accept their comments! This is not a time to defend either your pride or your writing. Successful grant proposals are clear to the reviewers on the first reading, and you want yours to be successful! Remember that the reviewers are completely in the dark about your situation and your project.

In developing the budget, be as detailed as you can be. The granting agency wants to know what their money will be used for, so show them precisely what you plan to buy and what services you plan to purchase. If a summary budget is all that is required, prepare a detailed budget and attach it as an appendix if at all possible. And, above all, check your arithmetic!

The third rule for preparing successful grants is to show how your proposed project will make a difference in the science education of the children in your class and how you are going to measure its effectiveness. For example, it is not good enough to write that children will love their new science computer program. You must show how the proposed purchase will improve their achievement in science.

The fourth rule of good grantsmanship is to persevere. If at first you don't succeed, try again. Very few proposers are awarded grants the first time they submit one. Refine your proposal the next time you submit it, or revise it and submit it to a different granting agency. Contact the granting agency that rejected your first proposal and ask for feedback; incorporate their feedback into your next proposal. Remember that if you believe your proposed project is a good one, there *are* granting agencies that also believe it is a good one and are willing to fund it . . . if they know what it's all about.

There is money out there for projects that cannot be funded internally. This money is yours for the asking, but you have to ask through clearly written proposals.

THE EARLY CHILDHOOD SCIENCE EDUCATION TEACHER AS RESEARCHER

The National Association for Research in Science Teaching has coined the phrase, "Every Teacher a Researcher" ("ETR"). This phrase captures the fact that a large amount of valid, meaningful, and relevant research can be done by teachers in their own classrooms.

There are many ways teachers can get involved in research. One way is for them to participate in collaborative efforts with college and university faculty. Another, equally powerful way, is for teachers to do it themselves.

Every teacher truly is a researcher. At a minimum, teachers reflect on lessons they teach, assess the strengths and the areas that were weak, and make changes to strengthen them. They revise the instruction to accommodate the interests and changing needs of children. They reconstruct lessons to ensure that every child is successful. They develop assessment techniques that are authentic. They share successful teaching strategies with colleagues.

The time may come when teachers want to try out a whole new system, such as a different methodology or a different approach to curriculum. They often do this informally, comparing the results of two classes, or this year's class with last year's class. If the results seem to be better, the new system may be adopted.

Often, however, the research done by teachers never leaves the classroom or the school. It is considered experience, not research. Yet these very ideas that have been tried and proven in individual teachers' classrooms can comprise a large portion of the research base. The ultimate goal of all effective research in science education is improving classroom practice. How do children best learn science? What works? What doesn't work? How effective are various teaching techniques and new and innovative teaching strategies? Teachers can and should play a significant role in that research.

Concerning the science teacher as researcher, van Zee (1998) offers several "beliefs":

▌ Prospective teachers can and should learn how to do research as they learn how to teach.

▌ Beginning teachers can and should conduct research in their own classrooms.

▌ Both beginning and experienced teachers should conduct research that documents and articulates positive aspects of their practices.

▌ University faculty should create opportunities for interactions among prospective, beginning, and experienced teachers so all can learn by sharing experiences and insights with each other.

▌ Teachers possess unique knowledge that should be articulated and contributed to development and application of new theories of teaching and learning in guiding reform efforts (246–247).

The research done by teachers studying their own classrooms is called *action research* or *applied research*. This type of research seeks to determine effectiveness of classroom practice. The term "action" comes from the idea that the teacher is a participator in the development of the new knowledge that results from the study; the study occurs while the teacher is teaching, and the teacher is part of the group under study. Action research is essential if changes to teaching practices are to occur, for it is action research that determines the ultimate effectiveness of any proposed change in classroom practice.

In action research, you systematically inquire into practice in your classroom and document the results in accordance with the principles of sound scientific inquiry. However, common sense investigation is not enough; to qualify as research, investigations must possess validity, and this occurs through systematic inquiry, documentation, and analysis of data.

The steps taken in action research are as follows:[2]

1. *State the hypothesis or problem.* The hypothesis may be a simple statement of what you think will happen as a result of doing what you plan to do, such as, "If I implement a hands-on approach, children should become more interested in science." Or it may be a statement of a problem such as, "I wonder what would happen if I took children outdoors every day to observe their natural surroundings?" In action research, the hypothesis or problem frequently emerges when a teacher notices a reaction to something being done in the classroom, such as "I notice that when I provide simple hands-on activities, children get very involved in their own inquiries."

2. *Read the current literature* available on the subject to see what other researchers have found out and how they proceeded. There are many resources where you can find the research that has been done by others

in the field of education. First try the Educational Resources Information Center (ERIC) database. Your college or university should have the ERIC databases. If not, access ERIC through the Internet. The address for ERIC is http://www.ericsp.org/. In addition, you may wish to search other sources of information such as *PSYCHLIT, Education Abstracts, Social Sciences Abstracts,* and other pertinent databases.

3. *Identify the information needed to solve the problem.* The information you need may include changes in student achievement, attitude, and interest, or changes in teacher attitude and interest, or, frequently, both. The information needed normally is cited in the problem or hypothesis statement. For example, suppose you had noticed that children seemed to do better on their science activities if you have pizza parties on Fridays. The statement of hypothesis might read something like this: "If there are classroom pizza parties on Friday afternoons, student achievement on science activities is greater than it is during weeks when there are no pizza parties on Friday afternoons." The information needed would include several consistent measures of student achievement on science activities, dates and times of science activities, dates and times of pizza parties and pizza party announcements, and the like.

4. *Select or develop instruments to gather the needed information.* It is important to identify the kinds of information available to you that will help you answer your question. Many objective tests are available to help the researcher gather quantitative data. Or you may wish to design your own. Attitude and interest surveys can be used. Videotaping, student journals, open-ended interviews, teachers' journals, observations, children's work samples, written records of formal discussions, numbers of times children go to the science center on their own, numbers of trips taken with parents to local museums, and so on are all valid kinds of information that can be collected. You will want to collect the information that bears on the problem or hypothesis. But because you don't always know in advance what data is going to be the most informative, it is a good idea to keep track of everything.

5. *Select the sample or group.* In action research, the group most often used is your own class. Much has been written about the questionable validity of researchers using preselected samples of children such as the researcher's own class. There normally is nothing that can be done about this situation, and the consensus within the educational research community is that the disadvantages of using a preselected sample are outweighed by the insights gained from action research. Because you are using your own class, you must be careful to be as objective as possible. Ask a colleague to help in the research project to be sure your own feelings do not color the data or conclusions. You must also be careful not to generalize the results of your work to all children. What worked in your class may and may not work in someone else's class. However, when published, your research makes a significant contribution to the literature, and when many action researchers have studied the same type of

problem, generalizations can be made; these generalizations often are more valid than those made from carefully selected random sampling of subjects in one location.

6. *Design the procedure for collecting the data.* In action research you do not need to utilize complicated statistical techniques; instead, you can utilize a qualitative approach that involves systematic and thorough descriptions of what you did and what the responses were. Keep notes, student portfolios, grades, records, student work, opinion surveys, attitudinal assessments, and so on. Most action researchers keep daily journals in which they record their daily procedure and reflective interpretations. Videotapes of lessons can be analyzed objectively when it comes time to analyze the data. Again, it is well to collaborate with a colleague when analyzing the data, for your colleague will often be able to lend an objective eye. Your colleague can also run the camcorder for you, focusing on scenes that are germane to what you are seeking to learn, freeing you to concentrate on the teaching. You will have to spend time designing your investigation; your review of the literature may give you ideas. You will need to consider many factors such as when to implement the new system, what time of day to collect information, whether you need help (camcorder operator, objective observer, someone to write information down as things happen, etc.), the format for the data (journal formats, assessment formats, questionnaire formats), and so on. The key to this step is to have an advance plan for how you will analyze the information. Then you can work backward to be sure you get the right kind of data to enable you to do the analysis. However, if what you are doing does not seem to be answering your question, you can revise the procedure.

7. *Collect the data.* This is the implementation phase. You might want to get used to the idea that Murphy's Law will be in full force during this stage: "If anything *can* go wrong, it *will*." Many action researchers do a short version of the project called a *pilot study* before they do the full-fledged implementation, to work out the snags. However, you must be certain that whatever you do as a pilot program does not provide either the children or you with preconceived notions that could contaminate the data once you start the real procedure. Many researchers implement the pilot program with one class and then implement the full study the next year with a different class, having refined it on the basis of what they learned from the pilot.

8. *Analyze the data.* This involves poring over all the information you obtained to see what makes sense. You have already planned to some extent how you are going to analyze the information, so now you do it. However, much new information that you never considered previously will present itself. Thus, it is entirely possible that you may find unexpected results. Sometimes these results are valid and become part of the analysis; sometimes they suggest additional avenues of new research or ways of continuing the original research. Enlisting the assistance of an

unbiased colleague to examine the data independently helps ensure valid interpretations.

9. *Prepare the report.* Whatever research you do, it is imperative that you get the results out to others. "Teachers can and should communicate their findings in local school meetings, regional and national conferences, and publications . . . Reports of such teacher research can contribute to reform efforts by drawing attention to issues important to teachers and providing documentation of their successes in implementing reform approaches to instruction" (van Zee, 1998, 247). This means sharing your work with focus groups at your school, preparing your work for publication in professional journals, or presenting it at professional conferences. The typical research report contains the following elements:

▮ Statement of problem or hypothesis
▮ Survey of relevant literature
▮ Detailed description of procedure, with instruments identified, the kinds of data collected, and an indication of the reliability and validity of each
▮ Your analysis of the data
▮ Implications for the classroom teacher

Articles submitted for publication and proposals submitted for presentation at professional conferences are normally reviewed by individuals who are familiar with the topic of the research. This is referred to as "peer review" and is done blindly, which means that the reviewers do not know who submitted the proposal, and the author does not know who the reviewers are. In evaluating quality of research, reviewers look at the following:[3]

1. The match between the research questions and the method employed
2. The match between the research questions and type of data collected and the analysis of the data
3. Successful and appropriate application of data collection and analysis techniques
4. Value of the study to classroom practice
5. Ability to withstand critical analysis (Conclusions have to be warranted from the data presented; are there additional or different conclusions or explanations?)

Student teaching is a good time to work on an action research project. Select a mentor from your college, and ask your cooperating teacher for permission and assistance. Fueyo and Koorland (1997) suggest that the strand of teacher as researcher be included throughout the preservice teacher preparation program.

You may have noticed during the course of your professional studies that much research is conceived, planned, controlled, executed, and analyzed by college- and university-based researchers with little, if any, collaboration with practicing teachers. They select the questions to be investigated, design the experimental method, and formulate conclusions from the application of statistical procedures to show the significance (or lack of significance) of outcomes on the research hypothesis. The studies are published in journals teachers probably do not read, using language and statistical manipulations unfamiliar to teachers, about problems teachers are probably not faced with in the first place, and suggest solutions teachers would probably not find useful to implement. These investigations are perceived by teachers as not relevant, and much of this research fails to help science teachers improve their science teaching.

However, research conceived, executed, interpreted, and written by teachers themselves is meaningful and relevant. It is this action research that ultimately will put professional "teeth" into science education reform. It is hoped that you will participate in action research and thus take advantage of part of your professional privilege.

EXCELLENCE IN SCIENCE TEACHING

What constitutes excellence in science education? Several characteristics of excellence in science teaching and science programs have been identified by the research, and are summarized in Figure 24.2.

Standards for excellence in science teaching and science programs are provided in the *National Science Education Standards* (National Academy of Sciences, 1996). It is hoped that all science teachers will become familiar with these standards and use them to guide the development and implementation of their science programs.

SOME CHARACTERISTICS OF EXCELLENCE IN SCIENCE EDUCATION

1. Excellent science teachers give up on textbook-oriented science and develop their own programs that are relevant and responsive to the needs of children and the community. Programs are discovery in orientation and hands-on in nature.
2. Excellent science programs focus more on process than on content.
3. Excellent science teachers reach out and seek new ideas.
4. Excellent science teachers participate in professional growth experiences such as inservice programs and conferences.
5. Excellent science programs provide much inservice training and have strong central and building administration support.
6. Excellent science programs are in a continuous state of evolution.
7. Increased preparation in science content is not a significant factor in differentiating between the most and the least effective science teachers.

FIGURE 24.2 Some characteristics of excellence in science teaching and science programs
Adapted from Penick & Yager, 1993, and Yager, 1998

SUMMARY

As an early childhood science educator, you will make many professional decisions. Among the most important are decisions about curriculum, about methodology, and about continuing your professional development and contributing to the profession. Decisions about curriculum and methodology must be based on sound pedagogical theory, research, the standards of the professional societies, and your own constructions of the elements of quality science education. The science content that is included in the program is used as the vehicle through which children's skills in the scientific processes and in inquiry are developed and is selected to meet the interests and needs of the children in the class.

Workshops and inservice institutes are provided by school districts, colleges, and professional organizations to enable early childhood science teachers to keep up with new curricular materials, new ideas about pedagogy, and current developments in the profession. Many opportunities are provided by national, state, regional, and local science teachers associations for early childhood science teachers to attend conferences where they can share their experiences and expertise with each other. Financial resources are available for science programs through granting agencies. Successful grant proposals are clear, succinct, and to the point and address the granting agency's objectives.

Research in science education is vital to establishing the best ways of teaching science and the most appropriate curriculum. The professional educator is in a unique position to undertake action research projects and share the results of this research with the professional community through conference papers and publications. Through such activities, the professional early childhood science teacher develops and maintains science programs of excellence and engages in lifelong learning.

AFTERWORD

Teaching early childhood science is not difficult. Children love science, and successful teachers encourage them to wonder, to explore, and to construct their own meanings. Excellent early childhood science teachers stimulate children to ask their own questions about phenomena that are meaningful and interesting to them, to develop their own methods of investigating these questions using the scientific processes, and to validate their conclusions through connections with their prior knowledge and through the presence of both explanatory and predictive power. Excellent early childhood science teachers challenge children to do science the way scientists do science. Excellent early childhood science teachers involve *all* children in scientific inquiry, regardless of gender, ethnicity, academic ability, or any other factor.

Much professional and public attention is being given to ways of achieving excellence in science education. In 1998 the National Science Resources Center (NSRC) launched a long-term nationwide initiative called "Leadership and Assistance for Science Education Reform" (LASER) to foster and sustain progress in achieving excellence in science education ("NSRC Initiative," 1999). In 1999 the National Commission on Mathematics and Science Teaching for the 21st Century was formed. Chaired by former astronaut John Glenn, the commission will review the current status of mathematics and science education in the United States and will recommend specific actions for improvement. The participation of the science education community is encouraged[4] ("Secretary Riley," 1999).

Anderson ("An Interview," 1999) was asked what he thinks the classroom of 2025 will look like. He replied,

> Unless the test-obsessed politicians continue to mess things up, cooperation (instead of competition) will become the hallmarks of learning situations . . . The fact that all children can learn will finally be accomplished, and therefore we will see many definitions of competency and many opportunities for success. (p. 45)

By using the constructivist approach suggested in this book, you can develop an early childhood science program that meets the needs of all children, provides the foundation for the academic challenges that lie ahead for them, and prepares them for a lifetime of successful learning.

> I assure you that you can pick up more information when you are listening than when you are talking.
> E. B. White, *The Trumpet of the Swan* (New York: HarperCollins Children's Books, 1973).

Notes

1. The entire May 1999 (volume 56, number 8) and May 2000 (Volume 57, number 8) issues of *Educational Leadership* are devoted to professionalism and ways of supporting new teachers.

2. Adapted from D. Ary, L. C. Jacobs, & A. Razavieh (1990, 381).
3. From a seminar on Contemporary Research Paradigms held at the annual meeting of the National Association for Research in Science Teaching, Boston, MA, March 12, 1992.
4. For information on how you can help the National Commission on Mathematics and Science Teaching in its work and influence the direction of science education improvement, visit the Commission's website at http://www.ed.gov/inits/Math.

WEBSITE ADDRESSES FOR PROFESSIONAL SCIENCE EDUCATION SOCIETIES

American Association for the Advancement of Science
  http://www.aaas.org/
American Junior Academy of Science
  Refer to http://www.aaas.org/AAAS/affil.html
Association for Childhood Education International
  http://www.udel.edu/bateman/acei/
Association for the Education of Teachers in Science
  http://science.cc.uwf.edu/aets/aets.html
National Academy of Sciences
  http://www.nas/edu/
National Association of Academies of Science
  Refer to http://www.aaas.org/AAAS/affil.html
National Association for the Education of Young Children
  http://www.naeyc.org/default.htm
National Association for Research in Science Teaching
  http://www.narst.org/
National Research Council
  http://www.nas.edu/nrc/
National Science Teachers Association
  http://www.nsta.org/

References

American Association for the Advancement of Science. (1994). *Benchmarks for science literacy.* New York: Oxford University Press.
American Association for the Advancement of Science. (1997). *Resources for science literacy.* New York: Oxford University Press.
Ary, D., Jacobs, L. C., & Razavieh, A. (1990). *Introduction to research in education* (4th ed.) Forth Worth, TX: Holt, Rinehart and Winston, Inc.
Chaucer, G. (1995). *The Canterbury tales.* San Marino, CA: Huntington Library Press.
de Regniers, B. S. (1974). *The enchanted forest.* Atheneum (out of print).

Fueyo, V., and Koorland, M. A. (1997). Teacher as researcher: A synonym for education. *Journal of Teacher Education, 48*(5), 336–344.

Glasser, W. (1992, May). The quality school curriculum. *Phi Delta Kappan,* 690–694.

An interview with Robert H. Anderson. (1999). *The Educational Forum 64*(1), 41–45.

Joubert, J. (1966). *Pensées.* Paris: Union Général d'Editions.

Lowery, L. F. (1997). *NSTA pathways to the science standards, Elementary school edition.* Arlington, VA: National Science Teachers Association.

Martin, D. J. (2000). *Elementary science methods: A constructivist approach* (2nd ed.). Belmont, CA: Wadsworth/Thompson Learning.

McIntyre, M. (1984). *Early childhood and science.* Arlington, VA: National Science Teachers Association.

National Academy of Sciences. (1996). *National science education standards.* Washington, DC: National Academy Press.

National Science Resources Center. (1996). *Resources for teaching elementary school science.* Washington, DC: National Academy Press.

NSRC initiative serves as model for science education reform. (1999). *NSTA Reports! 10*(6), 10.

Penick, J. E., and Yager, R. E. (1993). Learning from excellence: Some elementary exemplars. *Journal of Elementary Science Education 5*(1), 1–9.

Schoenfeld, A. H. (1999). Looking toward the 21st century: Challenges of educational theory and practice. *Educational Researcher 28*(7), 4–14.

Secretary Riley announces members of National Commission on Science and Math Education. (1999). *NSTA Reports! 11*(1), 1–14.

van Zee, E. H. (1998). Fostering elementary teachers' research on their science teaching practices. *Journal of Teacher Education 49*(4), 245–254.

White, E. B. (1973). *The trumpet of the swan.* New York: HarperCollins Children's Books.

Yager, R. E. (1988). Differences between most and least effective science teachers. *School Science and Mathematics, 88*(4), 301–307.

Activities Cross-Referenced to Content Standards Outlined in the National Science Education Standards

Most of the activities can be referenced to more than one content standard; the referenced standards are the most appropriate ones.

UNIFYING CONCEPTS AND PROCESSES—STANDARD

SYSTEMS, ORDER, AND ORGANIZATION

Do the Buttons Match?	(Chapter 4)
Classifying Stuffed Animals	(Chapter 3)
Classifying Plastic Food	(Chapter 3)
The Grocery Store	(Chapter 3)
The Hardware Store	(Chapter 3)
Fingerprints	(Chapter 4)

EVIDENCE, MODELS, AND EXPLANATION

What Did You See on Your Way to School Today?	(Chapter 2)
What Did You See on Your Way to School Today That Has Always Been There but Which You Never Noticed Before?	(Chapter 2)
What Did You See on Your Way to School Today That Made You Wonder about Something?	(Chapter 2)
What Did You See Today?	(Chapter 2)
What's That Smell?	(Chapter 2)
A Mystery Box	(Chapter 1)
Making Sense Out of Data	(Chapter 12)
What Do You Mean by . . . ?	(Chapter 11)
Goldilocks and the Three Bears	(Chapter 22)
Hibernating Teddy Bears	(Chapter 14)

How Thick Is the Earth's Atmosphere?   (Chapter 14)
How Smooth Is the Earth?   (Chapter 14)

CONSTANCY, CHANGE, AND MEASUREMENT

Which Is Longer? Which Is Shorter?   (Chapter 5)
How Many Pennies?   (Chapter 5)
A Four-Year-Old's Measurement of Height   (Chapter 5)
Measuring Your Partner's Height   (Chapter 5)
How Long Is My Arm? How Long Is My Foot?   (Chapter 5)
Body Measurement Olympics   (Chapter 5)
How Long Is a Kilometer? How Long Is a Mile?   (Chapter 5)
Which Holds More?   (Chapter 5)
How Many Cups of Sand Does a Coffee Can Hold?   (Chapter 5)
How Much Soda Is in a Liter?   (Chapter 5)
Which Is Heavier? Which Is Lighter?   (Chapter 5)
How Much Does a Penny Weigh?   (Chapter 5)
Who Has the Biggest Cookie?   (Chapter 5)
How Long Does It Take Sand to Run through a Funnel?   (Chapter 5)
How Long Does It Take to Run across the Playground?   (Chapter 5)
How Can We Increase the Speed with Which Sand Flows
    through a Funnel?   (Chapter 9)
Measuring Rocks   (Chapter 5)

EVOLUTION AND EQUILIBRIUM

How Big Were the Dinosaurs?   (Chapter 14)
How Long Were the Dinosaurs?   (Chapter 14)
Teaching about Dinosaurs Using Multiple Intelligences (Chapter 17)

FORM AND FUNCTION

Tell About the Bubbles   (Chapter 4)
Blowing Bubbles   (Chapter 13)
Experimenting with Bubbles   (Chapter 13)
How Many Peas Are in a Peapod?   (Chapter 12)

SCIENCE AS INQUIRY—CONTENT STANDARD A

ABILITIES NECESSARY TO DO SCIENTIFIC INQUIRY
All activities in this text foster ability to do scientific inquiry;
those specific for this standard are listed.
Ways of Communicating   (Chapter 4)
What's in the Bag?   (Chapter 4)
Twenty Questions   (Chapter 4)
Funny Figures   (Chapter 4)
Predicting What Would Happen If . . .   (Chapter 6)
A Wordless Story   (Chapter 7)
What's That Unknown Object?   (Chapter 7)
Keeping a Paper Towel Dry in the Water   (Chapter 7)
Raisin Dance   (Chapter 20)
Why Do Cans of Soft Drinks "Explode"
    When They Are Opened?   (Chapter 23)

Hidden Figures   (Chapter 17)
What Is Your Comfort Zone?   (Chapter 17)
What Is Your Dominant Learning Modality?   (Chapter 17)

UNDERSTANDING ABOUT SCIENTIFIC INQUIRY

All activities in this text foster understanding about scientific inquiry.

PHYSICAL SCIENCE—CONTENT STANDARD B

PROPERTIES OF OBJECTS AND MATERIALS

Sink? Or Float?   (Chapter 6)
The Case of the Mysterious Crayons   (Chapter 6)
Do Crayons Sink or Float?   (Chapter 6)
Sinking and Floating Fruits   (Chapter 18)
Floating Eggs   (Chapter 9)
What Kinds of Materials Absorb Water?   (Chapter 6)
Mixing Liquids with Water   (Chapter 6)
Cleaning Pennies   (Chapter 11)
Making Egg Shells Soft   (Chapter 4)
Investigating the Reaction of Vinegar with Materials   (Chapter 18)
How Much Sugar Dissolves in Water?   (Chapter 10)
What Affects the Amount of Sugar That Will
    Dissolve in Water?   (Chapter 9)
How Can We Make Salt Crystals?   (Chapter 9)
Process-Oriented Activities Using The Popcorn Book
    by Tomie dePaola as the Introduction   (Chapter 22)

POSITION AND MOTION OF OBJECTS

The Inclined Plane   (Chapter 13)
Jake, the Train, and the Inclined Plane   (Chapter 13)
How Long Does It Take a Toy Car to Roll down
    a Ramp?   (Chapter 5)
Balloon Rockets   (Chapter 12)
Investigating Parachutes   (Chapter 11)
Falling Balls   (Chapter 15)
Bouncing Balls   (Chapter 11)
The Pendulum   (Chapter 9)
An Investigation into Friction   (Chapter 13)
Defying Gravity   (Chapter 15)
Gravity, Friction, Inertia, and Force   (Chapter 16)
Exploring Gears   (Chapter 17)

HEAT, LIGHT, ELECTRICITY, AND MAGNETISM

What's Hot? What's Cold?   (Chapter 11)
How Does Ice Affect the Temperature of Water?   (Chapter 5)
Effect of Different Kinds of Cups on the Temperature
    of Water   (Chapter 10)
How Long Does It Take an Ice Cube to Melt?   (Chapter 12)
Freezing Water   (Chapter 20)

How Can We Increase the Rate of Evaporation of Water?   (Chapter 10)
Does the Color of the Cover Affect How Fast Water
    Heats up in the Sun?   (Chapter 5)
What Happens to Chocolate Chips Left in the Sun?   (Chapter 5)
Mixing Colors   (Chapter 6)
Mouse Paint   (Chapter 22)
Investigating Reflection   (Chapter 17)
How Long Is My Shadow?   (Chapter 5)
Shadows   (Chapter 7)
What Can I See with the Magnifying Glass?   (Chapter 4)
Transparent-Translucent-Opaque   (Chapter 6)
What's Magnetic? What's Not Magnetic?   (Chapter 3)
An Investigation into Magnetism   (Chapter 13)
Where Are the Poles on a Strip Magnet?   (Chapter 7)
Naming the Poles of a Magnet   (Chapter 15)
Batteries and Electricity   (Chapter 16)
What's That Sound?   (Chapter 2)
Listening for Different Sounds   (Chapter 2)
What Sound Is Louder?   (Chapter 2)
Sounds of Rubber Bands   (Chapter 17)

LIFE SCIENCE—CONTENT STANDARD C

THE CHARACTERISTICS OF ORGANISMS

Observing Animals   (Chapter 2)
What's That Animal?   (Chapter 7)
Classifying Animals   (Chapter 3)
Classifying Leaves   (Chapter 3)
Animals Classification Interactive Bulletin Board   (Chapter 19)

LIFE CYCLES OF ORGANISMS

What Can Sprout and Grow?   (Chapter 6)
Observing Seeds   (Chapter 2)
Classifying Seeds   (Chapter 3)
Observing the Insides of Lima Bean Seeds   (Chapter 22)
"Seed Museum" Interactive Bulletin Board   (Chapter 19)
Growing Marigolds   (Chapter 4)
What Causes Plants to Grow to Be Healthy?   (Chapter 9)
Graphing Plant Growth   (Chapter 5)
What Falls out of a Flower When You Shake It?   (Chapter 4)
Outdoor Gardens   (Chapter 20)

ORGANISMS AND ENVIRONMENTS

Animal Camouflage   (Chapter 14)
Mealworms   (Chapter 10)
Endangered Species Interactive Bulletin Board   (Chapter 19)
Do Plants Move?   (Chapter 6)
Playing Music to Plants   (Chapter 12)
How Old Was That Tree?   (Chapter 7)

Rainforest Interactive Bulletin Board   (Chapter 19)
Pets   (Chapter 19)
Ant Farms   (Chapter 19)
Aquariums   (Chapter 19)
Plants   (Chapter 19)
Terrariums   (Chapter 19)

EARTH AND SPACE SCIENCE—CONTENT STANDARD D

PROPERTIES OF EARTH MATERIALS
The Rock Hunt   (Chapter 2)
Which Rock Is Mine?   (Chapter 2)
Classifying Rocks   (Chapter 3)
Classifying Rocks into Two Distinct Groups   (Chapter 3)
Classifying Rocks into Subgroups   (Chapter 3)
Favorite Rocks   (Chapter 4)
Making Mud   (Chapter 16)
What's in the Dirt?   (Chapter 2)
Classifying Materials in Soil   (Chapter 3)
The Origin of Soil   (Chapter 7)

OBJECTS IN THE SKY
Why Does the Moon Shine?   (Chapter 14)
Model of the Solar System   (Chapter 14)
Daytime Sky Watching   (Chapter 20)
Nighttime Sky Watch   (Chapter 20)

CHANGES IN EARTH AND SKY
What Season Is It?   (Chapter 7)
What Is the Weather Today?   (Chapter 2)
What's the Weather Outside?   (Chapter 7)
The Weather According to the Internet   (Chapter 21)
Recording Time and Outdoor Temperature   (Chapter 5)
Is It Warmer in the Sun or in the Shade?   (Chapter 5)
Wind   (Chapter 7)
Weather Charts and Graphs   (Chapter 4)
How Much Will It Rain? How Much Will It Snow?   (Chapter 6)
How Do Clouds Form?   (Chapter 14)
Distance of Thunderstorms   (Chapter 5)
Locations of Volcanoes Interactive Bulletin Board   (Chapter 19)

SCIENCE AND TECHNOLOGY—CONTENT STANDARD E

ABILITIES OF TECHNOLOGICAL DESIGN
How Smooth Is That Cloth?   (Chapter 2)
The Video   (Chapter 23)
A Technology Inventory   (Chapter 21)
Exploring Tutorial and Interactive Computer Programs   (Chapter 21)

Using Desktop Publishing   (Chapter 21)
Using Spreadsheets and Graphing Programs   (Chapter 21)
Sending E-mail   (Chapter 21)
Surfing the Web for Science Sites   (Chapter 21)

UNDERSTANDING ABOUT SCIENCE AND TECHNOLOGY

Making Butter   (Chapter 10)
Space Snacks   (Chapter 16)
Exploring NASA   (Chapter 21)
Science-Technology-Society Topics   (Chapter 23)

ABILITIES TO DISTINGUISH BETWEEN NATURAL OBJECTS AND OBJECTS MADE BY HUMANS

Most of the activities listed in Content Standard B (Properties of Objects and Materials), Content Standard C (Characteristics of Organisms), and Content Standard D (Properties of Earth Materials) overlap with this standard.

SCIENCE IN PERSONAL AND SOCIAL PERSPECTIVES—CONTENT STANDARD F

PERSONAL HEALTH

Charting Food Groups   (Chapter   4)
What Affects Our Heartbeat Rate?   (Chapter 10)
What Happens to Our Hands When We Leave
    Them in Water?   (Chapter 11)
Study of Bacteria   (Chapter 19)

CHARACTERISTICS AND CHANGES IN POPULATIONS

Local Demographic Changes   (Chapter 17)

TYPES OF RESOURCES

Many of the activities used in early childhood science classes reflect this standard.

Regions Where Food Is Grown Interactive Bulletin Board   (Chapter 19)

CHANGES IN ENVIRONMENTS

Causes of Soil Erosion   (Chapter   7)
Investigating Erosion   (Chapter 20)
A Walk around the School   (Chapter 20)
Sidewalk Ecology   (Chapter 20)
Schoolyard Ecology   (Chapter 20)

SCIENCE AND TECHNOLOGY IN LOCAL CHALLENGES

Many of the activities used in early childhood science classes reflect this standard when relevance to local situations is included in the lesson.

HISTORY AND NATURE OF SCIENCE—CONTENT STANDARD G

SCIENCE AS A HUMAN ENDEAVOR

Many of the activities used in early childhood science classes reflect this standard.

What Is a Scientist?   (Chapter 17)

APPENDIX B

Selected Sources of Free and Inexpensive Materials

There are many sources of free and inexpensive materials. This list is just a beginning. You are urged to develop your own list of materials available to you that are also useful in your science program. Some of the content below may have copyright protection.

American Association for the Advancement of Science (AAAS)
1333 H Street NW
Washington, DC 20005
http://www.aaas.org/

> The AAAS sponsors a number of educational programs and also maintains networks of scientists who visit early childhood school classrooms. Write for information.

American Textile Center
P.O. Box 12215
Research Triangle Park, NC 27709

> Free and inexpensive teaching materials are available about manufactured dry goods.

Campbell Soup Company

> Send for the Campbell's "Free Stuff" catalog that details their "Labels for Education" program and for information about available free educational materials.

Labels for Education
P.O. Box 4552
Monticello, MN 55565
Tel: 800-424-5331
http://www.labelsforeducation.com

Colgate-Palmolive Company

> An inexpensive oral hygiene teaching/learning kit with activities, posters, a teacher's guide, a videotape, and a take-home card in English and Spanish are available.

Colgate *Bright Smiles, Bright Future*
c/o JMH Communications, Inc.
1133 Broadway, Suite 1123
New York, NY 10010
Tel: 800-334-7734
http://www.colgate.com

Discovery Channel
http://www.discovery.com/

> The Discovery Channel broadcasts a wide variety of science-related television documentaries. Check their website for schedules and highlights.

Fas-Track Computer Products

> Send for their catalog of an extensive listing of computer hardware, software, and technological accessories. Fas-Track is a division of Educational Resources.

Educational Resources
1550 Executive Drive
P.O. Box 1900
Elgin, IL 60121-1900
Tel: 800-624-2926
http://www.edresources.com

National Academy Press
2101 Constitution Avenue NW
Washington, DC 20418

> The National Sciences Resource center in collaboration with the National Academy of Sciences and the Smithsonian Institution has published an extremely valuable book entitled *Resources for Teaching Elementary School Science* (National Academy Press, Washington, DC, 1996) that will prove to be invaluable to the early childhood science teacher. The book is available online (free) at www.nap.edu/readingroom/enter2.cgi?0309052939.html

The following science references are also available online (free):

> *National Science Education Standards* www.nap.edu/readingroom/enter2.cgi?0309053269.html

> *Introducing the National Science Education Standards* www.nap.edu/readingroom/books/intronses

> *Every Child a Scientist: Achieving Scientific Literacy for All* www.nap.edu/readingroom/enter2.cgi?0309059860.html

> *Science for All Children* www.nap.edu/readingroom/enter2.cgi?0309052971.html

National Aeronautics and Space Administration
http://www.nasa.gov/

> NASA operates Teacher Resource Centers throughout the country to provide educators with NASA-related materials for classroom use. Materials include classroom activities, lesson plans, teacher guides, slides, audiotapes, and videotapes. Contact the NASA center that serves your state or

George C. Marshall Space Flight Center
One Tranquility Drive
Huntsville, AL 35807

National Association for the Education of Young Children
1509 16th Street NW
Washington, DC 20036-1425
Tel: 800-424-2460
www.naeyc.org

> *Resources for Developmentally Appropriate Practice: Recommendations from the Profession* by Gail Perry and Mary S. Duru, editors (2000), contains an extensive listing of resources available for early childhood teachers and young children.

National Science Foundation
1800 G Street, NW
Suite 527
Washington, DC 20550
http://www.nsf.gov/

> Ask to be placed on their mailing list to receive information about science events pertinent to your grade level.

National Science Teachers Association
1840 Wilson Boulevard
Arlington, VA 22201-3000
http://www.nsta.org/

> *NSTA Science Education Suppliers* is an annual catalog of educational services, computer software, media materials, and print materials endorsed by the NSTA.

> The NSTA *Science Teaching Resources Catalog*, published annually, contains a listing of science education student material and teacher material books endorsed by the NSTA.

> NSTA also publishes *NSTA REPORTS!* Each issue contains several pages of sources of free or inexpensive materials.

Natural Resources Conservation Service
http://www.nrcs.usda.gov/

> Check the federal government pages of your telephone directory for local listings. Materials are available on the uses and conservation of water.

Ohio State University
ERIC/CSMEE
1929 Kenny Road
Columbus, OH 43210-1080
http://www.ericsp.org/

> CSMEE stands for ERIC Clearinghouse for Science, Mathematics, and Environmental Education. Ask to be placed on the mailing list for the *CSMEE Horizon,* a newsletter that describes new publications on science and mathematics education available through ERIC.

Public Broadcasting System
http://www.pbs.org/

> Check the PBS website for listings of televised programs appropriate for units you are teaching.

Smithsonian Institution
National Science Resources Center
Arts and Industries Building, Room 1201, MRC 403
Washington, DC 20560
http://www.si.edu/

> Ask to be put on the mailing list for the *NSRC Newsletter.* The NSRC collects and disseminates information about exemplary teaching resources, develops curriculum materials, and sponsors activities to help schools develop hands-on science programs.

Office of Elementary and Secondary Education
Smithsonian Institution
Arts and Industries Building
Room 1163, MRC 402
Washington, DC 20560

> Write for the free *Resource Guide for Teachers* that offers a listing of classroom media available for language arts, visual and performing arts, science, and social studies.

> Also ask for the free quarterly publication, *ART to ZOO.* Each issue covers one topic and includes general background information, lesson plans, classroom activities, and resources for teachers. An English/Spanish page is included.

State Departments of Natural Resources often have excellent collections of free or inexpensive materials about state natural resources and state parks. Ask for information.

U.S. Environmental Protection Agency
401 M Street SW
Washington, DC 20460
http://www.epa.gov/

Write for a list of educational materials. A wide variety of available information about the environment is free or very inexpensive.

The Weather Channel
300 Interstate North Parkway NW
Atlanta, GA 30339
http://www.weather.com/twc/homepage.twc

Free materials are available on weather and teaching weather. Many documentary videos are available for dubbing; write for information.

Listing of Children's Literature

	Chapter
Aardema, V. *Bringing the Rain to Kapiti Plain: A Nandi Tale*	22
Aliki. *My Feet*	3
Aliki. *My Five Senses*	2
Anson-Weber, J. *Snuffles*	2
Arnosky, J. *Crinkleroot's Guide to Knowing the Trees*	3
Baker, K. *Who Is the Beast?*	7, 22
Barrett, J. *Cloudy With a Chance of Meatballs*	4
Bash, B. *Desert Giant: The World of the Giant Saguaro Cactus*	6
Baxter, N. *Hot or Not*	11
Behn, H. *Crickets and Bullfrogs and Whispers of Thunder*	2
Bell, S. *The Hundred Penny Box*	5
Berenstain, S., & Berenstain, J. *The Berenstain Bears Grow-It: Mother Nature Has Such a Green Thumb*	6
Berenstain, S., & Berenstain, J. *The Berenstain Bears on the Moon*	14
Berger, M. *All about Seeds*	2
Blankly, F., & Vaughn, E. *Mickey's Magnet*	3
Bogacki, T. *Cat and Mouse in the Rain*	6
Bogacki, T. *Cat and Mouse in the Snow*	6
Bond, M. *A Bear Called Paddington*	7
Brenner, B. *Mr. Tall and Mr. Small*	5
Brett, J. *Goldilocks and the Three Bears*	22
Brett, J. *The Mitten: A Ukrainian Folktale*	7
Brown, M. W. *Goodnight Moon*	14
Brown, M. W. *The Noisy Book*	2
Burningham, J. *Mr. Gumpy's Outing*	6
Burton, V. L. *Mike Mulligan and His Steam Shovel*	23
Carle, E. *The Grouchy Ladybug*	20, 22
Carle, E. *Little Cloud*	20
Carle, E. *The Very Busy Spider*	22

Carle, E. *The Very Hungry Caterpillar*   22
Carle, E. *The Very Lonely Firefly*   22
Carle, E. *The Very Quiet Cricket*   22
Carroll, L. *Alice's Adventures in Wonderland*   8
Carroll, L. *The Walrus and the Carpenter*   19
Carter, D. A. *Feely Bugs: To Touch and Feel*   2
Cauley, L. B. *Jack and the Beanstalk*   22
Challoner, J. *Hot and Cold*   11
Chanin, M. *Grandfather Four Winds and Rising Moon*   7
Chapman, C. *Barney Bipple's Magic Dandelions*   4
Climo, S. *The Egyptian Cinderella*   22
Cole, J. *It's Too Noisy!*   2
Cole, J. *The Magic School Bus Gets Baked in a Cake: A Book
    about Kitchen Chemistry*   18, 20
Cole, J. *The Magic School Bus in the Time of the Dinosaurs*   14
Cole, J. *The Magic School Bus: Inside the Human Body*   10
Cole, J. *The Magic School Bus Plays Ball*   13
Cole, J. *You Can't Smell a Flower with Your Ear!:
    All about Your 5 Senses*   2
Collay, R., & Dubrow, J. *Stuartship*   22
Conrad, L. *All Aboard Trucks*   13
Cooke, A. *Weigh It Up, Bear's Playschool Kits*   5

de Regniers, B. S. *The Enchanted Forest*   24
de Saint-Exupéry, A. *The Little Prince*   5
dePaola, T. *The Cloud Book*   14
dePaola, T. *The Popcorn Book*   22
DeRolf, S. *The Crayon Box That Talked*   6
Dewey, A. *The Sky*   20
Dodd, A. W. *Footprints and Shadows*   5
Dodson, P. *An Alphabet of Dinosaurs*   14
Dorros, A. *Ant Cities*   19
Dorros, A. *Feel the Wind*   7
Dorros, A. *Follow the Water from Brook to Ocean*   7
Dragonwagon, C. *Brass Button*   4
Dunbar, J. *The Sand Children*   9

Edwards, F. B. *Troubles with Bubbles*   4
Ehlert, L. *Moon Rope*   22
Elffers, J. *Play With Your Food*   3
Emberly, E. *Ed Emberly's Great Thumbprint Drawing Book*   4
Ets, M. H. *Gilberto and the Wind*   7

Faine, E. A. *Little Ned Stories: A Chapter-Picture Book for Kids*   9
Fuchs, D. M. *A Bear for All Seasons*   7

Garis, H. R. *Uncle Wiggily's Storybook*   18
Gibbons, G. *Bicycle Book*   17
Gibbons, G. *From Seed to Plant*   22
Gibbons, G. *The Pumpkin Book*   22
Gibbons, G. *The Seasons of Arnold's Apple Tree*   4
Gibson, G. *Playing with Magnets*   13
Gibson, G. *Pushing and Pulling* (in *Science for Fun*)   5
Ginny, S. *Uncle Lester's Lemonade Lure*   3
Ginsburg, M. *Mushroom in the Rain*   5
Greene, C. *Ice Is Whee*   10
Grossman, B. *Tommy at the Grocery Store*   3
Grossman, J., & Dunhill, P. *Nonsense and Commonsense:*
   A Child's Book of Victorian Verse   3

Hamley, D. *Hare's Choice*   15
Hayward, L. *The Biggest Cookie in the World*   5
Hayward, L. *Wet Foot, Dry Foot, Low Foot, High Foot: Learn about*
   Opposites and Differences   10
Heide, F. P. *Timothy Twinge*   14
Hennessy, B. G. *The Dinosaur Who Lived in My Back Yard*   14
Hesse, T. *Come On, Rain!*   6
Hoban, R. *The Mouse and His Child*   6
Hoban, T. *Is It Red? Is It Yellow? Is It Blue?: An Adventure in Color*   3
Hoban, T. *Is It Rough? Is It Smooth? Is It Shiny?*   3
Hoban, T. *Look Book*   22
Hoban, T. *Shadows and Reflections*   7
Hopkins, L. B. *Click, Rumble, Roar: Poems about Machines*   2
Hubbard, P. *My Crayons Talk*   6
Hulme, J. N. *Bubble Trouble*   4
Hutchins, P. *Clocks and More Clocks*   5

Isadora, R. *I Touch*   2

Jansson, T. *Finn Family Moomintroll*   13
Johnston, T. *We Love the Dirt*   2
Jordan, H. J. *How a Seed Grows*   4
Joyce, W. *Bently & Egg*   4
Juster, N. *The Phantom Tollbooth*   4, 10

Kalman, B. *Dirt Movers*   13
Keats, E. J. *Whistle for Willie*   22
Keller, H. *Will It Rain?*   2
Kids Livin Life *The Homeless Hibernating Bear*   14
Krauss, R. *The Carrot Seed*   5
Kroll, S., & Bassett, J. *The Biggest Pumpkin Ever*   6
Kroll, V. L. *Hands!*   11
Kudlinski, K. *Animal Tracks and Traces*   7

Larson, G. *There's a Hair in My Dirt! A Worm's Story*   3
Lear, E. *The Owl and the Pussycat*   23
Leedy, L. *The Edible Pyramid: Good Eating Every Day*   4
Leonard, M. *Swimming in the Sand*   9
Lionni, L. *Inch by Inch*   5, 22
Lobel, A. *Fables*   2, 9
Lodge, B. *The Half-Mile Hat*   5
London, J. *Like Butter on Pancakes*   10
Lowry, L. *Number the Stars*   21
Lyon, G. *Come a Tide*   7

Macaulay, D. *Black and White*   12
Maestro, B. *Why Do Leaves Change Color?*   3
Maestro, B., & Maestro, G. *Temperature and You*   5
Maki, C. *Snowflakes, Sugar, and Salt: Crystals Up Close*   9
Martin, B. Jr., & Archambault, J. *Here Are My Hands*   11
Mason, A. *Mealworms: Raise Them, Watch Them,
    See Them Change*   10
McClintock, M. *Stop That Ball!*   11
McLerran, A. *Roxaboxen*   20
McMillan, B. *Sense Suspense: A Guessing Game for the Five Senses*   4
Merriam, E. *The Wise Woman and Her Secret*   4
Mitchener, C., Johnson, V., & Adams, P. *Water Magic*   11
Mitton, T. *Roaring Rockets*   12
Morgan, R. *In the Next Three Seconds*   5
Morris, T. *Growing Things*   9
Morris, W. *Just Listen*   2
Myller, R. *How Big Is a Foot?*   5, 22

O'Brien, R. C. *Mrs. Frisby and the Rats of NIMH*   11

Palazzo, J. *What Makes the Weather?*   4
Parnall, P. *Winter Barn*   5
Peters, L. W. *The Sun, the Wind, and the Rain*   20
Phillips, B. *Beanie Mania II: A Comprehensive Collector's Guide*   3
Phillips-Duke, B. *What in the World?*   4
Plourde, L. & Schoenherr, J. *Pigs in the Mud in the Middle
    of the Rud*   16
Polacco, P. *Boat Ride with Lillian Two Blossoms*   7
Pope, S., Stilwell, S. & Ward, H. *On the Move: A Study of Animal
    Movement*   7

Rainis, K. G. *Exploring With a Magnifying Glass*   4
Ramsay, H. *Hot and Cold*   12
Reid, M. S. *The Button Box*   4
Rey, M. *Curious George Goes to a Chocolate Factory*   5
Roop, P. *Keep the Lights Burning, Abbie*   6

Scarry, R. *Mr. Fixit's Magnet Machine*   13
Selsam, M. *Benny's Animals and How We Put Them in Order*   3
Selsam, M. *Eat the Fruit, Plant the Seed*   2
Selsam, M. *Seeds and More Seeds*   3
Sendak, M. *Where the Wild Things Are*   20
Serfozo, M. *What's What? A Guessing Game*   7
Seuss, Dr. *Green Eggs and Ham*   4
Seuss, Dr. *Oh, the THINKS You Can Think!*   12
Seuss, Dr. *Oh, the Places You'll Go!*   1
Seuss, Dr. *One Fish Two Fish Red Fish Blue Fish*   17
Shapp, M., & Shapp, C. *Let's Find Out What's Light and What's Heavy*   5
Sharmat, M. *Gregory, the Terrible Eater*   4
Silverstein, S. *The Giving Tree*   7
Silverstein, S. *Where the Sidewalk Ends*   22
Simmons, J. *Daisy and the Egg*   4
Smith, M. W. *Goodnight Moon*   14
Snyder, Z. K. *Changeling*   16

Taylor, B. *Everybody Needs a Rock*   2
Taylor, B. *Bouncing and Bending Light*   17
Taylor, B. *I'm in Charge of Celebrations*   2

Vagin, V. *The Enormous Carrot*   4
Van Allsburg, C. *Two Bad Ants*   20, 22
Van Cleave, J. *Dinosaurs for Every Kid*   14

Wald, D. K. *How Teddy Bears Find Their Homes*   3
Wallace, K. *Eyewitness Readers: Whatever the Weather*   7
Walsh, E. S. *Mouse Paint*   6, 22
Walter, M. P. *Ty's One-Man Band*   17
White, E. B. *Charlotte's Web*   22
White, E. B. *The Trumpet of the Swan*   24
Wildsmith, B. *Brian Wildsmith's Wild Animals*   2
Wolkstein, D. *8000 Stones: A Chinese Folktale*   22

Yashima, T. *Umbrella*   2

Zubrowski, B. *Soda Science: Designing and Testing Soft Drinks*   23

Glossary

accommodation—Forming new schemata or splitting off new schemata from existing ones to accommodate new information

advance organizer—An introduction to a lesson that foretells the lesson's nature and objective and stimulates interest

assimilation—Enlarging schemata with new information

attribute—A characteristic of an object

buoyancy—The ability of a liquid to cause something to float in it

calcium carbonate—$CaCO_3$, the chemical name for calcite, found in bones and shells and used for making Portland cement and lime

chromosome—A cluster of genes that contains the blueprints for the function and reproduction of cells

circumference—The distance around an object

clownfish—A small saltwater fish

cognitive disequilibration—A state of mental uncertainty about the explanation of an occurrence

cognitive equilibration—A state of mental satisfaction

continental drift theory—An outmoded theory that suggested that continents wandered about on the earth's crust

conventional units of measurement—Units of measurement based on the standardized foot as the standard; formerly known as the British system

cumulus cloud—Massive puffy cloud with a flat base

deciduous tree—A tree that loses its leaves seasonally—usually in the autumn

didactic—An approach to teaching in which material is presented for students to learn

discrepant events—Events that are different from what was expected

DNA—Deoxyribonucleic acid: the building blocks of genes and chromosomes

earth and space science—The study of the earth, the solar system, and the universe

earthquake—A trembling of the earth that is usually caused by volcano eruptions or plate movement

ginkgo tree—A deciduous tree with fan-shaped leaves and yellow fruit; native to eastern China

great circle—An imaginary circle surrounding the globe that passes through both the north and south poles

hardware—The computer and its accessories

heft—Hold an object in one's hand and move the hand up and down to feel the weight of the object

igneous—Rocks formed from magma; includes granite, pumice, basalt, obsidian, and others

inclusions—Pieces of nonnative materials imbedded within pieces of rock

interpolation—Inferring information between two known points, such as inferring temperature between labeled marks on thermometers

life science—The study of living things and their interrelationships with each other and the environment

meta-analysis—Analysis of a group of similar studies previously published

metamorphic—Rocks formed from changes in other rocks caused by high temperatures or high pressures or both; includes gneiss, schist, quartzite, slate, marble, and others

meteorologist—Scientist who studies weather

metric units of measurement—Units of measurement based on the meter as the standard

mutually exclusive—Characteristics of different objects or concepts that do not overlap

nontraditional—Units of measurement based on items chosen by children.

opaque—A material that does not permit light to pass through

pedagogy—The science, art, and profession of teaching

period (of a pendulum)—Time it takes a pendulum to make one complete back-and-forth swing

phototropism—The bending of a plant toward a light source

physical science—The study of matter and energy; includes the study of mechanical energy (energy of motion), heat, sound, light, electricity and magnetism, nuclear energy, and matter and chemical energy

plate tectonics—A theory of crustal movement of the earth's continents and ocean basins

plates—The crustal material on which the earth's continents and ocean basins sit

pollen—Fine dust in a seed plant whose function is reproduction

receptor systems—Systems in living organisms that enable them to detect stimuli

schema—(pl. **schemata**) A cognitive structure

scientific literacy—The ability to understand science in its day-to-day context

sea anemone—A shallow-water, saltwater stationary animal with bright colors and clusters of tentacles that resemble flowers

sedimentary—Rocks formed from materials that have settled and become cemented together; includes sandstone, limestone, conglomerate, shale, gypsum, and others

serrated—Sawlike edges

software—Programs that are operated by a computer

stamens—Slender stalks on flowers with pollen-bearing sacks on them

stratosphere—The layer of the earth's atmosphere where passenger jet planes fly; 16–30 miles above the earth's surface

translucent—A material that permits scattered light to pass through but not whole images

transparent—A material that permits clear images to pass through

volcano—A structure or vent on the earth's crust from which molten rock and gases emerge or formerly emerged

Index

AAAAS. *See* American Association for the Advancement of Science

Aardema, Verna, *Bringing the Rain to Kapiti: A Nandi Tale*, 331

Academics of Science, 371–372

Accommodation, 186

Accuracy, 101

ACEI. *See* Association of Childhood Education International

Action research (applied research), 376–379

Adult literacy, 15

Advance organizer, 326

Advertising, 306

AETS. *See* Association for the Education of Teachers in Science

African Americans, 224–226

Afrocentric literature, 331

Agassizi, Jean Louis Rodolphe, *Geological Sketches*, 153

Alice's Adventures in Wonderland (Carroll), 124

Aliki
  My Feet, 54
  My Five Senses, 40

All Aboard Trucks (Conrad), 169

All about Seeds (Berger), 44

Allergies, 259, 277
  database for, 311

Alphabet of Dinosaurs, An (Dodson), 180

American Association for the Advancement of Science (AAAS), 12–13, 359, 363

Amphitheaters, 274

Animal observation, 39

Animals, 117

Animals, 302

Animals, stuffed, 54

Ant Cities (Dorros), 263

Ant farms, 263

Applied research (action research), 376–379

Aquariums, 260–261

Arch, 74

Aristotle, 186

Arm length, 82

Arnosky, Jim, *Crinkleroot's Guide to Knowing the Trees*, 57

Arsenopyrite, 259

Asbestos, 259

Asians, 224–226

Assessment, 235–252
  attitude, 244–245
  content, 245–246
  indicators of proficiency, 237–238
  inquiry, 242–244
  process skills, 237–242
  reporting to parents, 248–250
  science portfolio, 247–248
  of teacher and program, 250–251

Assimilation, 186, 188

Association for Childhood Education International (ACEI), 372
  Bibliography of Books for Children, 330

Association of Childhood Education International (ACEI), *Childhood Education*, 330

Association for the Education of Teachers in Science (AETS), 371

Association for Women in Science (AWIS), 224

Assuage epistemic hunger, 190

Astronomers, 101

Atmosphere, of earth, 176–177

Atoms, 174–175

Attitude assessment, 244–245

Attributes, 49–51, 54

Auditory learning. *See* Learner differences

Audubon Society, 372

Ausubel, D.P., Novak, J.D., Hanesian, H., *Educational Psychology: A Cognitive View*, 183

AWIS. *See* Association for Women in Science

Bag contents, 67–68

Baker, Keith, *Who Is the Beast?*, 121, 329

Balance, 89

Balloon rockets, 159–160

Banners, 306

Bar graphs, 155, 162

Barrett, Judi, *Cloudy with a Chance of Meatballs*, 69

Bash, Barbara, *Desert Giant: The World of the Saguaro Cactus*, 107

Batteries, 367
  and electricity, 197–198

Baxter, Nicola, *Hot or Not*, 151

Beanie Babies®, 54

Beanie Mania II: A Comprehensive Collector's Guide (Phillips), 54

Bear for All Seasons, A (Fuchs), 116

Bear Called Paddington, A (Bond), 112

Behavior management, 264–266

Behn, Harry, *Crickets and Bullfrogs and Whispers of Thunder*, 39

Bell, Sharon, *The Hundred Penny Box*, 82

Benchmarks for Science (American Association for the Advancement of Science, 1993), 13

Benchmarks for Science Literacy, 365

Benny's Animals and How We Put Them in Order (Selsam), 55

Bently & Egg (Joyce), 65

Berenstain, Stan and Jan
  Berenstain Bears Grow-It: Mother Nature Has Such a Green Thumb, 105
  Berenstain Bears on the Moon, 182

Berenstain Bears Grow-It: Mother Nature Has Such a Green Thumb (Berenstain), 105

Berenstain Bears on the Moon (Berenstain), 182

Berger, Melvin, *All about Seeds*, 44

Bernard, Claude, *Bulletin of New York Academy of Medicine, Volume IX*, 164

Berra, Yogi, *Yogi Book: "I Really Didn't Say Everything I Said,"* 235

Bibliography of Books for Children (Association of Childhood Education International), 330

Bicycle Book (Gibbons), 217

Biggest Cookie in the World, The (Hayward), 91

Biggest Pumpkin Ever, The (Kroll), 103

Binoculars, 275–276

Biology, 8

Black and White (Macaulay), 161

Blankly, Franklin and Vaughn, Eleanor, *Mickey's Magnet*, 56

Bloom's higher levels in questioning, 26

Blowing bubbles, 165–166
Boat Ride with Lillian Two Blossom (Polacco), 120
Bodily-kinesthetic intelligence, 228–230
Body Measurement Olympics, 79–80
Body temperature, 92–93
Bogacki, Tomasz
  Cat and Mouse in the Rain, 108
  Cat and Mouse in the Snow, 108
Boilerplate information, 318–319
Boiling point of water, 92
Bond, Michael, *A Bear Called Paddington*, 112
Bouncing balls, 151
Bouncing and Bending Light (Taylor), 215
Brainstorming, 129
Brass Button (Dragonwagon), 66
Brenner, Barbara, *Mr. Tall and Mr. Small*, 81
Brett, Jan, *The Mitten: A Ukrainian Folktale*, 116
Brian Wildsmith's Wild Animals (Wildsmith), 39
Brief History of Time, A (Hawking), 1
Bringing the Rain to Kapiti Plain: A Nandi Tale (Aardema), 331
Brown, Margaret Wise, 182
  The Noisy Book, 42
Bruner, Jerome, 8
  The Process of Education, 32
Bubble Trouble (Hulme), 64
Bubbles, 63–64
Bulletin boards, 255–257
Bulletin of New York Academy of Medicine, Volume IX (Bernard), 164
Buoyancy, 136
Burgess, Gelett, "The Purple Cow," *Nonsense and Commonsense: A Child's Book of Victorian Verse*, 47
Burningham, John, *Mr. Grumpy's Outing*, 104
Burton, Virginia Lee, *Mike Mulligan and His Steam Shovel*, 356
Bush, George, 14
Butter, making, 139–140
Butterflies, 281
Button Box, The (Reid), 66
Buttons, 66

Calendars, 268
Canterbury Tales, The (Chaucer), 361

Carle, Eric
  Little Cloud, 274
  The Grouchy Ladybug, 278, 329
  The Very Busy Spider, 329
  The Very Hungry Caterpillar, 329
  The Very Lonely Firefly, 329
  The Very Quiet Cricket, 329
Carroll, Lewis
  Alice's Adventures in Wonderland, 124
  Walrus and the Carpenter, The, 253
Carrot Seed, The (Krauss), 84
Carter, David A., *Feely Bugs: To Touch and Feel*, 38
Cat and Mouse in the Rain (Bogacki), 108
Cat and Mouse in the Snow (Bogacki), 108
Caterpillars, 281
Cauley, L.B., *Jack and the Beanstalk*, 327
CD information programs, 301–304
Celsius, 92, 98
Census Bureau, 299–300
Center for the Study of Books in Spanish for Children and Adolescents at California State University in San Marcos, 330
Centimeter, 77, 98
Change
  conceptual, 192
  of scientific knowledge, 5
  of variables, 165–168
Changeling (Snyder), 196
Channin, Michael, *Grandfather Four Winds and Rising Moon*, 116
Chaperones, 281
Char, Renè, *Leaves of Hypnos*, 124
Charlotte's Web (White), 324
Charts, 69–71
Chaucer, Geoffrey, *The Canterbury Tales*, 361
Chemistry, 8
Childhood Education (Association for Childhood Education International), 330, 372
Children with disabilities, 231
Children's Book Council, 330
Children's literature. *See* Literature
Children's magazines, 332–333
Chinese proverb, 34
Chocolate chips, 98
Chromosome, 5
Cinderella, 331

Cinnabar, 259
Circumference, 77
Citizenship, 14
ClarisWorks, 310
Class roster, 310
Class website, 300
Classifying (basic scientific process), 9, 47–60, 125, 237
  groceries, 57–58
  hardware, 59
  leaves, 56–57
  magnetic objects, 55–56
  photographs, 55
  plastic food, 52
  rocks, 48, 50–52
  seeds, 53
  soil, 58
  stuffed animals, 54
Classroom organization, 254
Classroom science. *See* Constructing science in the classroom
Click, Rumble, Roar: Poems about Machines (Bennett), 42
Climo, Shirley, *The Egyptian Cinderella*, 331
Clocks, 95
Clocks and More Clocks (Hutchins), 97
Cloud Book, The (DePaola), 180
Cloud formation, 179–180
Cloudy with a Chance of Meatballs (Barrett), 69
Clownfish, 4–5
Coffee can, 87
Cognitive disequilibration, 189–191, 200, 325–326
  See also Constructivism
Cognitive equilibrium, 186–187
Cognitive itch, 189
Cognitive perturbation, 189
Cognitive structures, 186
Coin collection, 50
Cold and hot definitions, 150
Cole, Joanna
  It's Too Noisy, 39
  Magic School Bus series, 329
  Magic School Bus in the Time of the Dinosaurs, 180
  The Magic School Bus: Inside the Human Body, 144
  The Magic School Bus Plays Ball, 171
  You Can't Smell a Flower with Your Ear!: All about Your 5 Senses, 40
Collay, Ryan and Dubrow, Joanne, *Stuartship*, 327
Colors, mixing, 103, 328–329
Columns, 306–307, 310

Come On, Rain! (Hesse), 108
Come a Tide (Lyon), 122
Comer, James, P., 267
Comfort zone, 212
Communicating (basic scientific process), 9–11, 61–75, 125, 237
  bag contents, 67–68
  bubbles, 63–64
  button matching, 66
  charting food groups, 71
  fingerprints, 73–74
  funny figures, 72
  growing marigolds, 66
  making egg shells soft, 65
  material that falls out of flowers, 64–65
  and rocks, 62
  seeing with magnifying glasses, 67
  "Twenty Questions," 68
  ways of, 63
  weather charts and graphs, 69–70
Communications skills, 300
Community resources, 270–271
Comparisons, 78, 86, 92
Computer technology. *See* Technology
Computerized teaching, 302
Conceptual change, 192
Conrad, Lynn, *All Aboard Trucks*, 169
Constructing ideas
  animal camouflage, 174
  assessment, 236, 250
  batteries and electricity, 197–198
  blowing bubbles, 165–166
  classifying, 59
  comfort zone, 212
  constructing pairs of words, 20
  data, 154–155, 163
  defining operationally, 152
  defying gravity, 184–185
  desktop publishing, 306
  e-mail, 313
  earth smoothness, 177
  experimenting, 171
  explaining your science program, 369
  falling balls, 191
  formulating and testing hypotheses, 144
  gender bias, 222
  Goldilocks and the Three Bears, 325
  hidden figures, 220
  identifying and controlling variables, 131, 136
  inferring, 122
  intelligence, 229
  investigating parachutes, 10–12

learner differences, 212
learning modalities, 213, 218
local demographic
  changes, 225
meanings of words, 20
measuring, 99
measuring rocks, 77
metaphors, 27, 369
microteaching, 209
models, 182
multidisciplinary unit, 347–348
mystery box, 22–24
naming poles of magnets, 194
NASA, 315
observing, 45
philosophy of early childhood
  science education, 27–28
predicting, 101, 111
reactions to free discovery, 200
remembering science, 3
rock classification, 48, 50–51
rock hunt, 34–36
rocks and communication, 62
spreadsheets and graphing, 309
sugar dissolving in water,
  138–139
surfing for science sites, 315
teaching the content of
  science, 366
technology inventory, 297–298
tutorial and interactive
  computer programs, 304
unexpected questions, 4
weather on the internet, 315
what did you see on your way
  to school today?, 37
"what do you mean by"
  questions, 147
wordless story, 113
Constructing models,
  173–182, 238
examples of, 174
Constructing science in the
  classroom
animals, 117
arm and foot measurement,
  82–83
bag contents, 67–68
balloon rockets, 159–160
bouncing balls, 151
bubbles, 63–64
button matching, 66
cleaning pennies, 149–150
cloud formation, 179–180
daytime sky watching, 274
dinosaurs, 180
erosion, 279–280
exploring gears, 216–217
fingerprints, 73–74
floating eggs, 133–134
flowers, 64–65
food group charting, 71
friction, 170–171

funny figures, 72
graphing plant growth, 84
groceries, 57–58
growing marigolds, 66
hands left in water, 149
hardware, 59
healthy plants, 135
hearing, 39, 42–43
heartbeat rate, 143–144
height measurement, 81
hibernating teddy bears, 179
hot and cold, 150–151
inclined plane, 168–169
investigating reflection,
  214–215
leaves, 56–57
listening, 38
long and short
  measurement, 81
magnetic objects, 55–56
magnetism, 167–168
magnifying glasses, 67
making butter, 139–140
making egg shells soft, 65
mealworms, 142–143
measuring length using
  objects, 82–83
melting ice, 142
miles and kilometers, 85–86
mixing colors, 103
mixing liquids with water, 106
moon shine, 181–182
peas in a peapod, 161–163
photographs, 55
plant movement, 105
plastic food, 52
rain and snow, 107–109
rate of water evaporation,
  140–141
salt crystals, 134–135
sand through a funnel, 132–133
schoolyard ecology, 278
seasons, 116
seeds, 53
senses (several), 40–41
shadows, 85, 118
sidewalk ecology, 277
sight, 39, 42, 43–44
sinking or floating, 104, 106
sinking and floating fruits, 239
smell, 40
smoothness of cloth, 38
soft drinks exploding, 353–354
soil, 58, 121
soil erosion, 122
sounds of rubber bands, 215
sprouting and growing, 103
stuffed animals, 54
temperature, 93–94
time measurement, 95–98
transparency, translucency,
  opaqueness, 109–110
tree age, 121

"Twenty Questions," 68
unknown objects, 120
vinegar reactions, 243–244
volume measurement, 87–88
walking around the school,
  278–279
water absorption, 107
water temperature, 160–161
weather, 120
weather charts and graphs,
  69–70
weight measurement, 90–91
wind, 119
Constructivism, 183–195,
  200–207, 336–337
background, 183–186
conceptual change, 192
disequilibration, 189–191
multicultural, 226–228
nature of, 186–189
principles of, 365–366
prior beliefs, 191–192
right and wrong, 193–194
validity of self-constructed
  conceptualizations,
  192–193
See also Process-oriented
  inquiry
Constructivist-oriented
  multicultural approach,
  226–228
Constructing models, 131
Content assessment, 245–246
Continental drift theory, 5
Control, locus of, 218–219
Controlled experiments, 12
Controlling variables, 11,
  128–136
Conventional units, 77–78
  vs. metric units, 98–99
See also Measuring
Cooke, Andy, Weigh It Up,
  Bear's Playschool, 90
Cookies, 91
Crayon Box That Talked, The
  (DeRolf), 106
Crayons, 106
Creative writing, 340–341
Crepe paper, 256
Crick, Francis, 5
Crickets and Bullfrogs and
  Whispers of Thunder
  (Behn), 39
Crinkleroot's Guide to Knowing
  the Trees (Arnosky), 57
"Crocodile in the Bedroom"
  Fables (Lobel), 128
Cubic centimeter, 86
Cubit, 80
Cultural differences, 224–228
  characteristics of learning by
    race, 226
  statistics of race, 224–225

Cumulus cloud, 274
Cup, 86
Curiosity, 1
Curious George Goes to a
  Chocolate Factory
  (Rey), 98
Curriculums, 368–369
Cutouts, 48–49

Daily weather chart, 41
Daisy and the Egg (Simmons), 65
Daisy interdisciplinary model,
  347–350
Data, 11, 378
Data interpretation. See
  Interpreting data
Data tables, 155, 162, 166, 169,
  171, 308, 340
See also Interpreting data
Databases, 310–312
  for allergies, 311
  for birds, 312
de Regniers, Beatrice, The
  Enchanted Forest, 361
de Saint-Exupéry, Antoine, The
  Little Prince, 76
Debugging, 318
Decay, 357
Defining operationally,
  146–152, 238
Defying gravity, 184–185
Demographic changes, 224–225
See also Cultural differences
dePaola, Tomie
  The Cloud Book, 180
  The Popcorn Book, 327
DeRolf, Shane, The Crayon Box
  That Talked, 106
Desert Giant: The World of the
  Saguaro Cactus (Bash), 107
Desktop publishing, 304–306
Developmentally Appropriate
  Practice, 15–18
See also National Association
  for the Education of
  Young Children
Dictionary of the English
  Language (Samuels), 61
Didactic, 365
Digital cameras, 300
"Digital Divide," 299–300
Dinosaur Hunter, The, 302
Dinosaur Who Lived in My
  Back Yard, The
  (Hennessy), 180
Dinosaurs, 174, 177–178, 180,
  229, 305
  databases for, 311
Dinosaurs for Every Kid
  (VanCleave), 180
Dirt, 43
Dirt Movers (Kalman), 169
Disabled children, 231

Discovery, 9–10
Discovery Channel, 317
Discrepant events, 189–190
Discussion and explanation, 9–10
Disequilibration, 189–191
  See also Constructivism
Disraeli, Benjamin, *Vivian Grey,
  Book II*, 146
DK Interactive Learning, 302
DNA, 5–6
Dodd, Anne Wescott, *Footprints
  and Shadows*, 85
Dodson, Peter, *An Alphabet of
  Dinosaurs*, 180
Doing science, 8, 235–236,
  301, 363
Dorros, Arthur
  Ant Cities, 263
  Feel the Wind, 119
  *Follow the Water from Brook
    to Ocean*, 122
Dragnet, 113
Dragonwagon, Crescent, *Brass
  Button*, 66
Drug-free schools, 15
Dunbar, Joyce, *The Sand
  Dunbar*, 133
Dunhill, Priscilla, 48

E-mail. *See* Electronic mail
Early Childhood Longitudinal
  Study, Kindergarten Class
  of, 1998–99, 267
Early Childhood and Science, 365
Early childhood science
  education professional,
  361–384
  curriculum and content,
  362–367
Earth, 88
  smoothness of, 177
Earth and space science, 7
Earthquake, 5
Earth's atmosphere, 176–177
Eat the Fruit, Plant the Seed
  (Selsam), 44
Eating questions (exercise), 24–25
Eclipses, 277
Ecology, 277–278
*Ed Emberly's Great Thumbprint
  Drawing Book*
  (Emberly), 74
*Edible Pyramid: Good Eating
  Every Day* (Leedy), 71
Education Abstracts, 377
Educational Leadership, 382
*Educational Psychology: A
  Cognitive View* (Ausubel,
  Novak, and Hanesian), 183
Educational Technology, 318
Educational Technology
  Quotient (ETQ), 297–298

Edwards, Frank B., *Troubles
  with Bubbles*, 64
Egg shells, 65
Eggs, floating, 133–134
Egyptian Cinderella, The
  (Climo), 331
Ehlert, Lois, *Moon Rope*, 332
8000 Stones: A Chinese Folktale
  (Wolkstein), 332
Einstein, Albert
  Ideas and Opinions, 253
  Out of My Later Years, 128
Elective Affinities
  (von Goethe), 47
Electricity, and batteries, 197–198
Electronic mail (e-mail), 312–313
Elementary School Edition, 365
*Elementary Science Methods:
  A Constructivist
  Approach*, 365
Elementary Science Study (ESS), 9
"Elephant and His Son, The"
  Fables (Lobel), 32
Elevation, 88
Elffers, Joost, *Play With Your
  Food*, 52
Emberly, Ed, *Ed Emberly's
  Great Thumbprint
  Drawing Book*, 74
Enchanted Forest, The
  (de Regniers), 361
Endeavour, 88
Enormous Carrot, The
  (Vagin), 66
ERIC, 303, 377
Erosion, 279
ERT. *See* "Every Teacher a
  Researcher"
ESS. *See* Elementary Science
  Study
Essays (Eyquem de
  Montaigne), 211
Essential vs. nonessential
  information, 220–221
ETQ. *See* Educational
  Technology Quotient
Ets, Maria Hall, *Gilberto and
  the Wind*, 119
"Every Teacher a Researcher"
  (ETR), 375
Everybody Needs a Rock
  (Taylor), 44
Evidence, 113
Excellence in science
  teaching, 380
Excite, 314
Exosphere, 177
Experimenting, 164–172, 238
Explanatory power, 204
Exploration, 9–10
*Exploring with a Magnifying
  Glass* (Raines), 67

Expository methodology, 199
  disadvantages of, 199
Expository-discovery
  continuum, 198–199
External locus of control, 218–219
Eye color, 156–159
*Eyewitness Readers: Whatever
  the Weather* (Wallace), 120
Eyquem de Montaigne, Michel,
  Essays, 311

Fahrenheit, 92, 98
Famine, Edward Allan, *Little
  Ned Stories: A Chapter-
  Picture Book for Kids*, 134
Falling balls, 191
Feel the Wind (Dorros), 119
Feely Bugs: To Touch and Feel
  (Carter), 38
Field dependence and
  independence,
  219–222, 301
Field trips, 270, 281–286
  destinations and learning
  opportunities, 285–286
  planning elements, 284
Fingerprints, 73–74
Finn Family Moomintroll
  (Jansson), 164
Flashlight, 118
Floating, 104, 106
"Floating coffin," 189–190
Flowers, 64–65
Fluids, 364
*Follow the Water from Brook to
  Ocean* (Dorros), 122
Food groups, 71
Food pyramid, 71
Foot, 78
Foot length, 82
Foot measurement, 80
Footprints, 113
Footprints and Shadows
  (Dodd), 85
Formatting, 304
Formulating and testing
  hypotheses, 11, 130,
  137–145, 238
Free discovery methodology,
  200–201
  disadvantages of, 201
Freezing point of water, 92
Freezing water, 289–290
Friction, 170–171
Frisch, Max, *Homo Faber*, 295
From Seed to Plant
  (Gibbons), 328
Fruits, sinking and floating, 239
Fuchs, Diane Marcial, *A Bear
  for All Seasons*, 116
Funnel, 95, 132–133
Funny figures, 72

Galena, 259
Gallon, 86
Gardens, 280–281
Gardner, Howard, 228
Garis, Howard R., *Uncle
  Wiggily's Story Book*, 235
Gears, 216–217
Gender bias, 222–224
Geological Sketches
  (Agassizi), 153
Gibbons, Gail
  Bicycle Book, 217
  From Seed to Plant, 328
  The Pumpkin Book, 327
  *The Seasons of Arnold's Apple
    Tree*, 72
Gibson, Gary
  Playing with Magnets, 168
  Pushing and Pulling, 97
Gilberto and the Wind
  (Ets), 119
Ginkgo tree, 37
Ginny, Susan, *Uncle Lester's
  Lemonade Lure*, 59
Ginsburg, Mirra, *Mushroom in
  the Rain*, 86
Giving Tree, The
  (Silverstein), 121
Globes, 177
Goals 2000: Educate America
  Act, 14–15
Goethe, 137
Goggles, 259
*Goldilocks and the Three
  Bears*, 325
Goodnight Moon (Brown), 182
Gram, 88
*Grandfather Four Winds
  and Rising Moon*
  (Channin), 116
Grants, 287, 373–375
Graphing applications, 306–310
Graphs, 69–70, 84, 154–159,
  162–163
  See also Interpreting data
Gravity, 88
  defying, 184–185
Great circle, 78
Green Eggs and Ham (Seuss), 65
Gregory, the Terrible Eater
  (Sharmat), 71
Groceries, 57–58
Grossman, Bill, *Tommy at the
  Grocery Store*, 58
Grossman, John, 48
Grouchy Ladybug, The (Carle),
  278, 329
Group agreement, 193
Group organization, 264
Groups, 50–52
Growing Things (Morris), 135
Growth of plants, 103

Guided inquiry methodology, 201–202
Gummy bears lesson, 19

Hair color, 158–159
Half-Mile Hat, The (Lodge), 86
Halley's Comet, 13, 101
Hamley, Dennis, *Hare's Choice*, 183
Hand measurement, 80
Handedness, 214
Hands! (Kroll), 149
Hands left in water, 73, 149
Hardware, 59
   definition of, 299
   See also Technology
Hare's Choice (Hamley), 183
Harvard, 8
Hats, 49
Hawking, Stephen, 5
   Stephen W., *A Brief History of Time*, 1
Hayward, Linda
   The Biggest Cookie in the World, 91
   Wet Foot, Dry Foot, Low Foot, High Foot: Learn about Opposites and Differences, 141
Hearing, 38–39, 42–43
   See also Senses; sound
Heartbeat rate, 143–144
Heft, 34
Height, 81
   See also Length; Measuring
Help cards, 265
Hennessy, B.G., *The Dinosaur Who Lived in My Back Yard*, 180
Hesse, Karen, *Come On, Rain!*, 108
Hibernating teddy bears, 179
Highlights for Children, 219, 220
Hispanic literature, 331
Hispanics, 224–226
Histograms, 156–157, 161–162
   See also Interpreting data
Hoban, Tana
   Is It Red? Is It Rough? Is It Smooth? Is It Shiny?, 53
   Is It Red? Is It Yellow? Is It Blue?: An Adventure in Color, 53
   Look Book, 329
   Shadows and Reflections, 118
Hoban, Russell, *The Mouse and His Child*, 100
Home page, 314, 316
Home science, 283, 287–292
Homeless Hibernating Bear, The (Kids Livin Life), 179
Homo Faber (Frisch), 295

Hopkins, Lee Bennett, *Click, Rumble, Roar: Poems about Machines*, 42
Hot and cold definitions, 150
Hot and Cold (Ramsay), 161
Hot or Not (Baxter), 151
How Big is a Foot (Muller), 82, 329
How a Seed Grows (Jordan), 66
How Teddy Bears Find Their Homes (Wald), 54
http:// (HyperText Transfer Protocol), 313
Hulme, Joy N., *Bubble Trouble*, 64
Hundred Penny Box, The (Bell), 82
Hutchins, Pat, *Clocks and More Clocks*, 97
Huxley, Thomas Henry, *Our Knowledge of the Causes of the Phenomena of Organic Nature*, 112
Hypermedia software, 300
HyperText Transfer Protocol (http://), 313
Hypotheses. *See* Formulating and testing hypotheses
Hypothesis, 376

I Touch (Isadora), 38
Ice, 94
Ice cubes, melting time of, 142
Idea Factory, Inc., 170
IDEA. *See* Individuals with Disabilities Act
Ideas and Opinions (Einstein), 253
Ideas for teachers. *See* Constructing ideas
Identifying and controlling variables, 11, 128–136, 238
Igneous rock, 35
I'm in Charge of Celebrations (Byrd), 42
In the Next Three Seconds (Morgan), 95
Inch, 98
Inch by Inch (Lionni), 81, 329
Inclined plane, 168–169
Inclusions, 34
Index finger, 73
Individuals with Disabilities Act (IDEA), 231
Inferring (basic scientific process), 9, 112–123, 126, 238
   definition of, 113
Infoseek, 314
Insects, 277
Instructional objective, 125

Intelligences, types of, 228–230
Interactive bulletin boards, 255–257
Interdisciplinary integration, 345–360
   daisy model, 347–350
   rose model, 350–355
   science, technology, and society (STS), 355–358
   significance of, 358–359
Internal locus of control, 218–219
International Society for Technology in Education (ISTE), 321
Internet, 313–317
Interpersonal intelligence, 228–230
Interpolation, 93
Interpretation, 11
Interpreting data, 130, 153–163, 238
Intrapersonal intelligence, 228–230
IQ tests, 228
Is It Red? Is It Yellow? Is It Blue?: An Adventure in Color (Hoban), 53
Is It Rough? Is It Smooth? Is It Shiny? (Hoban), 53
Isadora, Rachel, *I Touch*, 38
ISTE. *See* International Society for Technology in Education
It's Too Noisy! (Cole), 39

Jack and the Beanstalk (Cauley), 327
Jansson, Tove, *Finn Family Moomintroll*, 164
Jeopardy!, 220
Jerome Burner Telling Stories to Make Science: Karplus Lecture Excerpts, *NSTA Reports!*, 273
Jigsaw puzzles, 50
Johnson, Samuel, *Dictionary of the English Language*, 61
Johnston, Tony, *We Love the Dirt*, 43
Jordan, Helen J., *How a Seed Grows*, 66
Joubert, Joseph, *Pensées*, 361
Journal of College Science Teaching (National Science Teachers Association), 370
Journal of Computers in Mathematics and Science Teaching, 318

Journal of Elementary Science Education (Association for the Education of Teachers in Science), 371
Journal of Research in Childhood (Association for Childhood Education International), 372
Journal of Research in Science Teaching (National Association for Research in Science Teaching), 371
Journal of Science Teacher Education (Association for the Education of Teachers in Science), 371
Joyce, William, *Bently & Egg*, 65
JumpStart Learning System series, 302
Junior Academy of Science, 372
Just Listen (Morris), 38
Juster, Norman, *The Phantom Toll Booth*, 61

Kalman, Bobbie, *Dirt Movers*, 169
Karplus, Robert, 9
Keats, Ezra Jack, *Whistle for Willie*, 331
Keep the Lights Burning, Abbie (Roop), 110
Keller, Holly, *Will It Rain?*, 41
Kennedy, John F., 295
Kennesaw State University, 80
Kids Livin Life, The Homeless Hibernating Bear, 179
Kilogram, 88–89, 98
Kilometer, 77, 85–86
Kinesthetic learning. *See* Learner differences
King, Jr., Martin Luther, *The Strength to Love*, 345
Knowledge
   ownership of, 22–27, 200
   of science of early childhood teachers, 3–8
Knowledge Adventure, Inc., 302
Krauss, Ruth, *The Carrot Seed*, 84
Kroll, Steven, *The Biggest Pumpkin Ever*, 103
Kroll, Virginia, *Hands!*, 149

Language, 61
   See also Communicating
Larson, Gary, *There's a Hair in My Dirt: A Worm's Story*, 58
LASER. *See* Leadership and Assistance for Science Education Reform
Laser videodiscs, 218

Leadership and Assistance for Science Education Reform (LASER), 382
Leaning Company, 302
Lear, Edward, *The Owl and the Pussycat*, 345
Learner differences, 211–234
  auditory learners, 212–218
  children with disabilities, 231
  cultural differences, 224–228
  external locus of control, 218–219
  field dependent, 219–221
  field independent, 219–222
  gender bias, 222–224
  internal locus of control, 218–219
  kinesthetic learning, 212–214, 216–218
  multiple intelligences, 228–230
  visual learners, 212–215, 217–218
Learning, 188, 191
  See also Constructivism
Learning Cycle, 9–10
Learning modalities. *See* Learner differences
Learning styles. *See* Learner differences
Leaves, 49, 51–52, 56–57
  types of, 57
Leaves of Hypnos (Char), 124
Leedy, Loreen, *The Edible Pyramid: Good Eating Every Day*, 71
Length, 77–86
  Body Measurement Olympics, 79–80
  conventional units, 77
  definition of, 77
  metric conversion table, 78
  metric units, 77
  See also Measuring
Leonard, Marcia, *Swimming in the Sand*, 133
Lessons, introducing, 326–328
Let's Find Out What's Light and What's Heavy (Shapp), 90
Life science, 7
Lifelong learning, 15
Light bulbs, 197
Lightning, 95
Like Butter on Pancakes (London), 140
Line graphs, 154, 161, 163
  See also Interpreting data
Linguistic intelligence, 228–230
Links, 314
Lionni, Leo, *Inch by Inch*, 81, 329

Liquids, 86, 106
Listening, 22, 62
  for different sounds, 38
Liter, 86, 88
Literacy, 324–344
  adult, 15
Literature, 325–333
  cognitive disequilibration, 325–326
  evaluating, 331
  introducing lessons, 326–328
  magazines, 332–333
  multicultural, 331–332
  presenting factual information, 329
  providing practice in the processes, 329
  sources of children's, 329–331
  validating conclusions, 328–329
Little Cloud (Carle), 274
Little Ned Stories: A Chapter-Picture Book for Kids (Faine), 134
Little Prince, The (de Saint-Exupery), 76
Living graphs, 156
Living laboratories, 259–263
Lobel, Arnold
  "The Crocodile in the Bedroom" *Fables*, 128
  "The Elephant and His Son" *Fables*, 32
Locke, John, 186
Lodge, Bernard, *The Half-Mile Hat*, 86
Logical-mathematical intelligence, 228–230
London, Jonathon, *Like Butter on Pancakes*, 140
Look Book (Hoban), 329
Loop, 74
Loudness, 39
Lowry, Lois, *Number the Stars*, 295
Ludovici, Anthony M., 137
Lycos, 314
Lyon, George, *Come a Tide*, 122

Macaulay, David, *Black and White*, 161
McClintock, Mike, *Stop That Ball!*, 151
McLerran, Alice, *Roxaboxen*, 279
McMillan, Bruce, *Sense Suspense: A Guessing Game for the Five Senses*, 67
Maestro, Betsy and Guillo, *Temperature and You*, 96

Magazines, 332–333
Mager, Robert, 125
Magic School Bus: Inside the Human Body (Cole), 144
Magic School Bus Plays Ball, The, (Cole), 171
Magic School Bus series (Cole), 302, 329
Magic School Bus in the Time of the Dinosaurs (Cole), 180
Magnetic/nonmagnetic chart, 144
Magnets, 55–56, 114, 167–168, 367
  poles of, 194
Magnifying glasses, 67
Maki, Chu, *Snowflakes, Sugar, and Salt: Crystals Up Close*, 135
Malcolm, Shirley, 224
Mammals (National Geographic Society), 303
Man-made environment, 2
Maps, 255
Marigolds, 66
Mason, Adrienne, *Mealworms: Raise Them, Watch Them, See Them Change*, 143
Mass, 88–89
Materials and equipment organization, 256–257
Mealworms: Raise Them, Watch Them, See Them Change (Mason), 143
Mealworms, 142–143
Measuring (basic scientific process), 9–11, 76–99, 125, 238
  length, 77–86
  metric vs. conventional units, 98–99
  temperature, 92–94
  time, 95–98
  volume, 86–88
  weight, 88–91
Mediations on Quixote (Otega y Gasset), 196
Mental equilibrium, 187
Merriam, Eve, *The Wise Woman and Her Secret*, 68
Mesosphere, 177
Meta-analysis, 266
Metamorphic rock, 35
Metaphors, 27, 369
Meteorologist, 101
Meter, 77
Methodologies, 198–203, 367–369
Metric units, 77–78
  vs. conventional units, 98–99
  See also Measuring

Mickey's Magnet (Blankly and Vaughn), 56
Microsoft, 302
Microsoft Office, 310
Microteaching, 208–209
Middle finger, 73
Mike Mulligan and His Steam Shovel (Burton), 356
Mile, 78, 85–86, 95
Milliliter, 86
Millimeter, 77
Mitchener, Carole, Johnson, Virginia, and Adams, Phyllis, *Water Magic*, 150
Mitten: A Ukrainian Folktale, The (Brett), 116
Mitton, Tony, *Roaring Rockets*, 160
Models. *See* Constructing models
Montessori schools, 200
Moon, 88, 277
Moon Rope (Ehlert), 332
Moonshine, 181
Morgan, Rowland, *In the Next Three Seconds*, 95
Morris, Ting, *Growing Things*, 135
Morris, Winifred, *Just Listen*, 38
Mosquito, 88
Mountain ranges, 177
Mouse and His Child, The (Hoban), 100
Mouse Paint (Walsh), 103, 328
Mr. Fixit's Magnet Machine (Scarry), 168
Mr. Grumpy's Outing (Burningham), 104
Mr. Tall and Mr. Small (Brenner), 81
Mrs. Frisby and the Rats of NIMH (O'Brien), 146
Mt. Everest, 177, 182
Mud-making, 206
Muller, Rolf, *How Big Is a Foot*, 82, 329
Multicultural children's literature, 331–332
Multicultural education, 224–228
  characteristics of learning by race, 226
  general characteristics of effective, 227
  strategies for, 227
  See also Cultural differences
Multiple intelligences, 228–230
Museums, 281
Mushroom in the Rain (Ginsburg), 86

Musical intelligence, 228–230
Mutual exclusivity, 50–51
My Feet (Aliki), 54
My Five Senses (Aliki), 40
"My Name Is Stegosaurus," 229
Mystery boxes, 22–24

NAEYC. *See* National
    Association for the
    Education of Young
    Children
NARST. *See* National
    Association for Research
    in Science Teaching
National Association of
    Academies of Science, 371
National Association for the
    Education of Young
    Children (NAEYC),
    15–18, 372
National Association for
    Research
    in Science Teaching
    (NARST), 371, 375
National Commission on
    Mathematics and Science
    Teaching, 382
National Commission on
    Science Education
    Standards and Assessment
    (NCSESA), 12, 14
National Geographic, 39
*National Geographic Kids
    Network*, 316
National Geographic
    Society, 303
National Geographic World, 39
National Research Council, 211
    *National Science Education
        Standards*, 6–7, 13–14
*National Science Education
    Standards*, 6–7, 13–14,
    202, 236–237, 267, 301,
    363, 380
National Science Resources
    Center (NSRC), 382
National Science Teachers
    Association (NSTA), 12,
    14, 267, 330, 367,
    370–371
    "The Use of Computers in
        Science Education," 301
National Wildlife, 39
Native American literature,
    331–332
Native Americans, 224–226
Naturalist intelligence, 228, 274
Nature, 1–2
    observing, 42
Nature trails, 274
"Net Generation," 299

Netiquette, 316
Networking, 318
Newsletters, 267–268
Nietzsche, Friedrich, *The Will to
    Power*, 137
Nobel Prize Internet
    Archive, 223
Noisy Book, The (Brown), 42
Nonessential vs. essential
    information, 220–221
Nontraditional systems, 9
NSCESA. *See* National
    Commission on Science
    Education Standards and
    Assessment
NSRC. *See* National Science
    Resources Center
*NSTA Pathways to the Science
    Standards*, 365
NSTA Reports!, 318, 370
NSTA Reports! (Jerome Bruner
    Telling Stories to Make
    Science: Karplus Lecture
    Excerpts), 273
NSTA. *See* National Science
    Teachers Association
Number the Stars (Lowry), 295

O'Brien, Robert C., *Mrs. Frisby
    and the Rats of
    NIMH*, 146
Observing (basic scientific
    process), 9–11, 32–46,
    125, 237, 239, 241
    hearing, 38–39, 42–43
    senses (several), 40–41
    sight, 39, 42, 43–44
    smell, 40
    texture, 38
    weather, 40–41
Oh the Places You'll Go
    (Seuss), 2
*Oh, the THINKS You Can
    Think!* (Seuss), 153
*On the Move: A Study of
    Animal Movement*
    (Pope), 117
1–2–3 system of behavior, 265
Opaqueness, 109–110
Optical illusions, 21
Organizing, 253–272
    behavior management,
        264–266
    bulletin boards, 255–256
    the classroom, 254
    community resources,
        270–271
    groups, 264
    living laboratories, 259–263
    materials and equipment,
        256–257

parent resources, 266–270
    for safety, 258–259
    time, 257–258
Orpiment, 259
Ortega y Gasset, José,
    *Meditations on
    Quixote*, 196
Ounce, 86, 88
*Our Knowledge of the Causes
    of the Phenomena
    of Organic Nature*
    (Huxley), 112
Out of My Later Years
    (Einstein), 128
Outdoor learning centers,
    274–280
Outdoor temperature, 96
Owl and the Pussycat, The
    (Lear), 345
Ownership of knowledge and
    thought, 22–27

Pace, 80
Palazzo, Janet, *What Makes the
    Weather*, 69
Pallotta, Jerry, 329
Paper towels, 117
Parachutes, 10–12
Parallel construction, 50–51
Parent nights, 269
Parent resources, 266–270
Parent volunteers, 267
Parental participation, 15
Parents, reporting to, 248–250
Parnall, Peter, *Winter Barn*, 94
*Pathways to the Science
    Standard* (National
    Science Teachers
    Association), 14
Patterns of fingerprints, 74
PBS (Public Broadcasting
    System), 317
Peanuts, 45
Peas, 161–162
Pedagogy, 362
Pendulum, 129
Pennies, 82–83, 90
    cleaning, 149–150
Pensèes, (Joubert), 361
Perceptions, 21
Peters, Lisa W., *The Sun,
    the Wind, and the
    Rain*, 280
Pets, 259–260
Phantom Toll Booth, The
    (Juster), 61
Phillips, Becky, *Beanie Mania II:
    A Comprehensive
    Collector's Guide*, 54
Phillips-Duke, Barbara J., *What
    in the World?*, 68

*Philosophy of the Inductive
    Sciences* (Whewell), 100
Photographs, 55
PSYCHLIT, 377
Physical science, 7
Physics, 8
Piaget, Jean, 49, 86, 186–187,
    189, 195
Pinhole projectors, 275
Pinkie, 73
Pint, 86
Planets, distance from sun, 175
Plant nursery, 282
Planting, 280–281
Plants, 135, 261
    graphing, 84
    growth, 155–157
    movement of, 105
Plastic bags, 255
Plastic food, 52
Plate tectonics, 5
Plateaus, 177
Plates, 5
Plato, 186
Plausible explanation, 192–193
Play, 1
Play With Your Food
    (Elffers), 52
Playground, 97
Playing with Magnets
    (Gibson), 168
Polacco, Patricia, *Boat Ride
    with Lillian Two
    Blossom*, 120
Pollen, 64, 74
Popcorn Book, The
    (dePaola), 327
Pope, Joyce, *On the Move: A
    Study of Animal
    Movement*, 117
Popular Lectures and Addresses
    (Thompson), 76
Pound, 88, 98
Power-Point, 300
Predicting (basic scientific
    process), 11, 100–111,
    126, 192, 238
    definition of, 101
    rainfall, 107–109
    snowfall, 107–109
    "what would happen if"
        questions, 101
Predictive power, 193, 204
Prior beliefs, 191–192
    See also Constructivism
Problem-centered studies, 351
Process approach, 9
Process of science, 8–12
Process skills
    assessing, 237–242
    graphs of assessment, 308–309

Process-oriented activities using *The Popcorn Book* (dePaola), 327

Process-oriented inquiry, 196–210
 descriptors of, 203
 lesson planning for, 203–208
 See also Constructivism

Process-oriented objective, 124–127

Professional development, 15

Professional organizations, 369–372

Proficiency indicators, 237–238, 243

Program Standard D, 267

Program Standard F, 267

"Project 2061," 13

PSYCHLIT, 303

Public Broadcasting System. *See* PBS

Pumpkin Book, The (Gibbons), 327

Pumpkins, 49

"Purple Cow, The," *Nonsense and Commonsense: A Child's Book of Victorian Verse* (Burgess), 47

Pushing and Pulling (Gibson), 97

Qualitative data, 154
 See also Interpreting data

Quantitative data, 154, 306
 See also Interpreting data

Quantum (National Science Teachers Association), 370

Quart, 86

Quinney, Donni, 80

Rainfall, 107–109
 homemade rain gauge, 108–109

Rainforest, 256

Rainis, Kenneth E., *Exploring with a Magnifying Glass*, 67

Raisin dance, 287–288

Ramsay, Helena, *Hot and Cold*, 161

Ranger Rick, 39

Reader Rabbit series, 302

Reading and writing, 324–344
 See also Literature

Realgar, 259

Receptor systems, 36

Recycling programs, 358

Reggio Emilia, Italy, 200

Reid, Margarette S., *The Button Box*, 66

Reflection, investigating, 214–215

Remembering science, 2–3

Reports, 379–380

Research, 375–380

Resources for Science Literacy, 365

Resources for Teaching Elementary School Science, 365

Reward-punishment system, 265

Rey, Margaret, *Curious George Goes to a Chocolate Factory*, 98

Rhythmic method of counting seconds, 95

Right vs. wrong, 19–22, 193–194

Ring finger, 73

Roaring Rockets (Mitton), 160

Rock hunt, 34–36

Rocks, 44
 classifying, 48, 50–51

Roop, Peter, *Keep the Lights Burning, Abbie*, 110

Rose interdisciplinary model, 350–355

Rows, 306–307, 310

Roxaboxen (McLerran), 279

Rubber band scale, 170–171

Rubber bands, sounds of, 215

Safety, 257–259, 275, 283
 basic rules for, 258
 with insects, 277
 and outdoors, 278

Safety contract, 258

Safety goggles, 259

Sagan, Carl, 1, 12

Salt crystals, 134–135

Sand, 87, 95
 through a funnel, 132–133

Sand Children, The (Dunbar), 133

Scarry, Richard, *Mr. Fixit's Magnet Machine*, 168

Schemata, 186–188

School completion, 14

Schoolyard ecology, 278

Science
 definitions of, 7
 doing, 8, 235–236, 301, 363
 and knowledge of early childhood teachers, 3–8
 knowledge explosion of, 5
 process of, 8–12
 remembering earlier grades, 2–3
 women in, 222–224

Science for All Americans, 13

Science center, 254–255, 349

Science and Children (National Science Teachers Association), 330, 370

Science in the classroom. *See* Constructing science in the classroom

Science Curriculum Improvement Study (SCIS), 9

Science Education (Association for the Education of Teachers in Science), 371

Science Education Standards, 365

Science journals, 338, 340

Science Newsletter, 341

Science portfolio, 247–248

Science Scope (National Science Teachers Association), 370

Science smock, 259

Science, technology, and society (STS), 355–358

Science text evaluation review form, 339

Science textbooks, 332, 334–338
 activity-oriented, 335
 constructivist approaches, 336–337
 textbook review, 335, 338–339
 traditional, 334–335

Science workshops, 372–373

Scientific inquiry, 6–7

Scientific literacy, 12

Scientific process, 329

SCIS. *See* Science Curriculum Improvement Study

Scoring, 241–242
 See also Assessment

Sea anemone, 4–5

Sea level, 88, 92

Search tools, 314

Seasons, 116

Seasons of Arnold's Apple Tree (Gibbons), 72

Seconds, 95

Sedimentary rock, 35

Seed Museum, 255

Seeds, 44, 53, 255

Seeds and More Seeds (Selsam), 53

Self-assessment, for technology, 297–298

Self-determined criteria, 52

Self-empowerment, 22

Self-identified criteria, 56

Self-referencing behavior, 265

Selsam, Millicent
 Benny's Animals and How We Put them in Order, 55
 Eat the Fruit, Plant the Seed, 44
 Seeds and More Seeds, 53

Seminars, 372–373

Sendak, Maurice, *Where the Wild Things Are*, 273

Sense Suspense: A Guessing Game for the Five Senses (McMillan), 67

Senses, 38–40, 40–41, 120

Serfozo, Mary, *What's What? A Guessing Game*, 120

Serrated edges, 52

Seuss, Dr.
 Green Eggs and Ham, 65
 Oh the Places You'll Go, 2
 Oh, the THINKS You Can Think!, 153

Shade, 93

Shadows, 85, 118

Shadows and Reflections (Hoban), 118

Shapp, Martha and Charles, *Let's Find Out What's Light and What's Heavy*, 90

Sharmat, Mitchell, *Gregory, the Terrible Eater*, 71

Shoebox guitar, 216

Shoebox model, 181

Shoebox science, 256

Sidewalk ecology, 277

Sierra Club, 372

Sight, 39, 42, 43–44

Silverstein, Shel
 The Giving Tree, 121
 Where the Sidewalk Ends, 326

Simmons, Jane, *Daisy and the Egg*, 65

Sinking, 104, 106

SIS. *See* Supported Inquiry Science

Sky watching, 274
 nighttime, 290–292

Smell, 40

Smithsonian, 39

Snappy investigation, 170

Snappy spring scales, 170

Snowfall, 107–109
 measuring, 108–109

Snowflakes, Sugar, and Salt: Crystals Up Close (Maki), 135

Snyder, Zilpha Keatley, *Changeling*, 196

Social Sciences Abstracts, 377

Socrates, 186

Soda, 88

Soda Science: Designing and Testing Soft Drinks (Zubrowski), 354

Soft drinks, 352

Software
 definition of, 299

evaluating, 318–319
sources of, 321–322
See also Technology
Soil, 58
erosion of, 122
origin of, 121
Solar system model, 175
Solzhenitsyn, Alexander
Isayevich, 324
Sorting, 49–50
Sound, 38–39
Space snacks, 207–208
Spaceships, 88
Spatial intelligence, 228–230
Spell-checking, 304
Spreadsheets, 306–310
Sprouting, 103
Sputnik, 8
Stamens, 64, 74
Stereotypes, 222
See also Gender bias
Stewardship, 327
Stimuli, 188
Stop That Ball!
(McClintock), 151
Stratosphere, 176–177
Strength to Love, The (King), 345
STS. *See* Science, technology,
and society
Stuartship (Collay and
Dubrow), 327
Stuffed animals, 54
Subgroups, 50–52
Sugar, dissolving in water, 131,
138–139, 154–155
Sun, 93, 94
and eye protection, 275–277
Sun viewer, 275
*Sun, the Wind, and the Rain,
The* (Peters), 280
Supported Inquiry Science
(SIS), 231
Surfing the net, 314
Swimming in the Sand
(Leonard), 133

Take-home science kits, 283, 287
Taylor, Byrd
Everybody Needs a Rock, 44
*I'm in Charge of
Celebrations*, 42
Taylor, Barbara, *Bouncing and
Bending Light*, 215
Teacher education, 15
Teacher and program
assessment, 250–251
Technology, 295–323
databases, 310–312
electronic mail, 312–313
evaluating computer software,
318–319

getting started, 320–321
internet and world wide web,
313–317
inventory, 296–298
reasons to use computer-
based, 298–301
software sources, 321–322
spreadsheets and graphing
applications, 306–310
statistics, 298–300
tutorials and CD information
programs, 301–304
video, 317–318
word processing and desktop
publishing, 304–306
Teddy bears, hibernating, 179
Telling time, 95
Temperature, 92–94, 98, 160
See also Measuring
Temperature graph, 70
Temperature and You
(Maestro), 98
Terrariums, 261–262
Testing hypotheses. *See*
Formulating and testing
hypotheses
Textbooks, 332, 334–338
Texture, 38
The Case of the Mysterious
Crayons, 102
*There's a Hair in My Dirt: A
Worm's Story* (Larson), 58
Thermometer, 160
Thermosphere, 177
Thinking, valuing children's,
24–27
Third International Mathematics
and Science Study
(TIMSS), 7, 15
Thompson, William (Lord
Kelvin), *Popular Lectures
and Addresses*, 76
Thought, ownership of, 22–27
Thumb, 73
Thunder, 95
Time, 95–98
See also Measuring
Time organization, 257–258
Tommy and the Grocery Store
(Grossman), 58
Ton, 88
Translucence, 109–110
Transparency, 109–110
Trees, age of, 121
Troposphere, 177
Troubles with Bubbles
(Edwards), 64
Trumpet of the Swan, The
(White), 382
Tutorials, 301–304
"Twenty Questions," 68

Two Bad Ants (Van Allsburg),
277, 326, 329
Ty's One-Man Band
(Walter), 216

Ultraviolet rays, 275
Umbrella (Yahsima), 41
Uncle Lester's Lemonade Lure
(Ginny), 59
Uncle Wiggily's Story Book
(Garis), 235
Unconventional measurements, 79
Uniform Resource Locator
(URL), 313, 316
Unit measurement, 83
Unknown objects, 42–43
URL (Uniform Resource
Locator), 313, 316
U.S. Department of
Education, 267
"Use of Computers in Science
Education, The" (National
Science Teachers
Association), 301
User friendly, 318

Vagin, Vladimir, *The Enormous
Carrot*, 66
Validating conclusions, 328–329
Validation, 192–193, 194
Van Allsburg, Chris, *Two Bad
Ants*, 277, 326, 329
VanCleave, Janice, *Dinosaurs
for Every Kid*, 180
Variables
and experiments, 165–168
identifying and controlling,
128–136
Very Busy Spider, The
(Carle), 329
Very Hungry Caterpillar, The
(Carle), 329
Very Lonely Firefly, The
(Carle), 329
Very Quiet Cricket, The
(Carle), 329
Video, 317–318, 351
Vinegar reactions, 243–244
Visual learning. *See* Learner
differences
Vivian Grey, Book II
(Disraeli), 146
Volcano, 5
Volume, 86–88
See also Measuring
von Goethe, Johann Wolfgang,
Elective Affinities, 47

Wald, David Kenneth, *How
Teddy Bears Find Their
Homes*, 54

Wallace, Karen, *Eyewitness
Readers: Whatever the
Weather*, 120
Walrus and the Carpenter, The
(Carroll), 253
Walsh, Ellen Stoll, *Mouse Paint*,
103, 328
Walter, Mildred Pits, *Ty's One-
Man Band*, 216
Water, mixing with liquids, 106
Water evaporation, 140–141
Water Magic (Mitchener,
Johnson, and Adams), 150
Water temperature, 160–161
We Love the Dirt (Johnston), 43
Weather, 40–41, 120
Weather Channel, 317
Weather charts and graphs,
69–70
Weather vane, 119
Web browser, 313
Websites for professional science
education societies, 383
Weigh It Up, Bear's Playschool
(Cooke), 90
Weight, 88–91
See also Measuring
*Wet Foot, Dry Foot, Low Foot,
High Foot: Learn about
Opposites and Differences*
(Hayward), 141
What Makes the Weather?
(Palazzo), 69
"What We Need to Know"
list, 352
What in the World?
(Phillips-Duke), 68
"What would happen if"
questions, 101
*What's What? A Guessing
Game* (Serfozo), 120
Where the Sidewalk Ends
(Silverstein), 326
Where the Wild Things Are
(Sendak), 273
Whewell, William, *Philosophy
of the Inductive
Sciences*, 100
Whirl, 74
Whistle for Willie (Keats), 331
White, E.B.
Charlotte's Web, 324
The Trumpet of the Swan, 382
White House Millennium
Evening, 4
Who Is the Beast? (Baker),
121, 329
Wildsmith, Brian, *Brian
Wildsmith's Wild
Animals*, 39
Will It Rain? (Keller), 41

Will to Power, The
    (Nietzsche), 137
Wind, 119
Winter Barn (Parnall), 94
Wise Woman and Her Secret,
    The (Merriam), 68
Wolkstein, Diane, *8000 Stones:*
    A Chinese Folktale, 332
Women in science, 222–224
Wonder, 1
"Woods Hole" conference, 8
Word processing, 304–305

Wordless story, 113
Words
    constructing pairs of, 20
    meanings of, 20
Workshops, 372–373
World Wide Web, 313–317
Writing, 338, 340–341
    on computers, 341
    creative writing, 340–341
    recording children's
        responses, 338
    science journals, 338, 340

Wrong vs. right, 19–22,
    193–194

Yahoo, 314
Yahsima, Taro, *Umbrella,* 41
Yard, 78
Yogi Book: "I Really Didn't
    Say Everything I Said"
    (Berra), 235
You Can't Smell a Flower with
    Your Ear!: All about Your
    5 Senses (Cole), 40

Young Children (National
    Association for the
    Education of Young
    Children), 372
Your Big Backyard, 39

Zoobooks, 39
Zubrowksi, Bernie, *Soda*
    Science: Designing and
    Testing Soft Drinks, 354